4321 5325

A∅
2010
2K

AN ANGEL FROM HELL

AN ANGEL FROM HELL

Real Life on the Front Lines

RYAN A. CONKLIN

BERKLEY CALIBER, NEW YORK

THE BERKLEY PUBLISHING GROUP
Published by the Penguin Group
Penguin Group (USA) Inc.
375 Hudson Street, New York, New York 10014, USA
Penguin Group (Canada), 90 Eglinton Avenue East, Suite 700, Toronto, Ontario M4P 2Y3, Canada
(a division of Pearson Penguin Canada Inc.)
Penguin Books Ltd., 80 Strand, London WC2R 0RL, England
Penguin Group Ireland, 25 St. Stephen's Green, Dublin 2, Ireland (a division of Penguin Books Ltd.)
Penguin Group (Australia), 250 Camberwell Road, Camberwell, Victoria 3124, Australia
(a division of Pearson Australia Group Pty. Ltd.)
Penguin Books India Pvt. Ltd., 11 Community Centre, Panchsheel Park, New Delhi—110 017, India
Penguin Group (NZ), 67 Apollo Drive, Rosedale, North Shore 0632, New Zealand
(a division of Pearson New Zealand Ltd.)
Penguin Books (South Africa) (Pty.) Ltd., 24 Sturdee Avenue, Rosebank, Johannesburg 2196,
South Africa

Penguin Books Ltd., Registered Offices: 80 Strand, London WC2R 0RL, England

This book is an original publication of the Berkley Publishing Group.

The publisher does not have any control over and does not assume any responsibility for author or third-party websites or their content.

AN ANGEL FROM HELL

FIRST EDITION: April 2010

ISBN: 978-0-425-23394-8

An application to register this book for cataloging has been submitted to the Library of Congress.

PRINTED IN THE UNITED STATES OF AMERICA

10 9 8 7 6 5 4 3 2 1

Penguin is committed to publishing works of quality and integrity. In that spirit, we are proud to offer this book to our readers; however, the story, the experiences, and the words are the author's alone.

In memory of
Corporal Andrew J. Kemple,
Sergeant Benjamin J. Miller,
and
Specialist Darren Subarton
"Ne Desit Virtus"

INTRODUCTION

My name is Ryan Allen Conklin. I was born in the very small town of Marshall, Michigan, on April 1, 1985. All my life I've been asked whether I was truly born on April Fools' Day, but I take that as a compliment to my keen sense of humor. I am the youngest of three siblings: one sister and one brother. I lived what anyone would call an average American life. I played more backyard sports than league sports, attended church regularly, and was surrounded more by family than friends. My immediate and large extended family lived in close proximity in and around Battle Creek, Michigan. Nicknamed "the Cereal City," it is the home of cereal manufacturers Post, Kellogg's, and General Mills. On most Sundays, we held family gatherings. This gave me, my brother, and our cousins continuous adventures in my grandparents' endless acres of woods, while we abandoned the adults who sat inside and talked. The girls would pretend they were princesses and the boys all played Army in the woods. Little did I know then that all of us who played Army would eventually join the Army and play it for real. None of my female cousins became princesses.

In 1996, my parents sought a lifestyle change and moved to the historic town of Gettysburg, Pennsylvania. Gettysburg could not have been a better place for my family, because we were all devoted history nerds and drawn to community activities. It was a perfect place for us to grow.

High school was the time when I really started to come out of my shell. I picked up the guitar, flirted with girls, gained a passion for film-making, and focused more on making my peers laugh than on my studies. Jokes don't get you far in high school, but they landed me a spot on the Homecoming Court and sealed the deal with my being voted the Class Clown. High school was also a time when we all sought out where we would be pursuing higher education after graduation. I was undecided on what to do or where to go. But all these questions were silenced during my junior year, on the morning of September 11, 2001. I was sitting in English class when two classmates of mine stormed in crying and stated that "the World Trade Center is getting attacked. I think we're getting attacked." It was fair to say that that drove everyone's attention away from the day's lesson, and we all looked to the teacher for guidance. On that morning no one could accurately ascertain what was truly going on. Teachers were instructed to keep the televisions off for the rest of the day and proceed with normal activities. How normal was anything for anyone on that day?

It wasn't until I got home from school, and watched from the edge of my couch as the news unfolded on television, that I really began to put it together. Even then, it took about a week to fully grasp what was happening to my country. As I listened to countless stories of tragic loss and cunning heroism, I wanted to contribute. I wanted to do something. This was my generation's Pearl Harbor. I knew military actions would soon be launched, and I decided that the military would also be the route for me.

My senior year I chose to enlist in the Army. I did not come from a military family, but when my country called upon men to fight in time of war, my ancestors had never hesitated and always answered the call. The war in Afghanistan was raging and I didn't want to miss the action. There was even talk that Iraq could see an invasion from U.S. troops. I wanted a job where I would be guaranteed to "put boot-to-ass," so I sought to join the infantry. I was only seventeen, under the legal age, when I decided to join, so it took a lot of persuading my parents to allow me to go. With great resistance, they eventually came around and realized it was a path that I wanted to take. My mom always said that when she signed her name on my enlistment papers, it was "the heaviest pen to hold and the hardest signature to write." That was all before the war in Iraq kicked off. I can only imagine how much heavier that pen would have felt had I needed her signature after the invasion of Iraq.

I graduated from high school in June of 2003, three months after that invasion. On September 10, I reported to Fort Benning, Georgia, for my basic training. My first full day there was the two-year anniversary of the day that changed so many lives. I spent several weeks in utter pain and misery learning what would become my new life. The Army broke me down to build me up their way. I took it all in stride because it was something I had chosen and really wanted.

Basic training was definitely no walk in the park for me. It tested me beyond limits in a way I'd never thought possible. There were a few soldiers who just gave up when the yelling, pain, lack of sleep, and stress rose. I never wanted to be that guy. I was reliable and I didn't let things get me down. I must have wanted it more than others. From my stern drill sergeants I learned things about myself that I will forever be thankful for: strength, pride, mental toughness, honor, dedication, and teamwork.

I completed basic training and became an infantryman on December 17, 2003, just days after learning the news of Saddam Hussein's capture in Tikrit, Iraq. Upon graduation from the Infantry Training School, my company truly believed that we all would miss the war and that it would soon be drawing to a close. Like the rest of America, we would be in for a long process of realization.

After Christmas 2003, I reported to Fort Campbell, Kentucky, home of the 101st Airborne Division (Air Assault) Screaming Eagles. The division patch was modeled after "Old Abe," the bald eagle carried by Company C of the 8th Wisconsin Volunteer Infantry during the American Civil War. This story was legend to avid Civil War buffs but was special to me because my great-great-great-uncle served in that famous Company C.

When I reported to Fort Campbell, I found the base practically deserted because my division was at the time serving in Iraq. I lived day-by-day wondering if and when I would be sent there. The time never came, because the division returned within a few months. I spent the next twenty-one months stationed at Fort Campbell, where I trained vigorously with my unit, the famed 3rd Battalion, 187th Infantry Regiment (Rakkasans), whose pride it is to be one of the most decorated regiments in the Army. I served in Angel Company the majority of my time. The company carried the nickname of the "Angels from Hell."

It was there that countless days and weeks would be spent training in the rain, cold, heat, and mud. We slept in muddy foxholes and wore camouflage paint on our faces until the sweat rubbed it away. Our continuous training prepared us with knowledge of infantry tactics designed for Vietnam-era warfare and helped us build camaraderie with our fellow soldiers, on whom we all soon would need to depend.

It was not until we received our new brigade commander a few months before deployment that our training was revamped to an increased level of intensity. Colonel Michael Steele, a well-known and respected officer whose actions as a Ranger captain during an incident in Somalia in 1993 spawned an actor's portrayal of him in the movie *Black Hawk Down*. Steele changed the way an infantry regiment preparing for war was to be trained. We Rakkasans sarcastically forged for ourselves the unofficial nickname of the "Lost Ranger Regiment." We adopted several new techniques, perfected field exercises, conducted hand-to-hand combat, and attended countless courses with specialized instructors outside of the military. There's no other way to describe Steele other than to say he was legendary. It was his job to turn us into rough and tough warriors, and he excelled at the task. His first day as our commander was rumored to have sent a few soldiers to the hospital after he made platoons grapple each other in a vicious "Predator Pit," which put two platoons at a time in a small ring and commenced a fight which ceased only when there was one group of men, all from the same unit, inside. It was brutal, but I loved every second of it. Men in my regiment separated themselves from others in the division and took pride in what it was to be a Rakkasan.

Incidents where Steele interacted with fellow soldiers were a common springboard of conversation. I wish there'd been someone who followed him and documented his witty comments and anecdotes. He was a fearful-looking man, and the stories told behind his back made him even more of a mythical god to us. One morning I saw Steele pull his own pickup truck with a rope in the parking lot for physical training.

I was in Weapons Squad, First Platoon, Angel Company, 3rd Battalion, 187th Infantry Regiment, 3rd Brigade, 101st Airborne Division, Eighteenth Airborne Corps, United States Army. During my two years as a Screaming Eagle I was lucky enough to have experience in every role there was in a platoon. I spent time as a rifleman, grenadier, machine gunner, assistant machine gunner, team leader, and even an RTO.[1] I attended Air Assault School and courses called Combat Communications, Eagle First Responder, and Hand-to-Hand Combatives, and I even earned the coveted Expert Infantryman's Badge. As an infantryman, I knew my shit.

I could go on and on about what we did, how hard it was, and how much we hated it at the time, but I won't. Overall, it made us who we were. We were the best regiment in the division. That was apparent when it came to the Eagle Challenge before deployment, when the Rakkasans would frequently beat the other brigades in numerous competitions involving marksmanship.

The guys I worked with were the same guys I lived with. My company was the largest family I have ever had. We worked hard and we played hard. We survived all of our rigorous training together, our treacherous road marches, our sleepless nights in the rainy backwoods of Fort Campbell, and our boisterous drunken downtime escapades, which were oftentimes more dangerous. By the time we were being deployed, we all knew each other better than some parents know their own children.

We were tough, young, and filled with a vibrant passion to kill anyone who stood in our way. Rakkasan. This is my story.

---

[1] RTO stands for radio telephone operator. In each infantry platoon, there was one man designated to constantly monitor the radio, and to transmit and relay messages to different frequencies in a proficient manner.

THE DEPARTURE

"I'll be seeing you, America."

The day of September 14, 2005 started very early for me. Those of us in Angel Company who resided in the barracks had decided to spend our last night in America drinking. Anyone who ever served in the infantry knows that infantrymen drink like fish. Hours before our first formation, men were running up and down the hall screaming their favorite country songs and high-fiving each other with strong drinks in their hands. Everyone was drunk and pumped for our endeavors to begin. I stumbled by one room and witnessed a buddy of mine drink a shot of dish soap on a dare. Another soldier was head-butting his entertainment center to show how tough he was. At one point, some of my buddies and I chased each other through the hallways with knives and slashed away the last set of civilian clothes we wore. I was practically naked all night but for the shredded shorts I wore, which looked like the Incredible Hulk himself had worn them. What a sight we must have been in the barracks. Here we were, the pride of the 101st, drunk, naked, and drinking dish soap, hours before being sent into a combat zone.

Around 3 A.M., the ceiling light in my empty room flickered on. Still feeling the effects of a lot of alcohol, I scanned the room while the light burned my half-opened eyes. A blurry image came to me of my closest friend in the platoon, Specialist Ryan Avery, standing by my door giggling. I was completely naked on my bare mattress, remembering the time a few hours before when we ripped and shredded the last pair of civilian clothes we owned.

Avery was not the most typical New Englander I had ever met. Born and bred in the backwoods of New Hampshire, he had a neck as red as Superman's cape. At twenty-three years old, he had already served time as an infantryman in the Marine Corps before he joined the Army. He was a man of many practical talents and that was what I loved the most about him. Avery and I were inseparable during off-duty time. I learned so much from him. He knew it all when it came to liquor, beer, hunting, automobiles, guns, engines, and fixing things. Yes, in that order.

"Conklin, get up. We got a plane to catch," Avery said, before he walked back out of my room.

I uttered nothing more than mumbles. Naked, I crawled out of bed and attempted to adjust to the light that felt like the sun directly in the eyes. I put on what would be my uniform for the next year, which was our newly issued Army Combat Uniform (ACU). You know, the uniform whose camouflage pattern blends better into gravel stones than into anything found in a desert environment. I moved slowly because I still felt a little drunk. I grabbed my assault pack, my rucksack, and one duffel bag, which were all packed to the brim. I shut the light off in my empty room and walked through the hallway to find other zombie-like comrades looking the same way I was feeling.

I walked across the street, from my barracks to the company area, where we dropped our gear and waited for the first formation of the day. No one was really talking much. Most married soldiers spent their last seconds with their wives, while the single soldiers dealt with hangovers and couldn't bear the sound of their own voice.

My platoon, First Platoon, had thirty-five soldiers in it. Angel Company consisted of four platoons. During our first formation in the early morning, my company was all present except for one: Specialist Aric Hilmo. Soldiers were looking at me because I'd been drinking with him hours prior. I knew his drinking was out of control and figured he had probably passed out in his room at some point. He usually was the last man standing when we drank.

I ran across the street to the barracks and found him just like I had envisioned. He was an apparent victim of the clothes slashing, because he was lying spread-eagle and naked on his bed. The morning had just started too quickly and too early for me.

I dressed him as if he were a flexible mannequin. The entire time, Hilmo's eyes were shut while he mumbled anything but English. A few moments passed before others from my squad showed up to help out. Two soldiers escorted Hilmo across the street while I carried his bags. Our squad leader, Staff Sergeant Jimmy Poston, did the normal protocol and tried to discipline him in physical exercises; "smoking" as it was called. That only resulted in Poston being shown what Hilmo had had to drink hours prior. Poston eventually gave up and returned Hilmo to the squad. We had to supervise him long enough to get him and his bags on the plane.

As the sun rose over the Fort Campbell skies, we collected ourselves and our gear and headed back across the street to do a final formation behind the barracks. Families and friends all gathered to hug and kiss their loved ones off. Others, like myself, who had no one come down to wish us luck, either sat in silence and took the whole situation in or called home one last time on cell phones borrowed from people gathered around. Avery and I just sat there together and kept an eye on a napping Hilmo.

It was a surreal moment for me. I tried to take the whole situation in. Seeing fellow soldiers say good-bye to their small children who were too young to comprehend the situation was a little depressing. Private First Class Brice held his wife ever so tight. Specialist Taylor Edwards was trying to convince his mother that he would come back just like he did after his first deployment to Iraq. This was my first deployment and I felt every emotion imaginable. Eager, scared, anxious, curious, gloomy—you name it. Your mind just goes crazy at a time like this. My hands were sweaty, my muscles twitched, and I tried hard to hold back tears. Minutes felt like hours, but soon it was time to board the buses that filled the parking lot in front of our chow hall.[2]

---

[2] *Chow hall* was the name for our soldier cafeteria. Another common name was *DFAC* (dining facility). They were modern-looking cafeterias that were often decorated in sports posters and Army propaganda, or themed to the current holiday.

We left our formation in single-file lines and walked toward the buses. Families cheered and yelled, and several shed tears. I was glad my own family was not there. I could barely hold back seeing the other families, and I just knew I would be crying if mine were present. So, as if this emotional baggage were not enough, and still suffering with hangovers, we crammed into a bus that was too small for all the equipment we were wearing. My personal luggage consisted, in part, of helmet, body armor, weapon, assault pack, and tripod bag for my machine gun. No one was comfortable while we wedged our bulky bodies together in order to fit two to a seat.

The trip from the barracks to the airfield was spent in almost utter silence. Taylor, a twenty-three-year-old specialist from North Carolina, who had a keen love for redneck activities and nicotine, was about to embark on his second tour in Iraq. I plopped down next to him in what was left of the open seat that he occupied.

"Man, that was tough," he whispered. "I cried."

"I don't think anything less of you, man," I said straightforwardly. Not another word was said.

When we arrived at the airfield, we spilled out of the crowded bus. Once inside the main building, we all had to sign a lot of paperwork. I didn't know what any of it was; I just signed my name and went on my way. We then had to sit around in the building for what, to most of us, seemed like forever. For others, like Hilmo, the time was very short, for he was next to me sound asleep. I wondered if he knew that he was actually about to board a plane bound for overseas. Major General Thomas Turner, the commanding general of the 101st Airborne Division, managed to give us one last speech before we left. Apparently, we were the first infantry element to leave from the division. My company alone, along with some other attachments, stood before Turner as he recited words of encouragement, which were not really reassuring at all. He just reminded us of all the bad stuff over in Iraq that we were sure to encounter. Perfect timing. His words hit me like bricks. Because of my bad hangover, I almost passed out from standing at the position of attention.

The time finally came when someone from the aviation unit began calling out names in alphabetical order. When my name was called, I sounded off with an unenthused "hooah," picked up my stuff, and filed out of the door onto the large, open airfield. I was greeted by the refreshing, clean air of Fort Campbell. The air was crisp and pretty warm for September. Both were conditions I was about to miss.

As I neared the long single-file line leading into the plane, I tried to take everything in one last time. This was when I kept reassuring myself, *Surely this will not be the last time I will smell this air, or walk on U.S. soil.* I was convinced that I would make it back home, but it still was an eerie feeling. Slowly those steps got closer and closer. I was staring at my feet the whole time, just admiring the ground I was walking on, even though it was just the tarmac below my boots. It was tough to part with the soil of my native land, to know I was going to walk into a very foreign country to fight a war. I took the cards I'd been dealt and kept walking. As I got to the steps, I gripped the railing, took a breath, and then stepped onto the stairs leading into the plane. There was no looking back, only ahead. I whispered very softly to myself, "I'll be seeing you, America."

CAMP BUEHRING, KUWAIT

"Hotter than Hell itself."

Between the long night I had had, and the sleeping pills issued on the plane by our platoon medics, the trip over passed quickly. It was not until our stop in Frankfurt, Germany, to refuel that I saw Hilmo again. He had finally comprehended where he was during the flight to Germany.

Everyone was ordered off the plane as soon as we landed, at what looked like an abandoned airport out in the middle of nowhere. Of course there was no time, or freedom, to go anywhere other than where we were shuttled to. We were housed in a small, plain building, which housed the most primitive German souvenir shop and an equally lame coffee shop. There were bathrooms and phones, both of which soldiers lined up to use. I talked to one of the young female workers at the coffee shop, mainly because I was drawn to her German accent. Apparently I was not the only one; she was also being bombarded by several other men from my company. We all knew it would be one of our last opportunities to interact with a female for a long time, so we relished it.

We were barely in Germany long enough for the smokers to have that last lick of nicotine before the journey continued onward to Kuwait.

I enjoyed the flight by watching the inside of my eyelids and listening to tunes from my iPod.

When we finally landed in Kuwait City, it was impossible to ignore the heat. In fact, as soon as we got off the plane and were on the ground, everyone was looking for water. I was unaware of what time it was, but it felt like the middle of the afternoon. As we disembarked, we were greeted by some local Kuwaitis who were probably used to the routine of servicing American soldiers into their country. They came packed with the welcoming sight of ice-cold bottled water.

After a quick check on personnel and to ensure that we all still had our equipment, we were whisked aboard buses. Comfort was apparently last on everyone's agenda; we were crammed to full capacity onto non-air-conditioned buses, in a country that was hotter than Hell itself. The sweat and the heat were enough for Taylor and me to complain loudly. It was a discomfort that was being shared by everyone, but we made it our job to make a bad situation more miserable by complaining. This was the start of a new relationship between Taylor and me—we were now the new complainers, about anything and everything, for the duration of the deployment. It was the venting that helped us keep our sanity.

During an endless bus ride from Kuwait City to our camp, I got to see my first view of the barren desert sands of Kuwait. The blinds were pulled down over the windows, with orders to not raise them, but this did not stop me from moving the blind a bit to see nothing but sand. From all that I saw, Kuwait would be a one-day visit if any tourist wanted to see the country.

Nearly two hours passed before we finally arrived at Camp Buehring at close to midnight. The rest of the night and early morning consisted of a series of short but boring briefings, pay issues, a formal welcoming into the country, and the stress of keeping our mouths shut on what we said to family back home.

There was one briefing that changed everyone's mood. My company was seated on wooden benches inside a tent where we were to view a short film on combat in Iraq. Most of us were sleepy from jet lag, but when the movie started, everyone's eyes were glued to the projection screen. The movie consisted of countless raw footage showing the current form of attacks in Iraq. Improvised explosive devices, or IEDs as they were called, were complex and innovative roadside bombs, and their use against coalition forces was really starting to increase all across Iraq. Attack after attack was shown on the screen; scenes of military vehicles just ripped open by these hidden creatures of death. The film was very eye-opening and a little surreal. The song "Wonderful," by the band Everclear, accompanied the footage, which made for an unforgettable and effective montage.

I thought of trying to find comfort from the more superior person in my team of three, my team leader, Specialist Brendan Fooks, who had already been deployed to Iraq during the initial invasion. He beat me to the punch when he leaned in and said, "This is the real shit." At the time, that statement wasn't what I was looking for, but I realized it was also just what I wanted to hear. It meant I was not alone.

Fooks went on to say, "That movie got me scared, but that's exactly what you need to be. The more worried you are, the more alert you are. The more in the game you get, the better the chances of stopping these fucking things."

The rest of the early morning was spent with a drastic attitude change. Our company was ushered into two giant white tents in the corner of dozens of tents neatly organized like a planned community. First Platoon and Headquarters Platoon were housed in one, and Second and Third Platoons were in the other. After the routine and annoyance of checking our equipment and random assigned details where we low-ranking enlisted soldiers downloaded our company's gear, we finally got time to download and organize our personal equipment around our own cots. We got as comfortable as possible. Those of us who were on our first deployment kept inspecting the disgusting smallpox shot in our arm, which was beginning to pus-up underneath our Band-Aids. I just put on my headphones and went to sleep. It became my first sleep in a foreign country, thousands of miles away from home. It was an unusual feeling that I will never forget. This side of the earth had just become my new home for the next year. I knew that the key to survival was the ability to adapt to anything that came my way.

The best thing about our stay in Kuwait was that the tempo of a day's work was much slower than what we were accustomed to. We slept in, without any mandatory wake-up call in the morning. We did not conduct any mandatory physical fitness routines. Our first goal in Kuwait was adjusting to the heat. I don't know of any other place that can be as sweltering, as desolate, and as dry as the deserts of Kuwait. It never rained in the two weeks we were there. I can't even give an accurate average temperature, but it was easily not anything below 120 degrees. The heat was so unreal that when I had to utilize the port-a-potty, I would break a sweat walking the fifty feet to it. Once inside, the plastic walls became a sauna, and the aroma of human waste covered my sweaty body in steady streams of perspiration that continued for the duration of the walk back to the big white tents. It kept everyone for as much time as possible comfortably inside the tent, where the air-conditioning was being pumped nonstop. It was also just our luck that our tents were inconveniently the farthest tents away from the chow hall, which was over a mile distant.

My squad leader, Staff Sergeant Poston, did manage to get our Weapons Squad out to run in the heat. It was, I guess, to get us acclimated to the dry heat and to learn the importance of proper hydration. Drinking water was strictly enforced. It was not uncommon for Poston to inspect our empty bottles before we threw them away. Crates of bottled water would be dropped off next to our tent and it was the responsibility of all of us to keep the cooler filled with ice and water.

Our time in Kuwait did focus on some last-minute training. Angel Company practiced convoy procedures on roads and even ran through an IED obstacle course that was set up not far from the base. We also spent time at several different ranges out in the desert far from Buehring, where we zeroed all of our weapon systems for one last guarantee before we put them to the real test of accuracy in Iraq. At one of the ranges, I bumped into members of the other companies from my battalion and was grateful for one last chance to talk to my closest friend in the Army, Specialist Derek Borden, of Charlie Company. Borden and I had met our very first day back in basic training in September of 2003, and we'd been inseparable ever since. I didn't know if his company and mine would be together at all the whole year, so we wished each other luck when we parted ways on that range.

At Camp Buehring, I got my first taste and a lasting disdain for a certain crowd. It was the soldiers who were permanently stationed at Kuwait. How jealous I was. But the jealousy turned to hatred by my entire company. Those soldiers did not know or appreciate how good they had life. Kuwait was still considered a "combat zone," so they were getting paid just as much as we were. But nothing ever happened in Kuwait. They were safe and sound and made just as much money as we who were about to be thrown in the dragon's lair in Iraq. I will forever hold a grudge against those pogues,[3] who heckled my company for not saluting their officers. Their only discomfort was the heat. The list of reasons for our disdain could have filled an empty diary. As Rakkasans, and especially as infantrymen, we were cocky, and the pogues knew it. We had a right to that, based on how well and how often we trained. We had a very rough-and-tough mentality. Our motto was "If you ain't infantry, you ain't shit."

---

[3] The term *pogue* is an offensive military slang used by every infantryman to describe all non-infantry or non-combat soldiers and support units. Pogue is the pronunciation of POG, which is the acronym for persons other than grunts.

TRAINING WITH THE DEVIL

"You get in front of that door and you're dead, motherfucker!"

My squad leader organized our entire squad one night to walk along the sand berms that marked the perimeter of the base. We practiced patrolling with our NODs[4] and perfecting hand and arm signals. Our company also continued an occasional afternoon training session outside the compounds of Buehring, which gave us more exposure to the heat with all of our gear on. We also did convoy training, to practice reacting to IED attacks, and plenty of urban combat training. We would break down into squads and do run after run of entering a room, clearing any threat, and securing a building. They were tiresome drills in the heat, but a valuable and necessary refresher. Most of all, the training built extra confidence within myself and my squad. We worked well as a team.

My platoon sergeant, Sergeant First Class Quinn, had been with my platoon for almost twelve months before we deployed. He was, by far, a different breed from anyone else we were ever exposed to in the shoes of a platoon sergeant. Anyone who has served in the military has probably

---

[4] NODs is the acronym for night-vision optical devices. They are also referred to as NVGs, the acronym for night vision goggles. They are a singular optic lens that is attached at night to the helmet and pulled over the soldier's nonfiring eye.

come across those of higher rank who act rash and sometimes out of line, leaving everyone to contemplate their credentials. This man was one of those who inspire such concerns.

Quinn had served with several different units, having been bounced around the Army for various reasons before finally landing a job at Fort Campbell as our platoon sergeant. We heard through the grapevine that he'd been promoted in his old unit in order to oust him and was then picked up by ours. He came to us as a soldier with as much combat experience as I had: none. But during the past several months leading to the deployment, Quinn had begun convincing himself that he had been places and done things that could not be explained. A majority of my platoon knew from working so close to him that he had some possible mental health issues, but we were soldiers not doctors and there was little we could do. We just brushed it aside because he outranked us all. Behind his back, we recited absurd euphemisms for him and quoted him in the best impressions we could muster. I could see that he was a bit of a loose cannon. The slightest pressure or stress would set him off, to become a crazed maniac stuck in a moment of pure torture. Prior to deployment, it had been a hot issue that was kept quiet and under the rug but weighed heavily on everyone's mind.

One day at the urban combat training course at Camp Buehring gave my platoon another in an ongoing series of glimpses of a powder keg bound to explode. The squads took turns running through a mock house-to-house combat scenario. The day went normal for the other three squads, complete with Quinn dishing out verbal commands and "firsthand experience" that was just made up on the spot. All of his rants usually went through one ear and out the other for us.

When my eleven-man squad's turn came, we blazed through with splendid cohesion and performed with great professionalism. We crept stealthily from building to building in perfect tight stacks and covered all possible angles of attack with our muzzles. It was not until we came along the side of a building with a closed door that Quinn intervened. Our procedure for this was to have the first man in the stack halt the team and search for possible booby traps or anything rigged on the door. It was also his job to check if the door was unlocked, for a possible entry point. I happened to be the first man in the stack, so the responsibility came to me. I halted my team while I began to check the door and felt for anything rigged up.

Quinn was watching us from a few feet away. He quickly came charging at me like a hungry panther. He shouted words that sounded like gibberish. He was caught in yet another flashback to a scene he had never lived. I felt a stern grip on my shoulder as Quinn wheeled me around and slammed me against the wall. My team looked on, puzzled and fearful but sadly accustomed to his outbursts.

"You get in front of that door and you're dead, motherfucker!" he screamed, sprinkling my face and sunglasses with his spit.

"I was checking the door, Sergeant," I said, while showing proper respect with my hands behind my back.

"My first soldier was killed while checking a door in Afghanistan doing exactly what you were doing!" Quinn barked back. "An RPG right in his gut!"

"Roger!" I tried so hard to hold back. In order to survive with him commanding, we all had to keep changing how we ran things because it was one way one day, and the next he would change everything. It was almost impossible to work with him.

From the quiet and creepy babble talk with dangerous eyes that never looked in ours when he recounted war stories, to his fueled war-mongering King Kong stance, Quinn continued to be the main object of wisecracks and impersonations by many in the platoon. Only when he was not around, that is. I could go on for days based on some little quirk that showed his mental status to be a little disconnected. We just dealt with it by joking and tried to ignore him. We found most of the real leadership from our squad leaders, who had excellent advice, competence, and charisma.

DRIVER'S LICENSE TO KILL

"Oh shit, this is it, boys."

Other than trying to survive the daily and nightly heat, life was pretty good and safe. There were phones and computers that we had to pay to use and a small gym on the base to work out at any given time. Four meals were served a day in satisfactory chow halls, and water was always readily available. Our platoon even found time to organize a couple games of tag football. We naturally also moved toward the more violent games such as "King of the Hill" atop a large dirt pile and a rougher version of rugby played in organized piles of dirt and stones. It was all in good fun. There was really only one time in Kuwait where we actually feared for our lives.

Every so often our company would go out to somewhere in the middle of nowhere and train. We journeyed to and from the ranges via shuttle buses driven by locals. We were all a little worried the first day when we realized that an Arab man would be our driver. To us he looked no different than the common Iraqi that we trained against and had dehumanized in our minds. None of the hired drivers could speak English, so all the demeaning gibberish and tireless rants we would dish out to them fell on deaf ears.

The day that scared us all was a trip to the convoy training course. Getting to the range was a normal, if alarming bus trip. The ride took about forty-five minutes, out to the middle of nowhere, over some roads of the open desert. When there was no road present, the driver did not slow down his speed at all. You could feel the bus drift left and right over the loose sand, but the driver went on, oblivious to us telling him to slow down. We all believed that this Kuwaiti knew better than any of us how to drive in the desert, so we just hung on for the ride. It was not until we were at the end of our day and leaving the range that we got back on our bus, ready to go on another ride from Hell across the desert. The two buses our company filled sped off as if the drivers were late for work.

Everyone in our bus was yelling for the driver to slow down. At first, we all thought this whole situation to be quite comical. It was not until the endless hard left and right turns that we began to feel the bus wheels come off the ground. There was not a single soldier who was not yelling at the bus driver, yet he did nothing. Sharp turns soon made helmets and gear that were stored above us fall onto us. I was sitting in the middle of the bus, and I tried desperately to stand up and look through the front windshield, but all I saw was the bus in front of us suddenly halted in the desert.

"Oh shit, this is it, boys," said the squad leader from First Squad, Staff Sergeant Hodges, an Angel Company legend. "The Hodge" was a legend in the company because of both how long he had been in it and his knack for sticking into every pause in his speech a "but, fucking" instead of the common "um."

Our bus driver slammed on the brakes, which ground my face into the seat in front of me. From the sound and swear words that echoed throughout the bus in almost perfect unison, I knew everyone was being crushed into the seat in front of him like a domino effect.

Miraculously, we stopped just inches away from the other bus, which was stuck in the sand. Our Kuwaiti driver then began to back up to give the other bus room. We soon collected ourselves, assessed each other's condition, and then breathed a sigh of relief that we were still alive. All of the smokers in my company filed out of the bus to smoke a much-desired cigarette. I got off my bus to see how bad the first one was stuck in the sand.

Avery and I tried to joke about the whole situation, but we could not get over the fact that we were absolutely out in the middle of nowhere. No roads, no homes, just gentle rolling slopes of sand like a beach without an ocean. No one had a radio either to call anything in. This day could not get any worse.

My prayers were soon answered when the first bus weaseled its way out. Everyone quickly loaded back up and we headed out. For a second, my bus got stuck, but the driver maneuvered in a way to get us out. In the end, I guess the Kuwaiti really did know desert driving better than we did. And this isolated incident did not change the way they drove in the desert.

We all talked later that night about those drivers who owned the potential to really hurt some U.S. soldiers. Their carelessness and reckless driving could really hurt, if not kill, some soldiers if the bus did in fact overturn.[5]

---

[5] Sadly, about a month later, I read in the *Stars and Stripes*, a paper distributed to deployed soldiers, that a bus in Kuwait did overturn in the desert and one U.S. soldier was killed in the rollover.

USO SHOW

**"I could feel the eyes of all the soldiers
in the audience around me shift to look at me."**

A few days before we "went downrange," as it was referred to, a USO show was sponsored at our camp. Growing up, I remember watching film clips of Bob Hope entertaining thousands of soldiers in almost all of the wars of the twentieth century. Now it was my turn, and I was thrilled to hear that Dave Attell, a comedian who was very popular in my platoon, would put on a show. His television show and stand-up comedy albums had often been recited among the platoon since way back before we knew he would be performing for us.

Avery and I had to be the first ones there, and we arrived an hour before performance time. I made sure to have the best seat in the camp, front row center. Before the show started, more men from my company came and joined us, along with others in the division. The tables in front of the stage soon filled up.

Another comedian, Scott Kennedy, was the opening act before Attell. Kennedy was hilarious. He was doing his routine while interjecting his monologue with his thankfulness for what we were doing for our country. The best part of his act was that he used audience participation. Well, out of all the hundreds of attendees at his disposal, who did he pick on? Me.

"What's your name, sir?" he asked from the stage.

"Ryan." I shouted back. At this time I could feel the eyes of all the soldiers in the audience around me shift to look at me. Others from my company shouted from interspersed pockets in the crowd, calling my name.

"What do you do in the Army?" Kennedy asked.

I let out a loud and thunderous "Infantry," which was followed by numerous "hoo-ahs" from all my fellow grunts.

Kennedy then asked me, "How long have you been in the Army?"

"Two years," I replied.

"What did you do before you joined the Army?" Kennedy questioned.

"Nothing," I said with a smile.

"Oh, man, Ryan, I was trying to relate to you. Let's see, do you masturbate?"

The crowd, along with me, just started laughing.

"Hell yeah!" I shouted.

"All right, now we have something in common." He shouted, "Whacking Ryan! It's good to meet you, Whacking Ryan."

And of course, for the rest of the week this nickname surfaced from time to time among my company. The remainder of Kennedy's set went off just great. He was very entertaining.

Dave Attell came on stage next. Being a fan of his stand-up, I knew that he would usually drink during his shows. This show was different because proper hydration was our friend, so he was drinking water. Naturally, the ban on booze spun into his act. He put on a very humorous show, with lines that were destined to be recited among my buddies through the entire deployment.

GOING "DOWNRANGE"

"Don't worry about prayer at that moment of truth."

The morning of our departure broke like every other morning in the Kuwaiti desert: hot and sweaty. We all awoke in a different mood, for we were departing from Kuwait and hoping to escape the heat. The night prior, our company had made sure to pack everything nice and tight. It made for a quicker movement.

The first step to the morning consisted of our first battalion formation since Fort Campbell. Now that the rest of the battalion had caught up with us, we all formed up among the rows of tents. Our battalion commander gave us the standard motivational speech. He recapped stories of our long months of training and how hard it had been, with the remainder of his talk on how far we had come and how ready we were. He reiterated over and over, "You're ready!" We all strongly agreed.

Our battalion sergeant major informed us of how separated our battalion was about to become. He mentioned that this might be the last time our battalion would be all together in formation with each other. He said to expect casualties. It was something nobody wanted to hear, but we had to accept it. The sergeant major strongly urged us to be patient regarding the group we would be attached to. He told us that we were headed to Baghdad to be attached to part of the 3rd Infantry Division, already nine months into their deployment. The Angels from Hell became the first company to leave that day. We were the first to leave from the battalion, the brigade, and the division. It was a hell of an awesome feeling.

The end of the formation came with a different pace. The battalion chaplain invited us all to bow our heads as he led us in prayer. It was a somber moment, praying for safety over the next twelve months, reminding us to watch out for each other and ourselves. Everyone then sounded off with a unison "amen." Before we broke ranks, the chaplain got our attention to reiterate one last point.

"When you get face-to-face with the enemy, don't hesitate. Kill the bastard. Don't worry about prayer at that moment of truth, for I will be in the rear saying the prayers so you don't have to. You know what to do. May God be with you all." The chaplain finished and walked off.

With spirits high in the air, our first sergeant, First Sergeant Holland, gave his shot at a motivating speech to our company. I found Holland uninspiring; he lacked charisma and was not personally close to anyone in our company. He was new to our group and had given little effort to learning who he was leading. His speech did nothing more than go through one ear and out the other.

Around nine o'clock in the morning, it was time to grab all our belongings and head toward the buses for our staging area. We packed ourselves into the bus tightly and uncomfortably. We then left Camp Buehring and headed to an Air Force tarmac somewhere about twenty miles south of our current base.

By the time we downloaded at our new staging area, I was sick of toting around all my gear and constantly checking all of the sensitive items to ensure that nothing was left behind. It felt like we had to check the gear every ten minutes. I understood the reason behind it, but I was carrying a duffel bag, rucksack, tripod and gear in a bag, ballistic vest, helmet, assault pack, weapon, laser-sight, and NODs. They were all tightly packed and secured, so it became an annoyance to keep whipping it all out. With all our gear on, Avery said it best himself by saying that "we could sink the *Titanic* just by standing on it."

We were housed in an air-conditioned tent for the afternoon until our plane arrived. We quickly packed our rucksacks and duffel bags on a platform that was tied down to be loaded in the rear of the plane. Then we did what all infantrymen are notorious for doing with any given downtime. We all crammed into a nearby tent and slept. It made the time go fast to have a place to relax and escape the heat. I and some of my same-rank buddies slept as far away from the upper ranks as possible, to avoid being picked out for stupid details. Those of us who had been in the Army for a few years knew the techniques to avoid being selected. Some of the everyday details tasked to the lower enlisted consisted of getting water for everyone, sweeping, or anything that someone with higher rank wanted done. I just put in my iPod earbuds and took a nap.

BAGHDAD, IRAQ

"Expect contact on the ride over!"

"Get up. Get your shit on and get outside next to the buses. Team leaders, do a good sensitive items check," shouted the platoon sergeant.

This time I was ready. I'd already had my equipment out for inspection for my team leader prior to the call. Call it a sixth sense, but it was more force of habit. We got all our items looked at and boarded a bus that took us to our plane. I was one of the last ones on the bus, so I would not have to contend with wiggling my way to a seat with gear pouring off of me.

"Give me a thumbs-up on all your sensitive items," said Quinn. In my head I was screaming, *Are you kidding me?* Nothing could have vanished from the five steps I'd taken from the ground to my seat. Either way, we were all good to go, enabling our bus to move out.

We arrived at our C-130 around noon. In typical Army fashion we had to "hurry up and wait." The air conditioner did not work, naturally, so there was no place to hide. We were waiting for the Air Force personnel to load our bags up and get the plane ready for flight. So there we were, stuck with all our gear on and too lazy to take it off while we waited for the thumbs-up.

My luck, the thumbs-up came when I'd left the bus in order to relieve myself. Halfway through a good piss I had to stop midstream. I ran over to the C-130 while my platoon filtered in. As I ran to the plane, I was only thinking of how bad I had to pee and how much it stung to stop midway. While I buttoned my pants, it never crossed my mind that I did not have my black assistant gunner's bag, which contained my tripod and other essentials for a gun team. I'd left it in the bottom compartment of the bus I was riding. As I took my cargo-strapped seat in the plane and got situated, I began to check all my gear.

Before I could say *shit!* in my head, I heard Sergeant Caruso, a team leader in Second Squad, yell.

"Conklin!"

"Right here, sarnt!" I yelled back, knowing full well what was coming.

"I got your AG bag. You'll pay when we touch down," Caruso yelled as everyone began to look at me with smirks on their faces like children in an elementary school who've witnessed someone swear. Everyone looked at me except my team leader, who looked like he was at fault.

"Sorry, Fooks," I said to him across the sardine-packed plane.

"You know I'll have to smoke you for this," he replied.

"It's a great day for it," I said cheerfully and sarcastically.

A wise man once said false motivation is better than no motivation at all. I tried to embrace it, but could not really portray it. The flight lasted two hours, but it was much longer for me than it was for anyone else.

The two-hour plane ride was spent in silence. With the plane's engine, it was too loud to talk to anyone. Most were asleep or listening to their iPods. I just sat there in self-meditation, waiting for the plane to land so I could collect my bag and do whatever stupid task my team leader could think of.

After a long, hot, boring flight, we landed around two in the afternoon on Iraqi soil, at the Baghdad International Airport (BIAP), the former Saddam International Airport. As I exited the plane, the first thing I did was grab my AG bag from Sergeant Caruso and apologize.

As my company filtered in a long line to our rallying point, I took a quick 360-degree glance around the area. All the buildings had been reinforced by the military, but they were pockmarked with plenty of battle scars. The horizon of the city was filled with both tall and smaller buildings. The sound of scattered police sirens could be faintly heard. Smoke plumes from unknown sources filled the sky with black clouds that rose above the buildings in the distance.

As my company gathered in a makeshift picnic area made up of tables and umbrellas, I saw Fooks and knew what time it was.

"What's on the agenda?" I sarcastically asked him.

"Leave all your stuff on and come with me," he said very comfortably with his gear off. It must have been nice, but it was my fault, so it was time for me to man up.

I did quite a few push-ups, low crawls, jumping jacks, and anything else he deemed necessary. It did not help that I was already soaking wet from the excessive heat while loaded down with all of my gear, but now the sand from the crawling I did clung to my sweat-soaked body in crevices where I did not need sand to be.

As I slowly crawled like a bear in the sand, I realized that not only was I the first soldier from my platoon to be smoked in Iraq, but possibly the first from the entire 101st Airborne Division. I was attempting to poke fun at my predicament, and it was enough for me to laugh about it and even crack a smile on the others in my squad.

The festivities ended after about twenty minutes for a much-needed water break, but the punishment lingered, as I was not allowed to take off any of my gear. This proved to be the worst punishment because the temperature was just as hot as it was in Kuwait, and with all my gear on it made for an uncomfortable initiation into Iraq.

On the afternoon agenda, we waited for the sun to go down, which ensured a safer flight to our forward operating base (FOB) at night. Excluding me, getting comfortable was the order. I did, however, get indoors to an air-conditioned room and watch some rerun football game from America on the television while sitting with some guys from my platoon. The afternoon was filled with sarcastic comments and jabs from my company as I sat with all my gear on.

"Keep laughing, because if this building gets mortared tonight, I'll be the sole survivor, and I'll tell your families what assholes you all were in your last moments on earth," was the phrase I used all night. Being the center of attention in my platoon was nothing new to me, so I pulled it off just fine.

There was one sincere moment that I'll never forget. It came from my squad leader, Staff Sergeant Poston, who I always found had a personality hard for me to understand. Usually a very calm and reserved person, Poston let some time pass before sitting beside me to talk.

"You must want to take your gear off pretty badly?" he jokingly asked.

"Oh no, I love it. I've been wearing it for about five hours now. I think it has become a part of me."

"The importance of keeping track of your gear is a real concern for all of us," Poston tried to preach.

"I understand. I was just caught off guard before getting on the plane, sarnt."

"You feel pretty silly wearing that?" Poston asked.

"Fuck yeah," I replied.

"Go ahead and take it off. Catch a break before we move out." Not a second passed before I'd dropped everything at my feet, as if I had a quick release button, and sat back down to relax.

Poston went on to say quietly, "You afraid at all?"

This was the first time anyone in my platoon had asked me if I was scared.

"Yeah. Hell yeah. It's a totally new situation for me, and all I can do is embrace whatever comes my way and hope I react the way I was trained," I confided in him.

"Don't worry, Conklin. I am too," Poston said before moving to a different seat. That short conversation with him left me in self-reflection. I felt confident and not alone. Even if it was his second tour in Iraq, we were all there now. Together. Come what may.

At the onset of dusk, we gathered our company outside for further instructions. We waited for our ride into the Green Zone by flight on a Chinook helicopter. I stood outside and admired my first night in the cradle of civilization. Avery and I just scanned the panoramic view of the skyline. The sound of helicopters in the air and the scattered sight of short-lived tracers streaked through the night sky at random times.

"Two minutes out!" shouted my platoon sergeant, which signaled us all to gather our gear and prepare to load our bird. I stood quasi hunkered down from all the weight that was bearing down on my knees. Sweat poured from my face, making no room for comfort. At times, a little adrenaline was enough to ease any pain.

"I think our helicopter just got shot at or something," Avery said to me.

"What do you mean?" I said with concern.

"I could have sworn I saw tracers go up at the helicopter. They're dropping some kind of flares along the way to disrupt something," he explained.

"Please God don't tell the platoon sarnt." As soon as I uttered this sentence, Quinn's booming voice resounded.

"Make it a quick load. Expect contact on the ride over!" Quinn yelled. The only thing in my head was *damn it, shut up*. There was nothing I could do but shut up myself and move on.

The Chinook landed about 250 meters from our staging area. The thumbs-up was given and away we went toward it. The whole scene was an incredibly inspiring sight, much like a Hollywood movie. The blades of the chopper were pumping like a hard, steady drum. In single-file formation, my platoon ran with equipment stacked on our backs.

As I neared the bird, my hearing was deafened by the blades of the aircraft. The hot air vent from the helicopter made a toasty resistance as we neared the rear of the Chinook. We followed each other like ducks in a row until we dropped our gear in an orderly fashion and packed it tight. As I ran back empty-handed, the resistance from the vent felt like someone was pushing me with a mighty force. Occasionally, I saw someone tumble in the dark when he was unable to negotiate with the boost. I could not help but laugh. I returned to the staging area to grab more equipment and reversed the order back to the Chinook for another load-up.

"This is the shit I've been training for! I've waited my whole life for this!" screamed an overexcited Specialist Ramirez. "Ram" had a sketchy background and was disliked by quite a few people in the platoon. His self-glorifying talks of his time in a Mexican gang in Los Angeles separated him from people who didn't take pride in being an asshole. His smile-for-violence attitude made it hard for me to bite my tongue at times around him, but I did. His training was a sore subject for me from the past. He was someone I never trusted. When things got bad in training, he always seemed to get "injured." Here we were, seconds from being fed to the lions, and he was already acting like a loose cannon.

"Let's just pack this shit and get going!" I yelled back.

All the gear was packed, which left my platoon the last to be loaded. My platoon donned what equipment we had left and walked slowly to the freshly refueled Chinook. There was plenty of yelling, people pointing in all directions, screaming, and confusion as we all packed in. After several last-minute pleas to "scoot down," we settled in and prepared for liftoff. Unlike any helicopter ride I had ever been on prior, I could not see the row of men opposite me. A pile of rucksacks and duffel bags divided us like the Berlin Wall. The tangled mass of bags was all I saw, since our backs were to the windows.

Not a word was uttered, because of the overpowering sound of the blades chopping through the air. The lights were turned off as the Chinook lifted off the ground. This was the part where my heartbeat could be felt through my ballistic vest plate. I cannot speak for anyone else on the aircraft, but I was 50 percent scared and 50 percent adrenaline-rushed.

As I sat there in pitch-black solitude, I reached into my shirt and pulled out my dog tags. Affixed on the chain was a religious emblem of the Virgin Mary that my grandfather had worn on his dog tags during his service in World War II. I was now airborne above the most violent city in the world and it was all in God's hands from there on out.

It was only a ten-minute flight into the city, but four minutes into it my heart skipped a beat. A bang, like a firework, outside of the aircraft lit up the interior of the bird in a red flash from the rear. I could see the tail gunner on our Chinook perfectly silhouetted for a split second like someone had flickered a light in a darkened room. I could not tell what was going on. Asking anyone was out of the question since it was so loud in the hull.

I twisted my head as far as I could to the left to look out the porthole to see the view. What I saw looked very similar to Miami at night. Streetlights, roads, cars—the city was lit up much like any American city would be. The view was cut short when another small pop sound near the aircraft was accompanied by another flash in the sky. I was not sure whether we were getting shot at, flares were being dropped, or something else. I just sat there and thought a million things. I thought of my family at home, possibly enjoying a good football game on television. I envisioned my friends probably drunk at college somewhere, having the time of their lives. Now here I was, a million miles from home sitting helplessly in a pitch-black helicopter dodging unknown explosions in Iraq. It was the first time I regretted my decision to join the Army.

The feeling of the Chinook touching down on ground was comforting. The reverse process of unloading broke out like clockwork. In less than five minutes the carcass of the helicopter had been emptied and we were out gathered on the tarmac.

"Welcome to LZ [Landing Zone] Washington," shouted a stranger from the 3ID. "Grab your gear and wait over by our Humvees. We'll let you know more on when we'll drive you to your FOB."

"What? Fooks, this isn't our FOB?" I asked my team leader.

"Nope. We still have to drive to our final destination," he replied.

As everyone else settled down and waited for our next block of instructions, the smokers gathered for a much needed cigarette. I walked over to the crowd to hear everyone asking questions about what were the explosions or flares in the air. Some people thought they were tracers being shot at our flight. In any case, my mind was thinking a mile a minute, and I needed something to release me.

"Avery, give me a cigarette," I demanded from him.

"Holy shit! Conklin's smoking," Avery shouted, which drew the eyes of others. No one had ever seen me smoke before, but I needed something, anything, just to escape.

"It's going to be a long year, Avery, and cancer is the last thing on my mind right now," I muttered as I inhaled a drag from the cigarette.

About a quarter to eleven at night, our escorts arrived. Eight Humvees run by men of the 3ID came to drive us to our new FOB. This was our first glimpse of an armored Humvee and how it was manned. My platoon was all split up as we tried to load all our guys into any available seats. I was on the first wave to go and I was paired up with Fooks.

We threw our gear in the back of the Humvee and got in. Fooks sat behind the driver, and I to his right. We must have looked like some kind of rookies to the now veteran 3ID men. They were relaxed, calm, and could not wait to get to bed. As for Fooks and me, we were wide-eyed, wearing earplugs, and locked, cocked, and ready to rock. As soon as we pulled out of LZ Washington, all I could think about was the video montage of convoys blowing up that we'd viewed in Kuwait. I looked over at Fooks for reassurance and saw him shielding his eyes in case the windows exploded. I put my clear-lens goggles on, but my main concern was, well, my crotch. So I just protected my manhood with my hands and tried to get a view of Baghdad at night as we drove around.

It was a short trip to our new base, but it felt longer because I was just waiting for something to explode. To my surprise and thankfulness, we arrived safely at FOB Union III, our new home. We exited the vehicle as soon as we got inside and then cleared our weapons. As a sergeant from 3ID was inspecting my weapon, I said to him, "Is this the place?"

"Welcome home," he said. Fooks and I gathered our gear and walked to the nearest building, which we were told was our sleeping quarters.

As I entered, I dropped my gear in a pile. Slowly but surely the rest of my platoon filtered inside and gathered together in the main lobby. The building we were staying in used to be an old school during Saddam's reign and definitely still looked the part. Once we were fully reunited in our new building, we were greeted by a few members from our company who'd left days before us as the advance party. It was their job to coordinate the sleeping arrangements in our company and plot out where everything was located on our base.

"Good to see you guys. This is our building where we shall be staying. I don't know how long we'll be here. I don't know how they are going to use us yet. We're playing it day by day as we figure things out. This FOB did receive a couple mortars near the dining facility last night, so try to stay indoors as much as possible. Barbershop is located across the street, and it looks like many of you could benefit from it. Midnight chow is about to open so go get something to eat," spoke our Executive Officer (XO) from Headquarters Platoon.

Sergeant First Class Quinn designated what rooms were to be for what squad. Weapons Squad, being the largest one in the platoon, received the largest room. They were old schoolrooms filled with poorly constructed bunk beds. That was better than the cots we were used to, so we took them with open arms. I had a broken bunk, so I did not have to share with anyone.

Before bed I got a bite to eat at the nearby chow hall, about fifty feet from our building. I came back tired, threw myself into my bed, and listened to some music to calm me before I drifted off. I closed my eyes, thanked my lucky stars, and fell asleep.

FOB UNION III

"Pretty in its own way."

When I awoke the next morning, there was no alarm. No one else was moving from bed. We slept in for several hours. We had no agenda until further notice. There was no schedule of training or places we had to be or anything. It was near noon and no one was awake, so I went back to sleep because I refused to be the first person to wake up.

It was not long after that that Avery decided to put his boots on.

"Where are you going?" I asked him.

"Going exploring. I'm gonna see what this place looks like," he said.

"I'm gonna tag along," I said as we both grabbed our boots.

As we walked out of the school building, we were practically engulfed in the shadow that was cast from the large Ba'ath Party Building. It was located in the center of our FOB and towered over the Green Zone of Baghdad. Prior to the invasion in March of 2003, it was the headquarters for the Ba'ath Party regime. After a few severe direct hits from heavy bombs that penetrated the center of the complex and gutted it, it had since been vacant.

The building now housed the offices of all the commanders of 1st Battalion of the 76th Field Artillery Regiment, part of 3ID. This was the unit that we were now attached to at FOB Union III. Over the course of the month, my company would refer to them by the acronym of "FAGs," which stood for "field artillery guys." Inside the heart of the building was a large-scale gym, filled with state-of-the-art equipment organized all over the main floor. Nearby we located the Internet room, phones, and a room with a large-screen television. I was pretty excited about the whole building.

It was not until Avery and I reached the roof of the building that this whole experience really set in. The view of Baghdad was magnificent. The architecture of the palaces and mosques that stood out was just amazing. In some ways, it reminded me of any bustling big city in America. The main differences were the architecture, the lack of grass, and the fact that instead of oak or maple trees there were palm trees budding out of random streets. The city was void of any vibrant color and looked like everything had been painted with a sandy khaki mixed with dust. Just outside the walls of our FOB I could see a construction site with newly broken ground. I found out that it was the site of the American Embassy that construction had just started on. There were several tall buildings in Baghdad, but few were more than twenty-five stories in height. The city stretched in every direction. The skyline was dotted with streaks of smoke that poured out from unknown origins, either from burning garbage or the aftermath of explosions. The Tigris River shined and reflected the ever-present and blistering sun. The numerous and once-proud palaces from the Hussein reign were all pockmarked with damage from numerous bombing raids. Most of the palaces had since been converted to American headquarters. Right outside the perimeter of our FOB loomed the powerful and intimidating "Hands of Victory" crossed sabers arch. Built out of the weapons from the Iraq-Iran War and with hands sculpted from Saddam Hussein's, the arch was an iconic symbol of Baghdad and the centerpiece of Saddam's parade grounds. As a kid I remembered seeing him on television surveying his military might during pass-and-review parades under these sabers.

Each corner of the rooftop had a suitable observation post constructed out of sandbags and plywood. In each were two soldiers from an Australian army infantry unit. We sparked up some conversation to pass the time and found these men very charming. They held the same bitterness toward being an infantryman. Over the next couple of months, our relationship with the Aussies proved more enjoyable and rewarding than the one we had with anyone in the 3ID at our FOB.

Avery and I returned to our school building barracks and continued our survey of the grounds. We ventured down into the basement of our building, where we found crude jail cells that were more like torture chambers, with 100 percent isolation. The question of the purpose for such madness in the basement of a school can only be answered by the powerless regime of Saddam Hussein.

The course of the next few days consisted of self-amusement. The rest of the company joined us and settled into other classrooms on October 1. We were all still awaiting our next command to reveal what our purpose on FOB Union III would be. Most of our time was spent sleeping, chatting, or working out—luxurious time that we would all soon miss. Some nights I would go to the roof of the Ba'ath Party Building either alone or with others and just talk about anything and everything.

One night I was on the rooftop with Specialist Avery and Private First Class Alex "Sunny" Sundberg, when Sergeant First Class Quinn came out of what must have been a shadow. He was creeping around with binoculars, convinced there was terrorist activity on the other side of the highway, at the old soccer stadium between the crossed sabers. I think he forgot we were in the middle of the highly fortified Green Zone.

"Do you hear that, men?" whispered a lurking Quinn.

"What? The dog barking?" replied Avery, confused like the rest of us.

"You know what that means—dogs only bark at people they don't like," Quinn went on to explain.

It was dark out, but there was enough moonlight to see the confused looks on Avery's and Sunny's faces. They were equally as perplexed as mine. I also wanted to punch Quinn. We were all too used to his split personality by now and his made-up stories. They were usually the most dramatic, absurd, and unbelievable because they were just that.

"I'm going to go alert the guards!" he said sternly as he crept off. He left in good time, for the three of us went on to discuss how crazy he was and shared past stories of his mental status. At his expense, Quinn was the best conversation topic in the platoon. Within hours, the three of us were retelling the story of his latest head-case incident throughout our platoon.

In one of the rooms of our schoolhouse barracks that Third Squad was staying in, they shared the story with a captain who was attached to our company as our medical advisor. He was an amusing and knowledgeable man who had more downtime than any of us combined. We never said a bad thing about him because he was a former Special Forces soldier and we were in awe of that tab. The best part was he knew some of the units in SF that Quinn would frequently talk about, and the captain had never heard of him before. It was way too apparent that Quinn fabricated most of his stories, and the captain would hear the stories from us and discredit them. Quinn never dared mention a word around the captain though, in fear of being called out. Not only did we see symptoms of mental illness brewing in Quinn's mind, but the captain began to write examples down for his own work on Quinn.

Over the next few days, rumors of our purpose at FOB Union III floated around our ears. The one rumor that kept surfacing was that Saddam Hussein himself was about to come to our FOB for his highly anticipated trial. There was a building adjacent to the Ba'ath Party Building that had a courtroom in it that saw daily construction done to it. The proof was everywhere.

Our initial tasks eventually came down, and the company was split up around the FOB to reinforce the guard posts. It was looking more certain that something big was going to occur at FOB Union III. Over the course of a few days, Second Platoon filled thousands of sandbags and constructed a large-scale bunker at the front gate. First and Third Platoons constructed observation posts around the rooftops of buildings. My platoon also helped thoroughly clean the entire school we were living in. Headquarters Platoon constructed another observation post out of countless sandbags on top of the arch at the front gate.

After a week of constant construction on our fortification, the place was starting to look and feel safer. The Islamic holiday of Ramadan was beginning, and the rumor of the trial being hosted at our FOB was enough to keep everyone's head on his shoulders. We did get some help in small labor from hired Iraqis, but we always had to have an armed guard to keep an eye on them.

In the first week of October, we were told for certain that Saddam Hussein's trial was in fact going to be located at our FOB and that was the purpose of the buildup around the post. We now had to post a guard on the passageway to the back door of the courthouse for around-the-clock presence. Fooks and I would start to get the late night to early morning shifts.

I'll never forget my first guard shift in Iraq. Around 3:45 A.M., the mosques that encircled our FOB poured out the sound of imams shouting out prayer through amplified speakers. It reminded me of movies I'd seen before deployment, about Arabic cities. The loud prayers from mosques scared me every time, and they occurred five times a day. It was very creepy, but also pretty in its own way. The anticipation of expecting some type of suicide attack to occur when the prayer ceased could only be attributed to watching too many war movies.

By mid-October, the Ba'ath Party Building had around-the-clock security from my platoon. Second Platoon guarded the main entrance and Third Platoon occupied the surrounding observation posts. With many floors and parts of the building to guard, we were stretched thin, with about eight men off-duty at any given time. We had it down to about six hours on guard, six off, six on, six off, and so on. It started to take a toll on our sleeping habits.

Any free time that came occurred in between guard shifts. Men from my platoon still managed to organize some games of volleyball. Any recreational sport we did as a group usually broke eventually into name-calling and internal roasts. It wasn't really demeaning, because we were really close; it was almost like a weird fraternity. Some soldiers were victims of constant ridicule and jokes, but it was all in fun. There was a reason too that we were soldiers and not volleyball players. A few times people digested more sand than they'd expected. Others seemed to have flimsy arms and constantly sent the ball bouncing several yards away from our net.

During volleyball, or anytime for that matter, there was always one easy target to poke fun at. Avery. I was like his little brother and pestered him relentlessly. It was all out of love—and I would frequently tell him that. When he would get excited, his voice sounded like the cartoon character voice of an ogre.

"The ball hit almost in the parking lot," Avery said in his signature voice, which sounded like there was a sock in his throat, excited that the volleyball had sailed twenty-five yards away from play.

Everyone paused and looked at each other, quickly debating who would laugh first. A second later, everyone burst into laughter simultaneously. I could barely breathe I was laughing so hard. As I tried to peek through my eyes now filled with tears, I could see Avery lower his head and mumble, ". . . oh shit . . ."

After a few minutes passed and most of our laughing subsided, we continued to play the game. But I could not help but replay the audio of Avery over and over in my mind. We all seemed to be having a case of the giggles at Avery's expense.

As I never let go of the situation, Avery began to get perturbed. It got to the point that he kept threatening me, but every time he spoke, I reiterated everything in the best Avery impression I could muster.

Since I was like a pestering little brother testing the limits to the brink, it was only a matter of time before Avery snapped. He came charging from the other side of the net toward me while I continued to laugh hysterically. He first attempted to kick sand up to my eye with his right foot, to temporarily blind me. As the sand hit my face, I peered through my squinting eyes as best I could and caught his foot, which was now high in the air. I immediately yanked his leg higher into the air, which unbalanced him. Avery flew up and landed on his back. I secretly felt like Jackie Chan performing a karate move. But with the sound of his body slamming into the sand, all surrounding laughter ceased.

Without a word spoken from anyone, we all paused and waited for what might happen next. Avery slowly struggled to pick himself up and stand. Instead of lashing out and continuing the attack, as I thought was imminent, he composed himself, brushed the sand off, and limped all the way back to our barracks without saying a word. I could faintly hear the sad theme song from *The Incredible Hulk* television series playing in my head.

"Way to go, Conklin, you killed Avery," Fooks said to me with a smile.

"Dude, he is pissed!" Taylor said, still laughing.

We continued the game as usual, but I could not help but feel bad. It was funny still at the time, but Avery was the closest friend I had in the platoon. I later checked up on him, and he was in a lot of back pain, but not pissed. So went the relationship of Avery and me. We were a one-of-a-kind duo.

If volleyball was not someone's way to vent his boredom, there were many other outlets people partook in. Watching bootleg movies that were bought cheaply across the street at the haji[6] shop was something everyone did. One soldier would buy a video, and within two days it seemed that the entire company had viewed it. Masturbating to porn was always something to pass the time. Beer was nowhere to be found in the country, but we did have access to nonalcoholic beer in the chow hall. Like most guys, the gym became my closest ally. I wasn't one of the guys who received daily shipments of diet supplements, powders, and pills, working out until my heart exploded, but I found the opportunity almost every day to work out during time on my own. There was plenty of the latter.

---

[6] *Haji* is an adjective used by soldiers to refer to anything made or owned by Iraqis. There are haji cars, haji shops, haji food, haji clothes, haji homes, etc.

ON GUARD

"The sound or visual observation of explosions became an everyday occurrence in Baghdad."

It was not until October 14 that we received our individual guard duty assignments for the upcoming trial. Fooks and I would again be paired up to sit and guard OP (observation post) 11. This guard post was located on the northeastern corner of the rooftop of the Ba'ath Party Building. Being on this routine guard did give us a chance to get into a somewhat regular sleep schedule. Our shift time was from 3 A.M. to 11 A.M. until further notice. At first I was pleased by the time, but then I realized that it would be hard to be awake during the chow hall hours. We soon found ways around that and got into a rhythm.

Being on an OP was fun for about a day. The remaining days felt like every other day, but seemed to get progressively longer as they went on. An average day would consist of getting up at 2 A.M. and putting my uniform and its countless bits of gear on. We would then gather in the lobby of the school, where the sergeant in charge of the daily guard shift would check us all to ensure we had the right equipment and were able to function for guard. Fooks and I would then head out about 2:45 A.M. and start our long trek up the bombed out and crumbling stairs of the Ba'ath Party Building. I hated trekking up those six flights of broken steps in the black of night with all the odds going against me. With as much gear as we had on our backs, it was dangerous maneuvering through the dark, especially when we were unmotivated, hungry, and sweaty.

Once we completed the first task of making it to the top, we rested for a breather. We would then climb a wobbly ladder by which we finally made it to the corner guard post. At the changing of the guard, we were briefed by the men we replaced about any activities that we needed to be aware of. Most of the time there was nothing to report, but it was always done with a hint of sarcasm. Once the trade-out was complete, we began the long drudgery of sitting idle until 11A.M. Battling to stay awake proved to be one of the most difficult tasks while on a guard position.

On guard with the same person day in and day out, I learned more about Fooks than his own mother probably knew. Fooks and I had a lot in common, so it made for a much more relaxed and enjoyable time together. He was two years older than I and grew up in a small Pennsylvania town about an hour away from my home. He was my team leader and was destined to become a sergeant during the deployment. This was his second tour in Iraq, and October actually marked the month that should have been his release from the Army, but they'd seen things differently and "stop-lossed" him, which kept him in indefinitely. His aspirations to be promoted made him a stickler for standards. He would become what I referred to as "Der Fuehrer," comparing him to a Nazi.

When we would come on guard at three in the morning, the two men we would replace most of the time would be Sergeant Ethan Woods and Specialist Andrew "Drew" Kemple from Third Platoon, two great soldiers who relaxed some rules a bit while on the OP. They rarely had their NODs out by the time I was reporting, yet their entire guard shift was spent in the dark. They even joked that they would sometimes initiate a sleep schedule but I was skeptical as to whether that was their sarcasm or reality. Most noticeable was that I can't recall them ever wearing clear eye protection during night hours, which was fine with me but not for "Der Fuehrer." I know it was Fooks acting with the best of intentions, but it made something as tedious as guard all the more uncomfortable. There I sat, with my NODs on my helmet, scanning left and right, while wearing clear glasses. I got used to it, but would have loved to take my helmet off at times.

The view we had of Baghdad from OP 11 was outstanding. Tall buildings, the Hands of Victory, the bridge over the Tigris River, and the mosques that dotted the horizon were enough to stimulate the eyes.

An occasional explosion or sporadic gunfire could be heard throughout the city at any given time. Our job was to report the distance and direction to headquarters, and anything else that could help. When we did report any activity we witnessed, we would usually be told to "keep monitoring the situation" and nothing would be done. The sound or visual observation of explosions became an everyday occurrence in Baghdad. Each time I experienced one, I would think to myself that it marked one less terrorist in the world to worry about if it was a suicide bomber.

One morning, I saw an explosion just outside the Green Zone walls. By luck, I happened to be staring directly at that section of the city when a car exploded in the far distance and sent a large smoke pile and debris flying up through the air. I grabbed my compass and got an azimuth to calculate the distance and direction, while Fooks relayed my description on the radio up to higher. After that, the situation was out of our hands. I never heard what all had transpired.

One of the most anticipated days for enemy activity occurred on October 15. That was the date for the referendum on the new Iraq constitution. We were told every night in our squad meetings leading up to this date to be the utmost vigilant then. The Green Zone was reported to be a high target for mortar and rocket fire, and we were even told that there might be a coordinated attack by the enemy to attempt to puncture the Green Zone. As badass as this sounded—and even with us trigger-happy grunts secretly daring them to try—October 15 passed as an ordinary day, with a couple common explosions heard in the distance. There were dozens of American patrols that ran outside our walls, babysat by Abrams tanks at strategic points of entry around FOB Union III. The Alamo was untested.

Two days later a mortar landed within FOB Union III, in the Aussies' camp, which was only a stone's throw away from our company's building. No one was injured, because the mortar did not detonate after it landed. No one even knew it had happened until it was mentioned in the evening meeting.

Conversations with the person you serve guard with pass the time and usually have the tendency to get pretty deep. Fooks and I would open discussions about anything and everything. We talked about what future events could transpire in the course of the year, past memories, future desires, girls, or games that we made up to pass the time. Every day on guard we would try to find new things to talk about and get lost in. Fooks and I would make up games such as "The Six Degrees of Ben Affleck" or "Name That Tune." We also talked about ongoing operations and casualties within our division that we read about in the paper. Eight hours a day with the same individual grew a bond that became unbreakable. I think we had enough time to talk about every issue possible. We discussed music, The Beatles, our families, and even dreamed about the day when we both would be out of the Army for good. Then the subject would always come up of what we would do next. Fooks flirted with the idea of returning to college. I too dreamt of the day I would be back in school. I even joked that I would become a cast member of a reality television show.

GUARDING THE TRIAL OF THE CENTURY

"I did not want to miss my chance to watch history unfold."

On October 19 the "trial of the century," as some called it, kicked off right beneath my feet. Saddam Hussein and seven other former Iraqi officials were put on trial by Iraqi authorities. They were being charged with the killing of 148 Shiites that had occurred nearly twenty years earlier. The world and specifically Iraq knew that Hussein faced a litany of other charges that were just as gruesome.

The monumental day was a little different from normal days because the entire platoon was manning guard shifts all throughout the FOB, some in guard towers, others next to the courthouse door, and some in the basement of the Ba'ath Party Building. Shortly after Fooks and I arrived to OP 11, the normal calm morning routine of guard was altered. Around 3:30 A.M. two Black Hawk helicopters came over us and landed in the middle of our FOB. The LZ was near the chow hall and past the opposite corner of the Ba'ath Party Building, so I could not monitor the hubbub until the armored bus came by the bottom of the building below me leading up to the courthouse. I did not want to miss my chance to watch history unfold, so I hung my head over the edge of the rooftop and looked down. I saw several three-letter-agency American security teams everywhere. The bus parked for a few moments and soon began to pour out prisoners.

It was hard to tell who was who from their heads, because they were wearing body armor. I wanted so badly to go downstairs a couple floors and get a closer look. Fooks did not like the idea of leaving one person at the post, but we'd done it every time before when one of us had to use the bathroom, which was located at the very bottom of the building. I told him I would return quickly and sprinted back in the building and down the stairs. Because every man in the platoon was stationed all through-out the place, there were a couple people from my squad on one of the landings, in the dark stairwell that overlooked the alley to the back door. When I showed up, I saw Taylor, and he kept saying how he saw Hussein and how creepy it was. I pulled my camera out and tried to take a picture, but I forgot to turn the flash off and I saw at least three heads from the personal security team look up. I freaked out because we'd been specifi-cally instructed not to take pictures. I pleaded with Taylor to lie if anyone asked and tell them that it was a flashlight accidentally triggered. Not a word was ever mentioned and the photo didn't even turn out. I ran back up to my post while the prisoners were swiftly escorted in through the back entrance of the courthouse. Hussein and the others were safe inside, but I was not going to be content until I saw him with my own eyes.

I returned to Fooks sweaty and out of breath. "Damn. Maybe tomor-row" became a catchphrase on that guard post.

This method went on the exact same way for every day afterward that they came to our FOB. It was all very exciting, being a part of this trial. I would see them load into the building in the morning, and after my guard shift I would go get lunch in the chow hall and see the trial on a live television feed that the entire world was watching. It was a unique feeling knowing that this international news event was occurring only a couple hundred feet from where I slept.

The trial went off uncompromised throughout its entirety, but during the early morning I would watch as all of the judges, lawyers, and other personnel shuffled into the courthouse, and within the first few weeks of the trial I read in the paper about how one of the attorneys was as-sassinated somewhere in Baghdad. He would become the first of several individuals to lose their life over the course of the trial.

REALITY CHECK

"The concussion was felt throughout my body."

After two weeks of doing the same routine guard shift every day, we all started to grow tired of what we were doing. We began to feel complacent, bored, and unused. In fact, we were uncertain if we were ever going to get utilized to our full ability in Iraq. Guarding was something an infantry unit that trained as hard as we had hated in a hurry. Every day became the same for me. Walk up the stairs, sit for eight hours, and walk back down. During one of the descents Fooks and I made after guard, down the countless flights of crumbling stairs of the Ba'ath Party Building, I managed to injure myself. As we gingerly stepped on the shifting cement steps, a crumbled chunk I stepped on shot out from under my right foot. The weight I was carrying throughout my body sent me falling down the stairs, buckling my right ankle severely. I heard a popping sound as I went rolling.

When I finally stopped tumbling and the dust settled, I tried to catch my breath as I clutched my ankle. Fooks swiftly moved toward me and immediately inspected my foot.

"Shit, you OK, man?" he inquired.

"FUCK! Son of a bitch! This is a classic move on my behalf," I tried to say sarcastically, but I was in obvious pain. I reached for my canteen and took a large drink of water while I surveyed my situation. I tried to isolate my ankle. I felt around the outside of my boot and knew that I had not broken anything, but I was seconds away from severe swelling. I quickly tied my boot extremely tight to keep pressure around my ankle before I tried to walk back to the school barracks.

"Do you think you can make it down?" Fooks asked. "I'll help you down. Come on." He stretched out to pick me up. The two of us limped down the remaining flights of stairs. I had rolled my ankle numerous times throughout my life, but this one was far worse, mainly owing to the countless pounds of gear that weighed me down. I saw the doctor to get it inspected as soon as I got back. He reassured me that my ankle was not broken but said that I'd stretched my ligament pretty severely. I took my swollen ankle and limped back to the school barracks, where I propped my foot up with pillows and went to sleep. I only missed one guard shift, because I did not want to screw anyone else over with extra duty. The following day, I was back up at OP 11 with my feet propped up on some sandbags while I watched Baghdad usher in the morning.

Guard continued on in its normal fashion. Only the small things that occurred made the time easier to pass. One morning, soon after the prayers from the mosques wrapped up, a shot rang out from the general direction we were watching, near a building about three hundred yards away. Fooks and I were in the middle of a conversation, but within the next second we were both instinctively on the ground. It was a cautionary reaction when a rifle was shot. After a few seconds on the ground we peered over the sandbags around our gun and surveyed the city like wide-eyed prairie dogs. We also aimed our machine gun in the direction of the shot. Fooks was already on the radio sending it to higher. There was nothing more we could do than to sit and wait until our guard shift was over. The next day I spent most of my time while on guard refortifying the position with more sandbags, a metal door, and other scrap materials I found on the Ba'ath Party Building rooftop. I worked up a hell of a sweat, but it passed the time and strengthened my confidence in the OP.

In mid-November, our company rearranged our guard rotation shifts. First Platoon shifted to guard the front main entrance. Being on a gun team, I sat behind the machine gun with Fooks again for another eight hours a day, this time inside a concrete pillbox which was surrounded by countless sandbags giving the appearance of a pyramid. The gun pit had no room to stand up and no chairs to sit on, so we had to create a make-shift sandbag stool. We still did eight hours on and sixteen off, only this time our rotation was from 10 A.M. to 6 P.M.

A few days into our new rotation, I was off duty and sleeping when I was suddenly awoken shortly after 8:00 A.M. to a sound seared into my memory. The day was November 18 and I was sound asleep, dreaming of things far better than where I was. Being a light sleeper, the slightest noise would usually wake me up. This particular morning I awoke believing I heard a muffled explosion far away but still close enough to be concerned about. I glanced around the room to see if anyone else had been awake to hear that. I made eye contact with Fooks, who was still in bed, but was just as wide-eyed as me. We did not speak a word, but I could tell from his eyes that he'd heard something too. Before I could open my mouth to speak, *BLOOOOM!* came the sound of an extremely loud explosion. The windows shook violently next to my head, and I instantly covered my face, fearing the glass would shatter onto me.

"Mortars! Take cover!" yelled my crazed platoon sergeant from the adjoining room.

Instantaneously, everyone in my room flew out of bed. As I flipped out of mine and onto the floor, my peripheral vision saw everyone doing the same.

"Eddie, no!" Avery yelled in vain up to Taylor, who was now mid-flight from his upper bunk, on his way to landing on top of him.

"Get your shit on!" yelled Sergeant First Class Quinn as he weaved in between our beds on his way out of the room. He had his weapon in his hands, and his body was dripping in gear and ammunition.

I was still trying to grasp the situation. It had been so serene just five seconds ago, and now there was all this commotion. I grabbed my helmet and put it on while I reached for my weapon. What happened? I kept asking myself that question. I knew everyone was thinking the same thing. My first reaction was that the main gate had to have gotten hit by a suicide car or something. The explosion sounded right on top of us. It was so incredibly loud and the concussion was felt throughout my entire body. In a hurry, Fooks and I were the first ones from our squad's room into the lobby, waiting to hear from anyone who knew anything.

We started getting a hodgepodge of reports, but one thing stood out: The main gate was secured. The explosions had happened right across the river, at the Hamra Hotel where foreign journalists stayed. Some insurgents drove a car rigged with explosives up to the security wall of the hotel and detonated them. This was the first explosion I heard, the one that initially woke me up. The plot was then furthered by a more powerful truck filled with explosives that detonated at the same spot near the hotel, killing eight Iraqis and wounding over forty more. The Tigris River that separated us from the situation amplified and carried the sound over to us.

We were put on high alert, but eventually we were given the all clear on our FOB. My squad quietly returned to our building. The smell of explosives and fire still lingered in the air that the soft wind brought over. Fooks and I paused before entering our room, a little tired but still filled with adrenaline, to converse. We paused and both started laughing when we realized our appearance. Though Fooks and I had been the first of our squad out of the room and ready to do whatever necessary, we were both in nothing more than our PT shorts, unlaced boots, helmets, and protective vests, with one weapon and one ammo mag each. Had the insurgents hit our front gate, they would have been greeted by two tired, disgruntled, half-naked men with rifles. It was one of those moments where we just had to laugh. It was what kept us sane.

SAME SHIT, DIFFERENT DAY

"We lost track of what day it was."

Our platoon continued to manage the front gate for the next two weeks. Those were boring times babysitting that entrance, but luckily they were filled with some of the most in-depth conversations about anything and everything. Fooks and I also snuck in plenty of Sudoku puzzles that I would cut out from the *Stars and Stripes* newspaper each day. Fooks and I would often challenge each other on who could finish first, in pen.

The boredom of sitting in a gun pit for hours on end led people to do mischievous things. Some soldiers would constantly stab sandbags with pens and knives, an activity that did not benefit anyone. I drew a picture of a giant Indian warrior on a sandbag to poke fun at Private "Chief" Estrada, a proud Native American and fellow member of my squad. In the long run, my platoon's destructive activities led to an impromptu investigation by our sergeants as to who was doing the slaughtering of sandbags.

We initially all believed it to be our platoon scapegoat, Specialist Wilson Ly, who was notorious for getting caught for mischievous and random acts of poor choice. Sadly, no one officially declared he was the one stabbing the sandbags. I admitted to the drawing because it actually was a really good picture and it hurt nothing.

In the long run, we were all punished as a group for the phantom sandbag stabber. After our shift we all had to fill sandbags for over an hour and replace the giant gun pit's damaged bags. Our platoon learned the lesson and never repeated the activities—except for drawing—in guard positions.

Saddam's trial resumed on December 5, after a week's delay, and finally gave my platoon a break. Everyone except my gun team, that is. Apparently my platoon leader, Second Lieutenant Adam Scher, made a rookie mistake. He decided to give a break to another gun team in another platoon, and used mine instead. Scher was a recent addition to our platoon and was fresh out of West Point. He was as "by the book" as new "butter bar" lieutenants came. The fact that he looked eerily similar to a grown-up Ralphie from the classic Christmas movie *A Christmas Story* didn't really work in his favor either. Detailing our gun team out to another platoon was the first of many stunts that Scher would pull that pissed me off.

So when the rest of the platoon was guarding the basement of the Ba'ath Party Building about four hours a day, Fooks, Chief, and I continued to roast in the gun pit of the front entrance. We were attached to Second Platoon and had to follow their rules. They came up with the most exhausting shift rotation ever. Eight hours on, eight hours off, eight hours on, eight hours off, eight hours on, and thirty-two hours off. Time spent for inspections, meals, and random tasks that came my way during the day was not factored in, and that left very little free time to do anything. The point was to keep a constant rotation without setting a pattern. Well, I may not have been an officer, but I knew that this new rotation had a pattern in itself. All I could do was complain to myself and my gun team. A couple days into the new rotation, we found it impossible to get any kind of sleep. It deteriorated everyone's alertness.

Spending every waking moment in the gun pit seemed to freeze time. It was the most monotonous time of my life and it was a struggle to stay sane. I could feel brain cells literally simmer within my helmet as I sat like a broken robot. Fooks, Chief, and I engaged in intellectual conversations about the most random stories of our past in order to keep our brains working and the time passing. Most conversations, however, centered on the female anatomy, porn, or our drunken pasts.

Sometimes we made up little games to pass the time, such as urine competitions. Since we were unable to leave the gun pit while on shift, we resorted to urinating into the empty water bottles that surrounded us. A competition was born in which at the end of the shift we would declare the winner to be whoever could fill the most bottles with urine. On average, we each would fill almost two one-liter bottles. In hindsight, what we did sounds incredibly stupid, but given the situation, there was nothing else to do.

With Saddam's trial continuing on our FOB, I was still adamant about seeing him with my own eyes. I would see the prisoner bus come through our gate late at night, but it was always empty, since the prisoners were flown in. On one of the last mornings I knew Saddam would be on our FOB, I stayed awake at night before my guard shift and walked outside after I heard the blades of a Black Hawk churning. Based on routine, I knew that this was the time that he would be driven to the helicopter pad and transferred into the helicopter. I walked down near the chow hall and got a good vantage spot within a shadow of a building. Either nobody cared or everyone was sleeping, because I was the only one around watching the switchover. As soon as the prisoner bus rolled up with Humvee escorts, my eyes were glued. Quickly, a strange moment in time, I saw Saddam whisked away into the helicopter. I saw him! I was so thrilled to actually see the world's most notorious dictator in the flesh. I smiled, turned around, and went back to my building to nap before guard.

Guard duty continued in its own unfashionable and unmotivating way. Day in and day out, we lost track of what day it was. The only thing that kept us interested other than the standard chitchat was the rumors that were in the air of the next step for our company. One thing was certain: We knew that we would leave soon to a new FOB. We were even told to start packing. This was a good sign but did not help the torture of a monotonous guard shift twice a day. Fooks and I were running out of things to talk about. We needed something different.

That something different did come on one of our last guard shifts at the front gate. It was just like any other night on guard. Fooks and I were sitting on the gun, with Chief sitting underneath facing the opposite way. We were busy trying to spark up a good conversation topic. Around ten o'clock at night, as if at the drop of a hat, the entire sky of Baghdad around us was covered in bullet tracers.

"What the hell is going on?" was everyone's verbal reaction, but the phrase fell upon deaf ears. No one knew what was going on. I backed away from the gun to get a better view in the open, while Fooks stayed under our cement bunker. I climbed atop some sandbags to get to a more elevated position and peer over the walls of the FOB. Red bullets filled the black sky and were randomly fired into the air in all directions. It looked just like an old movie clip of the Battle of Britain, when all the tracers lit up the skies.

"Let me get a look!" Fooks said impatiently to me.

"All right, go. I'll get the gun," I said to him as he went out the back of the pit to where I'd been standing.

Red tracers, green tracers, and the sound of sporadic automatic gunfire filled the night sky. It was, ironically, so beautiful.

"Iraq just defeated Syria in a soccer game. It's celebratory fire. Don't be alarmed," shouted the sergeant in charge of our shift. "Stay under a good roof because these people don't understand the laws of physics."

As soon as the words left his lips, a bullet came straight down and struck the ground near where the sergeant was standing. The dirt and dust that was kicked up convinced me to stay inside the gun pit to continue my view of the tracer show. This celebration went on for about twenty minutes, but opened a floodgate for conversation the rest of the shift. The occasional smack of a dead bullet impacting the pavement outside sparked a smile from me whenever one landed nearby.

The next day, soldiers on guard on the roof told tales of countless bullets that ricocheted all night long on the roof. They too had sought out cover during the rain of lead. I read in the paper the day after that forty-six Iraqi civilians were injured from falling bullets during the celebration. I concluded that the Iraqi people desperately need a new form of expressing victory.

HURRY UP AND WAIT

"Within seconds everyone was suited up and hugging the ground."

I saw my last guard shift in Baghdad on the 12th of December, and it came and went as boring as the rest. With the responsibility of guarding the base passed back to 3ID, our next task became our packing. We spent about four days moving duffel bags and other items out of the school-house and into large metal railcar-looking containers called Conexes that were then shipped to our next location. Packing my multiple bags to the fullest proved the hardest and most time-consuming task. Not a centimeter of space was left in any bag.

Once packing was completed, all we had to do was wait. If not at the chow hall, everyone could be found in his bed just lying there trying to find things to do. One night as I lounged in my bed, I could hear Taps being played on a trumpet in the building adjoining my squad's room. The unit we were attached to had lost one of their officers from a roadside bomb and was having his memorial service. As I lay there in my bed, it really sunk in that now we were going to be the guys out there doing what they were doing. It was a somber and surreal moment. Poston broke the silence when he spoke out loud to himself and said, "Makes it all seem real." That it did.

On the 17th of December, we packed up our belongings and cleared out of the school that had been our barracks. The age-old "hurry up and wait" method set in and had us waiting forever in the afternoon sun outside the school. Cigarettes were smoked by the nicotine addicts and conversations ensued with everyone. I leaned against my gear next to Avery and enjoyed some pudding cups and Gatorade.

Eventually, a couple of deuce-and-a-half trucks came, picked us up, and drove us out of the FOB and down the road to LZ Washington. Some of our bags had left days prior on a convoy, to catch up to us when we got to wherever we were going. There was a rumor passed around our company that our Conexes were hit by an IED during a convoy up north. There was no confirmation as to whether any damage was done to our gear or not. Rumors led one's imagination to run rampant.

While at LZ Washington, we were briefly reunited with other members of our battalion whom we had not seen since Kuwait. Among these numerous friends, mostly from Bravo Company, was one that stood out from the rest. Specialist Richard "Scud" Scibetta had been a personal friend of mine for the past two years and was also very close with many members of my platoon. His personality traits mimicked the fictional character Rocky Balboa's, and Scud had become a sort of mascot to our platoon. We spent most of our time waiting at the LZ joking around with him before we headed out.

Our whole battalion left the Green Zone of Baghdad in Chinook helicopters that night, to regroup back at Camp Stryker in the Baghdad International Airport (BIAP). Our first night there, our platoon crammed into one tent that wasn't intended to hold as many bodies as were shoved into it. A succession of endless rows of tents for other platoons formed what was referred to as "Tent City." It was easy to lose track of which tent housed which platoon. From all of the constant moving of gear and the sporadic, recurring checks of sensitive items, our tiredness was enough to keep everyone asleep in his tent that first night.

Waking up in new places for the first time always brought new experiences. My first morning in Tent City was a rude awakening. I woke up near noon and rolled over in my cot to see if Fooks was awake yet. We exchanged a few words, until both of us stopped talking and lay there in silent reflection. Everyone else in the platoon was either still asleep or off in a musical oasis courtesy of an iPod. The environment was calm. The silence was broken with the sound of a rocket being launched in the distance, which sounded similar to a firework being sent up in the sky, before the explosion. As soon as I heard that initial sound, I opened my eyes and made direct contact with Fooks's. Without our saying any words, I knew in that split second we were both thinking the same thing: *Oh shit!* In almost the same split second I heard the voice of someone in my platoon utter, "That sounded like a . . . ," and before that person could say the inevitable, a loud and thundering *Kerploomf!* ripped through the tranquil scene.

"Get down!" was echoed by several people, but instinct moved quicker and had already sent everyone down to the earth. I spun out of my cot and landed quickly on the dusty wooden floor. Everyone in the tent rolled on the ground and weaseled his way into his vest and helmet at the speed of light. Within seconds everyone was suited up and hugging the ground. We expected another incoming rocket but prayed for it to be farther instead of closer.

As I was sprawled on the ground with Fooks and Avery by my side, we could not help but laugh and replay all of our reactions when we'd heard the initial launch of the rocket. The all clear was given on the loudspeaker after a couple of minutes. Avery and I left the tent to "kill the cat," as I called my quests of curiosity. The rocket had impacted only about two hundred meters from our tent, and had miraculously landed on the edge of Tent City, with the majority of its devastation destroying part of a concrete wall and a vacant truck. With another close call on the one-way road in life, Avery and I decided to do something. We got a haircut. We figured if we were ever going to kick the bucket while helplessly sleeping in our cots, we were at least going to look good.

We were scheduled to leave Baghdad that evening, to fly up north. Our final destination was set to be Tikrit, which would become our new base for the rest of our time in Iraq. Before we loaded up in our plane that night, our company was given time to stock up on some snacks and magazines for the road. As Avery and I walked to the AAFES[7] shop, I saw pass by me a familiar face that I'd never imagined I would see. I did

---

[7] *AAFES* stands for Army and Air Force Exchange Service, and is a military convenience store found on every military base in America. They sell everything a standard convenience store sells such as snacks, drinks, magazines, and odds-and-ends military equipment.

a double take. I turned around and saw my neighbor from back home in Gettysburg, Pennsylvania. Colin Wellborn, whom I grew up with and was friends with in high school was in the military and stationed at BIAP. How random it was to be at that particular corner of a large base at BIAP, let alone even just to be in the same place in Baghdad, or Iraq at all for that matter, a million miles away from Gettysburg, late at night, and here I found myself talking to one of my friends from back home. This fate-filled meeting proved a huge morale booster because for that small moment in time I felt far away from Iraq. Colin and I exchanged stories about our time there and stories of our hometown. I could have talked to him all night, but we both were in a hurry going opposite directions. I bid him the best of luck and we continued our separate missions in Iraq.

ARRIVING AT REMAGEN

**"The purpose . . . was to learn as much as
we could from the present unit."**

Our trip to Tikrit started at night on the 18th, when we flew out of BIAP. After a short flight and another cramped bus ride, we stopped for the night in a small plot of tents in an area we had no idea the location of. Later the next afternoon we packed ourselves and our gear into a Chinook helicopter for what seemed like a five-minute ride. Within that short trip in the air I saw a very different portrait of Iraq than I saw in Baghdad. The Tikrit area, located in the Al Saladhin province, was very flat, all desert, no trees, and scattered with random mud huts. It was a beautiful scene to see from the air, but in due time, I would grow tired of it.

We landed at the new place we would now call home. Two bases were located in Tikrit. One was FOB Speicher, which was huge and now the official headquarters of the 101st Airborne Division, and the other was a fraction of the size of Speicher and called FOB Remagen. The only occupants at FOB Remagen were my company, two battalions of field artillerymen from our brigade, and members of the 3ID whom we were replacing as they transitioned back to the United States.

We all finally got to move into a place of permanence in Iraq that first night at FOB Remagen. We were given trailers called CHUs.[8] At first, I shared a CHU, which normally housed two, with three soldiers from my squad. As more members from 3ID left, we would move into the vacant CHUs, which freed up the cramped ones. Soon, we had two men to a CHU.

The chow hall was an incredibly large tent, with hired workers from Africa who supplied delicious foods four times a day. I instantly knew that I would like it there at FOB Remagen. The only drawback to the chow hall was the fact that it was clear on the other side of the barren camp. A strategy to having a FOB located in open desert was keeping things separated in case of sporadic mortar or rocket attacks. As if walking the mile from our CHUs to the chow hall was not enough, it was a regulation from 3ID to wear your helmet, vest, and weapon at all times. This lasted for a couple of weeks after they left, but after some deliberation from higher command and plenty of complaints by all, the rule was eventually nullified and we soon were able to walk freely around FOB Remagen without all of our gear on.

The purpose of the first few days at FOB Remagen was to learn as much as we could from the present unit before they handed over all responsibility to us. Our first task at helping with the transition was to assist in occupying the guard towers around FOB Remagen. This was the last thing that any of us wanted to hear after our stay in Baghdad. Luckily, the task came down to the two lowest privates in our platoon, Private Rojo and Chief. We all knew they were picked because of their rank, but I would poke fun at them both and say, "Rojo, you were picked 'cause you can't speak English well, and Chief, um, you know it's 'cause you're Indian."

---

[8] *CHU*, pronounced "choo," stands for containerized housing unit. They are aluminum boxes roughly twenty-two by eight. They have linoleum floors and bunk beds inside. They're heated and contain an air conditioner. They also have two windows and one door.

WELCOME TO TIKRIT

"I found it quite exhilarating."

The first from my platoon to go on patrol were our squad leaders, lieutenant, and the platoon sergeant. This kept them out of our hair for a couple days. At night, they would regurgitate all that they learned and pass it on to us.

After some extensive map studying of the area and classes on how to perform our job as a mounted asset in Humvees, the lower enlisted started getting plucked from the bunch to go out on missions. My first mission came in the afternoon of December 21. A few men from my company were going to perform a dismounted patrol in the heart of Tikrit along with some men from 3ID.

We started off the mission with extensive driving all over the city. They were getting us familiar with the terrain, places of interest, and problematic areas. By late 2005, Iraqi civilians were all too used to the sight of convoys of military vehicles in their cities. I was impressed by how out of the way most cars would go at the sight of a Humvee. No cars could ever get close to us for obvious reasons. Sometimes, some cars refused to stop from either lack of concentration or the driver being just plain unaware. Our procedure, depending on the closeness of the vehicle, was to shoot what we called a "warning shot" with a shotgun from the man in the turret. After the first shot rang out that day, I realized that it was all real outside the wire.

The "sightseeing" tour was indeed eye-opening. One of the first structures I saw before rolling into Tikrit was a large photo-op structure sign that towered over MSR (Main Supply Route) Tampa with the words "Well Come to Tikrit" in English and Arabic on it. Streets were filled with old, rusty, dilapidated cars in the worst possible condition yet still drivable. It was not uncommon to see some with bullet holes. People packed the sidewalks and businesses. Men wore man-dresses called dishdashas.[9] Women were rare to see. The people would stop what they were doing and stare at us with cold, hard stares each time we drove by a circle of them. I'll never forget the sinister looks on their faces.

The streets were filled with scattered garbage, which was an obvious sign that no legitimate waste management system was in place. Grass seemed to be extinct, but trash filled that role. In the residential areas the streets were at an all-time slum of a condition. Sewage ran in the streets. The stench was only comparable to a large-scale septic tank. We drove through the market area, which was appalling. Animals were slain on the curbs and then cut and sold on the spot. Flies swarmed back and forth between the open meat and the civilians. The flies seemed to be more annoying to us than they were to the civilians. Businesses stood out with their faded shop signs that looked like they'd been created in the late 1970s. Most businesses appeared to be abandoned, but people came and went through their doors.

Children of all ages roamed the streets freely. The clothes they wore looked like they'd liquidated a town full of garage sales. Few children ever wore sandals or any type of footwear. Walking through the muck that ran in the streets never seemed to bother anybody. Most of the kids would run to our vehicles as we passed by and yell for candy, but the men in the turret would yell at them to stop and back off.

We stopped briefly to conduct a dismounted patrol in a residential area. Each vehicle dropped everyone except the driver and gunners so that they could continue to drive around while the dismounted walked.

---

[9] *Dishdasha* is the name for the traditional one-piece dress worn by Iraqi men. Soldiers often referred to them as simply "man-dresses."

As I got out of the vehicle, the putrid smell of feces in the air just intensi-fied and was mixed with the aroma of something similar to chalk dust. I just tried to get used to it because I knew that that smell was only going to linger.

Staff Sergeant David Hubert led the patrol through the streets, mak-ing me the second man, behind him. We walked all around the streets and battled the heat as our constant enemy. Call it a sixth sense, but for some reason I knew all would be fine, so I really was not nervous at all during my first patrol in the streets of Iraq. In fact, I found it quite exhilarating. I knew there was always the chance for anything to happen at any minute, but it was just that which I found intriguing. It's like what relic hunt-ing would be for an archaeologist or ocean diving if you were a marine biologist. You never knew what you could get into with every street you walked down.

The patrol saw us cross through a couple of abandoned homes, in-teract with reclusive locals, stop on street corners to do map checks, and frequently fence hop. I felt intrusive at first just walking into people's homes, but I realized that I was the law in Tikrit and the authority was something I had to accept. When we crossed through a schoolyard, I got my first close interaction with some Iraqi children. The moment we were in the yard, swarms of them came running out of the school like a fire alarm had gone off. In a heartbeat, I had fifteen or so kids clinging to me and pulling on my gear. I tried to keep eye contact with the other men in my patrol, but they had their own following of children attached to them as well.

"Mista, mista" uttered all the children. "Chocolaté, chocolaté!" went the cries as they tugged on every piece of gear I was wearing. I tried to stay nice, but I was also trying to perform my first patrol and I wanted to focus on what the sergeants were instructing. "Sorry, kids, you have no idea what I'm saying, but I don't have any chocolate," I said, know-ing that they were clueless as to what I was saying. "Give me, give me," replied other children.

The children began slowing me down. I needed to start pushing them away, and I pointed in different directions with my hand in hopes that they would leave, like throwing an invisible stick to an energetic dog. "Give me watch, mista," said this young boy, probably around twelve years old. "My watch? I need it to tell time. Sorry, buddy," I said to him as I pushed through the crowd to regroup with my patrol.

The other half of that patrol was spent going through people's homes and also a few abandoned ones. Every street seemed to have one or two abandoned homes. I guess real estate is easy to come by when your country is at war. As eye-opening as it was, after my first patrol I realized this was going to be a long nine months.

The next day was a scheduled mounted patrol in 3ID's Bradley vehicles. Only three soldiers were plucked from our platoon: The Hodge, Avery, and Specialist Vinse "Vinny" Edwards. There were also others from my company who represented their platoons. They went in the middle of the night to do an observation stakeout along a heavily utilized road that we called Route Clemson, where terrorists were known to place IEDs frequently. When the patrol came back in the early hours of the night, it seemed to have been just another ordinary successful mission, because Avery went straight to bed. We were sharing a CHU and he did not say a word when he got back.

I woke up before Avery, and I heard from others in the platoon what had happened on their patrol. At the end of their stakeout, they physically walked down the road on foot, back to their Bradleys. Then the Bradley Avery and the others were riding in threw a track and needed to be replaced. Avery and Vinny sat on the ramp while The Hodge made himself comfortable in a nearby ditch and they waited for a wrecker and QRF[10] to respond. When the other patrol was approaching the Bradleys, a 155mm IED exploded on one of the Humvees from the QRF and was followed by some small-arms fire. Buried and blended in with concrete to give the appearance of a poorly conditioned road, this booming arsenal of destruction had been camouflaged. Everyone jumped back into action, and 3ID began returning fire into a nearby house that bystanders were pointing at, indicating a man inside. After the patrol, they all mounted back in their Bradleys and headed down Route Clemson, back to the FOB.

When Avery woke up, I got the finished story from him. All he could keep replaying was his description of the enormous ear-shattering sound of the explosion on the outside of his vehicle and how it made his ears

---

[10] QRF stands for quick reaction force, a platoon on standby at all times on the FOB that also performs route clearances twice a day.

ring afterward. He also mentioned that because of the threat of another bomb in the road, they decided to stay inside the vehicle while the gunners opened fire on the nearby abandoned building. The gunners did manage to refrain from killing the man inside, but they arrested him. Further tests were done to determine if he did emplace the device himself. It sounded intense, and I could tell Avery was drained of all energy. He never left the CHU that day. I went to the chow hall and got him a to-go box with meatballs and noodles. He got about halfway through one meatball and fell asleep with the box on his chest and a meatball still in his mouth. I instantaneously picked right up on this and laughed hysterically while I gathered others in my platoon to see the spectacle. Avery continued to sleep through my laughter.

Though I was nowhere near this attack, it was my first real glimpse of the carnage that awaited me outside the wire.

GETTING INTO A GROOVE

"Merry fucking Christmas!"

With the 3ID giving up less and less personnel each day as they transitioned out, we kept filling the vacancies with men from our platoon. With just one infantry company running patrols in Tikrit, the Angels from Hell were constantly working. We were still waiting for a field artillery battalion from our brigade to join us, but they were still slowly moving into FOB Remagen as well. It came down to my company to take charge of everything.

We were all still hashing out standards and procedures as we went along. For almost two years prior to this deployment, we trained in light infantry tactics without the experience of being mounted with vehicles. We excelled at road marching, air assaults, door kicking, ambushes, etc. All of that went out the window, and we had to start fresh by learning how to operate as a mounted element in Humvees. It was definitely a learning experience for my entire company. We were all picking up the different roles that comprised an efficient Humvee element. Out of all the roles I could have filled in the truck, I got stuck being in the gunner's turret every single mission for a long continuous time. Each platoon was tasked out with running at least two missions a day. That alone kept us outside the wire almost the entire day. Did I mention we did night missions almost as regularly? There was no pattern to our patrols. It was all day every day.

Colonel Steele wanted constant patrols to keep us all on our toes. He wanted patrols to last at least six hours each time we left the wire. 3ID did not stay out nearly as long as Steele projected. It was a smart idea, but being on the short end of the stick took its toll on us all. It seemed that we would always have a patrol during a mealtime, so we never had time to enjoy food at the chow hall.

A mission could consist of anything at random and was not as glamorous as it sounded. Most times we were given a mission where we had to just drive around and be seen. These were known as "presence patrols." Others required more dismounting, which meant more walking. It gave the lieutenant a chance to talk to locals, to see if they would divulge information. Other times we had "route clearance," which had us drive around streets and remove trash and make sure nothing ever blew up on us as we drove. A common question always asked was "When are we going to get some sexy missions?" What we did became very boring very quickly.

When a mission came down, we'd spend an hour before prepping the vehicle. We made sure we had everything we needed for any situation. A close inspection to ensure the weapons on the truck were clean was the most crucial. No matter what, in a matter of seconds, sand always found its way into a gun's chamber. The RTO, the soldier responsible for radio transmissions, would check all the radios in the truck and make sure we had communications with all elements. We would then assemble everyone together for a mission brief.

First Lieutenant Scher loved to talk and would always give us an hour-long explanation of what our mission was, and we would all listen and study the map as he went along. At the end of the mission we had to refuel all the trucks, check all equipment, and clean all weapons and trucks and be ready for another outing. It seemed that by the time we got done cleaning out the trucks, it was about time to reload them and head back out. This method lasted for about three weeks before we had time to slow down, breathe, organize everything, and divvy up the missions more equally among the other platoons.

It was no surprise that within the first few days of constant missions Christmas crept up on us without any fanfare. I remember lying in my bed and hearing a knock on the door to my CHU. Fooks then entered the room singing a Christmas carol, and it only then dawned on me what day it was, as I laughed in my bed and threw my pillow over my face.

"Merry fucking Christmas!" Fooks said to me.

"Merry fucking Christmas to you too," I said in reply.

"Hey, you need to get out here, it's Christmas. There are presents every—" he began to say before I cut him off.

"Yeah, I'm sure there are."

"No, I'm serious. Third ID left today, and they took all their shit they didn't need and piled it next to all the bathrooms. Get out before everyone takes all the good shit," Fooks explained as he left my CHU to get more "presents."

Being able to distinguish between Fooks's honesty and bullshit, I quickly threw my boots on and walked outside. To my surprise, it was like numerous garage sales were going on along all the bathroom trailers, and everything had the price tag of free. Fooks was not lying. It was just like Christmas. I quickly began to sift through all the junk, finding numerous items to snag and run back into my room. I was rushing, partly out of being so thrilled, but also trying to beat the mad dash because the word was now being passed around all my guys. I found new computer speakers, a mirror, a brand-new pair of desert combat boots, a basketball, a football, an unused Iraqi wool blanket, an American flag, a box of bootleg DVDs, a camp chair, two dressers, and countless ammo cans full of assorted ammunition. I then decided to head back and enjoy my gifts from the departing division. Avery's lazy ass did not manage to wake up that morning, but I knew he was looking for a new pair of boots in a certain size that I did happen to find. So I gave him a Christmas gift of a brand-new pair of boots. Everyone soon woke up and began the frenzy of collecting someone else's trash as his treasure. The rest of the day, until our afternoon mission, I spent in my CHU blaring Christmas music from my computer on my new speakers, courtesy of 3ID.

Our afternoon mission on Christmas Day was mainly a retaliation mission. We had received some information from a local Iraqi concerning the IED that had hit Avery, The Hodge, and Vinny's patrol a few days prior. This was to be our first raid and only consisted of our platoon. While the higher-ups collected and organized all of the information, we lower enlisted men packed all the trucks up and got them ready to roll out.

After our pre-mission checks and our mission brief were completed in the afternoon, we were ready for our "Christmas Raid." I was still a permanent gunner on one of the four Humvees, so it was basically another day at the office for me. As we were leaving the compounds of FOB Remagen, all of our weapons were locked, cocked, and placed on safe like always.

We were headed to a small village along Route Clemson, but to get there we had to travel through downtown Tikrit and hang a right to leave our assigned sector. A few occasional shotgun blasts from the first truck helped clear the road of civilian cars. We loved our shotguns.

It took about fifteen minutes before we arrived at the house in question. The first and second truck circled around to the back of the house, while the fourth truck and mine secured the front. Each truck's gunner pointed in a different direction to have full security of the perimeter. All of the dismounts exited the Humvees at the same time and lined up against the outer courtyard wall.

Something to understand about Iraqi homes is that they were almost always surrounded by walls that divided their property lines. Every house had its own courtyard separating it from its neighbors. Iraqis chose to hide their houses behind walls instead of having open view homes like ours in America. Our interpreter mentioned it was also a way for the men of the family to hide their wife and/or daughters from outsiders.

The dismounts from my platoon quickly stacked against the gate of the exterior wall and tried to open the gate in vain. They were moving quick like we had done hundreds of times during training. After several hasty attempts to open the gate had failed, everyone realized the need to get inside as soon as possible. On the ground, Sergeant First Class Quinn organized the first truck to ram in the fence with their front bumper. After the driver quickly reacted and drove into the gate, the dismounted element freely ran into the courtyard with precision.

Once inside the courtyard, the men hastily stacked along the front door, with each man aiming his M4 in a different direction, a textbook orchestration of an almost 360-degree angle of protection. The leader in the front of the group, Sergeant Evan Pitchford, swung over his shotgun, placed it around the doorknob, and fired into the door. With the door now deemed unlocked in our fashionable way, the element pushed in the door and entered the house. From my vantage point in the Humvee's turret, everything just flowed as it had been done in almost every one of our thousands of practice drills. From all my training, I knew the situation inside the house was going as planned, because I never heard any more shots. That was a relief. I also kept a handset from the radio stretched and strapped to my helmet so I could keep up with the progress inside of the house.

In the turret I kept close observation of the curious neighbors. Families grouped together by the gates of their courtyard and tried to peer through holes in their walls to investigate. I had to deal with them by yelling at the onlookers and sending them back inside their homes. If something ever did go wrong in the area, I figured it would be safer for them to be inside.

About fifteen minutes had passed by the time the dismounted element came cautiously back out of the house with one man in handcuffs. All went well, judging from the radio transmissions, and all concern subsided when I saw everyone get back into his vehicle. With an empty seat in my truck, the prisoner was placed in our Humvee as we drove back to FOB Remagen. Being in the turret, I could not get over the fact of how bad this man smelled. The turret hatch acted as a funnel of funk that tickled my nose with everyone's body odor, but this detainee's smell was ripe. It was like a mixture of a locker room and a wet dog. I was just glad I was in the turret, which at least had some fresh air flow, and not down below like the other three men in my truck.

So with our first raid as a platoon, by ourselves, we did pretty well. There was really only one hiccup. After Pitchford shot the door for the initial entry, a couple small bits of wood chips flew back in his face, which gave him numerous small cuts. With our constant habit of wearing eye protection at all times since leaving America, his eyes were saved from injury. We even made it back to FOB Remagen in time to enjoy a Christmas feast at the chow hall. Though we all missed our own family during this holiday, we were once again massed together around the same dinner table as a platoon, our new family.

EXPLORING TIKRIT

"Like a scene in a movie set in biblical times."

Spare time between missions in my platoon was spent scavenging. First Platoon was notorious for finding and building things. Avery, I, and a few others in our platoon drove to the mechanics bay. We got in there as soon as 3ID left, but before the members from 3/320th Field Artillery arrived. Tools and parts were at our disposal as we all spent our free time fixing up our own trucks. We took a couple new bumpers and turret slings taken from disabled vehicles with severe shrapnel damage. I disassembled a side mirror from a Humvee and mounted it to the side of my own turret. This gave me the opportunity to see behind me as I traveled in my truck. Not being a very craft-handy person like Avery was, I felt proud of my addition to the Humvee. I also added two large empty ammo cans bolted to the side of my turret. This was soon copied by Humvees everywhere. I was not the first, but after I put them on mine, every turret had spare ammo cans bolted to their sides within days.

Our constant presence outside the wire gave us an ample amount of time to visit every square inch in and around Tikrit. We explored Tikrit and her adjoining villages, such as Ad Dwar, Kadasiyah, Owja, and dozens of scattered mud huts that formed small communities.

One small nameless community appeared to be more of an oasis to me. During one of our countless missions of just getting used to the area, we stumbled upon a small dirt road. This road stretched parallel to the Tigris River and ran into a dead-end village. The interpreter, being a native of the area, knew it was a peaceful stretch of homes. We were a couple miles away from Tikrit and already the landscape was shifting in appearance. We were now traveling through a real mountainous area. The land started to show vegetation the more we drove deeper into the hillside. Cows began to roam free in the fields and birds began to sing.

I felt completely impervious to danger, so I stood up tall in the turret and admired the passing scenery. I saw that the other gunners were down inside, but it wasn't because they were protecting themselves from possible IEDs; it was ass-cold outside. My truck cranked the heat inside, but in the turret I could not feel a thing. I was just being slammed by frigid cold air. I was oddly reminded of times when I froze in the bleachers of high school football games. The landscape was so beautiful that I did not really mind being so exposed or frozen. A lot of people are surprised that Iraq has the potential of being so hot but also being so cold. As in all climates, there are hot, cold, dry, and wet seasons in Iraq.

We finally reached the small village that really only consisted of three homes. It was like a blast from the past. No electricity was in sight. Donkeys and sheep freely roamed around the homes. Sheepherders were seen with their flock on the horizon of the mountains. Like a scene in a movie set in biblical times, but it was all happening in real time. Kids came clamoring out of their houses, and they cheered, danced, and gave us the thumbs-up. This could have been the first time these homes had ever even seen American soldiers, judging by their welcoming interest and excitement.

Staff Sergeant Poston was seated below inside the Humvee, near my right foot, and he handed me a bag of candy and told me to start throwing the kids some. This was the moment when I realized I could no longer feel my hands to even grab the candy. I stripped off my gloves and put my hands in my crotch to warm them up. Poston shoved my empty gloves inside the heated vent to warm them up. After some time of regaining feeling in my hands and putting on nice warm gloves, I proceeded with throwing candy to the youngsters. I felt like I was on a parade float rolling down Main Street. Though the children could not express their gratitude in English, their actions spoke louder than words.

Along the same road we eventually came across a large embankment where we stopped our vehicles. This gave everyone time to relieve himself and let the gunners warm up. We set up a small security zone, and I quickly dropped down into the truck and wrapped myself in a blanket. It was now sunrise, and the sun became a welcoming sight as it lit up the Tigris River with an orange fluorescent glow. A light fog that also hovered over the river created one of the most beautiful sights I had ever seen. My speculation that this spot was some kind of secret of Tikrit was debunked when I asked the interpreter if anyone around town knew of this beautiful area. He informed me that Saddam Hussein used to come to the very spot where I was busy relieving myself. He went on to explain that Saddam would throw hand grenades into the river. What a lousy fisherman, I thought, as I continued to urinate on Saddam's "fishing" spot.

We finished up that morning by making a pit stop at the nearby American base, FOB Speicher. We tried to make a trip there at least once a month. It had everything a deployed soldier would want or need, so we made a quick twenty-minute run to the PX[11] to stock up on goodies. When we drove through FOB Speicher, we always passed what looked like a junkyard, but it was made up of American military vehicles that had been severely damaged from roadside bombs. They were either stripped for parts or sent off somewhere else. Driving by the metal graveyard was always depressing and scary because there were ambulances, Humvees, Abrams tanks, you name it. They were all charred and ripped open like butchered cans. It always got quiet in the vehicles when we passed by the lot. We all tried to concentrate on what we would buy at the PX instead of seeing vehicles that were stained with death.

---

[11] PX stands for Postal Exchange and is another name for AAFES; a military operated convenience store.

BRINGING IN THE NEW YEAR

"Stay alert, stay alive."

Two days before the New Year we came across our first VBIED.[12] While out on one of our numerous "getting acquainted" missions, we received a call from company headquarters around 9 P.M., about an informant who'd called in about a car rigged with explosives. We were given an approximate location and the style and color of a car. The information described practically half the vehicles on the road: a white four-door, possibly abandoned, and very old and rustic-looking. We quickly snapped into action, checked our maps, and headed to the area, a hot spot of activity for the unit before us. We drove in slowly and looked for any white car in sight. After stopping two vehicles along the way, we found a car that matched the description. It was abandoned and off the side of the road at a bend that we referred to as Z Road. We were working on a tip that the car was possibly rigged to explode, so none of us were willing to go up close enough to it to visually verify. We had to call someone whose job it was to do so.

---

[12] *VBIED* (pronounced "V-bed") stands for vehicle-borne improvised explosive device. In more familiar terms, it's a car bomb.

We split the patrol up in half, with two vehicles on each end of the road to prevent traffic and keep the car within our cordon. When our area was secured, we called up the EOD (Explosive Ordnance Disposal) unit. These guys were highly trained and lived for these situations. They arrived about a half hour later equipped with little remote-controlled robots commonly called "Johnny 5s," nicknamed after the popular movie from the 1980s *Short Circuit.*

We sat in our Humvees in sheer boredom as four hours passed before we heard a lick of an update. It was nearly one in the morning when we were finally told by EOD that they had confirmed multiple artillery rounds in the back of this white car. Our attention level was very low after sitting for hours so idle and in complete darkness. We all just wanted to see the unit explode this car in place. We were men of short attention spans and who doesn't like to see things explode? After about six hours of being on scene, the car was finally detonated by EOD, which sent a loud and thunderous explosion across the desert along with an incredible fireball into the black night.

The explosion was pretty exciting for about five seconds, then most of the real entertainment came from inside of my truck. Poston tried his hardest to keep everyone in the vehicle awake. He tried very hard in vain. We rotated guard shifts in the turret to keep a watch out around our perimeter, but when you're tired and bored, sleep deprivation is a hard enemy to fight against. Randomly, Poston made us do small tasks such as Chinese fire drills around the vehicle. Private First Class Brice, our driver, got the ultimatum of a lifetime. In order to stay awake, Brice was asked to choose either eating a cigarette or sniffing chewing tobacco.

Since Brice himself needed to do something to stay awake, he willingly chose to sniff tobacco. It was very amusing for the rest of us in the Humvee but not so much for Brice. After that incident we were all newly energized. Poston kept messing with Brice, to all of our enjoyment. It helped pass the boring time we sat idle, waiting for EOD to finish. Brice, being practically narcoleptic and now with burning nostrils, still managed to keep falling asleep even on the drive home.

New Year's Eve was just another day that came and went. The first day of 2006 was a day that I can remember for all the wrong reasons. While at FOB Remagen, we set up a shooting range out in the desert as a chance to shoot off some bullets. We all just individually unleashed all kinds of ammunition. I shot from the turret mostly, to get acquainted with transitioning between the M240B and my shotgun and the M4 that I had in there with me. We even set up a scenario of all four trucks in a convoy turning into the range at high speeds and everyone letting loose, a hellish and powerful force as weapons of all types were unleashed at the same time. It was outstanding. Drivers and dismounts quickly poured out and hunched behind their doors or knelt for precision, while the turrets unleashed their powerful machine guns. It was a thunder of raining lead. I'm convinced even some of the die-hard grunts got erections.

Near the end of the shooting, I transitioned to my shotgun. While trying to stand on the floor base below me, now filled with spent ammo casings, I lost my grip slightly while still pulling the trigger on the Mossberg 500 shotgun. The slip of my footing jostled the shotgun closer to my face, recoiled the barrel after it fired, and sent it square into my mouth, which cracked my front tooth in half. I had had a bond on that tooth since 1995, when I tripped over a slide on the playground in the fourth grade, but now the bond had been knocked clean out. I also slightly chipped the permanent front tooth beside my shattered one.

After the cease fire was given, I just began to laugh. I knew the reaction I was about to receive from the guys. I slowly grinned a cheeky smile like the cover of *Mad* magazine as I looked over and began to make eye contact with the men in my platoon. The laughter I received when they saw my smile was unforgettable. I looked like a total idiot. I knew I was not in Iraq to attract the opposite sex, so my busted smile didn't immediately bother me. But I also knew that I would have to deal with looking goofy until I could get it fixed when I got home. I rationalized quickly that I was going to have to look like a goof for several months. Of all people, this dumb luck had to happen to me. The first day of 2006 and it was off to a great start.

Two days later, command staff at FOB Speicher passed on to us knowledge of a possible cache in the desert about a half mile from their front entrance. Being they were nearly a twenty-five-minute drive from our FOB and the home of the division, we thought they would easily send someone from their FOB to check it out since it was practically at their doorstep. Not the case when it came to my company. My platoon took the brunt of it and was tasked out for the mission. The location was an old military complex from the former Iraqi Army regime. The open desert was covered with tons of crumbled concrete slabs that eerily formed the perimeter of what once were buildings. The facade of a few buildings still existed, but with heavy bomb damage they had since been gutted and turned into homes for the poor. It was picture proof that bombing campaigns can be swift and incredibly accurate. It was like a movie set of a post–nuclear blast on a military base.

My platoon arrived across the street from Speicher in the forenoon, in a four-truck convoy to the area circled on our map. We were looking for a man from one of the scattered households that called in the report of the possible cache. I had anticipated this day for a while. Not only did I have high expectations of the bounty surely at hand, but I was finally given a break from the turret and released to walk as part of the dismounted element. As we shuffled from household to household, we utilized our interpreter to the fullest. We eventually found the man we were looking for, who filed the report.

It was impossible to distinguish the man's age because Iraqis seemed to age quicker than Americans. He talked about mortars and bombs that coated the landscape throughout the surrounding desert. He was unaware if the weapons were being housed by terrorists or not, but we knew what we were really doing there. This man was concerned for his numerous children who played around the area, and he wanted these toys of death disposed of properly. When I say numerous children, I mean that practicing safe sex obviously was not an option for these people, because there seemed to be twenty-plus kids of all ages walking around the home, all spawned from that man. This obviously was not the work of one woman per household either.

We were escorted by the man to the scattered foxholes that housed multiple mortar rounds. Most of them were inactive and inert, but we occasionally came across some with live fuses. We just kept marking each site with a fluorescent orange tarp. We broke out the metal detectors for a brief moment, but that proved to be an act in vain, seeing as this was an old military complex and metal bits and pieces were scattered everywhere across the desert floor. We just kept looking for the obvious.

Many in my platoon, including me, spent the rest of the daylight hours walking in circles with our heads glued to the ground. We found a couple of bunkers in the ground, which were empty. An occasional crate of decrepit AK47 rounds and numerous long-forgotten gas masks and tanker helmets were the more familiar finds of the day. I knew right then and there that we were not going to come upon a large cache, but only leftover trash from this ghost of a military base.

Before the sun set, I began to attempt to converse with the locals. I was quickly swarmed by little children who looked to be around twelve years old. One young boy eagerly shook my hand and gestured for me to follow him. He led me into his family latrine, which consisted of a concrete room with a hole in the floor. The smell was atrocious, but that's not why he brought me in there. Stacked in the corner were multiple crates of old unusable AK47 rounds. I took these and added them to the pile we had been building.

Before we ventured away from the houses, Avery, from the turret of one of the Humvees, decided to give me a box of MREs, which in turn I distributed to the youngsters. They went wild for these. I doubt they even knew what they were being given, but the smiles they had were priceless. I don't think I've ever seen such happy faces at the sight of a box of MREs as these kids had. We could not exchange words, but I placed my hand on my chest and attempted to say the Arabic word of "you're welcome," *Ahfwan*. I relished interactions with helpful Iraqi children.

For laughs, I showed them all my broken smile. The young girls were quick to point and giggle, and I was instantly sent back in time to my elementary school days. I tried to do my best impersonation of a mime in telling the story of how I broke the tooth in half. Knowing that I probably was not getting anywhere, I decided to pick up three rocks and show the young boys how to juggle.

We continued to comb that desert even as the sun was setting. It was apparent that this old military complex had already been picked over sometime before us. Upon sunset, we decided to call upon EOD and have them dispose of the ordnance that we had collected during the day.

We prepared for what we believed would be another long night with EOD. While the first of them was rigging C4 blocks on the small cache, I sat on the hood of the Humvee, consumed another MRE, and chatted with the guys. Around 9 P.M., it was time to "fire in the hole."

The overenergetic EOD expert selected the youngest kid from my platoon to push the trigger on the ordnance. Private Cody Emery, an eighteen-year-old Texan, loved the thought of blowing something up. Who wouldn't? EOD decided on a proper distance from which our platoon could enjoy the explosion. This was going to be our New Year's celebration, so no one remained in the vehicle. Everyone climbed out, pulled out his personal camera, and prepared to document the explosion.

"Fire in the hole" was yelled before Emery squeezed the trigger, which sent a fiery explosion of red and orange lights shooting high into the air. The concussion shook the core of my body, which felt awesome.

In typical fashion, just as we prepared to leave, my Humvee decided it didn't want to start up. Another truck crew went into routine action by connecting a tow bar from their truck to ours. It had been a long day, and everyone was feeling tired from searching in the heat of the desert. Though it was only a thirty-minute ride back to FOB Remagen, I could not stay awake long. What was worse was that Brice, the driver, kept falling asleep again. Though we were getting towed, it was not exactly the greatest idea for him or any of us to be nodding off, but it was tough to stay awake. Brice just got yelled at by Poston the whole ride home, which kept me awake because I could not stop laughing. I sat behind Poston and just admired and laughed at how easy Brice kept falling asleep. He learned his lesson as soon as we got home to Remagen. Instead of going to bed like the rest of us, Brice had to reorganize everything out of the truck, put it in a neat order, have it inspected, and put everything back in the truck. He had to repeat this process a few times. Stay alert, stay alive. That was a common phrase learned early in basic training.

QUESTIONABLE QUINN

"Quinn would tell us stories that we all threw out the window."

Days of uninterrupted sleep were nonexistent for all the lower enlisted personnel. Those of us who were not a sergeant or above had to do truck guard twenty-four hours of every day. We had been doing this since our arrival to FOB Remagen. Two soldiers at a time would babysit in the trucks to ensure no other American soldiers would come and take anything. There were locks on the trucks, but Sergeant First Class Quinn, being paranoid, utilized the lower enlisted to spend every waking moment babysitting them. We were the only platoon on the base to do this, and there never was a theft problem to begin with. It was incredibly redundant. This needless guarding prevented all of us from ever getting any good sleep, which in turn made us all tired during missions. Sergeants and above would always complain that the lower enlisted soldiers were always tired, but they failed to attempt to remedy the problem. As long as they were not doing the guard themselves, they were happy. This was just one of the thousands of short-changing conditions I shared with the lower enlisted soldiers during our deployment.

What little "downtime" we ever got was utilized doing something very time-consuming. Quinn decided his CHU did not have enough sandbags. His CHU was as protected as our CHUs were, but he mandated that if we were not on patrol, we would spend all waking hours filling sandbags and packing his CHU tighter with protection.

He mostly looked on as we vigorously stacked all day in the blistering heat. Quinn would tell us stories that we all threw out the window. He would celebrate how his father built a bridge out of sandbags when he was in Vietnam as a member of the Special Forces. Others dispelled the notion that his father was ever in Special Forces, or Vietnam for that matter. I went further and said he didn't even have a human father, having hatched from a deviled egg.

Sandbagging forced us to be around Quinn and hear his stories that only he believed to be true. Quinn would tell stories about his prior deployment to Afghanistan and how many Taliban he had killed with his bare hands. He even had the nerve to tell us he once had to pilot a Black Hawk and fire a machine gun at the same time at the Taliban. There was no convincing him otherwise. The stories were so far-fetched that a crooked jury wouldn't even believe them. Quinn would recount these stories so much that he would begin to believe them. We could always tell when he lied, because he was unable to look anyone in the eye and he rocked back and forth on his heels while his hands were tucked in his pockets.

Sandbagging his CHU soon progressed to everyone having to do his own CHU. Day after day, we would rather be on patrol than fortify our CHUs, as it was less tiring. I remember picking up one sandbag that had been sitting in a puddle and quite wet. As I placed it tightly on the growing wall against Quinn's CHU, he took notice. Quinn inspected the progress and bragged that we were doing such a great job. He said that the bags were so tight that they were beginning to sweat. I knew the bag was wet from the puddle I had just picked it out of, but I let Quinn have his moment. He then told us a whole fictitious history of sandbags and how if it was not for his supreme guidance over us, we would have continued making an unfit protection. We all just did what everyone in the platoon did and agreed with whatever he had to say so he would get it out of his system and move on. As soon as he walked away, I informed everyone of the obvious origin of the wetness.

He seldom left the wire with us. When he did join us, he added an element of stress that we did not need. He made us stop for every little thing near a roadway, even if it was several yards from the road and the size of a Pop-Tart. It was like he was putting us in a bad situation, especially when he made us physically throw a grappling hook at garbage on the side of the road, even though we could only throw the hook so many feet and it would have been inevitable death if someone had actually thrown one on an IED. During one early morning route clearance, I had gotten sick of the snail pace on MSR Tampa, when time was of the essence. We were running dangerously close to missing out on breakfast at our chow hall when Quinn made us stop for a small piece of flattened rubber from a torn tire. I immediately saw it wasn't a threat because I could see all around the rubber shred and it was the size of a standard piece of paper. I walked right up to it, picked it up, and threw it as far as I could off the highway.

"What the fuckin' fuck, Conklin!" Quinn screamed from a distant vehicle behind me.

"Not a threat. No wires, sarnt. Just a piece of rubber," I yelled while trying to display proper respect for his rank and nothing more.

"God damn it, last month two men from Third ID did the same thing and then their bodies were blown into a million fucking pieces. Don't act like a fuckin' hero or you'll be dead!" Quinn yelled while pacing toward me. I wondered how he hid his horns so well underneath his helmet. "Get in your truck, hero!"

I couldn't care less what he had to yell at me for. I knew there was no threat whatsoever. I also knew it was yet another bogus story he'd made up about 3ID. Unlike him, I actually prodded the unit we replaced and was thirsty for any stories they had about enemy activity and casualties that they took in our sector. They never mentioned the sort of crap, or anything close to it, that Quinn was saying. However, my buddies in my platoon kept calling me "hero" the rest of the day. Quinn's mindset was beginning to become less funny and more scary. Thank God he rarely left the wire with us.

The lack of Quinn's presence on patrol was obvious to everyone. Most of us saw it as safer that he stay inside the wire. He didn't really attempt any initiative to ensure a seat in a Humvee, and the issue wasn't really pushed. This was not the type of leadership anyone would expect from a platoon sergeant. Quinn went out maybe once a week, and that was less than anyone in the entire company. First Platoon needed a leader.

FIRST BLOOD

"Oh, we're doing just dandy!"

By January 8, some major issues had started rising around the need for truck repair. A trip to FOB Speicher was planned that day to collect much-needed parts for our decrepit Humvees. A day at FOB Speicher also meant the chance to buy some personal supplies at the PX and maybe get some food from either the Pizza Hut or the Taco Bell vendor that they had on post. There was not one soul in my platoon who ever wanted to miss a patrol that resupplied at FOB Speicher, except for Quinn. Plus, if we were not on the patrol, sandbagging was what we had to look forward to. I originally was not on the patrol list, but I opted to be the gunner for The Hodge's truck instead of my usual Humvee.

Normally I was the gunner on the second or third Humvee in a convoy of four. On this particular day, I was the gunner for the lead truck. We headed down MSR Tampa in normal fashion, without any incident along the way. Occasionally, like every patrol, we would stop when we spotted something in the road. It would then either be kicked or shot away from the road, depending on how we saw fit. We ran into a lot of garbage boxes this way almost every day.

Arriving at Speicher this day felt like being back at Fort Campbell,

Kentucky. There was a different atmosphere in the air. Fobbits were littered all over the massive post. "Fobbits" was the term given to soldiers who never left a FOB. Jealousy and animosity from us spread to all-out hatred for them. Life was so easy for them and they were never really in the face of danger. The kicker was that they collected the same paychecks as we did. We hated fobbits. I still do to this day.

After completing whatever tasks needed to be done at the mechanics shop, we all headed to get some much-needed supplies at the PX. We picked up such luxuries as chips, soap, shampoo, haircuts, magazines, tons of batteries, and a few movies. We all went a little hog wild, not knowing when the next trip to FOB Speicher would be.

When our gluttonous trip to the PX was finished, we saddled back up in our Humvees and prepared to drive back to FOB Remagen. Because we were the last crew to return to the trucks, The Hodge decided that we would be the trail vehicle instead of the lead truck. This would be my first time gunning for a trail truck, which I looked forward to. Less responsibility and hardly ever would I have to direct traffic. We were only going to drive down MSR Tampa, so standing up really was not in the cards. I just sat down on the thin sling that typically made my ass fall asleep as we headed home.

Typical truck discipline was conducted in our truck. Normally we would talk The Hodge's ear off, but today we were all in our own little boring worlds, I guess. I took a gander at my watch and saw that it was nearly 4:30 P.M. Whenever I checked my watch, I would habitually calculate the math in my head and figure out what time it was back home in Gettysburg. It was around 8:30 A.M. on a Sunday morning back home. I was picturing my parents in church at that time and figured they would be saying the opening prayer at that exact instant.

BOOOM! came unexpectedly ripping through the air. Everything went silent while the truck slammed to a halt. Taylor, who was sitting in the rear seat next to me, instantly locked eyes with me. We both grew pale and shared the same confused look of terror on our faces. As we both stayed locked on each other, I just whispered, "Oh shit." I sprang to my feet in my turret and embraced my M240B machine gun in the nook of my shoulder. I looked ahead of our convoy and saw a giant black smoke cloud concealing the road up ahead, cutting off the lead truck from my sight. Everyone paused to listen to any transmission but the radio remained quiet. The Hodge grabbed the hand mic and broke the silence.

"One-three, one-three, this is one-one, give me a status on your truck, over." He hastily questioned the first truck. We all knew what had happened, but not to what extent. The first truck in our convoy, which consisted of Sergeant Pitchford, Private First Class Sanchez, and Privates Heiple and Boster, had just been struck by an IED. Buried in a box and disguised as garbage, it had been tucked behind a guardrail on a small bridge on the highway. It was placed in just a way that if you were traveling south, which was the direction we were headed, the IED was completely blocked from visibility. It was spotted by Sergeant Pitchford and Private Heiple inside the vehicle at the last second before detonation. Before anyone could say "IED," the device sent thousands of shrapnel shards into their truck.

"Halt traffic and scan your sector for anyone running," screamed The Hodge to me while still awaiting word from Pitchford's truck. The Hodge, being the most senior leader in my platoon, took the initiative to send up the report to the company.

A million things were going through my head in these first few seconds. *How could this happen? Could there be another IED somewhere? Is the enemy still watching us? Is this the start of an ambush? Is everyone in the first truck OK? Am I trained for this?*

I flailed my hands to halt traffic hundreds of yards behind my vehicle. I was still locked tight into my gun when I peeked over my right shoulder to see the lead truck. The crest of the hill and the smoke cloud still cloaked the damaged truck from visibility.

"One-one, one-one, this is one-three, over," Pitchford called over the radio.

"Give me a status, over," replied The Hodge.

"Sanchez has slight wounds to the face. My truck is disabled, over," he explained while The Hodge orchestrated Brice, our driver, to pass the other trucks and become the lead truck. As we sped past the wounded Humvee, I noticed that Sanchez was still standing in his turret and operating the machine gun. Blood streaked down his face as we locked eyes for a split second. We both shared the same look of fear and anger, but his was much more intimidating. He looked like a boxer before a fight.

Brt-brt-brt-brt-brt-brt-brt-brt came the booming sound of an M240B operated by Vinny on the Humvee that was now third in line. What or who was he shooting at? I looked to his gun and saw he was shooting out to the western desert, in the direction of a singular farm in an empty desert. The distance was far, and it was hard to distinguish what anything was. I figured he'd had a good look at something, because he was unloading his ammunition into this farm.

Trusting that Vinny had seen something that motivated him to fire, I helped him out. Vinny's and my trucks were the only two equipped with M240Bs, and I knew that at this distance we could easily destroy anything. Spotting his tracers burn onto the farm, I matched what he was shooting at, and together we put some suppressive fire on the farm. It was textbook execution. We were making our weapons "talk" by having him shoot and pause, then me shoot and pause, and so forth.

As we both began to unload, everyone in the truck got out and together we were firing at two different targets. The farm was the main target of my gun and Vinny's, and the other was out in the desert not far from the farm, a little shack that was being peppered by the rest of the platoon from their SAWs and M4s.

Everyone in my truck was now outside the Humvee and propped against the hood, unloading his carbine into whatever target he chose toward the farm. The Hodge, with his M14 carbine, and Taylor and Private First Class Scott MacMillan on their M4s, blew away one magazine each. Before Brice exited the vehicle and moved his selector switch from safe to semi, I was yelling at him to get me more ammunition from inside the truck. I had already gone through four hundred rounds in about three minutes and was out of ammunition. I performed a quick barrel change in time to receive more ammo.

After a few minutes of firing while the damaged truck crew collected themselves, a cease fire was given. Two of our trucks moved out off the road toward the shot-up farm to further investigate. My truck and Pitchford's damaged truck stayed back and secured the highway. At this time, four Humvees from Second Platoon rolled up to join us.

"Thought you would need some help," yelled the gunner from Second Platoon's lead truck.

"Oh, we're doing just dandy!" I sarcastically yelled back at him.

Second Platoon also came on scene with EOD equipment. Sensing that the area was secured, the EOD unit went to work to determine what type of IED it was and to give the all clear.

While the farm was being inspected by two of the Humvees from my platoon's convoy, my truck went ahead and began to hook the disabled truck up to ours and prepare to tow it back to FOB Remagen. Being up close to the truck, I could now see the damage more clearly. The main impact of the IED had shattered the front left tire and engine area. The hood was completely shredded, the front tire was flat, and all of the windows on the left side were spiderwebbed and ticked with pebbles. Amazingly, the armor on the Humvee had denied any penetration of shrapnel into the hull.

By the time we began the recovery of the vehicle, Sanchez was out of the turret. He was stunned and sort of in a daze, the blood still streaking down his face. Apparently, in that frightened second of noticing the IED before it blew up, his face was so low in the turret that most of the shrapnel went right over his head. Only small bits of pebbles came swirling in and peppered his face. The eye protection he was wearing gave an impenetrable shield that saved his eyesight. The Hodge reassured us that Sanchez would be all right, but "he'll be picking fucking shrapnel out of his fucking face for the rest of his fucking life."

While the medical inspection of Sanchez's face and the truck recovery were under way, The Hodge still was not happy with the situation. He decided to go under the bridge by himself to see if anyone was hiding out. He came back a few minutes later empty-handed.

After about twenty minutes, the disabled truck had been hooked to my truck and was ready to be hauled in. The other half of my platoon returned to give the update on the two locations that we'd fired upon. The firing done by Vinny and me had slaughtered numerous sheep and chickens at the farm, but no triggerman. The farmhouse and a truck on the property were also riddled with bullet holes.

The EOD expert declared the blast area all safe and clear to proceed back home. He also mentioned that the IED was a single 130mm mortar round wrapped in TNT with rocket propellant. Luckily, it was buried too deep and sent the brunt of the shrapnel straight up in the air. Thank God for small miracles. As all units cleared from the scene and headed home, I realized another small miracle. I was supposed to be the lead truck's gunner, in Sanchez's position, had we gotten back to the vehicles earlier after our PX run at FOB Speicher. That could have been me.

When we returned to FOB Remagen, we all felt we needed to strengthen our Humvees better. The disabled truck was dropped off at the mechanics bay and rapidly stripped of its extra armor. We equipped all of our remaining trucks with extra Kevlar vest plates, tucking them inside the doors under the windows and fastening them with 550 Cord[13] and duct tape. It was crude what we did to our vehicles, but we needed to make the Humvees' protection thicker by any means necessary.

Another thing I noticed when we returned was the outpouring of help we received from the men in my platoon who were not on the patrol. I knew most felt bad not being there, but I knew they would all soon bear witness to what an IED attack was like. They all came pouring out of their CHUs like a Nascar pit crew to inspect the damage and hear our tale. Sergeant First Class Quinn was practically foaming at the mouth when we returned. He seemed almost jealous that he was not there. All he did was tell imaginary personal war stories that had never occurred but that if they had, would have trumped the day's event. Nobody wanted to hear anything from *him*—a platoon sergeant that rarely patrolled with us.

---

[13] 550 Cord is an infantryman's most used tool. It's made from a long, lightweight nylon green shoelacelike material and is utilized for just about anything and everything. The possibilities of its usefulness are endless.

COMPLACENCY RUNS THROUGH IT

"Making the best out of what we were given."

Most of our daily and nightly patrols shifted to focus more on the Kadasiyah neighborhood of Tikrit. Kadasiyah was the adjoining town that connected to the north end of Tikrit. It was a typical Iraqi neighborhood, filled with houses separated by fences and walls. A couple of scattered mosques, empty fields, half-built homes, and small stores formed Kadasiyah.

Constantly being in the turret during every patrol gave birth for me to new strategies on how to stay alert and not complacent. Whether it was throwing rocks at barking dogs that chased our Humvees or finding a kid wearing a shirt of my favorite sports team, I looked for anything to break the monotony. Kadasiyah had a high population of children. They made it their job just to follow our dismounted soldiers throughout their neighborhoods. Others chose to ride their bikes behind or alongside our patrolling Humvees.

Taylor and I were great at making the best out of what we were given. We both were very sore about pretty much everything we did. Instead of keeping complaints to ourselves, we verbally expressed them to any open ear. Most of the time we were just told to "shut up, Joe," or "I don't give a fuck," but the "bitching," as it was referred to, was our form of stress relief. Taylor and I continued to entertain ourselves, especially when we dropped off the dismounted elements in the truck and we were the only two left in the Humvee. That's when the iPod, speakers, and random conversations poured out.

During long patrols in which we seemed to drive in circles in Kadasiyah, Taylor and I would joke with the children. Sometimes we would come across a large group of children who shouted for "chocolaté." We would usually only throw candy to the girls, and it would drive the boys insane. Once the crowd of boys were pestered and pissed, we would throw one piece of candy into the horde of boys and watch them fight for it. The fighting was never terribly violent, but sometimes we saw the occasional sucker punch that we would just laugh at. It sounds cruel writing all this now, but at the time we were young, immature, and fueled with hatred toward everything we were doing.

Another sad game Taylor and I would always play was trying to converse with people. Few people in Kadasiyah understood English. We would ask any random child or adult if he or she knew English. Once the confused look came across the person's face, Taylor and I initiated our game. We would ask the most horrible and confusing questions that were only understood by the two of us. Questions like "Where can I find the Penis Museum?" "Help me find the town rapist, because he just won a free ham sandwich," or the classic, "Have you seen the big motherfucking dickhead running around with scissors lately?" Whichever of us laughed first was declared the loser. The act of actually asking these questions of someone was what got us rolling with laughter. Knowing that they had no idea what we were saying made us not feel so guilty for being so rude. It was a game that was played every day and always was a "Who Can Top Who Game." Oh, the games grunts played in a combat zone just to pass the time. You had to have been there to understand.

One of the classic memories I have of entertaining myself while in the turret came during a patrol in Kadasiyah. Occasionally, we would see semiattractive women. Most were covered up in cloth, but we would find the occasional young female who showed herself unveiled and was quite the looker. One girl was spotted next to the entrance to her fenced-in property, standing idle and watching us pass by. What she did not know was that we stopped right in front of her house because we were bored and she was cute. My truck parked parallel to her as she stood near the gate of her driveway, and I immediately made eye contact with her and startled her off guard. I started singing the chorus of "Can't Take My Eyes Off of You" by Frankie Valli. The look on her face was priceless. She probably did not know what I was saying, but she did not dismiss me. She just smiled as I sang out loud and proud. The neighboring property next door had quite a few men constructing a new house, and they did not seem to take too kindly to my singing. After they all stopped what they were doing, I assumed that they had to be related to the girl. Before they started walking over to her, we decided to keep moving on with our patrol.

THE SCHOOLTEACHER

"I finally felt my first bit of compassion."

Boredom and burn-out came easily to those who were doing the same job every mission. I was sick of gunning. Others were sick of driving or dismounting. Our platoon was still working out the kinks for a rotation of some kind to mix jobs around in the trucks. By mid-January we did start rotating to different jobs. I drove for a few missions, but that wasn't as exciting to me as dismounting was.

Dismounting let me stretch my legs from that cramped and compacted Humvee. It also gave me a more personal attachment to the city and interaction with the people. During one mid-January patrol, I was part of the dismount element for the day and the Humvees dropped us off and drove somewhere nearby in Kadasiyah.

I, along with Staff Sergeant Hubert, Sergeant Armstrong, and a few others, was resting among some bushes outside of someone's courtyard walls. We were watching one of the main roads that ran into Tikrit while we stayed partially hidden and shaded by the bushes. The sun was at its highest and the shade seemed a perfect place to take a knee. It was not long before the gate entrance to the walled-in property behind us opened from the inside. We all quickly stood up with eyes and weapons pointed at the opening gate.

There stood an Iraqi woman who looked to be mid-forties in age. She happened to speak English and invited us inside. We all quickly looked at each other, but Hubert did not hesitate and drifted right in. We all followed right in behind him.

Two soldiers went to the roof as an over-watch, while Armstrong, Lieutenant Scher, Hubert, and I lounged downstairs. The woman of the house pleaded with us to go in what she called the men's lounge of her home. It was simply a living room mainly used by her husband and his friends. She notified us that he was at work and would not be home for a few hours.

We sat comfortably on her couches with our helmets off. The woman again entered the room, this time with her fourteen-year-old daughter, who had her hands full of Arabic packaged chocolates and homemade chai. The small cup was very sweet with lots of sugar, and it was warm and full of flavor.

As we began to enjoy the snacks, the mother and daughter quickly began to exit the room. They both seemed nervous and almost afraid of us. I immediately recognized it. Here were soldiers in their house who were stacked with gear and weapons. I too would be scared. We all broke the ice as we stopped them and began to make small talk.

The mother quickly responded with joyous praise of our presence. I was all too familiar with it because all the Iraqis said that when they were face-to-face with American soldiers in their homes. The woman then began to open up emotionally. It turned out she was an English teacher before the war began. She spoke very well and her story struck me.

She explained that she had not been able to teach since the Americans knocked out Saddam's Ba'athist regime. Since she was a sworn Ba'athist, she was not allowed to teach anymore anywhere in Iraq. She pleaded with us saying that she was not a Ba'athist. She explained that living in Tikrit, Saddam's hometown, everyone had to sign allegiance to the regime. Not doing so could have resulted in the death of oneself or one's family. I quickly empathized with the dilemma she was facing and could not help but compare it to the times of the Nazi regime.

Coming from a family of teachers, I felt for her immediately. I finally felt my first bit of compassion and a realization of the twisted grips with which Saddam had controlled his people. The regime change was great for her now because it offered more safety, but she was also left in the dark and unable to better educate her own people due to a psychotic tyrant who was no longer even in power. She was permanently labeled something she never believed in.

Lieutenant Scher took as much information as he could. We even took pictures of her teaching certificates and degrees and tried to comfort her by saying the overused "we'll do the best we can" phrase. I knew right away there was nothing we could do. This wasn't our job, and we had no instructions for these types of situations. There wasn't even anyone we could report this to that could remedy the problem. I felt like an asshole because I looked her straight in the eyes and saw her sadness and I knew we were helpless, but I couldn't let her know that.

We retracted our rooftop element and all pushed to exit out of the house. As I was nearing the front door, I spotted a stunning painting on the wall. It was of a beautiful bald eagle. It looked similar to paintings of the bald eagle that were plentiful around Fort Campbell.

While I stared and admired the painting, my peripherals spotted the naturally pretty fourteen-year-old girl coming my way. I pointed at the painting, and then to my division patch.

"Screaming Eagles. I love your painting," I said to her. Before she spoke, she came closer to me and reviewed my chest. The young girl spotted my name tape on my chest.

"Conklin? Is that how you say it?" she questioned me.

"Yes. You got it." I congratulated her.

"Conklin, that's a beautiful name" were the last words she spoke to me as I was the last one out of the door. The kind words put a new spark in me and an extra kick in my step.

After we left the home, we met back up with the mounted element. We climbed inside our Humvees and parked in a security halt at the soccer field nearby. We had a few minutes before we drove away, so some of us walked over to the local haji shop and bought a few cases of soda. Buying soda with American currency, I was certain they did not know the exchange rate, because I bought a twelve-pack with a dollar, and was given Iraqi dinar back in change.

As we emptied out of the packed haji shop, we became magnets to the awaiting children outside. The broken record of "mista, mista, chocolaté,

chocolaté" was being yelled at us at a time when I was actually loaded up with candy. Nearing the end of our patrol for the day and still with a lifted morale, I passed out candy like it was Halloween to all the surrounding children, until my pouch was empty.

Boooom! The notorious sound of an explosion rocketed through the air and reverberated off the dirt houses. All of the kids immediately scattered like cockroaches in light. I started to yell at them and pointed in all directions for them to flee, but they were one step ahead of me. I dropped a couple of my newly purchased Arabic-labeled soda knockoffs as I ran the twenty feet back to my Humvee.

By the time I climbed into my seat, the situation was already being sent up to higher by our RTO. An IED had detonated on a passing convoy on MSR Tampa, the highway about a thousand meters to our front, and the smoke cloud still lingered in the distance.

It turned out that while we were in the haji shop, the passing convoy had noticed the IED and cordoned it off. With an EOD element attached to them, they initiated a Johnny 5 to deactivate the IED. The device detonated before the Johnny 5 could work his magic. The explosion was the sound we were reacting to.

The IED had been placed a few feet from the one that had hit my convoy the week prior. Not only was I glad no one was hurt, but I was glad that that area was now officially clear of IEDs, because we were about to pass over that highway moments later. If it had not been for that vigilant unit who spotted the device, it could have killed one of them or one of us.

So went another day of the thousands of patrols we did. We never did see that family again, but we drove by that house almost every day. I like to think the woman is teaching English somewhere to someone.

ESCALATION OF FORCE

"You think you're at the O.K. Corral?"

January continued to give a glimpse of all that Iraq had to offer. In typical fashion, while my platoon was on QRF, we were called upon at a moment's notice to head downtown after a shooting broke out among the citizens.

Once again, I found myself in the turret of the third vehicle. As we were leaving FOB Remagen, I went through the ritual of loading all three weapon systems in the turret just before we left the gate. As we were pulling out of the main gate and onto MSR Tampa, the lead vehicle's gunner signaled for all traffic to stop. All the reckless Iraqi drivers shifted off to the side and the lead Humvee proceeded out.

As soon as my truck was pulling out and turning left, I looked to my right and saw a bus hurtling down the road past the halted vehicles. I quickly enacted the steps of escalation of force that we'd been drilled so much in. I waved my shotgun in the air and stiffened my arm to instruct the driver to halt. When I started to yell for the bus to halt, I got the attention from all the other soldiers in my truck. My driver stopped in the intersection as I wheeled my M240B to aim it at the bus.

"Stop him, Conklin!" yelled Sergeant Armstrong from the front seat inside.

My brain was ticking so fast and my heartbeat sped up. Why was this bus passing all of the other vehicles that had pulled off the side of the road? How could he not see our convoy in the middle of the road? I transitioned from one escalation of force measure to the next. After a few seconds of waving in vain, I cocked my shotgun and shot a warning shot above the bus. This all happened in a matter of seconds. The bus did the opposite of stopping—the driver barreled down the highway and continued to pass all the other cars that had pulled off to the side.

The bus was about fifty yards from my truck and headed straight into my Humvee. I feared the driver was deliberately driving into the middle of my convoy and I thought he could be a suicide martyr. One second passed and I shot a round into the front window, right in front of the driver.

The window spiderwebbed and cracked throughout the entire front. I reloaded another shotgun shell and knew it was not birdshot. I shot another heavier round into the front windshield, at the driver, who was now merely twenty-five yards away.

"Move to your crew serve weapon!" I heard someone yell from inside the truck. The moment I grabbed my machine gun, the bus abruptly swerved over to the far right shoulder of the road. Once I made sure the bus was no longer a threat, we proceeded out of the intersection and we all pulled out safely.

As the rest of the platoon made it out onto the MSR, we continued with the original mission and proceeded toward downtown Tikrit. When the bus was idle, I could faintly see inside it from my turret. It was filled with women who were frantically running around inside. My eyes widened and I felt bad. Since we were on a quick reaction mission, we did not even stop to check out the damage.

As we pulled away, I could see the shattered front windshield and saw the male driver slumped over, holding his face. Others were moving inside around him. I could not even tell if he was dead or just wounded. We were gone in a matter of seconds after it pulled over.

"Damn, Conklin, you think you're at the O.K. Corral?" said one of the soldiers in my truck.

"No, but I'm willing to do whatever it takes to get me back home," I said, as I plopped back into my sling. I could not help but feel bad for a few minutes. I tried to convince myself that I gave him an ample number of warnings. I did what we had been trained to do. I felt threatened and actually believed the bus was preparing to ram into us. I reassured myself in the fact that I shot the bus right in front of an Iraqi hospital. All I know is later that afternoon when we came back into the FOB, the bus was nowhere to be found. I convinced myself that everyone was fine, so nothing would bother me subconsciously. I never heard a thing about it again.

During the drudgery of patrols, I found it hard at times to hold back my anger when things got frustrating. One particular night patrol in Tikrit I lost that battle. Our guys had stopped a car that was parked along the side of a road and raising our suspicion. We cordoned off the area, set our orange cones out, and proceeded to call out the occupants.

From the vantage of my turret I watched the scene unfold. Lit by a lone street lamp, out came a man about twenty-five years of age. A thorough inspection of his car had him come up clean. Staff Sergeant Poston searched the man himself and produced only a cell phone, which was not a crime. It was what was on the cell phone that stirred our blood. This man had a picture in his phone of the World Trade Center towers getting hit by one of the planes during the 9/11 attacks. This immediately set off Poston into a rant that the young Iraqi man surely did not comprehend. We did not have an interpreter that night, but I'm sure he could sense our mood. Some of the dismounts were yelling relentlessly at him while they brought him closer to our Humvee. As soon as I caught wind of what was on his phone, it set me off like a spark on gunpowder.

Soon, it was a whole squad yelling at him in some of the foulest language a rated R movie could ever have. The Iraqi just stood there straight-faced and took it. The fact that he displayed no emotion stirred my blood cold. Poston soon realized we had nothing on this man so we had to let him go on his way. I could not keep my eyes off him as I stared hard down on him from my turret. My hands were clenched so tight I could have flattened a stress ball. My platoon loaded back up in the Humvees and prepared to move out. It was then that the Iraqi man, before entering his car, turned around and smiled at me.

"You motherfucking beeb!" I screamed hysterically as I began to climb out of the Humvee.

"Stay the fuck in the truck, Conklin," Poston yelled back at me while he grabbed my leg. "As much as that motherfucker should be ass raped to death, we can't do it now."

I planted both of my feet back on the floor while my rage overpowered me. Before the Iraqi got back inside his vehicle, we continued to have a stare-down.

"You," I yelled as I pointed hard with my finger. "Someday, somehow, you're going to die. And if it's not by me, I hope your killer is wearing an American flag, bitch!" I finished just in time as our Humvee pulled away from his car. I had to bury my anger away. That same sour attitude seemed always to return each and every time I left the wire. As soon as I returned from a mission, I returned to my happy self. Patrols became a harvest of my inner hatred. I could never suppress it. I felt like my whole time outside the wire and in the streets of Iraq was a waste. We weren't getting through to these people no matter how hard we tried. It was beyond frustrating. They couldn't clean up their own neighborhoods. Their hearts weren't in it, so why should ours be? I was not out to win their hearts and minds. Personally, I felt that more than half of the Iraqis I encountered had no hearts to win in the first place.

CHERRY SOLDIER

"It made what little time off I had to shut my eyes excruciating."

My brigade commander, Colonel Steele, came up with a plan to revamp the armor on our Humvees called RAP. The Army's love for acronyms never ceased. This one stood for the Rakkasan Armament Program. It was an experimental test that he'd conjured up to slap some more steel on our already excessively heavy Humvees.

Forty-seven Humvees in the 187th Infantry Regiment had been hit by IEDs by month four of our deployment. Steele gathered most of the welders and mechanics from around the brigade and posted them throughout numerous FOBs. Their job became to strategically place reinforced steel on weak spots on all the Humvees. It was a time-consuming task for the mechanics, but the success was immeasurable.

Angel Company was also inundated with our first and only supply of new soldiers. We were always aching to receive new privates in the platoon, but the only one my platoon got was already a specialist. The other platoons received two or three privates, whereas we received one specialist with a little bit of experience.

His name was Edward Rodriguez, a thirty-three-year-old Brooklyn-bred man with the body of an NFL linebacker. He was married with two kids and was a very intellectual and kind man. "Rod" became my room-mate, instantly killing the fact that I'd had a CHU all to my own for so long. We had good conversations, and he was not like some of the other new "cherries" who came in thinking they knew everything.

All was well until it came time to sleep. Never in my life have I ever heard of someone who could snore so loud. It was pure torture. Every night, I would crank my music up to a deafening level, sleep with the lights on, and yell from my bunk to wake him up. All was in vain because not only did he snore, but he had other traits similar to a bear's—he truly seemed to hibernate. It made what little time off I had to shut my eyes ex-cruciating. There were several nights that I had to sleep in Avery's CHU, like a child invading his parents' room during a thunderstorm. Just for some peace and quiet.

Over time, Rod adopted a system of sleeping on his stomach and wear-ing a hat over his face that pulled his nose back. Drastic times asked for desperate measures and I'd had to put my foot down. Being a reasonable guy, he complied, and soon I could sleep in the same room, though it was never easy. His snoring never ceased, but it was subdued to a degree.

A MAN'S BEST FRIEND

"There goes my dream of getting a good night's sleep."

The weather in January marked the start of the rainy season. The heat morphed into a cold front that always required extra layers of clothing. The nights seemed to be almost unbearable at times, especially in the turret. When rain was added to the mix, it made for an uncomfortable patrol.

The rain brought on needs for certain necessities. Constant rain and dew added coats of rust on all of the weapons we used. It got quite annoying trying to keep up with the rust. After a patrol, our truck crew would all combine together and clean different parts of the machine gun, shotgun, and our own personal weapons. As soon as all was clean and dry, we seemed to always head back out for another rainy patrol. The whole process would then start over again.

January 17 marked the date of my first day since arriving a month prior at FOB Remagen that I didn't leave the wire, but it was strictly due to circumstance. All was going to plan during the preparation for another nightly patrol around midnight. We were scheduled to do the usual routine patrol of driving around Kadasiyah. After the inspection of the vehicle and weapon systems and the mission brief were completed, we headed to the gate to prepare to leave. We were also in the midst of a week of continuous rain, and this night showering did not seem to let up. I just did not feel like being on this patrol for some reason, but it was too late. I was driving that night and Taylor was gunning, so at least I had someone to bitch with.

As we prepared to load our weapons and drive out of the gate, my Humvee just sporadically began to spit out fluid from under the hood. Divine intervention. As Poston told me to stop, he also halted the platoon. While I could hear the exchange of countless cuss words between people, Taylor and I had a different reaction.

"Hurray! No mission!" I yelled as we passed a high-five to each other.

But Poston had a different idea in mind. He decided to cross load into the other three trucks and continue with the mission. I quickly solved the math of empty seats within the platoon and realized that two people would have to sit out this mission. Before I could come up with a suggestion, Poston delegated that Taylor and I would take the vehicle over to the mechanics bay and get it fixed immediately. This was how I got my first time off.

My dream of getting a good night's sleep evaporated when I had to spend my newly acquired free time in the mechanics bay. Rod was on his first patrol, and I knew there would have been a chance to get some quiet shut-eye. I quickly realized that there was nothing that would ever go my way.

So as the patrol left the wire without me for the first time, Taylor and I found ourselves working to fix our Humvee. We were there for moral support or any odd jobs we could do for the mechanics to help speed up the process and get the vehicle mission-capable. The job did not prove to be a quick one either. We were there for hours and ran into the early morning. Our displeasure quickly faded, however, when we were completely surprised in the bay.

It was near 3 A.M. when the giant bay doors of the mechanics warehouse opened up. Taylor and I turned to see one of my platoon's Humvees being towed into the bay. The windows on the driver's side were all white with cracks and dings and the wheels were all deflated. I quickly found someone in my platoon for an update.

I was told that my platoon had been in the Kadasiyah area of Tikrit when they came across what they perceived as a possible IED. Unbeknownst to them at the time, they were facing a dummy IED. A skilled terrorist had led my platoon into a trap where the soldiers would stop in front of a fake IED and then get hit by a real IED once they got out to investigate. It was evidence that the terrorists were learning our procedures quickly.

As my platoon investigated the dummy IED, a dead dog's carcass on the road that was filled with a 155mm artillery shell exploded on Third Squad's Humvee, in which were Caruso, Hubert, Poston, MacMillan, and my cherry roommate, Rod, the driver. All members were rattled a bit, and they all complained about the ear-piercing blast from the explosion, but there were no injuries.

So went another IED that rocked my platoon. I just barely missed it by sheer mechanical problems. That was fine by me. I knew there would be more in the future. I felt worried about Rod, as he was driving on his first patrol and had experienced that. I tried to convince him that it would not be like that every day. His spirits were fine and I knew he was one tough guy.

MELTDOWN

"No one was willing to listen to Quinn anymore."

By the end of January, there had been a lot of changes made to my platoon. We were quickly forming tactics and procedures to meet many different scenarios. We'd started to gel as a platoon but still lacked a sufficient platoon sergeant.

Quinn rarely, if ever, came on any missions with us. He never was on any missions where we had been hit by IEDs, yet he conjured in his thoughts that he was there. Quinn spoke in a first-person account about these events. His twist of lies was puzzling. He just could not reach reality, so he immersed himself in another world, full of lies.

Few ever sought out conversations with Quinn. We all wanted a leader, but we were stuck with someone who was never present. And when he *was* physically present, his mind seemed to be elsewhere. We preferred him back in his CHU, where he was not a liability. This far into the deployment, our company commander and first sergeant began to see our dilemma.

We didn't yet have a strong enough case to kick Quinn out of our unit. That is until the end of January came. One late night he ordered the platoon to form up in front of his CHU immediately. For no reason, he had us gather around him to hear another one of his random rants about his hatred for his platoon.

Quinn began preaching about how he thought we were considering ourselves heroes because we survived a few IED attacks. It sounded almost like he was jealous, and he seemed bothered that he had not yet received his Combat Infantryman's Badge. He then began to talk about how we were all "worthless sonsabitches" and that we should "continue to go out in the sector and keep getting hit by IEDs until you die."

We all began to look around at each other with the same confused look. It was a dark night, but the light shed through the open door from Quinn's CHU was enough to see his eyes. They began to turn almost black and he looked possessed. He just kept chanting out devilish thoughts that scared most of us. He then questioned us on some of the tactics that we were coming up with during IED attacks. The Hodge broke the silence and began to explain what worked. The Hodge was someone our entire platoon looked up to as our real platoon sergeant. He was knowledgeable, smart, funny, and he took care of his soldiers. This was something Quinn saw and loathed. Right then and there Quinn snapped on The Hodge.

I cannot remember all that was said by Quinn to The Hodge, but Quinn tried to rally support against him. When Quinn quickly realized that we were all on The Hodge's side, he ordered him, a staff sergeant, to cease talking and do push-ups. This had probably not been asked of The Hodge for a decade. When he refused, Quinn freaked out and we almost had to hold him back. The Hodge just walked away and went back to his CHU. Quinn, now furious and beyond comprehension, began to try again to rally us against The Hodge. No one was willing to listen to Quinn anymore. He started blaming Lieutenant Scher and The Hodge for stealing his platoon.

Quinn then committed the final straw that we were all hoping would come during his breakdown. He singled me and other soldiers out and said something to the likes of that he was going to kill Lieutenant Scher that night. Everyone quickly dispersed from Quinn, and we locked ourselves in our CHUs. The word quickly passed to Lieutenant Scher, who was at the time up at the company headquarters tent.

Within seconds, the first sergeant came down and took Quinn out of his CHU, seized his weapons, and placed him under armed guard up at the command post (CP) for Angel Company. That night it was like a whirlwind had come through our platoon and stirred us up. It put everyone in a state of shock. The other platoons were just as stunned and confused. That was the only night that everyone spent locked in his own room. Some even slept with loaded weapons in fear of Quinn entering their CHU.

The next morning, the squad leaders called the platoon together for a special meeting. As we all sleepily roamed into a large empty tent nearby our CHUs, we knew we were about to find out the seriousness of the whole situation at hand. Our squad leaders led us in an open discussion on the measures we needed to take. We were free to vent about any feelings we had about what should happen with Quinn. We were also informed that The Hodge had been permanently removed from First Platoon and that really saddened us. He was exchanged with another squad leader of the same rank from Third Platoon.

We decided to all fill out sworn statements that explained all of our own past experiences with Quinn and his mental health issues. I wrote about training exercises in the States where he would snap under the slightest pressure. I also wrote about the time in Kuwait when he slammed me into a wall and threatened my life. We all had a lot to write because it was so fresh in all of our minds. His quirks were our main form of conversation for over a year. I made it clear that I never felt safe with him in command and I would refuse ever to leave the wire with him in command over me. My detailed letter was one of many. I didn't hear of a single soldier who wrote a positive letter on Quinn's behalf. We all signed our own letters and turned them in to the captain, unsure of the possible outcome of the action we had just performed.

The letters proved to work wonders. Within hours, the battalion commander was notified and Quinn was removed from FOB Remagen for good. We never saw him again. First Platoon finally could breathe a sigh of relief. Angel Company Commander, Captain Jeffrey Lesperance was very pleased with how we handled the situation and seemed happy with the outcome. Staff Sergeant Ledbetter was transferred from Second Platoon over to us as our interim platoon sergeant. Things were finally looking good for my platoon.

THE BUS STOP

"I was almost frozen with fear."

Being on QRF not only meant that we conducted route clearances twice a day, but also that we were kept cooped up in an empty tent on FOB Remagen. The reason for that was so we were all consolidated under one roof in case of an emergency when we got spun up. It was a large tent with plywood floors and separated in two halves. The NCOs stayed on one side and the lower enlisted men stayed on the other. Cots were all that we were given, but we all brought our sleeping bags for the nights we stayed over. Of course, we still did hour-long guard shifts through the night, to monitor the radio and guard the trucks. No one ever enjoyed being awoken in the middle of the night to go babysit a radio.

Route clearances conducted by QRFs were done around six in the morning and four in the afternoon. QRFs were also charged with reacting to anything and everything in the Tikrit area at a moment's notice. Route clearances were always boring and repetitive. Battling to stay awake during them was the true challenge.

The morning route clearance on the 20th of January was yet another morning my platoon was graced by the presence of an IED. Sergeant Armstrong was in charge of my truck that day, and I really did not feel like gunning that morning. I took the job of a dismount, sitting in the back right seat position. Taylor was driving my truck while Sunny was up in the turret.

We were rolling south down the one place I always was most alert. "IED Alley" did not get its name for no reason. Business 1 was the official name of the full stretch of road, but the small portion that ran next to Kadasiyah and Tikrit's northern edge forged this notorious nickname as a hotspot for frequently placed IEDs. Up and down this road, yellow stars were laid out as flower beds in the sidewalk and medians for trees that no longer stood. These were places where IEDs were frequently hidden. We called them "exploding stars."

Halfway down IED Alley, we noticed an Iraqi man standing next to a bus stop. Our protocol was always to search any man standing by the side of the road, so I prepared myself to search him. As we slowed the patrol down, my truck being the first truck in the convoy, we had the final judgment on the course of action.

"I think he's waiting for a bus or something," I said to Armstrong.

"What's this motherfucker want?" Taylor fussed from behind the wheel.

"I don't see him much as a threat. Do you?" Armstrong questioned us. We all had breakfast on our minds and thought the sooner we got back the better chance there was for us to get some warm chow.

"No. Let's keep going," Sunny chimed down from the turret.

Armstrong unlatched his door and asked the now nervous man, "Bus or taxi?"

"Bus," the middle-aged man replied.

"All right. Sounds good," Armstrong said as he swung his door shut and relayed on the radio that we were going to continue the mission.

No more than ten seconds after we started moving from a dead stop, there came the all-too-familiar sound of an IED explosion behind us. The sound was ear-shattering. It reverberated in our chests and startled everyone. In these situations, everyone's first word was always—"Fuck!"

It turned out the bus stop was rigged with a 155mm IED buried deep under the ground. I had been no more than five feet from the spot ten seconds prior to the explosion. I saw nothing suspicious. Had Armstrong decided to search that man, I would have found myself practically standing on the impending doom.

Staff Sergeant Gibson's truck was behind us and took the brunt of the blast. Most of the shrapnel sailed over the truck or chipped into the side of their Humvee. No one was injured except for the common ringing of the ears. Vinny was driving and had stayed calm during the ordeal. The vehicle was still serviceable. Vinny drove it away from the explosion site.

As soon as the all clear was given and we found out no one was injured, we searched from inside our vehicle to survey the grounds for any secondary devices before we stepped out. As I sat helpless in the backseat, something snapped in my head. Thoughts rushed through my mind as I replayed the scenario over and over. How come I had not searched that man? We had stopped for less threatening things before. Poston would have had me out searching that man had he been in the truck that morning. These terrorists knew our tactics and were acting upon them.

As I sat quietly in my seat playing these "what ifs" in my mind, everyone in my truck began to verbally play the scene over again. The third vehicle had since gotten out and detained the man next to the bus stop for further questioning. I still did not move or utter a word. I was almost frozen with fear, and the conversations in my truck faded away from me. *Why did this device not explode when we parked almost on top of it? Why didn't I get out and search that man? Why did I not just die? How long will my luck continue?*

"Conklin, go put an orange cone out a hundred meters in front of the truck," Armstrong shouted and I snapped out of my fog. The cones acted as a final line for vehicles before they would be shot at.

Shit! I thought. *I have to get out and walk down this road by myself knowing the evil eyes are watching me?* The last place I wanted to be was outside the vehicle. Before I opened my door, all I could do was play a thousand terrible scenarios over and over in my head.

I exited my vehicle and grabbed the cone from the antenna off the back of the Humvee. Maybe I was paranoid, but I thought I heard the unmistakable sound of crackling AK fire from somewhere nearby in neighboring Kadasiyah. It sounded pretty sustained for a moment, but if it wasn't directed at us, it wasn't a threat at the moment. Almost in a trance, I walked slowly away from my Humvee about one hundred feet with an almost thousand-yard stare on my face. I kept replaying twisted thoughts in my head as I placed the cone down and walked back to the truck.

Halfway back, I paused and turned to the side of the road that had houses lined up and down facing the bus stop. It gave perfect visibility for a possible triggerman to watch our every move. I knew somewhere out there evil men were trying to kill us and watched us. As I stood there and surveyed the houses, I snapped.

"You fucking pussies! You can all go to Hell! Come out and fight, you fucking cowards! Sure, plant a bomb and hide out, that's real brave. I'm gonna find you and fucking kill you all!" I just kept screaming. Then I noticed an Iraqi Police station on the other side of the road, across from the bus stop. I then turned my attention from the invisible enemy to the Iraqi Police, who were now standing around like always, looking curiously at me.

"Hey, IP, you're all fucking useless, too! All of you! You all fucking suck!" I knew they probably did not know what I was saying, but I was venting things that were just building up inside me. If I was a teapot, I was whistling at this point.

"Get back in the truck, Conklin," Armstrong yelled back at me. I gave the finger to the Iraqi Police and climbed back into my seat. I felt so much better, but I could not stop replaying the scenario of the IED over and over in my head. I thanked Armstrong again for not making me search that man earlier. I then thanked him for saving my life.

Before we left the scene to head back to FOB Remagen, the Iraqi Army came out and parked their old white pickup trucks next to our vehicles. The bed of one of their pickup trucks contained the bodies of three dead Iraqis. A man, woman, and child were lying dead in the back of this truck.

The story was later relayed to me that our IED attack had all been a setup to distract us. While we sat on that road after getting hit, the sound of AK fire I'd heard in Kadasiyah was a murder. Some terrorists had dressed up like Iraqi Army and raided the home of an Iraqi Army S3 officer and his family. The real Iraqi Army then went and picked up the bodies and drove by us to tell us the situation. Sadly, there was nothing we could do. It was just one of many tragedies that happened every day in Iraq. It was the first time I really saw the strategy and orchestration that these terrorists went through. They were smarter than I'd ever thought possible.

A SANDY SUPER BOWL

"This sand was like talcum powder."

As I continued to seclude myself in my puzzling thoughts later that same night, FOB Remagen was hit with a sandstorm. Amid the rainy season, it was rare to see a sandstorm. Being on QRF meant that our weapons were always mounted on top of the Humvees to reduce time when we were called upon.

Within minutes, the black machine guns turned tan from the clinging sand. The sand that clung to weapons was unlike the typical sand one would find at any beach in America. This sand was like talcum powder: fine-grained and it stuck to every surface. It even found its way into every crevice imaginable. I only could imagine what my lungs would look like by the end of my deployment. My platoon spent all night vigorously cleaning all weapon systems. This was the last time we kept our guns permanently affixed during QRF duty.

The following evening, as we were downloading our gear from the Humvees and into the QRF tent, a unique sound came screeching over FOB Remagen. It was followed by a muffled explosion. We all knew right away it was a rocket of some sort. We were unaware of where it had hit.

We knew it was close, but not close enough to raise a fuss. We were continuing to download our gear when the FOB loudspeakers came on. They informed us of a rocket exploded near a guard tower at the front gate, but they gave the all clear.

Around the same time of the month, America was being immersed in Super Bowl hype. I did not even know until the day of the Super Bowl that Pennsylvania's own Pittsburgh Steelers were competing. This was always a big event in my household, and the lack of hype before the game became another reminder of how homesick I was.

While the Super Bowl raged on millions of people's televisions in America, I found myself trying to sleep on a cot in the QRF tent in Iraq. I woke up in the middle of the night to hear the voice of Lieutenant Scher announce on the radio, "Steelers have just won the Super Bowl." The lights were out and everyone was sleeping in the QRF tent. I believe I was the only one who heard the message. I just quietly whispered a faint and dismal "woohoo" and rolled over to grab any sleep I could. That was my Super Bowl experience of 2006.

One of the most unnecessary techniques we started to initiate on patrols was what we called "over-watches." What this consisted of was parking our four Humvees five hundred meters or so off MSR Tampa and into the desert. We just sat there and monitored the highway. Now, the officer answer to this was that "we were deterring the enemy from emplacing an IED on that stretch of the highway." This was stupid. The enemy would be insane to lay one within our sight. All this meant to me was that "Muhammad" was going to continue down the road out of sight and lay it there. I knew that in order for this tactic to actually work, we needed to be hidden or camouflaged. But what did I know? I was just a specialist who used common sense and not textbooks. It was an annoying tactic that went hand in hand with complaints from everyone except our lieutenant.

My theory proved right on the early morning of January 31. While we babysat the highway, a convoy passed through on MSR Tampa. As the pogue convoy crested the hill out of sight from us, they came across three Iraqis emplacing an IED near the road. The non-infantry soldiers captured the terrorists along with three AKs, grenades, and two 103mm rounds. Now, if we had been the ones who came across those men, we would not have captured them. They would have been dead. The fact that these pogues pulled this off on our stretch of the MSR angered everyone in my platoon. It was embarrassing. We stopped doing these over-watches after a few months with zero results.

RAIN, RAIN, GO AWAY

"There were no happy smiles."

The first week of February was sprayed with relentless rainstorms. We were submersed in Iraq's rainy season. Every day it rained, and it rained hard. No light drizzle or afternoon spray. It was constant downpour. Sand turned to muck and patrols became drenched. We all came back from patrols more wet than if we had swum in a lake the entire time.

Being almost drowned every patrol, I managed to find fun in any situation. On February 4, we were dealt the worst two days of the rainy season. Extreme high winds and heavy raindrops made the environment only comparable to a hurricane in Florida. The rain did not even seem to be falling from up above. The pellets of rain were thrown by the strong wind so much that it literally was raining left to right.

It was hard to find motivation to do an afternoon route clearance amid the downpour. Because of the way the cookie crumbled, I always had a reserved seat in the turret. Before our pre-mission checks, I just sprayed almost an entire can of WD-40 on every inch of all three of my guns. I grabbed my green camouflage rain poncho, slipped into my tight-fitting vest, put my helmet on, and walked out of my CHU and into a wall of rain.

Mud was caked up to my shins by the time I reached my Humvee. The vehicles were parked a short distance from our CHUs and that helped some people stay somewhat dry. Everyone who was not gunning poked fun at those who were. The thought of staying dry inside the Humvees delighted those who thought they would actually escape the sideways rain. I just took it in stride. I accepted that I was soaked and would someday be dry again. Until that day came, I just filled my turret up with gummy snacks sent from home and enjoyed the rain. The chance to be a part of such bizarre weather made everything almost enjoyable. Besides, we had found from past experiences that IEDs hardly ever went off in torrential downpours. It was bad for the Iraqi who emplaced it, but most of all it would make the IED practically inert.

During that drenching patrol, we stopped briefly on a bridge to have a closer inspection on some twisted metal debris we'd found on the roadside. I laughed in revenge when those inside the Humvee were called upon to move it off the roadway.

While we parked idle on the highway to clear the trash, I took the opportunity to experiment with the wind. Sheer boredom led me to grab one of my empty gummy snack wrappers and just loosen my grip of it. The wrapper immediately shot out like a bat out of Hell to my right and kept flying about a hundred yards in a straight direction. I watched it until it was out of view and I still never saw it hit the ground.

Another boredom act of testing the wind's power was more amusing than my last test. I placed my hand in front of my face no more than twelve inches away. I conjured up some good-sized saliva and spit it into my hand, but the wind was so strong that the wad never even reached my hand. By the time it left my mouth, it turned right and shot out into the countryside out of sight. The magnitude of the wind was just unbelievable.

We headed back to the FOB to attempt to dry out. I was lucky enough to have an extra pair of desert boots, courtesy of 3ID on Christmas. Others would just stay accustomed to their swampy boots.

That night was going to be another night spent in the dreaded QRF tent, home of zero luxuries except a cot. The torrential rainstorm continued, so we spent the evening inside cleaning all of our equipment and giving it time to dry. No one dared to leave the tent to use the bathroom unless it was a dire need, because most of us were wearing our last set of dry uniforms. While cleaning, we joked about how it was our luck to be destined to have to go out in the storm so soon for no particular reason. There was a reason we always joked about the worst-case scenarios—they always came true.

Around midnight the call we were all dreading came over the radio. We were all at first dumbfounded yet felt as if we'd known something like this was going to happen. Being on QRF duty, we were required to be able to roll out of the gates at a moment's notice. We slept in our uniforms to save time. Most of the time we were not even sure what we were responding to, but we always had to be ready for anything.

As soon as we filtered out of the QRF tent, our pace to the Humvees was incredibly hampered. It was almost like watching us move to our trucks in slow motion. The flooding rains had now turned the sand into boot-deep mud. So much for having dry clothes, but, especially, good riddance to my only other pair of dry boots. Everyone was suffering before we even got into the trucks.

Luckily for me, it was Taylor's turn at gunning, whereas I was a dismount. Armstrong was controlling the truck and Poston was finally going to drive. Taylor mounted the once dry gun. Everyone in the truck bitched in unison about everything that surrounded us. Instead of sleeping warm in our cots, we were outside at night, knee-deep in mud, and exposed to sideways rain again. Our platoon always seemed to receive the short straw.

We were ready after about five minutes of serious scrambling amid the mud and rain. We all got our order of movement and pulled away from the QRF tent. From there, we did not even make it halfway to the exit of FOB Remagen before our first Humvee in line got stuck in the mud.

We paused momentarily as the second truck in line attempted to pull the first truck out of the swampy mud. Before the second Humvee even got near the first Humvee, they themselves got stuck too. Pandemonium came screaming across the radio as we were now combat-ineffective.

I looked up at Taylor, who was now monitoring the situation from the turret. He could not hear a word I was saying since the wind and rain were too strong from his vantage point. As I sat in the back seat, the

Humvee was filling up with water at our feet. Rain trickled out of every crack in the structure, ensuring that no one was dry. Looking at Taylor, now wet as a dog, I could not help but realize how much the turret was like having a showerhead pour water inside the truck.

The call came over the radio to the last two remaining unstuck Humvees to attempt to pull out the submerged ones. Before we accepted the job, Poston and Armstrong decided to watch the third Humvee in their attempt. He aligned our truck and shined his headlights toward the submerged Humvees. As the third Humvee proceeded closer to the second stuck Humvee, they themselves got stalled in the mud. It couldn't have played out worse than this. We were now three-for-three Humvees in attempting to leave FOB Remagen. Instead of our Humvee driving forward into the inevitable muck, we decided to drive back to where we came from and get an oversized crane truck that specialized in towing vehicles.

While Poston and Armstrong physically ran into the CP to stir up someone to drive the crane truck, Taylor and I snuck away to the chow hall, which was currently serving midnight chow.

We could not stop complaining about the whole situation, but we felt like we were getting even with it all by eating while the platoon was figuring out the debacle. We did not stay long, because we kept overhearing some pogues complain about the rain. We knew that they did not have to go out in it, so it just pissed us off and we left the chow hall and headed back to the immersed platoon.

We linked back up with Poston and Armstrong and drove back to the scene of our entire platoon still submerged in the mud. We noticed all soldiers from each truck were on hands and knees in the rain, shoveling, pushing, and directing all these attempts in vain. One Humvee was so far in the mud that its doors couldn't swing open because the mud was so high. The occupants all had to climb out of the turret. It was total chaos for our platoon, and there was no way we were leaving the FOB anytime soon. Whatever was happening in Tikrit would have to continue without our aid because we were going nowhere but deeper into the earth.

After about an hour of watching the three trucks and their occupants turn brown from head to toe from the mud, we just laughed at everyone from inside our truck. We had since closed the turret, and Taylor sat inside with the rest of us. This did not prevent the rain from still trickling inside from the nooks and crannies of the Humvee. We all knew the alternatives just by looking at the others struggle. It was hilarious to see the whole situation unfold. We felt useless, but we did not need our last truck stuck.

Help soon arrived within the hour in the form of a crane that pulled the three trucks out of their holes. The mission was subsequently called off. It proved to be the messiest mishap for our entire company that night. Three out of the four trucks on QRF duty were completely stuck in mud no more than one hundred meters from our CHUs. We tried to laugh it all off, but it was now near 2 A.M. and we were all soaked head to toe, inside and out, caked with layers of mud. There were no happy smiles. It was a night from Hell.

We slowly and gingerly retreated back to the QRF tent, stumbling in with mud and rain that covered our entire bodies. The look of defeat and utter hopelessness graced the faces of all who had frolicked in the worst weather Iraq had to offer. We all looked like we'd lost the World Cup, and it had been played in a mud pit.

We only snuck in two hours of sleep before we headed back out for the morning route clearance. The rain had let up slightly, but the thick mud was still prevalent. We did at least make it out of FOB Remagen, but we happened to get a truck stuck at a farm adjacent to MSR Tampa.

Round two of being stuck was more embarrassing than the first. Indeed we had three Humvees stuck earlier that morning, but at least no one was awake to see us struggle. Now it was daylight and we had a Humvee stuck in a farmer's field. After a few attempts from the entire platoon to get it out of its rut, we caved in and asked the farmer himself for help.

With the use of our interpreter, we were able to have the Iraqi farmer start up his ancient tractor and pull us out. It was a bit embarrassing knowing that here we were, strong and powerful soldiers from America, begging for help from an Iraqi farmer with inferior equipment. The help was greatly appreciated, however, and we did manage to make it back to FOB Remagen.

We never again did see rain the likes of that terrible night, though we did get dripped on from time to time. After a few weeks the skies ceased to secrete anything but humidity.

DEALING WITH KIDS

"A lot of hand gestures and broken English got both of us by."

February's momentum of patrols started out just like January's had. By the second week of February, we started slimming down patrols to one a day unless on QRF duty. The decision was made after countless complaints of feeling depleted. It was a break that soon started reenergizing people.

With more time to refuel from a good night's sleep, apart from being awoken in the middle of the night to guard trucks, patrols began to be more bearable. They were not enjoyable. They never were. They just became more feasible because we were not so tired during them and constantly checking our watches.

By February, the job of being a gunner had become second nature to me. During security halts the dismounted element of the platoon would walk around the city while the mounted element would park in an open area and wait. The first activity we would do was converse with the driver. When conversations got stale, we would crank up the iPod that was connected to portable speakers above the radio mount.

My personal favorite thing to do in the turret while parked was interact with the children. When we were parked in a clearing, children always were in the area playing among and around us. Some brave boys dared to get close. Depending on our mood that day, we would either embrace them or yell at them to get away. All wanted candy, but most were also just curious about us.

During one patrol, we were parked in a clearing between villages in downtown Tikrit and were swarmed by children. The truck crew just consisted of Taylor and me, which most would consider a bad idea, but I would not have had it any other way. The kids came close enough to touch the truck. Taylor always yelled at the kids to get back, but I could see they were completely unarmed.

"Mista, mista, do you want chocolaté?" chimed one persuasive boy, around eleven or twelve years old.

I almost misinterpreted what he was asking me. I had to ask him to make sure, so I yelled back, "You want chocolaté or you can get me chocolaté?

The young boy on his bike spoke broken English at me, saying, "Give me Emreekie dollar. I give you air-a-biyah chocolaté."

Now because of the broken English and Arabic I had started to pick up by this point, I knew this kid was asking me to give him an American dollar so he could buy me some local Iraqi chocolate at the corner haji shop.

Knowing the power of the American dollar in his country, I also sensed this kid wanted to make a little bit of a profit. It was hot out and I was hungry, and as the old phrase goes, "When in Rome." I was craving some Iraqi chocolate.

I wanted to guarantee this transaction would happen correctly, so I again reviewed his task.

"I give you Emreeki, you give me chocolaté. OK?" I said, while gesturing as much as I could with my hands.

"Yes, mista." The kid was very anxious that he would lose the sale, because several other boys were picking up on the situation and also offering to buy me chocolate.

As soon as I grabbed out a one-dollar bill, all the kids' eyes widened with excitement. The first boy quickly seized the dollar and sped off on his bike. This set off all the other boys in their demands to buy me chocolate.

"I'm sorry, I don't have any more. I'm broke, kids," I said to the youngsters as they began to piece together that I was not going to hand out any more money.

While waiting for my chocolate, I conversed the best way I knew how with the kids. A lot of hand gestures and broken English got both of us by. Some kids would show me pictures of their brothers and sisters. They also would rub their two index fingers together, a form of sign language meaning relation to siblings.

A couple of kids in the distance were playing soccer when I yelled for them to come over. I opened my hands in preparation to catch the ball. For the next ten minutes, time passed quickly as I played the universal game of catch with these kids from my turret. The children were delighted to play with an American soldier. I didn't mind because I was actually enjoying it as well. It was better than acting like a vigilante in an area where I felt completely secure, especially surrounded by young children.

Before I knew it, the young boy on the bike pedaled his way back to my truck, directing other kids out of his way as if he didn't have brakes. I was getting first class treatment from "my client." To my surprise, instead of one piece of chocolate, this boy had two pieces of wrapped chocolate and two cold Pepsi cans. He even produced change in Iraqi dinar.

While looking at the money, I said *"La, la,"* which was the Arabic translation for the word no. As he was dumping off our snacks to Taylor in the driver's seat, I reached into my wallet and gave the boy another American dollar.

"Suchron. Suchron," I said while putting my hand on my heart. "Keep the change." The kid was in high spirits as he backed up from the vehicle and examined his American dollar as if it were the Golden Ticket to the Chocolate Factory. The other kids quickly gathered around him and studied it.

The kids were happy, Taylor was happy, and so was I. I enjoyed that chocolate, which actually tasted very good. I always relished patrols where I could get a lot of interaction with the kids.

ALL OUT OF LOVE

"Holy shit, Reese, someone just shot at me."

In the beginning of February, small-arms fire started to pick up in the city. It was never directed at us though. People would break out into firefights as soon as we left a certain part of town. There was one part of Tikrit referred to by us as Fortieth Street. It consisted of rows of shops that lined both sides of the street, a busy business street for people. Iraqi Police and Iraqi Army would frequently get fired upon and called us like we were their personal 911. Every time we showed up, all was quiet in the city.

It annoyed us when we showed up and nothing would happen. It was not that we wanted something to happen, but more that we knew there were evil people in the area and we wanted them dead or captured. It was frustrating. One day we decided to conduct a thorough patrol into every shop on Fortieth Street. It would be a long and tiring patrol for those who dismounted.

I did not mind if I had to go on that patrol, as long as I was dismounted. I was getting annoyed that I was always placed as the gunner in the turret. The night before the mission, it was looking in my favor to miss the whole thing. I looked at the projected list of who was going, and I did not see my name written on the dry-erase board in Lieutenant Scher's CHU.

The next day, I woke up excited that I would not have to go on this long patrol. I could not have been any more wrong. It turned out that the colonel of the 3/320th Field Artillery, who outranked everyone in my company, had ordered everyone on FOB Remagen to start filling sandbags. He put out an order that sandbags must surround the entire facade of every CHU, to the height of the door. My platoon was sort of at a head start, thanks to our old platoon sergeant Quinn. At the time, the sandbags were about knee-high around the CHUs. This was going to be a daunting task anyway, and of course, the finish date given was as soon as possible.

When I woke up that morning and noticed my name still not on the roster for the day's mission, I made it my job to be on that patrol. I didn't care if I was gunning or not. I did not want to stay on the FOB and fill sandbags in the heat all day. Before the mission started, I headed over to Poston's CHU.

"Sergeant Poston, I have a question," I said to him once inside his CHU.

"Hey, by the way, we're taking some Public Relations people out on patrol today. They have a Humvee to add to our platoon today and you're going to gun for them. Now, what's your question?" asked Poston.

This was exactly what I wanted, but I decided to milk the situation and look pissed. I figured it could benefit me to act like I got tossed around all the time. I lowered my head and tried to look angry, as I pondered finding a question.

"What's the deadline on having our CHUs complete with sandbags?" I pulled that question right out of nowhere.

"As soon as possible," Poston retorted.

"Roger, sarnt." I left Poston's CHU looking depressed, but I was rather gleeful that I would be on the patrol. I was an expert at always finding the shortcuts around monotonous chores. It was all a game and I knew just how to play it.

For the patrol in every shop on Fortieth Street, we now had five Humvees. Four were my platoon's, and I was gunning on the Public Relations Humvee, with Private First Class Justin Reese driving. I figured it would be just like every patrol. We would drop off our dismounted element on Fortieth Street and the mounted element would drive around close to the area, park for a little bit, and then continue to drive around to show our presence.

The patrol was standard to every other one I had been a part of except for one small addition: The Humvee I was gunning on was a brand-new model. I was used to older model Humvees with at least ninety thousand miles on them. They were the lowest of the lowest grade and always in much need of repair. Rumors had it that some of the Humvees we owned were vehicles from the Gulf War. The Public Relations truck was new, clean, and air-conditioned. It even had a car freshener that actually made the Humvee smell like pine instead of old wet laundry.

But one thing really set this Humvee apart from any other Humvee I was ever in the entire year. The turret was affixed with a bulky loud-speaker and attached to it was a hand mic for the purpose of broadcasting American propaganda in Arabic to the people. Now as soon as we dropped off the dismounted element, it was just Reese and I in control of our truck. The highest other ranking person in the mounted patrol was Sergeant Armstrong, and he was in another truck.

It was like leaving a fresh-baked pie in front of a hungry child. You know that child is going to taste the pie. Well, it was no different having this loud amplified system at my disposal.

Driving through the city, I would yell a lot of random stupid phrases for the enjoyment of Reese and myself and the other gunners in the patrol that could hear. After a couple quick random verbal rants, I pulled my iPod out of my cargo pocket and attached it to the stereo. It was like unleashing a can of worms. I quickly sifted through my iPod and selected the most devilish music possible. I was playing such death band songs as "Let the Bodies Hit the Floor" by Drowning Pool, "Enemy" by Disturbed, and "Break Stuff" by Limp Bizkit. This music was bouncing off every house as we drove slowly through the alleys between them.

It had to have had set a lot of people off. The volume was excruciating. Children were not running up to us, but running away. I was blaring some of the most infuriating songs imaginable. It was definitely a style of music that these people had never heard before. The looks I received were priceless. My broken-toothed smile went along great with the music.

Halfway through the patrol, Armstrong decided to halt the mounted element in a clearing shaped like a square and surrounded by homes. The clearing was filled with children, so it was an ample place to pause. Each truck was then systematically swarmed by crowds of curious children in awe of us. I had my iPod on pause as I tried to get the attention of Avery, who was gunning on the vehicle nearest to mine.

"Avery!" I yelled across the ways.

"What?" he replied.

"You enjoying the music?"

"These people are scared as hell at that shit," he chimed back with a laugh.

"I'm gonna change it up and give these kids a taste of good music," I yelled back at him as I sifted through my iPod's catalogue. I came across "Fool on the Hill" by The Beatles, then "Freebird" by Lynyrd Skynyrd.

The children were mesmerized by now, and I had almost fifty of them around my truck dancing and enjoying the music. I was dancing too, from inside my turret. Reese just laughed from underneath me.

I guess the Iraqis were not fans of the eighties because as soon as I started to play "All Out of Love" by Air Supply, fathers and mothers filed out of their homes and yelled for their children. My first reaction was total surprise. I also was kind of irritated when I saw fathers hitting their little children really hard in the face with closed fists. All because they were dancing to the music I was playing? What a shame.

Before everything got out of hand, Armstrong instructed me that I was done with the amplified speakers. I agreed and put everything away. We then decided to find a new place to set a security halt before some of the families lashed out at us in different ways.

After a few minutes of driving through the claustrophobic alleyways, we found ourselves in another rubble clearing. The rubble was typically the remains of a flattened square of real estate, a once-standing home. Rocks, bricks, and plenty of garbage were all that was left and they coated the ground.

While we parked in the new area, we again picked up the boring task of passing time. The first thing we usually did when we halted was quickly switch out gunners and drivers to give the gunners a chance to relieve themselves. In certain situations, this was impossible, so we got skilled at peeing in water bottles and just throwing them out into the garbage-infested streets or desert.

After a successful bathroom break, we began our normal task of talking about anything and everything. Once things quieted down, I yelled over to the Humvee to my right where Avery was gunning.

While I was leaning over the side of my turret in mid-conversation with Avery, the unforgettable sound of a single shot rang out. Only this time it came with three unique sounds. I'm unsure on the order of the three sounds because it was all almost instantaneous. The rifle shot was far away, the snap was next to my face, and the crack was the ground or wall behind my Humvee. It happened so fast.

My first reaction was that my legs collapsed. I hunkered down in my turret at lightning speed. My eyes were bugged as I tried to figure out what had just happened.

"Holy shit, Reese, someone just shot at me," I yelled.

"Where'd it come from?" he asked.

"Give me the radio. One-one Bravo, this is . . .one-four Golf. I had a shot ring out from my right, over."

"Roger, we heard it, keep eyes on, let me know what you see, over," Armstrong replied back.

"Roger, out." I dropped the radio and slowly peeked my head over the turret. I saw Avery in his turret a little lower than usual as well.

"Damn, Conklin, I've never seen you move so fast in your life!" Avery yelled while he laughed.

"Fuck you! That thing went right in front of me. I never knew a bullet so close made such a weird noise." I was talking a mile a minute; I just could not really comprehend what had just happened. "Dude, Reese, that thing made the weirdest sound, like a pop sound, with a whiz. I can't explain it. That was intense!"

I stood back up in the turret, lower than normal. I was determined to find where the shot had rung out from. The giant mosque in central Tikrit towered over the landscape in the direction from which the shot seemed to have originated. Nicknamed "Evil Mosque," it would have been the prime place to be but I was unsure. There were two streets to my front and dozens of homes with windows. It was a winless battle. By now, if the shooter was still around, he was long gone. Shoot and move; a sniper's tactic.

I scanned every window around me, but there were so many choices that I could not do much good except present another chance for someone. Thankfully, we ended up not staying long. I wanted to be anywhere else but there. By luck, the dismounted element was more than ready to be picked up after walking all of Fortieth Street.

We quickly linked back up with them in a clearing near the street. Little was said about the sniper attempt on me earlier that day. It was just a long day and everyone wanted to rest. It was the start of my personal struggle coming to terms with the reality that there could be a sniper anywhere in the city. I was convinced that he could strike again soon, but I never really brought it up. Everyone's notion was that if it was your time to die, it was your time.

THE REALITY OF WAR

"What is the name of the WIA?"

On February 12, daily patrols in Tikrit were slotted for First and Third Platoons. Second Platoon was taking over QRF duty that week. I, however, was not scheduled for anything that day because I was on my way to FOB Speicher. Captain Lesperance had asked me personally if I would like to get my tooth fixed. Instead of looking like a "Snaggletooth," I decided I would take the offer and go to Speicher and get that taken care of.

In the morning, I gathered my stuff and linked up with Second Platoon, who were preparing to do their morning route clearance and drop me off at Speicher. I walked by First Platoon, who were loading up their equipment for their patrol. Most of the guys were envious of me because they knew that I would spend most of the day at Speicher doing nothing.

"Get me some Taco Bell," Taylor said.

"Fix your smile, Chip," Sergeant Pitchford chimed in.

I just gave everyone the middle finger and walked to Second Platoon's staging area. On my way, I passed Third Platoon as well. While I was passing them, Kemple shouted out to me.

"C-iaaa-nklin." He said my name rather annoyingly to grab my attention.

"What's up, Kemple?" I asked back.

"Same shit, different day," Kemple said as he passed by to prepare for Third Platoon's mission.

I felt like I was taking a sick day. I was getting dropped off at Speicher to get my tooth fixed and I knew it would not take long. I knew I had until the evening, when I would be picked back up on Second Platoon's evening route clearance. I was planning on relaxing at the PX, watching some television at their MWR (Morale, Welfare, & Recreation) building, and maybe using their telephones.

Once I got to FOB Speicher, I wasted no time in running over to the dental office. The dentist equipment was primitive, but they said they could fix me up. The bond they gave me on my tooth did not really fit right. I didn't really like it either because it made a small gap between my teeth. But I had to make do with it.

I spent the rest of the afternoon by myself enjoying what Speicher had to offer. All the pogues on the FOB were by now all too sick of the "comforts" of Speicher. I took advantage like I did every time I came up there. I bought some CDs at the PX and stuffed my face with some fast food.

Around 5:30 P.M., I headed across the FOB to prepare to link up with Second Platoon, who were on their way back to pick me up. They found me standing by the dental office, which was located right next to the emergency field hospital. I walked through the triage tent and was glad to see it empty, except for staff. Those were the only people I wished would never work in Iraq. In a perfect world.

When Second Platoon rounded the corner, I spotted their lieutenant's Humvee. I hopped in and everyone in the vehicle was inquisitive on how I'd spent my free time at Speicher. I knew they were jealous, so I played on that. I told them I'd had a blast. I also told them that they all should break some teeth in exchange for a day at Speicher.

As we were traveling to the exit of Speicher, we had to go through a series of checkpoints. During the approximately fifteen minutes it took to make it out, transmissions over the company radio net started rapidly going off. We all went silent in the Humvee because Second Platoon was the QRF for the week. Their lieutenant, First Lieutenant Renard, sat in front of me and quickly seized the hand mic. He, like us, eagerly listened and tried to comprehend the transmissions.

It was hard to distinguish what was going on. I could hear voices yelling for Angel CP, my company headquarters. *Oh dear God,* I thought. I prayed that something fierce had not happened to my platoon. I knew they were out at the time along with Third Platoon. Without me.

I could distinguish The Hodge's familiar voice coming over the radio. Lieutenant Scher kept chiming back in succession. I was confused as to whether it was First or Third Platoon that was involved with something. Transmissions became unclear and sometimes broken. We needed to get good reception.

What is going on? I said to myself as I peered out the window toward Tikrit.

"Fire . . . American wounded. No nine-line, go to Speicher!" came frantically over the radio. Almost immediately everyone in my truck uttered the same "Oh, fuck."

"Angel CP, Angel CP, this is two-six, we're pulling out of Speicher now, do you need us, over," chimed Lieutenant Renard.

"Break, break, break, we're on our way to Speicher!" came The Hodge's voice over the net. I could hear the sound of a siren in the background of that last transmission. What the *hell* was going on?

Panic soon struck our convoy. Platoon internal transmissions began questioning our vehicle for clarification on what was going on in the city. No one knew. We all played the waiting game, hoping for the best but prepared for the worst.

As we pulled out of Speicher and turned right onto MSR Tampa, we started speeding down the road. Before we got to the "Twin Tits,"[14] one Humvee from our company and one Iraqi Police truck came blazing by us on the other side of the road.

"That was one of our trucks!" yelled the driver to the lieutenant.

"FUCK!" screamed Lieutenant Renard.

I had never seen one of our Humvees by itself before, let alone speed-

---

[14] *Twin Tits* was a nickname for two large arches that stood over both lanes of the MSR Tampa that was at the edge of Tikrit proper boundaries. It also served as an Iraqi police checkpoint in both lanes. It was natural for infantrymen to nickname anything that resembled the female anatomy to make it easy to remember as an identifiable landmark.

ing so fast on the highway. Somebody was hit. I sensed it. I knew that truck belonged to our company. I saw the company symbol painted on the turret shield. Now a million thoughts started rushing through my head. What had happened? Who was hit? First or Third Platoon? How bad was it? What was going on in Tikrit?

As QRF, we continued to barrel down MSR Tampa ourselves, toward Tikrit. News quickly became clearer on the radio. Captain Lesperance ordered us to standby mode instead of entering the city. We were a little confused about the order since we were QRF, but First Platoon was closer to the scene than we were. The last thing we wanted to do was put all our forces in one small area.

The cry for help was coming from Third Platoon, which was in the Fortieth Street vicinity. They were down to three Humvees since one of theirs had sped off to Speicher. First Platoon quickly showed up on scene to their aid, and the information began to filter over the net back to the company.

Being a part of Second Platoon's convoy, we found ourselves parked in the middle of the desert adjacent to MSR Tampa near Kadasiyah. We could not do anything other than listen to the radio. Everyone was silent in the truck and patiently listened to every transmission.

The conversation was now formulated between two people. Captain Lesperance was now in his Humvee with Headquarters Platoon and was leaving FOB Remagen to be on scene as well. This left the XO in charge at the headquarters to orchestrate the company's transmissions.

The Hodge's voice finally came back over the radio.

"Angel CP, Angel CP, this is . . . The Hodge. . . ."

"Angel three-one, this is CP, give me an update on what your current situation is, over," asked the XO. This was it; our worried questions were about to be answered. "What is the name of the WIA?" he fired off again.

Then came The Hodge's voice over the radio in a tone unlike him. It was hard to distinguish that it was actually him talking because his voice sounded so different. Very solemn, quiet, and choked up.

"Angel CP . . . the patient is Kemple," said a reluctant Hodge. "He's currently in surgery." Immediately, everyone in our truck whispered a prayer under his breath.

"What is his status, three-one?" the XO asked. A few seconds went by. The Hodge still didn't reply. Everyone in my truck was in his own little world and hung on to every word said on the radio while we simultaneously sent up a thousand prayers and hoped everything was all right.

"Three-one, tell me the status, over." The XO became impatient, as we all did. Not hearing The Hodge's reply was like watching an intense movie at its climax and having to go to a commercial break.

Seconds passed that seemed like minutes, but The Hodge finally broke the silence by replying. "Angel CP, he's a . . . um . . ." You could hear the tears in his voice as he struggled to talk. ". . . he's dead . . . Kemple's dead."

This could not be happening. This wasn't real. Kemple couldn't be dead. He was one of the toughest guys we had. I had just talked to him. This could not be happening.

"Shit!" screamed Lieutenant Renard as he threw the hand mic to the floor. The transmission from the XO continued as he orchestrated the lockdown of Fortieth Street. With the entire company now locking down the street, we knew that we probably would not be called upon. We just continued to sit idle in the middle of the open desert and listen to the radio in a daze.

What had happened to Third Platoon was that they were conducting the same patrol we had just conducted the day prior. Mounted elements were driving around Fortieth Street, while the dismounted men walked around. Kemple was gunning in the turret of one of Third Platoon's Humvees when a single shot from an enemy sniper echoed over the street. The bullet pierced Kemple's left collarbone, went into his neck, and traveled through his lungs. Instantly he fell to the floor of his Humvee.

Having this all unfold over the radio in my Humvee reminded me of similar scenes from our grandparents' generation. Everyone intently listened to the radio and didn't utter a word. I just sat in my seat and stared out the window in the direction of Fortieth Street, while I pictured what was going on. I tried to stay strong, but in the silence between the transmissions I could hear everyone in my Humvee faintly cry.

Tears streaked down my face as I continued to look out my window. The sun was now beginning to decline and create a beautiful sunset. I rapidly wiped my face dry and created a damp sleeve on my uniform. No one ever carried tissues.

As I sat in my seat, I tried not to make eye contact with anyone. They were all doing the same thing. Staring out of their windows and fighting back tears. I just clasped my hands together, took my helmet off, and began a long prayer for Kemple, his soon-to-be heartbroken family, and the rest of my company.

We continued to sit in silence, parked in place. Based on the transmissions on the radio, I began to picture what was happening in the city. First, Third, and Headquarters Platoons had locked the street down. They began a hectic and fast-paced search of every building. This was time-consuming, but I knew they were operating under a different attitude. Most of the men had no idea that Kemple was dead, but they knew that someone in the company was wounded. This promoted an adrenaline rush mixed with fierce hatred that ignited everyone that was conducting those searches. Knocking on doors was out of the question. They were just flowing in and out of buildings.

I will never forget how calm and steady Captain Lesperance commanded all his units that day. Higher commands from the 3/320th Field Artillery attempted to send two of its platoons in to help out. Lesperance quickly, sternly, and fiercely called back on the radio to tell him to stay away. The last thing he wanted was to create a crowded chaos of soldiers, which the colonel from the 3/320th was inadvertently attempting to do.

Rumors began to fly over the radio about a possible shooter in the top of Evil Mosque. The structure dominated the entire city and presented a perfect place for a sniper. This was where politics came in and stewed up Lesperance. As American soldiers, we were not allowed to go inside mosques. They were places of holy sanctuary that we had to respect and never enter. Lesperance tried for over an hour pleading to force Iraqi Army soldiers to go in there. This created a whole mass of confusion that only wasted time.

After a few hours had passed, Second Platoon was given the green light to break down our standby mode and head back to the FOB. The ride back was a bleak and quiet one for us. Going back to my CHU was like visiting a ghost town. No one was there because they were all still out on Fortieth Street clearing homes. I just sat quietly in my room and began to play the guitar that some stranger had sent me in the mail about a week earlier. It proved to be the greatest stress reliever I possessed.

Near midnight, First Platoon staggered into camp and looked just completely drained of energy. Their uniforms were covered in sweat mixed with dirt and their heads hung low. Everyone crept into his CHU and immediately went to bed. I went into the shower unit near our CHU and washed the day's sweat off me. I took a look at my new tooth in the mirror and realized that not only did it look very poorly done, but I knew that I didn't really care what I looked like. The thought also crossed my mind that like Kemple, I could be alive one second and dead the next. My appearance didn't matter. So I snapped it off and threw the tooth away. I was destined to go the rest of the deployment by the nickname "Chip."

Before I left the shower, Poston was on his way in.

"Let's see the smile," he sarcastically asked. I smiled to reveal that the chip was still present. He was totally confused. "I thought you got that fixed today."

"I did, but it was poorly done. Besides, it's not like I'm gonna be impressing any ladies around here. I'll fix it when I get home."

Poston accepted what I had to say and then began to shift subjects to the inevitable.

"Did you hear what happened tonight?" he asked me.

"Yeah, I was with Second Platoon and heard all the transmissions on the radio," I replied.

"Yeah, but do you know the entire situation?" he asked again.

"I was monitoring company net. He's . . . ah . . . I know he's dead," I softly explained.

"Well, keep that information to yourself because the boys don't know. They all think he's wounded right now. We're going to let them get some sleep and have an official formation tomorrow morning and break the news," Poston informed me.

I realized then that I held knowledge inside me that others didn't know. As I walked back to my CHU from the shower, a couple of soldiers in my platoon asked if I knew anything about Kemple's situation. It broke my heart, but I had to lie and tell them that I'd heard he was wounded. I didn't stop but continued on my way to my CHU and collapsed down in bed. It took me a long time to fall asleep. Many more prayers were said that night.

The following day, it was time to finally come to terms with reality. I slept through the first formation since I was not needed. Now everyone knew that Kemple had in fact died of his wound.

The task at hand for the day consisted of continuing the arduous chore of filling sandbags. It gave time for silent reflection, but also time to see how others were coping. As I held my shovel and scooped into the sandy earth, I realized that Sergeant Woods was digging close by. Woods was from Third Platoon and had been one of Kemple's closest friends. They were almost inseparable. I saw him concentrated intently on digging and he hardly even looked fazed by what had happen the evening prior.

I was torn up inside by what had happened, and Kemple was not even my closest friend in the company. I used to drink with him in the barracks before we deployed, and I would frequently pass time talking to him in his room. He got me started on Jack Daniel's and he loved classic rock music. Kemple's birthday was the day after mine, so we went out and celebrated our birthdays together. But Sergeant Woods knew everything about Kemple. Still he managed to look almost unaware of Kemple's death as he systematically filled sandbags.

Woods was a very religious man. He was the one who would always be found reading his little Bible everywhere he went. I knew that his deep faith was what gave him so much strength. I was curious about how he was coping better than the rest.

"What's your secret? How are you handling things so well?" I questioned him.

Without even putting down his shovel, he just said, "Everything happens for a reason," and he continued to fill up sandbags. It was true. With the mentality of everything happens for a reason, one cannot dwell in the past or question reality. This was the start of my new outlook on life.

FINAL SALUTE

"I want you to go out and kill the son of a bitch who did this."

Two days after Kemple's death was my first mission back out. Once again, I found myself in the turret. This patrol was unlike all the others prior to Kemple being killed. It was missing the normal joking around from the turret to the kids, or as much of the taunting and intimidation as I usually did. For me, and I know for others, the turret was the last place I wanted to be. But being one of the men in my platoon with the most experience serving in the turret, I found it hard for me to do any other job.

Our mission that morning was to conduct local checkups. This consisted of visiting gas stations and making sure everything was systematic and that the Iraqi Police were conducting their jobs. Our presence was also to deter people who filled up with more gas than they were allotted by using extra tanks in their cars and then selling it on the black market for absurdly high prices. We also had to visit all of the Iraqi Police checkpoints and stations. We were at each site no more than a half hour, but having so many different checkpoints to visit easily filled the slot of a six- to eight-hour mission.

My level of awareness was at an all-time high. I had a renewed sense of fear that I had not really felt since I entered Iraq. With Kemple's death

I found that not only had I had a false sense of security when out on missions, but we all had. After his death, people started to act differently, to scan more, joke less, and work harder. The grim consequence of not being so aggressive was what tuned us all in.

In the turret, every time we came to a halt, I ducked lower than usual. My fear was not only that I thought there could be a sniper somewhere in the city, but that I knew there was one. I also knew he could shoot. I wanted to be as small a target as I could because being in an open turret with no cover above me meant that all tall buildings now became my nightmare. At every halt, I had my eyes glued to a pair of binoculars and scanned every vantage point in tall buildings. I started to think through the mind-set of a sniper and realized just how easy it could be to terrorize us. I started doing what I'd never intended to do to myself, I was literally scaring myself to death, but if I got into the mind-set that I was already dead, there was little to fear.

While I was parked outside of an Iraqi Police headquarters parking lot, dismounted elements from my platoon freely walked the parking lot calmly. I tried to think that they were trying to prove that snipers would not scare us, but then I realized that they had the option of continuous movement. I was stuck in the exposed turret of a parked Humvee and could not move as I pleased.

Staff Sergeant Poston quickly realized by looking at my eyes how scared I was. I also wasn't talking normally. I wasn't throwing rocks at stray dogs like usual. I was paranoid, which was good, but out of character for me. Poston climbed up on top of my Humvee and decided to have a heart-to-heart conversation with me.

"Hey, you doing OK?" he asked to break the silence.

"I'm all right," I said nonchalantly.

"You're scared, aren't you?" he asked.

I quickly dropped my scanning eyes from the city and looked right into his eyes and said, "Fuck yeah!"

"Me, too, man. Me, too," Poston said in a calming voice. "We can't not do our job though. You're the eyes of this vehicle. You need to be up scanning constantly. I know it sucks, but we trust you in this role." He continued to talk to me.

I interrupted him with a trembling voice, trying not to break out in tears. "It's easy for you to say, when you're never in the turret. Feeling this exposed, with nowhere to go," I said while pointing at my turret.

"I'm scared too," he said.

"I would kill to do any other job than gun every day. But I'm here, and if I am here, why can't we use preventive measures like glass on the sides of our turrets. That would have saved Kemple." I stopped myself before I began to cry. My eyes became glossy as I fought back tears. Out on patrol was the last place anyone wanted to be seen as weak.

"No one else is complaining," Poston said, but I fired back with something quick.

"No one else is complaining because they don't want to waste their breath. Complaining does nothing around here except make the person feel better. Then they get in trouble for bitching. So the next time someone dies, I'm gonna be in the background and say, 'At least I tried to help.'" I ceased talking and took my eyes off him.

"Look, I know it sucks. If you can come up with a system that works, then do it, but don't drop security. Do you understand?" Poston questioned me, but I blatantly ignored him. Being undisciplined was not my nature and very out of character, but I was fed up and I realized that if I did not attempt to make a stand now, nothing would ever get solved and I could eventually die.

"Look at me. Do you understand what I said?" Poston sternly asked again.

I immediately retorted with "I can't look now, I'm watching my sector." A sarcastic phrase I said to him without dropping my concentrated eyes on the city.

"Excuse me? Specialist, you better lock that shit up." Poston's mood quickly changed, but I continued to ignore him. "You're being a real smart-ass right now."

I was still trying to hold my emotions in because now I felt that nothing could ever be done. I bit my lip and struggled to say, "I can't be a smart-ass right now, because I'm busy being a target, and I can only be one thing at a time." I stopped talking right there. Anything else from then on and I feared I would be in tears. I could tell that Poston was angry. Given the situation that Kemple had just been killed and we were all dealing with it our own way, tensions were high. He did not punish me like I should have been for being so insubordinate. The rest of the day's mission was spent in silence. Everyone was still angry and confused at how we were operating patrols.

On the 15th of February, our entire FOB paused operations for a short while to reflect on the life of Corporal Andrew J. Kemple.[15] We all knew it would be a somber day, but strength in others made it easy. Around eight-thirty in the morning, Angel Company was formed outside of our CHU area. My patrol was a little late because we were on duty for QRF and were just returning from our morning route clearance as the company was being formed.

We parked next to our CHUs and quickly downloaded all of our gear. Shouts from our sergeants were pleading with everyone to get slings on our weapons and grab our soft caps. We all dropped off and procured what was needed for the ceremony and ran over to join the company already formed on the helicopter runway.

Our stoic first sergeant stood in front of us in his usual wall of silence. First Sergeant Holland rarely intermingled with the company. I was convinced that without our name tapes on our uniforms, he would never even know anyone's name. He was a stereotypical first sergeant who only harped about proper haircuts, pressed uniforms, and standing at parade rest.

We noticed that the entire 3/320th Field Artillery congregated in formation on the other end of the tarmac. Before we headed over to join the rest of the battalion, First Sergeant Holland decided to open the floor up to anyone who would like to say some kind words about Kemple in front of our company. At a time like this, many found it disrespectful that the first sergeant himself did not say anything. I figured he didn't because he couldn't. When did he ever give time to learn anything about anyone?

Private Zuercher from Headquarters Platoon decided to say a few words about Kemple. Zuercher was the inner-city type Caucasian thug who never really seemed to care too much about anything. He was the only one that actually got in front of the company and said some really positive and kind things about Kemple. We all loved Kemple. We all wanted to share things that could have lasted all day, but no one else stood in front

---

[15] Kemple was a specialist but was laterally promoted to the rank of corporal after his death.

of the company to speak. It was a hard time, and we wanted to get the ceremony started, and completed, and get focused again on continuing the missions. It was our job. It was what Kemple would have done.

When we marched over as a company, we were placed in the front of the entire battalion of field artillerists on the airfield tarmac. In front of us stood the over six-foot-tall black memorial shadow box with the lonely pair of desert boots and an upturned M4, topped with dog tags and an ACU camouflage-covered helmet. At the top was a framed eight-by-ten picture of Kemple. The whole memorial was sandwiched between an American flag on the left and the regimental flag of the 320th Field Artillery on the right. I still believe it should have been the 187th Infantry regimental flag, because that was who Kemple belonged to and died with.

Standing in front of the memorial before the ceremony began provoked everyone in our company to begin his own silent reflection. I was at the front left of the formation, a couple rows from the front row itself, so I was able to get a good look at the memorial and see Kemple's picture. The weather was standard warm, but not hot. The clouds were gloomy and it looked like a storm was amid them, but rain never came.

We stood in formation for a few minutes, waiting for some key personnel from FOB Speicher to fly over to our FOB. They did so in the form of two Black Hawk helicopters which landed near our formation. Out stepped our hero for a brigade commander, Colonel Michael Steele, and our brigade sergeant major, Command Sergeant Major Vincent Camacho.

They wasted no time and gathered to the left of our formation. With myself near the front left of the formation, I surveyed the crowd of onlookers and saw some familiar faces. There was a hodgepodge of civilians that worked on the FOB in the dining facility and phone center. None of them knew Kemple, but we knew they were present out of respect.

With everyone in place and the mood set, the ceremony began like clockwork. It started with many words of prayer from the battalion's chaplain. He was subsequently followed by Captain Lesperance. He read of Kemple's military experience, past to present, and enlightened us on how passionate he was about being in the infantry, his loyalty to the Rakkasans, and his love of the M240B machine gun.

The last speaker was Kemple's closest friend. I thought Sergeant Woods would have been the one to give the eulogy, but the task was taken on by his other closest friend, Private First Class Darren "Sub" Subarton. He gave the following moving, inspiring, and happy reflection on Kemple:

Corporal Drew Kemple, DK, the "red-headed fury," ham slice, or just plain Kemple. He was many things to many people, and I can't stress how much of an honor it is to be able to speak about him right now. He glorified what an Iron Rakkasan is, and what Third Platoon is all about. It's kind of ironic that I'm not sure what to say about Kemple since there was always so much to say about him. He was always surrounded by a barrage of ball-busting; both incoming and outgoing. I do know that he lived for Weapons Squad, he lived for Third Platoon, Angel Company, and that he was all about being the best at his job in the most prestigious division in the Army, the most distinguished brigade, the most "in-your-face" company, and the heaviest squad of the best platoon. He loved drinking beer with all of us. The only things he liked more than drinking beer was kicking in doors, shooting stuff up, and being an Iron Rakkasan. That was Kemple's Army and that's what I'll tell my kids someday about this man, and this stand-up soldier that left us too early. He always had some smart-assed comment to make us laugh and he always had our back. He was dependable and reliable. You knew that if Kemple was gunning for you he was giving it his 187 percent. Kemple left us the way he lived: fighting for what he believed in. He was all blood, guts, and busted knuckles. He believed in dying on his feet rather than living on his knees. So this is where I find some comfort in his passing, that he died on his terms. He left this world in the company of his brothers, doing what he lived for, what he loved, what he excelled at, and in him we were in the company of greatness. The Irish say "it's better to say so long than to say good-bye" because good-byes are forever. Well, Corporal Drew Kemple, when I leave this madhouse and make it back across the pond to America . . . I'll raise a big glass of whiskey to you. We all will. You've made an impact on all of our lives and will live forever in our hearts. So, so long, my good friend. One day again we'll cross paths and tip a glass, share some laughs, and talk of the days we gave it our all for the men who served before us and the Iron Rakkasans to come. *Sláinte*. . . . We salute you.

After Sub's speech, the sound of the twenty-one-gun salute startled all of us. We all knew it was coming, but using my peripherals I saw everyone in formation around me jolt a tidbit. As soon as the honor guard ceased the three bursts of fire, our company was ordered to present arms to salute Kemple's memorial.

While we held our salute, the playing of Taps began and reverberated from a distance. I had heard Taps played a million times at funerals, ceremonies, and I had even played it for such occasions, but this time was different. It felt like I had never heard the call before. It was being played for someone I knew closely and whose passing I felt should have been avoided. A few tears streamed down my face as I tried to hold my salute. I could see others to the left and right of me going through the same tribulations. The whole ceremony was surreal for me. It was like I was watching a movie, but it was all personal to me. It was just a sad affair.

Following Taps, Colonel Steele and Command Sergeant Major Camacho proceeded in front of Kemple's memorial and each placed a regimental coin there in his honor. Each paused a bit, rendered a slow salute, left faced, and marched away from the formation area.

The last leg of the ceremony consisted of our company filing out from front to back in a single-file line to pay our last respects to Kemple. We played follow the leader, and each man took his turn standing before the memorial alone, rendering a prayer, a salute, and performing a left face and proceeding out of the ceremony. It took a long time for each man to get his chance at saying good-bye, but it was worth it.

As I stood by myself during my turn, I rendered a slow salute, bit my bottom lip, and whispered, "Good-bye." I performed a left face and continued to bite my bottom lip as a last-ditch effort to prevent myself from shedding more tears. As I walked toward the scramble of onlookers, I passed Colonel Steele and Command Sergeant Major Camacho, and they each saluted and patted me on the shoulder.

Once the whole ceremony was completed, we were once again formed near our CHUs, in company formation, and waited for the next guided word. It came when Colonel Steele approached our now demoralized-looking company.

"Gather round me, men. Everyone take a knee. That includes the captain on down," Colonel Steele commanded us. Everyone quickly slumped down on one knee and left Steele the only man standing, surrounded by Angel Company.

Steele began to speak in his own signature way, hard punching and with a stern look on his face. He had about as much charisma as a modern-day Patton.

"Look, today is the start of a new day. I hear great things coming from you guys every day. You all are doing a hell of a job." Steele spoke as he looked into the eyes of every man kneeling in front of him.

"There's one thing I want you men to do. There is one way you can still honor Corporal Kemple." He paused as he continued to look sternly into every man's eyes. "I want you to go out and kill the son of a bitch who did this."

"Hooah!" yelled some men from my company.

"We got a long way to go, men, and you're doing a hell of a job. These people know exactly who runs this show, and it's you Rakkasans."

"Sheepdogs!" yelled someone in the crowd, which was a nod to an analogy from a Steele speech back in February of 2005 during our JRTC rotation in Louisiana.

With his fists clenched and the tough, determined underbite to his jaw, Steele gave the order to fall back in. His words were always inspiring. In those short few moments it was as if everyone had gained a second wind. We were ready to go put some boot to ass right then and there, until the cold, hard return to reality, in the form of our lackluster First Sergeant Holland, took over.

As soon as we were out of earshot from Colonel Steele, our first sergeant began to lambaste us. He was addressing the fact that our uniforms were too dirty, that some people did not shave that morning, and the length of our hair was way too out of standard. We quietly began to look around with confused looks on our faces. Was he being serious? The sad thing was that he *was* being serious. He screamed and ordered that we all must have clean uniforms, hats, and haircuts by the time for dinner chow or we would be refused to eat in the chow hall.

I could not believe what I was hearing. Our uniforms were a dusty brown because we had just come off a morning mission and it never took long to collect dirt on them. I was livid. I found comfort in the fact that I was not the only soldier pissed off at our first sergeant. Minutes ago, we had just gone through one of the hardest events some of us would ever have to go through, and now we were being harped on for not being pristine. It took a lot of intestinal fortitude not to shout out, *Aren't we trying to fight a war, dumbass?* This was just one of many times that First Sergeant Holland stirred a pot that shouldn't have been stirred. That same night, there were soldiers from our company who were forced to stand near the front entrance of the chow hall to physically inspect everyone in our company that came in, to ensure that each of us was properly shaved and clean. War is hell.

ALL DAY LONG

"I fucking hate this shit!"

Two days after Kemple's ceremony, with our half-cleaned uniforms and horribly self-attempted haircuts, we were about to embark on another day of patrols in Tikrit. We were all hoping for a standard day of inactivity, and tempers among us were at an all-time high. It was my platoon's rotation on QRF duty, so we were hoping only to drive around for a couple hours for our route clearances and nothing more.

I was scheduled as the driver for that morning, so I went through the routine pains of checking the fluid levels, cleaning the windows, and making sure all was in place in the truck before we left the wire. After the repetitive safety brief, we headed out toward the staging area before we left the FOB. At the last possible second before we rolled out, Poston decided he wanted a change of scenery and that he would drive. This made Armstrong sit in the front and I behind him as a dismount. We were the second truck in line of the convoy. Specialist Ben "Doc" Gallegos sat in the back passenger seat opposite me. Sunny covered down as the gunner.

It was a typical route clearance, full of the boring passing scenery that we saw every single day. All the way up MSR Tampa to FOB Speicher and back again. Then we dreadfully had to drive through the main city of Tikrit. This was always our least favorite part. I was at least glad I had nothing to do in the truck but be a passenger.

As we prepared to drive through IED Alley, I assumed my standard seated position where I held my groin and tensed up and waited for the inevitable IED. There had been construction going on near a light pole on the median of the roadway, and there was quite a lot of built-up dirt in mounds along the road. It would have been a prime place for an IED. Then again, everything looked like a possible place for an IED. The terrain was one big mind game.

When we passed the first dirt mound, all was well. Our convoy had continued to travel down the road when all of a sudden I heard what sounded like a shotgun blast, followed by dirt that splashed all over the left-side hood of our Humvee.

"Any damage, Sunny?" Armstrong yelled calmly back at Sunny, thinking he'd just taken a warning shot with his shotgun.

"Me? No, I didn't do anything," he called back.

"I think we just got hit by an IED," I said.

"Holy shit," muttered Poston. He quickly realized the situation and that we'd cheated death, which made him chuckle. He slowed the vehicle to a halt.

"One-six, this is one-one Bravo, stop the convoy. I think we just got hit by an IED, over." Armstrong passed over the radio.

"What do you mean you think?" questioned the overeager lieutenant.

"It didn't go off completely. Something must have short-circuited or something, over," Armstrong retorted.

"Holy shit, Doc, you know if that would have gone off, it would have been in your and Sergeant Poston's laps. Then what would I have done if the medic went down?" I said with a laugh.

"Fuck it," the sarcastic but untalkative Doc replied.

"I fucking hate this shit!" I said, adding my two cents.

Our convoy stopped almost in place, but our vehicle pulled away from the dirt mounds. We called up EOD to come and better investigate the area with proper equipment. We locked down the roads with our "mighty" orange cones and pulled into the Kadasiyah neighborhood that lined IED Alley. Sometimes it took EOD a long time to make it to a location, so we prepared for the long haul. We knew breakfast was out of the question, so we all settled for the dreaded MRE.

Our waiting for the EOD element to meet us at our location gave ample amount of time to replay the scene over and over again. I started to realize how lucky I kept getting. Whatever was happening, I just wanted my luck to continue. Luck. It didn't matter how many schools you attended in the Army or how many push-ups you could crank out in two minutes, because IEDs had no preference. That was all that the Iraq War came down to. Luck.

EOD arrived after about twenty minutes. They came with their high-tech frequency jammers known as Warlocks. We had them too, but ours served no purpose other than to gargle radio transmissions. EOD pulled their truck next to ours and we told them what had happened. They pulled out Johnny 5 and drove him up to the dirt pile.

It was hard to view what Johnny 5 was doing in the dirt from the distance we were at, but there were no more questions regarding what was hidden when Johnny 5 pulled out a 155mm artillery round. Everyone in my vehicle, with a wide-eyed expression, all uttered under his breath, "Shit." Luck was on our side that morning.

Once EOD gave the all clear sign, Poston, Armstrong, and I went up to the dirt pile and inspected what hadn't killed us. We were told the IED did not explode because of two reasons: It was in poor condition, and it was rigged improperly. I was for the first time glad that these terrorists were dumb. Poston picked up the round, and for some curious reason he found some Iraqi money taped to it. No one had ever heard of such a thing. Poston took the money and deemed it lucky. Once back into the vehicle, he wedged the bill to the ceiling of our Humvee. Our lucky breaks soon turned a lot of people into superstitious believers.

As much as we would have liked to call it a mission complete and head back to base, we still had to drive up to the Twin Tits and turn around on the MSR and then drive all the way back to FOB Remagen. As long as it may have sounded, the day was just about to get longer.

As we pulled out of our halt next to Kadasiyah, we passed Second Platoon, who were rolling into Kadasiyah for a mounted and dismounted patrol. We passed them with the standard gunner's salute to each other, which consisted of a "rock-and-roll" gesture with the hands. Most times it was the typical middle finger gesture with a smile passed between gunners. It was our unique way of showing our bond with each other.

By the time we reached the Twin Tits, Second Platoon had suddenly come yelling over the radio back to the Company CP.

"Angel CP, this is two-seven, we're taking small-arms fire, over!"

That's all we needed to hear before Lieutenant Scher ordered us to whip around and head right back to where we were. We drove like Hollywood stuntmen and threw caution to the wind. Driving so fast through traffic usually meant gunners shot more "warning shots" than normal.

While we drove back to Kadasiyah, we started to form an idea of what was happening based on the radio transmissions. While Second Platoon was conducting their dismounted patrol in Kadasiyah, a maroon car pulled up on their street and shot off at them multiple rounds from two AK47s. The platoon was strategically scattered throughout the street in the busy market area at the time of the shooting.

An enemy bullet pierced Second Platoon's platoon sergeant through his smoke grenade, and shattered his radio to pieces, both of which were attached to his vest. Second Platoon's mounted element began opening fire on the car and nearby buildings as it sped away. The stunned platoon sergeant tried to separate himself from his shattered smoke grenade, which billowed green smoke. Second Platoon's 50-caliber machine gun, which did more destruction to nearby buildings than it did to the fleeing car with the gunmen inside.

About five minutes after the initial drive-by firefight had ensued, our Humvee convoy linked up with Second Platoon. Staff Sergeant Poston immediately slammed on the brakes and jumped out of the driver's seat.

"Switch with me, Conklin. Sunny, watch your sector. Armstrong and Doc, come with me and we'll link up with the other dismounted element," Poston hastily barked before he sped off.

I was quite perplexed. I was supposed to be a part of the dismounted element. Poston was driving. I had all my equipment ready to rock and roll, and here I was being traded when something went bad because Poston wanted to be where the action was. I took it as a slap in the face. What was the point in switching jobs if we were not going to perform them? I started to realize that I seemed useless in the eyes of Poston. He only saw me as a driver or gunner. I wanted to do what I had been trained my whole Army career to do, and that was dismounted patrols. This was the ignition of the powder keg between Poston and me.

All I could do was watch things unfold while I sat helpless in the driver's seat in the vehicle with Sunny. I was like an athlete on the bench during a big game. First Platoon's dismounted element went running through one alley, while Second Platoon's dismounted element went through between other buildings. Lieutenant Scher took the reins of the show after he placed the bewildered platoon sergeant from Second inside one of his vehicles in order to command transmissions back to CP. It also gave him a breather from his near-death experience.

After I moved my Humvee to be a part of the now eight-vehicle cordon, our "angels on our shoulders" arrived in the form of two Apache attack helicopters. They arrived on scene and tore through the air, which provided security and confidence for everyone on the ground. They were all over the skies looking for the maroon car in question. Since Kadasiyah was right next to MSR Tampa, a busy highway, we all knew those masked gunmen were long gone.

After about an hour of patrolling the immediate area without any threat from terrorists, the dismounted element came reluctantly back to our Humvees. Everyone was pretty pissed off knowing that these men had gotten away to fight another day. The Apache pilots were ever so persistent to keep looking, but we had to tell them that the threat was gone.

While Poston and the others returned to the vehicle, my temper was apparently written on my face. Though I didn't say a single word, they knew from my demeanor how furious I was. Poston tried to explain his reasoning, but I continued to look straight forward and bite my tongue as I drove.

Before we got into a heated argument, a call from the company came over the radio back at us. They had received a phone call from the Iraqi Police informing them that they had found an IED among garbage on the side of the road at the opposite end of Tikrit. The location was at what we aptly called "Stink Wadi," a swampy piece of land that ran under a bridge and smelled of the worst fecal waste aroma imaginable.

We cleared the scene from Second Platoon, headed across town, and again drove through Tikrit at a speed of utmost haste. I got my little jab at Poston before we drove off by asking him, "You sure you don't want to switch out again before we head to the next event, sarnt?" That was my way of displaying the tension that was in the air.

When we arrived at Stink Wadi, we could see that the Iraqi policemen had haphazardly cordoned off the area and halted traffic. Good thing EOD was still attached to us because not having to call them cut time right off. Our platoon of four trucks just secured the outer avenues of approach on the roads and encircled the possible IED.

My own theory of IEDs found by Iraqi Police did not instill any confidence in me. The police always proved to be useless as help in these matters. I was convinced that they themselves set out IEDs and then called us up to make it look like they were allies and cracking down on the devices. We were even notified that there could be many inside jobs done by the IP, so trust was never formed between us and them. Nevertheless, we did in fact have an IED on the bridge over Stink Wadi that afternoon, and it was now our job to remove it safely.

We did our standard stop and wait while Johnny 5 went to work to disarm the IED. Not only was breakfast and now lunch out of the question, but it was starting to look like dinner was going to be missed as well. It seemed that when time-consuming events happened, they only happened when First Platoon was on QRF duty.

Being stuck in the vehicle with the person I was now fed up with proved to be an uncomfortable situation. For this brief time in my Army career, rank went out the window and we went at a verbal joust with each other for about twenty minutes. I couldn't stop saying how badly I wanted to be placed out of his truck. All our bickering ended when I quit the fruitless argument and played the role of "I'm driving. I can't talk anymore. I need to focus on the road."

Shortly thereafter, Johnny 5 dragged two 155mm artillery rounds out of the side of the bridge and exposed the device. This IED did not seem to have any wires attached to it. EOD tried to explain that the terrorists may have been working in pairs, which let each man deliver one small piece of the device at a time, to limit their exposure on the spot where they emplaced the IED. Either way, EOD dragged the artillery shell out and loaded it into their vehicle.

Literally seconds before we all cleared the scene, Second Platoon came over the radio again and stated that they had just gotten hit by an IED on MSR Tampa. What the hell, Tikrit? What was it with the day turning upside down? Turned out Second Platoon had gotten hit at the same spot where we did a few weeks prior, as they were returning to FOB Remagen, which was on the opposite end of our sector from where we were now.

Since EOD was rigged with numerous Warlocks, we decided to follow their lead through town at their ungodly pace. Never had we driven so fast before. I loved having my foot to the floor racing to yet another action spot. This day had been full of surprises, so I was definitely more alert than normal.

When we arrived at the bridge on MSR Tampa, we could see that Second Platoon was already rigging up one of their vehicles that was disabled after the blast. Almost identical to our IED attack on the same bridge, the blast had ripped through their vehicle's engine. Thankfully no one was hurt. EOD quickly grabbed debris to determine what size of IED it was. By now, with the sun almost down, everyone was in a hurry to get back to the FOB. We did not want to spend all day and night out in the city.

With nothing more to gather or help, Second Platoon, First Platoon, and the EOD element drove back to FOB Remagen in one long convoy. Finally we called it a day, but only in a perfect world. Lieutenant Scher could not say no to patrols, so we ended up going on one more route clearance two hours later, after dinner. At the time, we wanted to beat Scher up badly, but I guess, looking back on it, there had to be some logic in it. Nothing came about during that route clearance other than the bitterness of having such a long, stressful day. This was how a two-hour mission turned into a twelve-hour mission.

THE SUCK

**"It seemed we never had time to take a breath
and relax in between patrols."**

As tensions began to fester between Poston and me, we had a new element added to daily patrols that raised the anxiety level. In mid-February we started incorporating the Iraqi Army into the patrols. The IA (Iraqi Army) had a base in the heart of Tikrit that for some unknown reason, was nicknamed the "Birthday Palace." I assume it got its name from being a gift either from or to Saddam at one point. It was the home of the Iraqi Army's Tikrit-based soldiers. We began to run into everyday problems with them, mostly due to their laziness and lack of motivation.

When we gave them a time frame to be ready by, we would show up at the Birthday Palace at that time to begin the mission at hand. More times than not, we would then spend the first hour physically waking them up. They would drag and crawl like snails to get things ready. After we had waited two hours, they would inform us that they were finally ready. I thought that that would cut into our patrol time, but Lieutenant Scher did not see it that way. So the extra time spent waiting for the IA to get ready just further extended our patrol and complicated relations.

Incorporating the IA into our patrols was something that had to be done during our deployment. It was all part of the greater picture of getting the country stabilized and fitted with trained soldiers of their own. The IA were never motivated. It was hard to inspire them to do anything during a patrol. They did have one soldier, First Sergeant Kobe, who proved to be quite intimidating and inspiring to his men. We came to enjoy seeing him put his boot in his soldiers' asses. He was the backbone of the Tikrit soldiers and he forced them to work. We liked Kobe.

The objective of patrols still remained the same, only we would incorporate two to three IA trucks among the convoy. Their trucks consisted of nothing more than a standard white pickup truck with troops loaded in the back bed. I was unsure whether they were stupid or brave to drive around in the open with the threat of IEDs so prevalent. I never felt comfortable even in our metal-strapped box on wheels that had been redesigned to take blasts, and here they were driving around in pickup trucks.

Now that patrols had gotten longer, time ticked slower and animosity between fellow soldiers in our company was beginning to brew to new levels. Our chain of command decided to spice things up with a new flavor. That secret ingredient would be to now conduct one hour of physical training (PT) every day. If doing endless patrols, lack of sleep from guarding empty trucks throughout the night, and going to the brink of fights among us daily were not enough, we were now being forced by people who rarely left the wire to sacrifice our precious time to do tedious PT that few of us wanted to do.

With Fooks still my team leader and unwilling to skirt around the PT issue, he made sure Chief and I did our daily regimens. We had to work around Chief's guard rotation because he was still guarding a tower with Private Rojo, but Fooks still found time to make us exercise. Whether it was running on the tarmac in the desert heat or going to the gym and lifting, he made sure we did it. I hated every second. It seemed we never had time to take a breath and relax in between patrols. Any free time we had was spent walking down to the computer room and waiting in line in a shack with no air-conditioning. That should have been enough PT, because I always broke a sweat. We would usually be granted, if we were lucky, what seemed like ten minutes to shoot off an e-mail using the slowest dial-up Internet ever. I could have complained forever if I'd had the time.

OPERATION BRICK HOUSE

"Shut up and smile!"

Aside from running daily joint patrols with the Iraqi Army platoons, we also decided to bring them up to speed on what an air assault operation was like. This would take my platoon cooperating to put together an air assault mission for our IA counterparts.

We called it "Operation Brick House" and we pulled it straight out of our asses. It was going to be a cakewalk for us, but we built it up to sound high-speed for the IA. Our mission would be to land at a brick-making factory on the corner of Z Road and MSR Tampa. It was a small factory that intelligence told us housed two families. No problems had been present in the past from this area and we expected nothing from the target area now.

The task of teaching the IA the procedures of getting in and out of a Black Hawk was the responsibility of the sergeants in our platoon. First Platoon was to incorporate two sergeants in each helicopter, and the rest would be filled with IA. Naturally, we were one sergeant short, so the shortest straw came to me. Now I was going to be a part of the assault element.

On the day of the raid, we got divided into our chalks.[16] Mine consisted of our interim platoon sergeant, Staff Sergeant Ledbetter, Sergeant McCaskill, and myself. The rest of the open seats were filled by seven IA soldiers. With the help of a translator, numerous hand gestures, and drawing in the sand, we were able to explain to the Iraqi soldiers how to conduct air assault operations. It was going to be a crash course test for the IA, but at least they were getting their feet wet during a cakewalk mission.

The birds landed at FOB Remagen in the morning and gave us time to give a close inspection of the helicopters to the IA soldiers. Many of them had their cameras out, and at times I felt like I was at a museum giving a lecture to uninterested children. Either way, I was just glad to be doing something different for a change during a patrol, instead of sitting in that Humvee with people I was seconds away from snapping on.

Before we kicked off the initial mission around eleven in the morning, we made sure all of the other follow-on forces were ready. The plan was to have our four Black Hawk helicopters touch down at the objective and allow us (the assaulting element) to run into the compound and search the area. Simultaneous to our landing, four Humvees would arrive on scene and secure the outer perimeter, shut down Z Road, and make a bypass for traffic on MSR Tampa.

The planning was quick and uncomplicated. I was just praying that I didn't get shot by some overexcited IA soldier. When the pilots cued up their rotary blades and we now had the green light to load up on the choppers, it was go-time for the IA's big show.

I was the last to board my Black Hawk, which made me the first one out the door in order to orchestrate the IA's dismounting procedure. As I took my seat in the chopper and affixed my seat belt, I tried to yell over the deafening blades and engine, which churned at top speed.

"Is everyone strapped in?" I yelled. Immediately I was greeted by the most confused looks on the IA men's faces. For that moment in time I had forgotten that they had no idea what I was saying. I paused, smiled at my stupidity, and gave the universal thumbs-up. The gesture was then

---

[16] The term *chalk* refers to all the soldiers that fit in one helicopter at a time. Chalks for Black Hawks have about nine soldiers.

returned to me, signaling that we were all set. As I was preparing to put my magazine into my M4, the IA soldier sitting next to me was nudging me on my arm to take his picture.

"Are you fucking serious?" I yelled in full knowledge that he didn't know what I was saying. "I'm going to war with a bunch of tourists!" I said out loud to myself.

"Mista, huh?" the soldier yelled right back at me. He was obviously confused with the language barrier between us. I grabbed his camera and yelled, "Shut up and smile!"

After the quirky photo opportunity, I finished loading my magazine into my weapon and displayed my actions so the IA would follow my example. As our helicopter began to lift off the ground, they all in unison loaded their AKs. My nerves began to heighten at this time because I never trusted Iraqis with loaded guns.

Once we were airborne, I got to view Tikrit from the best vantage point. I was sitting in the outside seat with the doors wide open. I felt like I was in a Vietnam War movie. Before I had much time to enjoy the flyover, however, we were descending upon the objective. I could see the mounted element already in place on the ground, so all was going as planned.

Touching down was our signal to bust out of the seat harnesses and move out. I immediately jumped out and turned around to ensure all got off safely. When the last man came running out, I ran after the group and signaled them to follow me. Ledbetter pointed at the front gate, so that was what we oriented to. When we arrived at the gate, I was pleased to see the IA quickly form into a stack and prepare to enter.

We entered the compound and immediately began searching the nearby house. Ledbetter, McCaskill, and I were now acting as nothing more than observers. We were free-floating and keeping an eye on how the IA conducted everything. I knew I was in Iraq doing a mission, but it honestly felt like I was in the U.S. doing a training exercise. There was no threat whatsoever, so everyone's guard was down. There were many children in the households who were actually quite playful. Our whole operation was also surrounded by the compound's twelve-foot cement wall, and behind that stood our parked Humvees. It was a walk in the park for me, except the walk was endless.

After we searched the inside compound and found nothing, we proceeded to the exterior of the wall and began combing the outside fields for some reason. There was junk everywhere, so it made metal detecting redundant. No surprise, we did it anyway. I plopped down next to a giant dirt mound and just watched these Iraqi Army soldiers wander around and kick the dirt for hours. I entertained myself by throwing rocks at wild dogs until they ceased approaching me.

After a while, one of the IA soldiers came over and sat next to me. He happened to speak a little English, so he broke the silence and began to talk about what soldiers talk best about.

"You got wife in America?" he questioned me.

"No, but I got fourteen girlfriends," I sarcastically replied.

"Girlfriends?" he asked, obviously puzzled by the introduction of a word unfamiliar to him.

"Yeah. Fourteen girlfriends. It's like having fourteen wives, only I don't have to do any dishes, argue, be yelled at for having dirty shoes, and I don't have to cuddle," I said before I began to laugh. He didn't respond for a while after that. I think I put him into shock with so many unfamiliar words.

"You live in New York or Los Angeles?" the soldier asked. I definitely wasn't going to tell him where I actually lived.

"New York. I'd invite you to come visit my house, but your cousin parked a plane in the building and now there's no room." My attitude definitely made it obvious that I didn't want to talk to him, but he responded differently than I'd expected.

"Oh no, no, no." He paused and attempted to read my name tape on my vest. "Conklin? Is that how you say it?" He went on to talk more. Out of sheer boredom I continued to talk to this soldier about random things as best as we could converse. His English proved to be better than I'd anticipated. He also indulged me with some packaged chocolate from Iraq which was very good. I grew up not far from Hershey, Pennsylvania, and I thought I knew chocolate, but whatever he gave me was tasty. I spent a good three hours talking to him while the other IA soldiers occupied their time "looking" like soldiers.

The mission ended just like it started, although a few hours overdue for reasons unknown. We only found two AKs, which were permitted since there were two households and each household was allowed one AK. We loaded back up in the helicopters and returned to FOB Remagen, where I felt satisfied that I'd conducted a "training mission" with the Keystone Cops without getting myself killed.

THE FINANCIER

"They all stormed into the house screaming and yelling like furies."

While my platoon conducted our Operation Brick House mission, Angel Company was busy putting together a real raid in Kadasiyah based on newly updated intelligence. They had received word through some investigation into the sniper that killed Kemple. I had no clue how they came across the information, but they knew his name and his whereabouts. He lived up in Bayji, a city to the north of us thirty-some miles away, where 1st Battalion of the 187th was stationed.

Apparently the sniper was a hired mercenary and was being paid by a man who lived in Kadasiyah. I did not care how they got this information or even how accurate it could have been. No one did. Enough was said about a connection to Kemple's death and that's all we needed. There was going to be vengeance.

Angel Company officers formulated the plan quickly because it was a time-sensitive target. We knew when the financier was going to be at a certain house and we hoped the sniper would be there as well. The mission was going to consist of the entire company working together. Headquarters, First, and Second Platoon would constitute the large mounted element that would engulf the surrounding perimeter of the house and street, while Third Platoon, followed closely behind by the IA, would be the assault element into the house.

Our company began rehearsals on the afternoon of the 23rd of February. Each platoon was rehearsing over and over their roles for the early morning raid. Being part of the mounted element, there wasn't much planning for my platoon. Poston instructed me of our route and it was pretty self-explanatory.

Poston also took the time to mention that he was going to initiate a rotation schedule with our truck in a way where I would be out on patrols with Sergeant Armstrong more than I would be out with him. I still reiterated my interest in being transferred to another truck. Taylor had just recently been taken out of my Humvee and sent to Lieutenant Scher's vehicle, so I was kind of alone during patrols. I assumed that Taylor and I were forming such an bond against Poston that he'd had to split us up. This was the last straw. I wanted out of Poston's truck desperately.

We awoke around midnight and loaded up our Humvees. Everyone drank an energy drink and those who smoked did so. We moved out around 2 A.M. and drove in the darkness toward the Birthday Palace, where we linked up with the Iraqi Army contingents. Surprisingly, they were ready, thanks to Iraqi Army First Sergeant Kobe, who'd made sure his men were prepared.

We were about to conduct our first nighttime raid under complete darkness. We were all rigged up with NODs attached to our helmets. The IA did not have this capability, so we had to revise our plan and keep them as outer security of the assaulting element, but still within the perimeter of our vehicles. Pretty much, they were useless standbys.

I was stuck being the driver for Poston's truck. We were just one Humvee in a mass convoy of Humvees. I had never driven at night with NODs on before. It was a skill to learn. I was a little apprehensive at first, but I've found that the best way to learn new things in life is by doing.

We turned off all of our headlights and went blackout. Only the sound of beefed-up mufflers indicated the impending power creeping through the tight alleyways of the pitch-black Iraqi night. As we got closer to the target house, roads were now nonexistent. We were driving through old crumbled homes, piles of garbage, and big ditches. We were going for total surprise on the house.

"Try to stay out of the holes!" Poston yelled at me.

"Kinda hard to see them without lights," I sarcastically yelled back. I tried desperately to look through my NODs to see what infrared light there was coming out of my Humvee. It was not amplified as well as it should have been. It didn't help either that I was the lead Humvee for our platoon, so I couldn't just follow someone. I just kept rolling forward into the now green and black world I saw through my eyepiece.

"Go left. Go left some more!" Poston tried to direct me. I felt completely blind. I frantically tried to adjust my right eye to the atmosphere since my left was under the NOD lens. I kept switching back and forth, but neither gave me the proper vision. I became frantic, especially when I kept running over large objects that I had no idea what they were.

"I hope they get what we're looking for, 'cause this blackout shit ain't working. I'm blind as a bat." I tried to explain my poor driving under the given circumstances.

"Take a right right here and go over this curb," Poston directed me. I had just pulled in the direction he'd given when all of a sudden he yelled, "STOP!" I slammed my foot on the brakes immediately, and the sound of the squeaky jam of the tires broke the silent night. Lucky I did, because it turned out Poston could not see very well through his limited visibility either, and none of us had seen that the hood of our Humvee was hanging off a sheer cliff.

"Holy shit!" I yelled as everyone in the truck began to laugh.

"Back out slowly and we'll stop right here," Poston said, coaxing me. We were in the vicinity of where we were supposed to be, but we'd never comprehended just how steep the slope was until we almost plummeted to certain death. We hadn't even seen it on the map.

Once we had parked, that was pretty much all that we needed to do for the mission. With the area now surrounded, Third Platoon dismounted and raided the house in question like a ferocious storm. *Wham* went the front gate as they kicked it in. They all stormed into the house screaming and yelling like furies. From my vantage point, all I could see was an occasional flashlight dance across a window, and all I could hear was the sound of several parked Humvee engines, which alone was pretty intimidating. Crashing glass, men screaming, women crying—it all resonated through the dead air of the once peaceful neighborhood. I could only imagine what was transpiring within. Third Platoon had been chosen as the raiding party because they were still working on a different kind of adrenaline after losing one of their own. Since this financier had had a hand in Kemple's death, I was wondering if they would take him alive.

We were still parked in the vehicle when the sun began to rise. We had been on the objective for almost two hours. I monitored Third Platoon's transmissions on the radio and knew they had no casualties and were busy processing five men that they had detained. Sadly, the sniper who killed Kemple was not among the men detained, so that put a damper on things. It continued my fear that this man was still on the loose and probably preparing to kill again another day. Shortly after sunrise they decided to pack things up, and everyone broke down the cordon and returned to FOB Remagen. At least I could see where I was going now with the sun up. When I passed the ravine that I'd almost plummeted down, the severity of its depth was shocking. Everyone in our truck took a good long look at it and thanked his lucky stars we didn't end up killed due to a mistake in terrain.

The five men were housed at the detainee shack on a remote section of FOB Remagen. For the next twenty-four hours our platoon would conduct armed guard on them. The shack was no more than the size of a railcar and got very hot inside. There were five stalls in there, each built out of plywood, with a door and a window so we could visually monitor each detainee.

Private First Class MacMillan and I had to guard these men in their eighteenth hour of captivity. Our job was briefly explained—they were not allowed to sleep, sit, or talk. If they needed to use the port-a-potty, then they would be escorted outside by one of us to use one. MacMillan and I were not excited about this babysitting detail, but we certainly were not going to slack off.

By the time I arrived at the shack, the detainees were extremely exhausted. They had been awake for a long time, but I didn't feel any sense of compassion. We stuck to the rules. With every passing minute, one of the detainees attempted to sit on the ground but was quickly greeted by either MacMillan or myself screaming at him to stand up, which he did. The financier stood in the center stall. Seeing him, knowing what he had done to help kill Kemple, brewed a different emotion than I had ever felt. I put my gun in the corner of the shack in fear that I would actually kill him. For about fifteen minutes, I stood in front of his door making eye-to-eye contact and ranting some of the most evil words imaginable while he just stared at me. I cursed him, his family; I trash-talked the Koran; I told him he was days away from death and he would never be a martyr. I vented for a long time before it got so heated that MacMillan told me to take a break. The financier did nothing except stand and stare at me with a blank face. The screaming did nothing to him, but it made me feel better.

In our instructions, we were told that we were to give them one MRE for dinner. Naturally, we chose the worst on the menu. We still wouldn't let them sit, since we were told it was forbidden. I may have gone too far when one of them began to pray and I kept yelling for him to "shut the fuck up" incessantly until he complied. I guess I was using the vague instructions as a safety catch to make sure I didn't commit a crime. I had no compassion for any of these men who harbored terrorists. I didn't care if some of them were victims of circumstance or not. My hatred for them seemed to be brewing to a breaking point, and that point was on the horizon. It was turning me into a monster.

When one of the detainees signaled with hand gestures enough for me to figure out he had to use the bathroom, I pulled him out of his wooden cell and flex-cuffed his hands, blindfolded him, and escorted him outside to the port-a-potty. I understood that it would be hard to piss in a port-a-potty while blindfolded, but he was wearing a man-dress, which would make the task extra hard. I opened the door and guided him in. I was not going to physically watch him piss or shit. After about a minute, I banged on the door and opened it up. I don't know if it's Iraqi custom to do this, but he was not seated on the toilet seat. He had both feet on the toilet and was standing straight up but pissing straight down. So here I was, eye level to an Iraqi penis. I screamed, "Oh fuck, man," as soon as the picture registered in my head, and I slammed the door. Then I tried not to laugh and attempted to regain my intimidation factor. I cleared my throat and put my angry face on like an actor about to step on stage. I gave him a few more seconds to finish up and then tried the door again. He was ready to go this time and I escorted him back into his cell. MacMillan got a kick out of the story as soon as I got back.

When the time came that our shift of guard was done, I was glad to leave. Before I did, there was one incident that will never escape me. One detainee was so exhausted from standing for so long that he went to sleep while standing up and smashed his head into the wall as he fell to the floor. With my emotions off my normal track, I found it perversely funny. MacMillan quickly threw open the man's cell door and yelled for him to stand up. When we turned over our shift to two others in our platoon, we turned the detainees over as zombies. I never had detainee guard again, and I am thankful for that. I don't know what would have happened if I had stayed in there an hour longer.

SUNNIS, SHIAS,
AND A PLATOON SERGEANT

"We immediately thought it was an IED."

At the end of February our platoon was greeted by a much-needed addition. We were given a transfer from 1st Battalion of our regiment up in Bayji. Sergeant First Class Crisostomo was placed in our platoon as our official platoon sergeant. He had been in the Rakkasans for a while and was well acquainted with our reputation and expectations. We welcomed him with open arms and he was a great asset to the platoon. He was a guy who really knew his job and loved doing it. He was very sociable with all the men in the platoon, regardless of rank. He was the polar opposite of Quinn.

Staff Sergeant Ledbetter did not immediately return to Second Platoon after Crisostomo's entrance. Ledbetter stayed with us for a few weeks to work along with him to get adjusted more easily. With a proper platoon sergeant back in First Platoon, I started to feel something I had not felt in months: confidence in our leadership.

Before the onslaught of February drew to a close, the ever-present bearer of bad news visited my platoon. On the 22nd of February, my good friend and the unofficial "mascot" of my platoon and battalion, Specialist Richard "Scud" Scibetta, was seriously wounded by an IED.

His company, Bravo, was operating in Samarra, the larger city to the south of Tikrit.

During a routine patrol, Scud was the gunner for one of their inadequately armored Humvees when an IED exploded on his left which sent a heavy load of shrapnel into his truck. Scud was peppered from his legs to his face. There were moments when medics said he wouldn't make it, but timely medical attention was applied and helped save his life.

By the time the news came to our platoon during our routine nightly meetings, Scud was already through Germany and on his way to the Walter Reed Medical Center in Washington, D.C. Once again the war had become more personal than ever. With Kemple dead and Scud now seriously wounded, our complacency during patrols had been deleted, and we kept asking, who's next?

The same day Scud was wounded, Samarra experienced what was to be a pivotal event in the war with Iraq. One of their holiest shrines, the Golden Dome Mosque in downtown Samarra, was host to sectarian violence, culminating in the mosque's signature golden dome getting blown up by Sunnis. Correspondence through MySpace with my best buddy Specialist Derek Borden in Charlie Company told me he was on guard in Samarra and had viewed the bombing firsthand. He explained that it was the loudest explosion he had ever witnessed.

News of the mosque bombing spread like wildfire through our chain of communication and also through the public back home. We were put on high alert and warned of possible retaliations from rival religious sects. This was exactly the last place I wanted to be—in the middle of a civil war.

On March 2, the Shias decided to retaliate for the mosque bombing in Samarra. I was just "lucky" enough to be on duty when they happened to do it, in Tikrit. We were parked in the compound of the Birthday Palace, and we found ourselves once again waiting on the Iraqi Army contingent, which gave my platoon time to relax, take our helmets off, and wait.

It was about eight in the morning when the calm sound of a new day was alarmingly altered. A large explosion reverberated through the air and seized the attention of everyone in my platoon. Being inside the compound, we could not see immediately what had happened or where it had happened, but we all waited a moment until the smoke plume rose above the buildings of the city.

We immediately thought it was an IED on a possible convoy passing through nearby. After Lieutenant Scher checked the Blue Force Tracker computer screen in his Humvee, he noted that there were no friendly patrols in the area. I then thought it could be a mortar attack from someone with terrible aim. Either way, our daredevilish platoon rolled out to investigate without the IA.

We followed the plume of smoke all the way to the origin, like storm chasers after a twister. The smoke led us straight into the graveyard at the heart of Tikrit. Among hundreds of headstones there stood a dominating dome that looked like a miniature mosque. It turned out it was a Sunni religious site, in which Saddam Hussein's father was buried. As we neared the bombed-out entrance of the dome, we saw debris thrown all around the graveyard. I was the driver for one of our vehicles, so I was not in a position to further investigate up close.

As I parked in front of the building, it was apparent from my vantage point what had happened. The doors were blown clean off and parts of the steps were crumbled from a large bomb. One of the squad leaders took pictures of the inside and showed them to me. It was evident that the bomb had been placed inside the shrine and was big enough to demolish the interior and crumble the grave itself into chunks.

Within minutes of our milling around the debris-scattered graveyard, Iraqi Police and firemen arrived to clean up the area. The expressions on the locals' faces made it abundantly clear that they were pissed. It was more fuel for the fire of the futile civil war. As I sat in the Humvee and watched the klutzy policemen walk around aimlessly, I wondered if Saddam would ever hear about his father's tomb being blown up. I didn't dwell on that thought long. My attention was diverted back to making fun of the Iraqi Police and, especially, firemen.

Two days later we had a case of déjà vu. While we were yet again parked inside the Birthday Palace waiting for the IA, around the same time frame as the explosion of the tomb, the same explosion sound went off somewhere in the city. As soon as we heard it, we all immediately had the same thought: not again!

This time we knew there were friendly patrols in the city. Second Platoon was rolling through Business 1 (IED Alley) and had just gotten hit by an "exploding star" IED. We immediately jumped into our Humvees and rolled the short distance to IED Alley, where Second Platoon was parked in a security halt on the street. When we arrived, two of their Humvees were already driving into Kadasiyah to look for a triggerman. The other two were rigging up the busted Humvee with tow straps. First Sergeant Holland happened to be riding with Second Platoon at the time and was in the very Humvee that got hit. No injuries were reported on the Humvee that was struck, so we immediately heaved the deep sigh of relief.

RED LIGHT AND RUMORS

"It was a dull day of sweat."

With the month of March just getting started, we all wanted something different than February. After such a troubling month, with no real sense of accomplishment, we had grown tired and fearful. I got the one break I was looking for when I was transferred to Lieutenant Scher's Humvee and away from Poston. I was happy about this. It gave me an opportunity to speak my mind to the most important man in the platoon. I complained quickly about how we were not doing anything more than driving around and getting blown up. Scher did mention one thing that I didn't believe at first. He mentioned that something was being planned that would involve the whole battalion. I didn't think anything of it, but he was pretty adamant about it. Naturally, when questioned, he could not say much more.

Around this time, we did experience our first "dry run" at a joint mission between our entire company and the 3/320th Field Artillery. "Operation Red Light" came about because of a tip received from a prostitute before she was murdered by some terrorists. They beheaded her somewhere in the western desert near FOB Remagen.

It was basically an afternoon mission where dozens of Humvees from many different platoons drove out into the desert and secured different roads, trying to consolidate any cars we came across in hopes of seizing caches in transit. There weren't any real roads there, so every platoon was basically spread out, setting up flash checkpoints along the horizon.

It was a dull day of sweat out in the sun except for one incident worth telling. At our position in the scheme of things we were busy searching cars and rounding up all of the occupants in a group area until the operation was called off, when out in the distance, we saw a white pickup truck do a 360-degree turn to avoid running into U.S. forces.

A local Apache helicopter in the sky was alerted and they immediately flew over and pursued the truck. It was almost all out of view, but we could still see what was transpiring. The helicopter opened fire near the fleeing vehicle to get the driver's attention to stop, but instead the truck picked up more speed and continued going. The pilot then sprayed hundreds of bullets into the truck, which halted it in its place forever.

Another platoon closer to the truck was called out to investigate. It came over the radio that the truck was full of weapons, IEDs, grenades, ammunition, and RPGs. The driver was dead on arrival. They took several pictures of the cache, and later that night I got to view them, and the bounty in the truck was amazing. That driver had made the dumbest decision when he decided to run. With this, I guess Operation Red Light was a success. Before the sun went down, we dismissed all the locals that we had been corralling and let them get in their vehicles and on with their lives.

As the days trudged on, so too did the camp rumor mill begin to swell back up involving an even bigger operation than Red Light. Being low on the totem pole of rank, I didn't expect to hear a lot of concrete evidence until closer to whatever was supposed to begin. Every day, the guys in my truck—Hilmo, Reese, Avery, Taylor, and I—would grill Lieutenant Scher for information no matter how large or small it was. We were curious soldiers, and Scher's ambiguous statements were enough to put together piecemeal that something was coming.

On the evening of March 11, our inquiries were answered when we got our first warning order for the upcoming "big" mission. During our evening brief, my team leader and newly promoted Sergeant Fooks gave a lengthy report on our upcoming task. Fooks was in charge of the squad temporarily while Staff Sergeant Poston was in the U.S. on his fifteen days of R&R. This bumped Taylor down as my gunner for the upcoming mission. My squad was all huddled in Fooks's CHU with pens in hand and anxiously awaiting the news of our next task.

Dubbed "Operation Swarmer," named after a large training exercise our regiment performed in the 1960s, it was the big mission we had been hearing rumors about. We were told as much as we needed to know, and that didn't accumulate to much. We were given a brief synopsis of what the entire company's roles and responsibilities were to be and where they were to be performed. We were also told of our specific jobs, and none of it made me excited.

The plan was to conduct a large-scale air-assault raid into an area south of us between Samarra and Tikrit. It was an area that contained scattered households that had never seen American soldiers yet. The mission brief for our platoon stated that we were to "conduct an air-assault raid at the home of a suspected terrorist leader, in order to capture or kill him, gather intelligence on anti-Iraqi operations, investigate suspected caches, and deny sanctuary for the enemy." Yeah, it sounded cool, but we knew what the reality would be. While we were busy with that, other companies in the battalion would be simultaneously landing at other places and doing the same thing. From there on out we were to conduct continuous raids from convoys all across the desert, until every home had been inspected. The brief called for a three-day mission, but I had been in the Army longer than a day and knew we wouldn't reach that goal.

The last part of the brief became the most daunting part of it all: the packing list. Fooks, who acted just like Poston in his place, planned for everything, which made our squad suffer. We were Weapons Squad and we bitched the most out of the platoon, because we carried the heaviest equipment of any squad. Now for this upcoming three-day-plus mission, it only got heavier. I had to carry a poncho, five field-stripped MREs, five liters of water plus one extra bottle of water, five hundred linked 7.62mm rounds in ammo cans. This alone was over twenty-five pounds and didn't include my helmet, vest, seven full M4 magazines, my M4 with M68 optic lens and PAQ-4 night laser, NODs, spare M240B barrel, traverse and elevation apparatus, pintle, tripod for the M240B, knee pads, elbow pads, flashlight, extra batteries, chem lights (glow sticks), snacks, camera, notebook, first aid pouch, sand and wind goggles, sunglasses, clear glasses, two pairs of extra white socks, pens, paper, Gerber, flex-cuffs, weapons cleaning kit, etc. I was carrying almost my entire body weight and was expected to move like a track star. It sucked. It sucked so bad that there is not an accurate word to describe how much it sucked. Oh, did I mention that it would be hotter than a burning sauna outside?

Going back to my CHU, Avery and I complained the entire time. We were both assistant gunners for this mission, so we were the "hump bitches" who carried the most weight in the squad. After packing the initial list in my assault pack, I tried to put it on to see how bad it was going to be. I think I woke up the entire camp when I put it on my back and screamed bloody murder from the excessive weight. I literally was slumped over and felt like I was carrying a professional wrestler on my back. I tried to come to terms with the weight, right before I realized I had yet to attach my AG bag, which contained my outdated Vietnam-era tripod that I had to carry for some reason only known to Fooks.

Within the next few days, after patrols, we spent our time going over countless rehearsals. From unloading from a Black Hawk, to entering and clearing a building, crew drills in the desert, and mounting the gun on the tripod, it took up all our free time. Each day that got closer to "D-Day," more information trickled in. We were told not to leak anything of this back home through e-mails.

STOP, STOP, STOP

"I have a bad feeling about today."

Our daily patrols still continued, with a slight change of pace for me. With our normal RTO, Private First Class Reese, sent home for his fifteen-day R&R, I volunteered to fill the role as platoon RTO since it was in the same Humvee I served in. I had been an RTO for dismounted infantry tactics for a year prior at Fort Campbell, so it was a role I easily picked back up. This was another reason I'd begged Poston to transfer me to the LT's truck earlier, so I could handle the role of a different task and help the overall efficiency of the platoon.

With my unimpressive luck, my first day as an RTO was spent dealing with a shit storm handed to me in Tikrit. On March 13, our platoon was once again on QRF duty. We were preparing to roll out of the gate at 5:30 A.M. for our normal route clearance when something inside of me triggered fear for no reason. I had never felt any type of premonition or bad feelings before any other mission, but for some reason this feeling almost subconsciously came out.

"Hey, LT, I have a bad feeling about today," I muttered from behind his seat.

"You just jinxed us, asshole!" Avery yelled back from behind the wheel.

I was still unsure about my ill feeling as we continued to do our standard route clearance of driving up and down MSR Tampa. After we turned around at the Twin Tits, we proceeded to go into downtown Tikrit. The sun was now up, making visibility for roadside hazards easier.

As we got deeper and deeper into the city of Tikrit, I was occupied on the radio in our Humvee relaying our position to the company. Halfway through my transmission, a large-sized explosion rocked through the air not far from where we were driving. I immediately relayed all of the information the lieutenant was telling me so I could send it back to the company.

Avery picked up the pace for the convoy and drove to the site where the loud explosion had been heard. By the time we arrived where the explosion originated, we had driven past several Iraqi first-responders to get to the site. Once we were on scene, it was a sight I would never forget.

It was a television repair shop that we drove by daily. Now the building had no front facade, as it had been blown out, with debris scattered all the way on the other side of the street. Our platoon immediately set up a perimeter and let the first-responders from Tikrit handle the situation. Lieutenant Scher and a couple others from our platoon walked among the police and firefighters to inquire what had happened.

While I was relaying information back to the company on their frequency, I was also busy on the other radio frequency trying to coordinate with an Apache helicopter pilot in the area to provide aerial security. The lieutenant also kept calling me on the handheld radio to tell me the information he was finding out. I felt like a switchboard operator. At times I had three different conversations going on and it was a bit stressful. Avery helped me out when I was overloaded with curious questions from people that at times I could not answer.

In between radio transmissions, I kept looking out the window at the shop to survey the situation that I was reporting. I could see what remained of numerous human bodies. Thick pools of dark red blood were scattered around the shop like puddles after a large rainstorm. Shoes, pieces of AK47s, hands, legs, torsos, and other chunks of meat were thrown around like some kind of whirlwind of death had struck. Firefighters quickly removed the bodies and hosed down the sidewalk with water. A flattened hand severed from the wrist was spotted on the floor with a set of keys still clutched in its grasp.

Lieutenant Scher came back to my truck to inform me of what information he had been finding out, so I could send it back to the company. Apparently some terrorists had come to this TV repair shop and killed the owner, then rigged his body with explosives and called the Iraqi Police. Once the police arrived and went inside the shop, they moved the body, which triggered the explosion and sent seven policemen into tiny pieces all over the room and outside the shop. Thirteen other policemen were wounded severely by the bomb.

We remained parked outside that hell for a couple of hours. Breakfast came and went, and then lunchtime was nearing. The scene was pretty much cleaned up enough for us by noon, so we didn't need to hang around. We proceeded back to FOB Remagen just in time for lunch to begin. When our platoon came into the chow hall, we sat together. When we sat in the chow hall full of clean fobbits, our dirty faces and sun-faded uniforms made it known who had the real jobs. We went through the line of food and sat down together at the long tables. After the hectic start of the day, several guys jokingly asked me if I was glad to be an RTO again. As busy, wild, and stressful as it was to be an RTO when the shit hit the fan, I was.

Before any one of us could finish what we had on our plate, a call came over our handheld radios from Captain Lesperance. He was asking us to take supplies over to the Tikrit hospital. We grudgingly stuffed our pockets with muffins, bananas, cereal, and energy drinks and departed the chow hall in one big mass.

Within fifteen minutes, we were back on the road and headed into the heart of Tikrit. We had the supplies we were supposed to deliver to the hospital in our Humvee. Once we arrived at the hospital, we sent our dismounted teams inside. I stayed outside in my non-air-conditioned Humvee with the rest of the mounted element.

After I'd sat in that Humvee for two hours, Avery, Taylor, and I had already run out of things to talk about. In silence, the bitching always picked back up. After the complaining ceased, we usually just sat quietly and thought about home and how bad we did not want to be in Iraq. During the silence in our unmotivated truck that night, a large explosion was once again heard, somewhere else in the city. I immediately snapped out of my boredom stare and checked the computer in our truck and found that there were no U.S. forces in the city.

Back and forth, Lieutenant Scher and I would ask each other over the radio if we knew anything more on that explosion, but we were both clueless. It was not long before anything worth reporting came into my lap. Fifteen minutes after the explosion, an Iraqi ambulance approached our cordon from around the hospital entrance. Without even questioning them, we let them through and into the hospital. I could see them unload a few individuals on stretchers. Scher was inside the hospital with some dismounts, so I relayed to him what I'd seen outside. He linked up with the delivered wounded inside to ascertain what had happened.

After a few moments, Lieutenant Scher called back to me and ex-plained that three civilians were wounded from a VBIED from somewhere in Tikrit. The sound we'd heard was confirmed as the recent explosion, so I relayed this information back to the company. A few minutes passed before I got the next update from Scher. He informed me that one of the civilians had died and we needed to medevac another patient to FOB Speicher for better care than what the crude Iraqi hospital could offer. After all my training as an RTO, I was finally ready to give an actual nine-line medevac call over the radio. I was pretty excited.

While I waited for the proper detailed information from Lieutenant Scher, I scanned the parking lot for a suitable spot for the helicopter to land. As soon as I found one, Scher exited the hospital and came over to our truck. As bad as I wanted to make the nine-line medevac call, I knew that Scher had all the answers already. Instead of wasting valuable time having him relay the information for me to write down and call up, I decided to let him call it up. Scher sent the request and had two squad leaders out in the parking lot with smoke grenades in their hands waiting to hear the medevac helicopter.

Simultaneous to the call, the patient was carted out of the hospital on a stretcher and waited with doctors and men from my platoon. On the radio, the pilots told me they would be in sight within seconds. The sound of the helicopter's blades prompted Poston to pop his purple smoke gre-nade in the parking lot to better direct the pilot.

The single bird came in quick and lowered to touch down. For some accidental reason, some flares were jettisoned from the helicopter and they bounced dangerously around like a fireworks show in the parking lot. Some of the flares were inches away from two of the guys. It was scary for a moment and led to a quick confusion between us as we watched the man on the litter get shoved into the open door of the Black Hawk while the men carrying him dodged flares. The helicopter's wheels had touched the pavement only seconds before the man was loaded, and the Black Hawk was back into the sky bound for Speicher immediately.

With all the proper care being administered to all the wounded civilians, it was now our job to proceed to the scene of the VBIED to make sure it was being cleaned up. We drove out north on Business 1 to the intersection of Saddam Boulevard. The roads were already locked down by Iraqi Police, but we just bypassed them and headed in.

We came to find two mangled skeletons of steel that had once been cars on the side of the road. One was impossible to recognize as having once been a car. It was more of a twisted metal ball with chips of white paint and recognizable car parts. The car on the other side of the street was a maroon four-door with holes and dents covering every square inch of it. It looked almost like a hunk of Swiss cheese on wheels. Not a single piece of glass remained.

The ground between the two cars had collected small puddles of blood mixed among scattered shards of metal. Behind the peppered maroon car was a sad image. I noticed a small child's abandoned bike with holes throughout it and traces of blood trailing away from it. The fate of that child will never be known to me.

We locked down the area with our security and dismounted some of our men to talk to the police, to inquire as to what had transpired. I needed to stretch my legs too, so I handed the mic to Avery as I went out with the lieutenant and interpreter "Jerry" to listen in. We didn't make it far from the vehicle before someone called out for us to halt and get back. Someone had spotted a secondary IED device tucked near a broken chunk of the curb. We quickly snapped around, ran back into the vehicle, and shut all the doors. All of the Humvees in our cordon pulled their gunners down at lightning speed.

As we waited for the inevitable to explode, nothing could be heard but our heavy breathing. We called EOD and decided to hold what we had and wait for proper disposal. Within a half hour, they arrived and as usual sent Johnny 5 out to capture and disarm the device. Thankfully, we averted disaster, due to someone's timely keen eye. It felt good to finally chalk one up for the good guys.

By the time we cleared from that scene and after all potential danger had been wiped clean, we talked Lieutenant Scher into letting us do our afternoon route clearance an hour earlier of our normal scheduled time since we were already in the center of the city. It took a lot of begging and some sucking up, but he caved in and decided to start where we were and head up Business 1, through IED Alley, and to the Twin Tits.

We carefully drove through IED Alley and were on high alert after the events that had transpired throughout the day. We didn't even make it a hundred yards into IED Alley before Staff Sergeant Gibson came screaming over the radio, "Stop, stop, stop, IED spotted in the median in between one-six and my truck."

We were unaware that we had just passed an IED, but hearing the advice from Gibson, we slammed to a halt where we were. It was hard to tell from our vantage point, but the IED was tucked alongside one of the decorative "exploding stars" in the concrete. These stars were always a perfect place to hide an IED and were always nerve-racking to drive by.

Moments after the IED was spotted, our convoy pulled off the road and into Kadasiyah. We split in half and sent two vehicles around one street and the other two around the other part of the neighborhood. We dropped off our dismounted elements while the mounted continued deeper into Kadasiyah. We were on the hunt for any person who looked suspicious, ran, had a camera, or was on a cell phone. After we had dropped off everyone but drivers and gunners, as the RTO I quickly found myself the only non-driver/non-gunner and in charge of the mounted element since I had the radios and controlled the trucks. With the mic hooked to my helmet and constantly pressed against my ear, I coordinated actions with Lieutenant Scher, who was randomly raiding abandoned buildings with the dismounted element. I orchestrated the outer exterior cordon around them.

I was the only one capable of exiting either of the two Humvees we had since the other Humvee consisted of just its gunner and driver. When I spotted citizens running away from the area, I threw down my hand mic and exited the vehicle in hot pursuit. I ran about twenty yards while I screamed loudly and as intimidatingly as I could in order to halt most of the people in their tracks. Several ran away, but I was only one person. I mostly stopped older men, then gathered them and searched them in place with haste. Avery and Taylor met me with our Humvee, so I wasn't alone. I only found cell phones, which I quickly flipped through, pretending to look for anything suspicious. The phones were all in Arabic, so I wouldn't have had the slightest clue if I had found something. I was "faking the funk." The Iraqis did not know what I was doing or capable of, so we were at a happy medium.

In my broken Arabic, I tried to ask what knowledge they had about the "boom" noise earlier in the day, or if they knew of any strangers who were in the neighborhood. I have had more success talking to blind and deaf people than I did with the Iraqis at that moment, so I sent them on their way and got back in the vehicle. After thirty minutes or so, the dismounted element called to say that they had turned up nothing in the abandoned houses. I instructed the mounted element to go back and pick them up.

Simultaneous to our impromptu raids, the EOD element that was already with us had started to disarm the found IED. It took them less than fifteen minutes to engage Johnny 5 on the ground and disarm the device. Instead of exploding it in place and adding to the deterioration of the road, they hauled it back to the FOB in their truck. That would be the last thing in the world I would ever want—to drive around Iraq with a live IED in my trunk.

With nothing further to find or investigate, First Platoon and the EOD element headed up to the Twin Tits, turned around, and headed south on MSR Tampa, to FOB Remagen. After that long and tiresome day, I remembered verbalizing my bad feeling early that morning and how it had proved accurate. From that moment on, I always listened to my instinct.

On the drive back to FOB Remagen, our truck full of "bitchers" played a new game we invented to pass the time. It was called "I'd Rather." All one had to do to play was use some form of the phrase "I'd rather ———— than be in Iraq." Everyone chimed in sequence and we laughed at each other's absurd versions of the sentence. The only one I remember saying to the other guys was "I'd rather be beaten up by Mexican hoodlums than be in Iraq." That continuous game back to the FOB ended yet another upside-down day in Tikrit.

OPERATION SWARMER

"This is gonna fucking suck."

In the early morning that followed our bloody day in Tikrit, we were supposed to kick off Operation Swarmer. Luckily, Colonel Steele decided to postpone the attack by forty-eight hours. March 16 was the new date we were given the green light for our "D-Day." The night before, we all went over back briefs in Fooks's CHU. It was hard to sleep that night, as anxiety and excitement twisted my gut. As usual, Rod's constant snoring didn't help either.

At 5:30 A.M., the dreaded knock on my door, from the "human alarm clock" that we still reluctantly had, woke me up. How unmotivated I was to wake up and make eye contact with my equipment. There it sat, neatly next to my bed, looking like an unmovable rock laughing at me. Knowing that I was moments away from strapping on this god-awful weight was a horrible way to start the day.

When I was finishing up putting all my accoutrements on, Avery met me at my door to give his two cents.

"This is gonna fucking suck," he said with a sad look on his face.

"You summed it up right there, buddy," I said as I attempted to put my assault pack on my back. Avery had to assist me as it was nearly impossible to pick up. With all of my Weapons Squad equipment and dismounted rifleman gear plus the extras I mentioned earlier, I was hunkered down.

"Avery, I can't put my arms down," I jokingly complained, alluding to *A Christmas Story*.

"I hope the helicopter lifts off," he replied.

The entire platoon was staged on the airstrip and awaited the arrival of helicopters. Avery and I attempted to take our time getting over to our staging area, because we were just so heavily equipped that we were walking like elderly men. Sergeant Nick Walters from Third Squad came out of nowhere and drove a half-ton truck right alongside us.

"Hey, your squad is supposed to be at the far end of the airstrip," Walters informed us. Weapons Squad took a hard look into the distance and it had to be half a mile. The complaining was triggered like a shot at the Kentucky Derby. "That's why I stole this truck," Walters said. "Get in, I'll take you guys down there."

"Whose truck is this? Where did you get it?" I asked him as we gladly threw our gear on the back.

"I saw it sitting over there between the two warehouses and I know what hell you're probably going through," Walters chimed back.

Thank God for that. He always was one of the sergeants who truly looked out for the lower enlisted. We weren't even in his squad, but he took care of everyone in the platoon. As he drove Weapons Squad down the tarmac, we kept passing our entire company, who walked the long trip to the edge of the airstrip. Constant smirks and occasional fingers were passed between us and the walking participants.

Once we disembarked, we dropped our equipment like an anchor on a ship. We all plopped down and waited for the arrival of the helicopters as the sun rose above the sand. As the men in my chalk met up with me, anyone who made the slightest joke about me getting a ride was invited to pick up my assault pack. They never made a joke after that.

When I looked down the tarmac, I could see that my platoon was at the farthest point away from the main camp. To top it off, my chalk was the farthest in the platoon. This made my helicopter the first bird in the assaulting element. I could see small groups of men gather for as far as I

Members of Angel Company training among their tents during their early days at Camp Buehring, Kuwait.

The bus that shuttled Angel Company to the ranges from Camp Buehring in Kuwait gets stuck in the sand out in the middle of nowhere after the local driver insisted on driving like a maniac.

Photos are courtesy of author unless otherwise noted.

Sergeant Aric Hilmo, First Platoon's Forward Observer, was always a source of entertainment, both deployed and stateside.
Courtesy of Evan L. Pitchford

The sandbag pyramid referred to as the "Gun Pit" outside the front entrance of FOB Union III in Baghdad.
Courtesy of Evan L. Pitchford

Specialist Ryan A. Conklin and Specialist Brendan Fooks on guard in the gun pit of the front entrance to FOB Union III in Baghdad. *Courtesy of Evan L. Pitchford*

Specialist Taylor Edwards was Conklin's partner in crime when it came to voicing their opinions about what they were doing— regardless of the repercussions.
Courtesy of Ryan Avery

Specialist Ryan Avery, Conklin's closest buddy in the platoon, is pictured on his cot at Camp Stryker just moments after a rocket impacted near the platoon's tent during their travel up north.

Staff Sergeant Jimmy Poston was a strict but knowledgeable non-commissioned officer and squad leader for Weapons Squad.
Courtesy of Vinse Edwards

"Well Come To Tikrit" was written on the sign that Angel Company passed every time they drove into downtown Tikrit.

First Platoon patrols through the streets of downtown Tikrit.

Conklin in his turret just moments after the platoon's first IED attack on January 8, 2006, on MSR Tampa in Tikrit.

Angel Company CHUs at FOB Remagen before the detail of filling and stacking sandbags to the roofs.

Conklin's Team Leader and Squad Leader, Sergeant Fooks and Staff Sergeant Poston, pose next to their Humvee. Conklin stands where he could usually always be found, in the gunner's turret.

First Lieutenant Adam Scher briefed First Platoon before every patrol.

When it rained in Iraq, it really came down hard. Small lakes sprang up all over the desert. Sergeant Evan Pitchford and Private Jeremy Heiple managed to get this Humvee stuck on FOB Remagen. *Courtesy of Justin Jirkovsky*

Conklin showing off the broken-tooth smile he received when he slipped, while firing a shotgun. He spent almost six months with this comical appearance, earning the nickname "Chip."

Corporal Andrew "Drew" Kemple, from Cambridge, Minnesota, was the toughest and strongest gunner. He loved everything about the M240B machine gun. He was killed by a sniper's bullet while in the turret of his Humvee in downtown Tikrit on February 12, 2006. *Courtesy of Darren Subarton*

The memorial box constructed on the FOB Remagen airstrip for Corporal Drew Kemple's memorial service. *Courtesy of Darren Subarton*

Conklin in the turret of the Humvee rigged with a speaker system that was used only once. After playing some choice songs, he was instructed to cease. The patrol ended with a single rifle shot toward his turret. *Courtesy of Wilson Ly*

Children typically gathered around platoon Humvees when they paused for breaks during mounted patrols.

Conklin served at times as the platoon RTO. It was not uncommon to have three different conversations on different frequencies with different people, all at the same time.

Gun Team 2 at the initial objective during Operation Swarmer consisted of Taylor and
Conklin. This was one of the few times Conklin used his heavy tripod that he carried
everywhere but rarely ever used.

An Apache helicopter provided aerial security while the platoon moved house to house rounding up male suspects during Operation Swarmer. *Courtesy of U.S. Army*

Conklin with a young Iraqi boy who wanted to try on his helmet. The boy and his brother cooked chai for the entire platoon when they inspected their home during Operation Swarmer.
Courtesy of U.S. Army

Conklin scans over the desert as the company sets up a patrol base to pass the night, a few days into Operation Swarmer.
Courtesy of U.S. Army

A Blackhawk helicopter takes off from the airstrip on FOB Remagen, stirring up fresh coats of sand on Angel Company CHUs.

Soldiers from First Platoon dig in a sand berm after finding an IED factory of hundreds of blasting caps, grenades, AK-47 bullets, and detonation cords during the April Fools' Cache. Conklin is seen top center looking over what was gathered as they continue to dig. *Courtesy of Justin Jirkovsky*

Dozens of South African 155mm artillery shells are pulled and displayed from this field during the April Fools' Cache. *Courtesy of Justin Jirkovsky*

Conklin acknowledges his twenty-first birthday while posing with several anti-tank mines found during the April Fools' Cache. He wears the pirate patch on his left sleeve that several members of First Platoon wore.

As a birthday gift for turning twenty-one, Conklin had the honor of triggering this massive explosion that detonated what was found during the April Fools' Cache.
Courtesy of Justin Jirkovsky

Sergeant Fooks and Staff Sergeant Poston stand before an Iraqi checkpoint on MSR Tampa, which the men referred to as the "Twin Tits." *Courtesy of Ryan Armstrong*

Homes owned by known insurgents were demolished, creating another incentive to refrain from fighting U.S. troops.

Angel Company Commander, Captain Jeffrey Lesperance and First Platoon's Platoon Leader, First Lieutenant Adam Scher discuss the day's action after bulldozing homes connected to insurgents. *Courtesy of David Hubert*

Conklin and close friend Derek Borden. They served together since their first day of basic training in 2003. Their companies were separated in Iraq. He served with Charlie Company in the same battalion.

After their initial landing at their objective during Operation Iron Triangle, First Platoon's LMTV broke down. While mechanics worked to repair the truck, the men caught some rest while they waited.

Lieutenant Scher talks through Jerry, our interpreter, to local shopkeepers for any leads on potential enemy activity in the area. By 2006, Iraqi-born interpreters who worked with U.S. forces still wore masks to conceal their identities because they feared being murdered or bringing harm to their families.

Combing the desert became a reality during operations such as this during Operation Iron Triangle.

Murals of Saddam Hussein dotted the country for decades. After three years of U.S. presence, it was rare to find one intact. This one was spared no mercy.

This is the face Conklin usually wore during the constant patrols. The heat, boredom and homesickness are clearly written on his face.

could see. The rest of the guys in my chalk and I dropped our gear mixed in together in a pile and shut our eyes.

Within minutes, the intimidating sound of numerous helicopters in the distance grew louder by the second, like a shifting storm. Once they were in sight, it was a beautiful display. About twenty-five helicopters came over to our positions and landed at their appropriate designated spots. It was a pretty cool thing to witness, especially knowing that we were about to be a part of the intimidating scene.

We were told that we had until 9:15 A.M., which was the initial planned time for takeoff. Naturally, "the Army way," we were prepared hours before we needed to be, so we had plenty of time to relax. We initially did a cold load of the helicopter, which just practiced our ability to get in and out of the bird in an orderly fashion and designate seats. We had some Iraqi Army soldiers with us, so we wanted to make sure they knew where they were going to sit and how to strap into the seat belt. I realized I was the last one in the helicopter, which made me, ironically, the first to get out. So this whole operation was going to begin as soon as my foot hit the ground. It was a pretty cool opportunity to fall in my lap.

After the cold load, we went back to lounging against the cement Jersey wall and waited for time to pass. Taylor and I would compare our mustaches, which we'd decided to grow days prior. A bunch of guys in the platoon grew them also, because we were never allowed to grow them in America. Iraq was the best opportunity. Taylor and I had horrible, dirty-looking mustaches. Mine looked like spider legs. Daily, we would ask people who had the nastier mustache. It was a fun game that lasted weeks, and the mustaches only got more hideous as time went by. While we lounged around, we also got to witness some gazelles run through FOB Remagen. They would certainly give an American hunter a run for his money, on account of their speed. We also monitored another Black Hawk helicopter that kept hovering over us. I was told that the helicopter was taking official Army photos, which later I got to see. I can clearly identify my helicopter as the first helicopter with a long line of others trailing behind it. Off to the left, you can see me and my group lounging around near the Jersey barrier on the ground.

While waiting for 9:15 A.M. to come around, I was first awakened from my nap by the sound of a four-wheeler coming toward our group. It was a sergeant major from the 3/320th Field Artillery. He was loaded up with muffins and bananas for us to take, which made me happy. It was the best thing the field artillery guys did for us all year. We each took a few and headed back down to eat them. Within minutes, I was back to catching up on some lost sleep.

Around 8:30 A.M., I was quickly awakened by a panic-stricken Sergeant Caruso.

"Get up. Get up now, everyone. Rakk-Six is here. Get up!" Colonel Steele himself was walking to each individual group before we began to load up. I stood up and brushed the dirt off my uniform, and tried to wipe my eyes awake.

When Steele approached, everyone was in utter silence. He was an intimidating person and we all respected him so much.

"Where's your name tape, Specialist?" Steele questioned Specialist Ly. His last name was so short that a pouch was covering his last name on his vest. He quickly exposed his name tape.

"Ly, take that do-rag off your head," Steele sternly said to him while he quickly seized it off Ly's head. I laughed briefly, which was enough to have him avert his attention to me. I froze when we made eye contact.

"You ready?" he asked me while he looked deep into my eyes.

"Hooah, sir," I said back to him.

"You don't look ready," he replied back.

I froze up and didn't know what to say. Colonel Steele was a living legend in our regiment and I did not want to say something stupid. But then it happened.

"I'm tired," I said. I quickly grimaced and bit my lip and knew that that was the last thing he wanted to hear from one of his soldiers. I had basically just told him I was a wimp, but I was legitimately tired and I could not come up with anything motivating to say. The awkward silence after my sentence certified my logic that it was stupid. Steele kept looking at me, studying me like a piece of art. I braced for something smart-ass to come out of his mouth.

"You're tired?" he asked me. *Oh God,* I thought. *Here it comes.* "Rack out before you leave, son," he said back and then walked away.

"Rakkasan, sir!" I sounded off as he left our group. Once he was out of earshot, I got the expected reply of snickers from the others in my chalk who were around me.

"*I'm tiiiiiired!*" Hubert said in the tone of a little girl.

"Yeah, I definitely looked like a big wimp in his eyes. Fuck it. Wake me up when it's time to go," I replied to everyone, and they were still cracking playful jokes. I settled on the ground, shut my eyes, and tuned them out.

Around 9:00 A.M. the sound of the first blades beginning to rotate chimed through the air. Within seconds, the rotary blades on all of the helicopters began to wind up. It was like the preliminary stage of a big race car competition when everyone started his engine. The sound of all the pilots preparing was our cue to don our equipment.

While putting on my heavy gear, I could faintly hear music playing behind the surging sound of the countless blades swirling. I looked around and noticed the same peculiar facial expressions of others, making clear that they could hear something as well. Upon further investigation, I looked down the tarmac and could clearly see a Humvee rolling slowly in between the helicopters and soldiers.

As it got closer and closer to me, the music was more audible. I could now distinctly hear what song it was. It was "The Ride of the Valkyries" by Richard Wagner. More people would recognize it as the song played during the helicopter raid in the famous movie *Apocalypse Now*. As soon as everyone could recognize the music being played, we all erupted in a loud and thunderous cheer. Men began to whistle, yell, and wave their weapons in the air. It was like a football team finishing up the greatest pep rally before a big game. Private First Class Ben Miller, Third Platoon's comic relief, ran alongside the music-pumping Humvee. He began to punch the air like he was in a montage from one of the *Rocky* movies. It was very humorous to all who saw the spectacle.[17] The Humvee continued to do laps around everyone and instill adrenaline in all. It was a classic Colonel Steele move that proved to work.

With the sound of the blades on all the helicopters churning at top speed and the music pumping from speakers adorned on the Humvee, we were finally given the thumbs-up to load up. Everyone in my chalk filed

---

[17] Benjamin Miller later deployed to Iraq with Angel Company again in 2007. Halfway through the tour he committed suicide on June 18, 2008.

in front of me and climbed aboard. I stayed in the back since I was last to load up. Instead of going through the hassle of putting on my assault pack for what was only a twenty-five-foot walk, I instead dragged it like a limp body to the helicopter.

I strapped into my seat belt and saw Taylor, the gunner for my gun team, lean forward and yell something to me. He was fighting a losing battle with the very ear-splitting blades above us.

"You got the bitch seat," he screamed.

"What?" I could barely make out what he was saying.

"You got the bitch seat. We're flying open door," he informed me. Somehow, I'd thought we'd be flying closed door since it was such a long flight. The bitch seat was aptly called this, because the outer seat in which I was seated, faced in the same direction as the helicopter. It was like a front row seat in a hurricane simulator. It sucked.

Once in the air, I asked Taylor what the scene behind us looked like as I could only see the direction in which we were flying.

"It's fucking beautiful, man. I can't even see the end of it." We were both pretty excited.

We were told that it was going to be a long flight, which proved to be the most accurate information I got for the assault. We flew for over thirty minutes, which was the longest flight I had ever taken in a Black Hawk. It gave me an ample amount of time to view the land of Iraq from the air. We passed countless scattered farms and villages. Occasionally I saw people pour out of the strewn houses to witness our large fleet flyover. The wind continued to pound my face. From behind my sunglasses, my eyeballs felt dry as the wind extracted tears from the corners of my eyelids.

After a while I knew we were getting close when we flew over the dried-up salt lake. After studying so intently the maps that had been handed out, I knew we weren't far away. We had to cross the large open desert after the lake, and then we would be within our target range. During our flyover of the desert, I noticed an old Iraqi tank out in the middle of nowhere. It had obviously been abandoned in some long forgotten war. The most curious thing I noticed nearby was a small herd of camels that ran through the desert. What was so remarkable about them was that one of them was pure albino and stuck out like a sore thumb. It was very cool to witness.

"Five minutes!" was yelled, and passed along by everyone in the bird, accompanied by the hand gesture of "five minutes." I looked over my gear one last time and locked and loaded my M4. I looked across to Taylor, and we were having a conversation without saying a word. The looks on our faces summed up exactly what we knew was about to happen. This was going to suck.

"Two minutes!" was yelled and passed. I peered out the door and could see the upcoming farmhouse in the distance which we'd code-named LZ Michelob. I kicked my bag closer to the door so I could grab it easier once we landed. As we began to descend, I prayed hard that no one would open fire. I kept thinking about the fish-in-a-barrel effect, like on the Normandy landings in 1944, and how guys could not even get off the Higgins Boats before they were targeted and slaughtered. I began praying that I would not clog the exit of our bird with my excessive weight and cause a domino disaster.

With our Black Hawk inches off the ground, I unbuckled my straps and grabbed my luggage. This was it. One small step from me and Operation Swarmer would be officially under way. With my M4 in my right hand and an open left hand ready to grab my rock-heavy bag, I stared out the door and waited for the familiar bump of when wheels hit ground.

Like hearing a starting pistol in a race, as soon as I felt that bump I sprang out of my seat, grabbed my bag, and swung it on my back. I made it a good twenty feet before the weight from my assault pack promoted me to teeter-totter like I was running on shifting ground. The wind from the rotary blades on the helicopter was enough to throw me off balance and away I went. Like a blooper in a war movie, I went flying forward like a car without brakes and hit the ground face-first hard. Like an idiot, I was spread-eagled on the ground. I was afraid I would trip someone else in getting up so I remained motionless as everyone passed me, pinned under my own gear.

The blades of the helicopter still churned and blew sand in my eyes. My sunglasses could only protect me so much. I did not need to see Taylor to make sure he made it out all right. The sound of his laughter as he passed me was enough clarification.

Sergeant Caruso was the last one out of the helicopter and he helped pick me up. The four helicopters that had dropped First Platoon off were back in the sky within seconds of downloading. While I scraped sand out of my eyes, I scanned the area and saw that all four squads had organized themselves into a wedge formation. I took notice of Taylor, who was now twenty-five feet in front of me. Caruso helped me up after being pinned by my assault pack and away I ran as if I was pulling a car.

"Fuck this!" I said immediately as I approached behind Taylor.

"That was some funny shit, Conk," he said.

Taylor and I stayed in the center of the line, behind Second Squad as they formed up and sprinted into the house. When they broke off, the two of us set up next to the water system on the farmhouse and faced away from the residence. It was a perfect place. There was a dugout berm for us already, and some trees overhead provided us with some shade. We had perfect vision in front of us of an entire empty open desert that stretched for days. I immediately cracked out the tripod just so I could get that self-satisfaction that I did not bring it in vain.

After the first five minutes, I didn't hear any shooting in the homes behind me so I knew all was going to be safe there. Taylor and I had nothing but flat empty desert all around us. The fear level ceased. We finally enjoyed the rare advantage of being in a gun team when you just lie there and watch nothing and talk to each other. The rest of the platoon was doing extensive searches of men and households. They were separating the men and interrogating them with the help of the interpreter. I didn't care what was going on. I was just exhausted. Taylor and I just chilled in our gun position.

We did not have any interaction with anyone except the occasional visit from Sergeant Fooks, who made sure we were not so bored that we killed ourselves. It was a long and unexciting day. The heat was out with a vengeance as well. We drank and poured water all over ourselves to beat the heat and lighten the load we were carrying.

Around 4:00 P.M., Headquarters Company came to our location driving our platoon's vehicles. They were a welcoming sight because I'd feared that we were going to be dismounted the whole week. I also knew that since I would be in a truck, I would not have to suffer carrying my excessive and needless weight on my back. Oh, how marvelous and welcoming those Humvees looked.

During the planning stage of Swarmer, we were placed in trucks with all the gun teams split up so each truck could have a member of Weapons Squad in it. By my luck of the short straw, I was placed in a truck with people I didn't have the least bit of interest in. Sergeant Adams, who was a recent transfer into our platoon, was unsociable and had the personality of a brick. Lifting weights and spacing out was what he did with most of his time. Ram was also in my truck. Together, we were like oil and water. We could work and get along, but there was too much buried animosity toward each other that prevented both of us from opening up normal conversation. Lastly, Staff Sergeant Ledbetter was in my truck. By then he was still floating around our platoon, since Sergeant First Class Crisostomo had been put in charge of our platoon. Ledbetter was all right to talk to, but not enough to have lasting conversations that humored me. The best part of being in that truck was that I was the permanent gunner in the turret, so standing up in the turret kept me away from whatever boring conversations they sparked up between each other anyway.

We stayed parked around the original main target of the farmhouse until 9 P.M. The sun was almost down before we started putting our dreaded NODs on our helmets. Once the other dismounted elements were completed doing whatever searching, documenting, and rounding up of wanted men they needed to do, we packed up and drove off.

Since this was the first time this stretch of desert had ever seen American troops, I had absolutely no fear of IEDs. No terrorist was going to wait in the same spot for three years for the chance to blow us up. Besides, there were no roads we were driving on, just open desert. This gave me the opportunity to stand in the turret fully exposed whenever and for however long I wanted. The wind gave me a great cool-down from the unnecessary heat on the drive that night. Best of all, I didn't even have the standard M240B in my turret. Instead, I had a Vietnam-era M60 mounted on it. It even had the butterfly trigger, so I kept both my hands on the handles around it to balance myself as we drove over the bumpy desert.

We drove for a while, until the lieutenant settled on an "out in the middle of nowhere" location on the map to set up a blocking position. In a straight line with fifty feet in between us and the next Humvee, we pulled out into a blocking position. We did this by having one Humvee pull left and park, the next one pull right and park, and so on, ensuring the proper interval in between each other.

Once parked, we immediately had a piss break and grabbed the closest MRE from the trunk of our Humvee. We had to have a man in the turret at all times, so Staff Sergeant Ledbetter initiated a plan of hourly rotations among the four of us in the Humvee. I started first, so I forced down my nasty textured and tasting MRE in the turret, with the moon providing ample amount of light.

We slept in that Humvee as best we could. It was an uncomfortable night. In such a cramped vehicle, there was only so much room to move. Everyone slept in his seat in awkward and uncomfortable positions. If we were not awakened every so often to pull our hour of guard in the turret, the pain of having our legs go numb kept us awake anyway. It was a rough night to get any rest. It also got cold that night, so feeling around in my assault pack to grab my handy poncho liner, aka "woobie," proved vital. But that only helped so much.

During one of my guard shifts on the gun, I monitored the sun coming up. I could now see how big our blocking position was. It consisted of all the platoons in my company. Once the sun was up, I found it impossible to sleep. I put my NODs away and grabbed another MRE for breakfast. I swished water around in my mouth afterward to substitute for brushing my teeth.

Around 9 A.M., Lieutenant Scher came over to each vehicle to run down how we would operate for Day Two of Swarmer. He was going to split our platoon in half: half to be dismounts in a Chinook helicopter to do multiple raids on homes in one direction, and the other half to stay mounted and move in the opposite direction. Although riding around all day in a helicopter sounded like fun, I did not want to tote around my assault pack. I was content with being stuck all day in a Humvee with such a delightful audience. To my surprise because nothing usually worked for my benefit, this time it did. I was going to stay in the mounted element and remain in the turret for as long as I could.

Day Two consisted of driving from house to house to house. Each house we approached, our dismounted element would run through the same routine. Search every square inch of every home and shack on each farm. I had the best part. I just stood in my turret and stared off into the abyss. Occasionally, I would steal snacks from MREs and kick back and eat while everyone worked tirelessly with the searching. The only thing I had to contend with was the ever-present sun that I was baking in. No one ever wore sunscreen except for Sunny, but that's because he was fair-skinned and I believe he could get sunburn from a flashlight because his skin was so sensitive. I took the punishment from the sun because I wasn't going to complain, in fear that I would be traded out with some-one on the dismount team.

We drove from farmhouse to farmhouse doing the same thing. Each one was separated by about a ten- to fifteen-minute ride. We didn't find anything worth reporting. Just a couple of old guns. It was a long and tedious task that we were doing, but our half platoon was just one little element in the larger group doing the same thing across the province.

Near dusk, we drove to our last farmhouse, which actually had a mounted element already there. It was the other half of our platoon, who apparently had stopped riding around in the Chinook and taken back their Humvees. After we all regrouped, we drove a long distance over the open desert back to the same desolate spot out in the middle of nowhere that we'd been at the night previous.

We slipped back into the same routine of guard shift that we had the night before. It was once again a night from Hell. The familiar and dreaded phrase of "wake up, it's your shift for guard" and the ever-recurring legs that grew numb every half hour uncomfortably passed the night. As rough as it was in that cramped Humvee, I had to thank my lucky stars that at least Rod was not in the same one. I wondered how bad the occupants in his Humvee wanted to smother him. I later found out they made him sleep outside and twenty feet away.

We started Day Three just as we had the day prior. I crawled from the Humvee a stiff man at seven in the morning. We all quickly ran through whatever morning routine we had. Mine consisted of scarfing down an MRE and then swishing water to rinse my mouth. Sometimes I would borrow other people's toothpaste and swish that around as well.

We picked back up exactly where we had left off the evening prior. We again split our platoon up to make better time in searching. As soon as all were ready, we headed out for more "trick or treating." Sometimes we would come across homes that had an "X" spray-painted on the side, which meant it had been searched. Sometimes we ran into houses that other units had forgotten to spray-paint or put engineer tape on the roof of. This made us search everything again and take longer.

By Day Three, everyone had his own aches and pains, but I was starting to have an irregular pain strike me. My big toes were really starting to hurt. I'd had this pain before because I was accustomed to not taking my boots off for days at a time, but this was *really* painful. Standing all day in the turret was only reinforcing it. Since complaining did nothing, I did what the old infantry phrase suggested in a situation like this: "Suck it up and drive on."

After the tedious task of going house to house, everyone had grown tired of coming up shortchanged. Word spread to us that Second Platoon had found a sizable cache hidden among the mud walls of a farmhouse. They found rockets, mortars, artillery shells, AKs, grenades, you name it. They bulldozed the house and continued their searching with a vigor that we lacked.

The course of my "Swarming" was rerouted when, to no one's surprise, our Humvee began to overheat. We stopped in the middle of the desert, in between farmhouses, when smoke began to pump through the hood. Avery, who was in Lieutenant Scher's truck, got out and he and Heiple, the two unofficial platoon mechanics, tried their best to fix the problem.

Through wear and tear, we had broken some cables, and our predicament was not going to be resolved because of the lack of supplies we had. To Lieutenant Scher's disgust and my excitement, they hooked us up to their tow straps and towed us back to the area where we had the company set up for our blocking position out in the middle of nowhere. Since Scher couldn't roll out with just two vehicles, they had to stay there at the blocking position and wait for the other half of the platoon to come link up with them.

Our rickety old Desert Storm trucks were ancient, and they ruined several patrols, but this one really put a damper on our operation. What this meant for me really was that, with us in it, our truck was going to be hauled back to the closest FOB, FOB Wilson, where we would work as fast as we could to fix, repair, and move back out.

It was like having a snow day from school. This meant that I would be able to eat some real food, sleep on a cot, check my e-mail, stretch my legs—oh, the possibilities. Jealousy stemmed from all the others whose trucks were not quite dead-lined like mine was. I was so excited.

"They're taking me out of the fight," I kept yelling at Lieutenant Scher. A phrase he would often say when we had to head back early from a mission.

While we waited for Headquarters Platoon to come pick us up and tow us in, I had plenty of downtime in the open desert to mess with the Iraqi Army guys. They loved Taylor for some reason. We would always joke that they were homosexuals who wanted to marry Taylor. Of course, Taylor went along and joked around with it.

One of the IA soldiers offered us some recently squeezed goat's milk that they had milked themselves from a goat they bought around the area. Taylor never really backed down from a challenge and lived by the unwritten rule of "I'll try anything once," and he did. The milk barely was in his stomach longer than five seconds before he threw it back up right in front of the Iraqi soldiers. They laughed like I had never seen them laugh before. Then, as if to gloat on how tough they all were, they consumed the milk like they were in a Gatorade commercial.

After milking the goat, they slit its throat and began to dig a pit to cook it in. They did not have to dig far before they accidentally ran across a heap of human remains buried lightly in the desert. These bones were old and had remnants of a dishdasha. The Iraqis just kicked everything to the side and cooked their goat.

With heroic timing, Headquarters Platoon came to us before the goat was fully cooked. They towed us on a long trip through the open desert back to FOB Wilson. I had been fantasizing about how grand this FOB would be and was shocked when I arrived. It was a dump. It was the ugliest, smallest, crudest FOB I had ever been to. I guess beggars can't be choosers, so I immediately passed my judgment and dealt with it.

It was near ten o'clock at night when we arrived, and we were literally dropped off at the mechanics maintenance bay. It was like a ghost town. Everyone who was permanently assigned to that building was nowhere to be found.

"Keep your sensitive items close by you. Find a cot somewhere. Go find something to eat. I'm in no hurry to fix this tonight. We'll fix it in the morning. I'm going to go find the Internet," Ledbetter said as he casually slipped out into the night.

This was fantastic. As bummed as I was about being a part of this crew, I was now glad I was with men who enjoyed shamming as much as I did. I was really going to relish the chance I'd been given. I took all my protective gear off and went in search of a cot. There was a pile in the mechanics bay so I took a few for the four of us.

After eating MREs for days, which clogged my bowels, they finally caught up to me. I was in hot pursuit of a port-a-john. With me not knowing where one was located on the foreign base and with the threat of the "MRE Shits" brewing, time was of the essence. I spotted one in the dark of night down a ways and sprinted toward it, but stopped twenty feet away. I could not wait. I ripped down my pants and went right then and there on a sidewalk. After a few moments I walked over to the port-a-potty and finished. I know several soldiers that shat their pants during deployment, but I did not want to be "that guy."

Near one in the morning, we all found our way back to the empty mechanics bay to sleep for the night. The night happened to be so incredibly freezing in that bay that I forgot about the pain in my toes until I began to take my boots off. It was always an orgasmic feeling when I let the tension out on my laces and loosened up my boots. After arduously prying them off my feet that night, the sight of dried blood painted over my once white socks made me sink low in my cot.

As bad as I wanted to get a good night's sleep for once, I knew it wasn't going to start anywhere before two in the morning. Unaware of what damage was beneath my socks, which were stuck to my toes from the dried blood, I knew I had to seek some kind of medical attention.

So off I was, walking, one-thirty in the morning, somewhere in Iraq, on an unfamiliar FOB, limping around in just my blood-soaked socks, my pants, and no clear idea as to where I was headed. I knew that if I wanted to know where anything was located on the FOB, who else would know better than a fobbit? And where else can a fobbit be found at any given time? The Internet room. So I headed there and received directions to the aid station.

"You're a sad-looking sight. What happened?" a female doctor said to me as I limped into the aid station.

"Not sure. I've been 'swarming' the past couple of days, and I finally took my boots off to find them stuck in blood to my socks," I tried to explain.

"Hop on the table and I'll see what you got," the attractive doctor said to me. This was the closest contact I'd had with a good-looking female in a long time, and her recent phrase of calling me a sad-looking sight kept replaying in my mind, and I began to chuckle out loud.

"What's so funny?" she asked me.

I kindly flirted. "Nothing. It's just, I'm so incredibly dirty, half my tooth is missing, and I smell like something died. It's almost two in the morning and you're so clean. I hope you're not offended."

Then, as if I'd dropped an ice cream cone, she said, "My husband is in the infantry. I totally understand." Soon after, a large male assistant walked in and addressed her as captain. I decided to shut up and have her do her job.

When the doctor cut my socks off, I could see, mixed with the blood, severe swelling in both of my large toes.

"Looks like you have two severe ingrown toenails on your big toes," she said, diagnosing my problem.

"What's an ingrown toenail?" I asked. I had heard of them before but never fully grasped what they were. She explained to me as best she could.

"So what is going to be done to fix this?" I questioned her.

"We're going to have to take both your big toenails off so they can re-grow properly," she calmly said, as if no pain was going to be involved.

"OK. Say you cut them out right now. Could I still rejoin my platoon tomorrow?" I regrettably asked.

"Oh my god, no. You'll have to be on a profile that would limit physical activity for a while," she said among her own chuckling.

As great as that sounded and how much relief it would give me, I knew that the crap I would receive from the other guys in my platoon would be too much. Not returning to them when they were at their worst would almost segregate me from the camaraderie we all shared. "Misery loves company" was the phrase we all lived by, and I just couldn't sit out like some privileged kid while my best friends were not as lucky. I wasn't trying to be selfless at all, I just would not want to see someone do that when I was out in the desert sucking away.

"Is there any way you can subdue the pressure, pain, or stall this operation so I can get back to my platoon tomorrow?" I asked.

"You grunts are all so hardheaded. Why is that?" she asked.

"We're just dumb, ma'am," I said.

"I can cut the corners of the nails out now, but tomorrow morning, you need to come in and we can take the rest of them out," she told me.

"So I'm not going to be able to rejoin them tomorrow?" I reluctantly questioned her.

"I'm afraid not. Not this time," the captain said.

So I let her do her job on my toes. The needles she punctured my big toes with went deep, until they hit bone. The pain was really bad, but the painkiller they injected worked quickly. Within a half hour, the corners of my nails were cut out and she'd squeezed out a lot of pus and blood. I was bandaged up and given extra gauze wrapping supplies.

As I was leaving, she ordered me to be back in at ten in the morning to finish the job. I said a standard "yes, ma'am" and a "thank you" and I walked out of the aid station. I also had a bag full of pain pills, so I knew I could at least drive on through the end of Swarmer. On my way back to the mechanics bay, I found the closest trash can and threw the piece of paper about my appointment away.

As hard as it was throwing away that "golden ticket," I knew I was doing the right thing. There was only one group of people I wanted to be with and share my agony with as soon as possible. My platoon. I limped back into the mechanics bay, wrapped myself in my poncho liner, and slept.

The next morning I woke up fully rested. It was something I had not done in a long time. I was up before Ram and Adams. Staff Sergeant Ledbetter was already gone, and I knew I could probably find him in the Internet room. As I assessed my feet, I put on a clean bandage, a pair of clean socks, and then my boots.

I had a noticeable limp that I tried to hide as I walked to the Internet room. I was keeping an eye out for any doctors from the previous night, because I wasn't going to show up for my appointment. While I scanned every room I walked into, I came across Third Platoon all gathered in an empty hangar. They all had their cots out and were just chilling. They had the greatest task of our company. They were the "Brigade Air Assault Response Force" or what we called "BARF." They were to be on standby in case anyone in the operation needed additional troops, then they would answer the call and air assault in. In other words, they sat on their butts in the hangar, smoked, and drank soda. They were the ones to be jealous of.

I spent some time that morning conversing with Third Platoon men about actions out in the desert. It was pretty boring stuff to pass on.

"Hey, Conklin, did you hear about Bravo Company?" asked Staff Sergeant Ching from Third Platoon, a recent transfer from Bravo Company of our battalion.

"No, what happened?" I asked back.

"Did you know Yates at all?" he asked me. I immediately knew something bad had happened to him.

"Just a little bit. We used to mop the halls sometimes back in the rear. I mostly interacted with him whenever us lower enlisted had to clean shit," I explained.

"He was killed yesterday, by a sniper," he sadly explained.

Specialist Nyle Yates was from Lake Odessa, Michigan. He was in Bravo Company in our battalion, Scud's platoon. Bravo Company was not involved with Operation Swarmer, but had instead stayed behind at their patrol base in Samarra. While manning his guard post, Yates was shot and killed instantly by a sniper.

News of occurrences like these, especially when they happened among our battalion, traveled like wildfire. That same day in Tikrit, FOB Speicher was hit with a mortar attack that killed two soldiers and wounded another. It always was a sad thing to go through, but it came with the job that we had. Every time it happened, we all would ask ourselves what we could do in the future to make sure something like that did not happen to us. All that really did was fuel more pent-up aggression toward the Iraqi people, our duty, and the overall deployment. "When it's your time, it's your time."

I remained with Third Platoon until the guys from my Humvee met up with me with my belongings in their hands. They too had decided to wait and chat with fellow Angels from Hell while our truck was being worked on. Later on in the early afternoon, four members from Second Platoon joined our growing crowd of laziness. They were going through the same problem of waiting for a disabled truck to be fixed.

Like a good disciplined soldier with some spare time on my hands, I decided to thoroughly clean my M60. The inside of the weapon was caked with very fine sand, much like talcum powder. I cleaned for about an hour before I decided to head into the Internet room. I began to search what the media was saying about "Operation Swarmer" and found it everywhere. There were reports of several large firefights ensuing during the searches. I did not know where they were getting their information from, because it was all quiet on the western front for my company.

As soon as I decided to send off an e-mail to my parents, Staff Sergeant Ledbetter came in to burst my bubble.

"Get your shit on and run out to the airfield, we're leaving with Third Platoon," he said in a hurry as he turned and walked out.

"How soon are we leaving?" I yelled before he was out the door.

"Right now!" he yelled back.

"I hate this shit," I said as I grabbed my gear and scurried out. All the pogues in the Internet room were just staring at me. I'm not sure if they thought it was funny or if they were jealous. They would have to be insane if they wanted to do what I was doing.

Back in the hangar, Ram and Adams were already dressed and holding my gear. I quickly dressed while walking out with them to the airfield.

"What's going on? Is our truck ready?" I hastily asked while jogging out to the hangar through FOB Wilson.

"Not sure. We're leaving the truck. We're air assaulting back with our platoon," Ram explained.

"What about my sixty?" I asked. "And my AG bag?" Since I was only carrying my M4, I wanted to make sure I did not have to lug around that heavy equipment.

"Ledbetter left it in the truck and locked it up. You're gonna be a rifleman now." I was delighted to be leaving all that stuff behind. I knew a move like that would have made Poston go insane, but that was part of the bonus of having him home on leave. Ledbetter outranked Fooks, so I knew I was safe.

Like always, we made it out to the airfield at a moment's notice, only to find that we had to wait for some time for the birds to be inbound. The momentary pause gave me more time to ask Ledbetter what was going on.

"Are you sure I should leave my weapons equipment in the truck?" I asked him.

"Yup, you won't need it where we are going. Ram, you stay behind and stay with the truck," he told him.

"Are you serious?" He always would ask that when given the opportunity to sham out of things.

"Where are we going, sarnt?" I asked Ledbetter.

"They extended our search area, and we're headed into the mountains. You're not gonna want that extra weight anyways," he said.

"Son of a bitch," I said, bracing for the upcoming "suckfest" trip through the mountains. Wait, did he say mountains? I didn't really see any mountains anywhere, so I was curious as to where exactly my platoon was venturing to, out in the desert.

I had plenty of downtime waiting under the shade of a wall. Most of Third Platoon's "BARF" element rolled out in the first wave of choppers, and my crew and the guys from Second Platoon were supposed to hop in that wave, but we were bumped because Colonel Steele and his entourage wanted on, so of course we obliged and sat back and waited for the next wave.

I didn't care. I was in no hurry to get out and "swarm." I took advantage of the extra time and went to the chow hall and grabbed some ice cream and a few extra Mountain Dews and put them in my bag. This was going to be my present to Taylor and Avery, who were hooked on the stuff. It was also my bribe to prevent them from talking crap about my "vacation." I could already see it coming.

With the overfriendly sun beating down on us as we waited, we all attempted to shut our eyes for as long as we could. This was an impossible task since the flies continued to land on our faces all at once. We would swat for a while, but they never seemed to stop, because there were so many of them. They were so annoying. We all tried the first alternative of covering our faces with something, but that made us sweat more. There was no defeating the flies in Iraq. They always won.

We had among us again some Iraqi Army soldiers who were going to go out with our group. They provided entertainment for us when two of them got into an argument. We watched in amazement as these two Iraqis got in each other's face and yelled. We didn't know or care what they

were fighting about. When one of them butt-stroked the other in the head
with his AK, everything got more entertaining. I laughed pretty hard. We
all did. We decided not to step in since it seemed to be a typical soldier's
fight. No one was seriously hurt, and their own Iraqi soldiers split them
up anyway and resolved the tension.

The second wave of helicopters did not come as early as we'd expected. In fact, they didn't even come until dusk, after we had been waiting for five hours. When they did land, we hurried up and into the Black
Hawk and clipped on our seat belts.

"Wait, hold up. We're missing one," one of the men yelled to the pilots before we took back off into the sky. We all looked around to find
who was missing. We spotted an Iraqi Army soldier in the same area we
had been lounging around in all afternoon. He had his boots off and was
on a prayer mat ceremoniously praying toward the east. What timing.
Here we were, with time of the essence, and we found ourselves waiting
on this Iraqi soldier to get done with his ritual. After about twenty seconds and four bows, he picked up all his stuff, threw on his boots, ran
into our chopper, and clipped in. It was actually a pretty interesting thing
to witness.

We were now flying in complete darkness. I never really enjoyed flying at night because I couldn't see anything. This time, however, I was
sitting in the front row behind the pilots, so I just stared at all the lights
in the cockpit and was amazed. I also kept using my NODs to see exactly
what the pilots were seeing. It was an enjoyable ride.

When they finally did drop us off, we found ourselves at another
blocking position much larger than the one we had made with our company out in the desert. This was the centralized blocking position for the
battalion. The members of our company, including the "BARF," were told
to wait for another fleet of Black Hawks who were to deliver us to where
our company was located. There was nothing better than being shuffled
around from place to place.

Outside the perimeter of the dozens of trucks in the blocking position
were trenches that stretched farther than I could see in the dark. They
were probably old trenches left over from numerous wars raged in Iraq.
The guys from my company and I just plopped down in them and talked
while we waited.

The moon was out, weather was cool and perfect, and the sounds of Army activity rustled through the air. It was a good time until I picked up a certain smell. I stood up and realized I was sitting in someone's shit. I sprang out of the dark trench and cursed up a storm. Everyone else immediately did the same and anxiously checked themselves. Lucky me, I was the only one who'd been sitting right on a fresh pile. I quickly began rolling around in the dirt and drenching water on my pants, but nothing would get the smell off of me. I also didn't stop cursing. I tediously worked as fast as I could to get as much of it off as I could, but there was no escaping it. It was now a part of me. These were the only pants I had along with me too, so I had to get used to it.

The wave of Black Hawks came in to pick us up much earlier than I wanted. As we all climbed in to find our seats, the pilots decided to shut the doors on our Black Hawks. I tried to yell that that would probably be a bad idea, but they closed them and we were on our way flying through the darkness.

Within seconds of being in the air, the aroma of my fecal-stained pants filled the helicopter.

"Who shit themselves?" someone yelled. Everyone reacted with the same disgusted look on his face. I just began laughing. It was a horrible smell, but I couldn't stop laughing.

"I sat in someone's shit down in that trench," I tried to yell in the loud chopper. I kept laughing, so I doubt anyone heard my explanation.

Sadly, the ride lasted ten minutes. It was ten minutes longer than I wanted it to be because the smell soon bothered me too. When we finally landed, I was glad to fling open the doors. It was hard to distinguish where the pilots had dropped us off, other than the middle of nowhere. It was kind of an eerie feeling not knowing where we were, and there were just fifteen or so of us. We quickly formed a file line, and my smelly pants took the rear of it. We looked through our NODs and searched for any infrared flash from the rest of our platoon, who were somewhere out in the general area.

We walked a few moments until we reached a farmhouse. Walking through their yard, I was a little uneasy as to what to expect. We tried to be as quiet as possible. The moon was now shielded by clouds, which limited our visibility. I hated being in the rear of a file formation because that meant I had to provide the rear security. I found myself mostly walking backward and feeling totally alone.

"Eeeeyaaww," came from a screeching donkey within five feet to the right of me. I opened my mouth almost to scream and raised my weapon. I quickly threw up my NODs and looked with my naked eye. I kicked the ground to make the donkey move while I tried to control my nerves. That stupid animal had surprised me so much I could have choked on my own heart.

We continued our patrol for over twenty minutes, until we walked right into First Platoon. The other members of Second and Third that we walked with split away to link up with their respective platoon. I was glad to see the guys from my platoon again as I passed through the line while they were all taking a knee. I kept hearing whispers of "Is that Conklin?" or "Pretty Boy, is that you?" and of course "Hey, Chip." They each said enough for me to identify who was asking me without seeing who it was. I was glad to be back. I quickly began asking each huddled pair I passed, "Have you seen Taylor?"

"Two more down," one guy would say as I continued my journey through the dark stretched line.

"What's up, guys?" I said to the recognizable huddle of Taylor, Avery, Vinny, and Fooks.

"Where's your shit at?" Fooks unsurprisingly asked me.

"What? No how are you? Just, where's your shit at? I lost it," I sarcastically said in reply. "No, Sarnt Ledbetter ordered me to leave it back. He said we were going through the mountains and I should leave it back with Ram."

"Mountains? What mountains? We're going through the same shitty desert that we've been in. Oh wait, you were shamming and you must have forgotten," Fooks jokingly said. It didn't take him long to get the first jab in me. Taylor and Avery soon followed too.

I walked over to them once I was out of hearing distance of Fooks and Vinny. "Hey, you guys don't say shit, here are some Mountain Dews," I said as I gave them their sought-after nectar. I also informed them about my feet. They both thought it was stupid of me to return to the line. I was happy to be back.

"How is FOB Wilson?" Taylor asked me.

"It's a dump. Seriously. Don't glorify it in your head, because it sucks," I said to him.

"Conklin, get over here." Sergeant Caruso came whispering from the dark. I left Taylor and Avery to meet up with Caruso.

"What's up, sarnt?" I asked him.

"You're a rifleman now. You're gonna be with me, Ly, and McCaskill," Caruso informed me.

And so it was. I was now a rifleman and was not carrying my dreaded gear, unlike Avery. He would later drop his assault pack off in a Humvee, so he too would share in the delight of less weight.

Our entire company ended up staying in the same general area in the wide-open field. We formed a large circle with two-man teams who were spread out every ten feet. Once given the word to rest for the night, we all immediately ate whatever MRE we had left and pulled out the woobie. Guard duty was an inevitable task, so every other hour one of each pair of us was awakened to watch his sector.

My first night back with my platoon was a grueling one. The wind came out like a hurricane-type gust. It was incredibly cold while we curled up out in the open desert. There was no time to dig holes to escape the wind, so mostly we would spoon to stay warm. If your partner was on guard shift, you would just roll up in a ball, cover your whole body with your poncho liner, and lie on the edges so it didn't blow away. I used an unopened MRE for my pillow, and my assault pack helped block the wind. It was a tough night in which no one slept well. A couple times I woke up to find myself shivering uncontrollably and my poncho liner blown off of me. Thank God I'd thought ahead and tied the strings of the liner to my boots to save it in the event that the wind decided to take it, or else I doubt I would have ever seen my woobie again.

The morning of Day Five of Operation Swarmer started off windy and cold. A sensitive items check forced everyone to wake up and accept the fact that his life sucked. Once I was awake, I mingled among other members of my platoon and crowded together with them to share blankets. The closer we all got, the warmer we all got.

The Iraqi Army contingent had a different idea and started a fire. We were not allowed to start one because our chain of command wouldn't allow us, but they didn't stop the Iraqis among us. Once again, this did not make sense, so we joined their fire, and soon it was crammed with cold soldiers and it became impossible to get close enough to feel the heat. Everyone burned his MRE trash in the fire, which quickly began to smell awful. Awful enough to leave, but then I realized that my pants did not smell as bad as they had the night prior. Either I'd gotten most of it off, or I had grown used to it. Either way, no one was asking me anything, so I didn't tell them.

Around 8 A.M., we gathered all our belongings and lounged around again. We waited for a series of Black Hawks to come and pick up each individual platoon one at a time and drop them off to scattered areas that still had not been searched. This started what turned out to be a hop-and-go day. We would get dropped off, thoroughly search a home and adjacent buildings, and then we would be picked up and dropped off at the next home. We did this countless times. Enough that I was actually getting sick of being in a Black Hawk, which was rare.

At one point in the afternoon searching, our operations were interrupted when Colonel Steele and Command Sergeant Major Camacho landed right next to a farmhouse we were currently searching. Within seconds of their landing, our platoon internal radios came alive with a command of "Look sharp, Rakk-Six is here." That warning provoked us all to act more vigilant. Luckily I was in one of the houses at the time with Ly, throwing blankets and going through drawers during a search. We did, however, miss locating an AK in one of the rooms; it was wedged within a tower of blankets, and one of the squad leaders found it and blamed Ly for not locating it. Ly was the best scapegoat.

With Steele and Camacho approving what they saw of us in action, they were up and off to go interrupt someone else's search. We continued our searches of the home, which produced no further results. We then flew to the next house to do the same, and then again, and again, and again. It was tedious, boring, and lackluster.

Toward the end of the long, drawn-out evening, we came to a household that only had two young boys living in it. They came out and were so incredibly happy to see us. They immediately ran inside their courtyard and began making chai for everyone in my platoon. These two brothers were happy kids, and their chai was absolutely amazing. The younger brother, about eleven or twelve years old, was curious about our gear. I let him wear my helmet, and Sergeant Armstrong let him listen to his iPod. It was a good change of pace for the day and made everyone mellow out a bit. We soon had to move on like we always did and proceed to the next area.

With the evening coming to a close, we instead patrolled in a modified wedge with our platoon, across open desert for about a mile and a half. We got to the outskirts of a little village and decided to call it a night as the sun began to set off in the skyline.

Before the sun went down, we all wanted to make sure we didn't have a night like we'd had the one prior, so we all began hastily to dig holes. Some dug shallow holes for two, whereas others dug pits to accommodate six or so men. Either way, we all had one thing on our minds: warmth.

All of the platoons linked up with us later that evening and added to our circle security. They too dug in. Headquarters, once again, did not have to, since they were all still mounted. If there was any platoon who did the least amount of work in the company, it was Headquarters.

We had our ritual guard duty through the night. During my guard shift I could hear multitudes of wolves or dogs howling out in the dark. They continued through the night and reminded me of nights spent in the woods of Fort Benning, Georgia, when the wolves would howl at the moon. After guard shift, it was back to spooning, which made for a warmer night than the last.

When we awoke the next morning, Day Six, we were happily greeted with the news that we were calling it quits on Swarmer. Some Black Hawks were expected to be coming for us in a few hours and to eventually take us out. Everyone was excited, and all were talking about what they were going to do when they got to FOB Wilson. I tried to explain to them that they better not put much thought into it.

I started off my day with an MRE and some pain pills that I had with me for my butchered toes. It was another cold, windy morning so I wrapped myself in my blanket and headed over to Avery and Taylor's pit. Our whole patrol base was out in the middle of nowhere, within sight of a small village off in the distance, but far enough for everyone to take all his gear off and relax. Captain Lesperance was doing it, so we all did too. No questions asked.

We sat around the open desert for quite a while. Hygiene, food, and weapons maintenance was how we spent those cold few hours until our birds were expected. When they did come, we were ready and willing to hop in. We were flown to the battalion-sized blocking position where I had landed two nights prior. Now, in the middle of the afternoon, I could see that the trenches stretched across the desert. I also could now clearly see that soldiers were relieving themselves in these trenches. I made it a point to others that they shouldn't sit in them. "Duh, people shit in them" was the general consensus that everyone shot back at me. Was I the only one who didn't know? I bet they wouldn't have had they been there at night.

At the blocking position, we were reunited with all of our company's vehicles. Even my truck was back up and running. I gathered my things and sat on my vehicle. We once again were given a few hours' time before we were to head back to FOB Wilson, so we all went on a cleaning campaign and extensively cleaned all of the mounted weapons on our Humvees. They were in dire need as they looked spray-painted tan because there was so much sand stuck to them.

After the hours had passed, we finally were given clearance for the entire battalion to break down their blocking position and drive back to FOB Wilson, a distance of fifteen or so miles. It was long enough for me to fall asleep in the Humvee and make it a minute-long trip.

Once at FOB Wilson, we parked inside and prepared for our convoy back home. We did not have much time to do anything but use the bathroom. Angel Company rolled out mid-afternoon for a long drive from FOB Wilson to FOB Remagen. I was unsure how long the trip was going to take, because, like any exhausted soldier, I fell asleep in the backseat. My Humvee was way in the back of the convoy, and the chances of my truck getting hit by an IED were slim to none. Many soldiers fell asleep during long drives, just few admitted to it.

Our trip went smooth, without any IEDs to hamper our drive to FOB Remagen. It was such a welcoming sight to see the FOB again and especially our CHUs. It was equivalent to being a sixth grader gone away at camp for a week and coming home to his parents' house. We were all glad to be done "swarming."

HUMAN ALARM CLOCK AND CHAI

"Mista, chai?"

We spent the first day back meticulously cleaning all of our equipment. We cleaned and inspected, and then cleaned it all again. We then repeated it all over again. Even the Humvees got a thorough scrub-down. Most were immediately dropped off at the mechanics bay for some much-needed repairs.

As soon as the daily patrols throughout Tikrit did kick back off, I timed it right to finally go get proper care for my toe problems. I filled out a sick-call request form the day we got back, so when everyone rolled out the next day, I limped to the aid station on FOB Remagen.

Once there, I had the medics assess my toes and they were amazed I'd let it go for as long as I did. They immediately poked me with needles and began to cut vertically down the center of my big toenails and lift the inward halves out. It was a little painful, but interesting to watch. I almost had to look away at times, but nasty stuff like that interested me.

When they were done, they wrapped me up and gave me more pills. Best of all, the medics gave me a "no-boot-wearing profile." This meant that I could not wear boots for a week. No PT, no boots, and best of all, no patrols. When I came back to the CHUs, I told my truck and squad my profile and their jealousy ensued.

Over the next couple of days I spent my time sitting in the Internet room, playing guitar in my CHU, reading, or sleeping, while the rest of my platoon ran patrols in Tikrit. I really caught up on some sleep. I did try to help others who weren't as fortunate by volunteering to pull other guys' guard shifts at night or doing errands for them.

After Swarmer and before the start of April, we were really growing tired of our guard shifts at night. No other platoon in our company was using a "human alarm clock" like we were, to wake everyone up for his designated patrol on time. Only the lower enlisted of course had to do nightly guard shifts. Some slacked off and fell back asleep in bed, while others just sat in the Internet room during their shift. It was a superfluous system implemented by Quinn that we still had not eradicated. We were the only platoon on the FOB doing it. Everyone else resorted to using actual alarm clocks and their system was working just fine, without forcing the lower enlisted to stay awake for the sake of staying awake.

There's an old phrase in the Army that says "you can always add to, but never take away," so this system was never going to be relinquished. Our sergeants were too stubborn. I quickly got so fed up that I started a petition and came up with alternate ways of ensuring we all got up at the proper times.

It was not until three weeks of fighting, yelling, and pleading my case that we finally did away with the old system of the "human alarm clock" and moved to everyone having real alarm clocks. With that struggle out of the way, everyone had a chance finally to get uninterrupted sleep at night and wake up at whatever designated time we had set by utilizing actual alarm clocks. I of course was exempt from passing uninterrupted sleep because I still had Rod, the snorer from Hell, as my roommate.

High maintenance on our weapons created a need for an abundance of cleaning products. This is where my parents came in to play a crucial role. We did not have such products at our disposal, like FOB Speicher did, so we relied on being shipped supplies from loved ones back home. Like many others in my platoon and company, I received multiple packages monthly from family and friends.

Mail call was still consistently the most anticipated event of each day. It really only occurred two or three times a week. Every day we would individually wander off to Company CP and peek in the tent to see if there was mail sorted out. It was the best chore to be called upon to grab a Humvee, drive to the CP, load up all the boxes and letters, and drive back over to our LSA and distribute them.

My parents were always willing to send anything I needed to improve conditions. Q-Tips, duct tape, baby wipes, food, and green scratch pads were constantly sent. It was hard to create a surplus of such needed items because we all shared in First Platoon.

My family and friends would also always send letters and pictures. Letters like theirs served as a way to lift our spirits. They kept me updated on things back home and brought my stress level down. The pictures I received I taped to the wall near my door. After a few months I had collected quite a mural of friends and family next to my bed. I spent many hours just staring at all the pictures and thinking about the things I'd done, should have done better, and would do in the future.

After Swarmer was a thing of the past, our company was once again shafted by the 320th Field Artillery. A National Guard unit from Puerto Rico that was on our base was scheduled to redeploy home. They had the job of maintaining the prison on FOB Remagen. With their absence, it now gave way for someone to fill that role. Of course the leadership in 3/320th was not going to task out their men to do it, so the job was palmed off on my company.

As much as everyone believed the job would come down to my platoon, the detail went to Second Platoon. As bad as that sounded, at least they wouldn't ever have to worry about IEDs or patrols anymore. This also meant that more patrols would be coming the way of First and Third Platoon, to cover Second's absence. We had just recently reacquired Third Platoon after their stint of guarding the Birthday Palace, and now we were losing Second Platoon.

Privates Chief and Rojo were finally pulled from their guard tower on the FOB that our platoon had detailed to them since our arrival. In March, Rojo was picked for his rotation of R&R leave time and sent back to America. Little did we know that he would never return to our platoon. From what we were told, Rojo went AWOL as soon as he landed and fled back to Mexico. I never saw him again.

My squad was glad to have Chief back. Fooks and I took on the task to train him in preparation for combat patrolling, but no matter how much knowledge you can pass on to someone, the best way to learn is by doing.

Chief's first patrol with us was a night patrol in Kadasiyah along IED Alley. I was in the turret and he was a dismount. He did fine throughout the mission until it came time to exit the vehicle and set a cone. Behind me, I heard him fire off a round from his M4 at a car that did not stop as soon as he wanted it to.

"Chief, what the fuck are you doing?" I snapped around and quietly yelled from the turret down the road to him.

"The car wouldn't stop, but he's turning around now," he said as he keenly kept aim on the now reversed vehicle.

"All right," I said to him as I grabbed a hand mic and relayed on the radio that everything was fine. "Chief, get over here."

"What? I did what everyone else does to people who don't stop," he replied to me from underneath his NODs.

"Not that. Where the fuck is your gear?" I said to him, trying to hold back laughter. Chief had forgotten to put his equipment on before exiting and had left it inside the truck. He was wearing his helmet, weapon, and vest, but had he gotten into a gunfight, his magazine pouches were at my feet inside the Humvee. Luckily, it was dark out and no one saw his mistake. It was quite comical and something I never forgot when it came to joking with him.

During that same patrol, another scene occurred that will live with me forever. As the dismounted patrol was off inside some residential homes, the others like me left in the trucks had to hang outside. Our four vehicles were far enough from the road and blended into the unlit neighborhood that I wouldn't have doubted if no one even knew we were there.

While I chatted with Taylor, the driver, I heard a soft voice near my vehicle. I thought it might be Chief asking for guidance, but I turned around and was surprised to see a little girl standing there.

"*Ah salam ay lakem,*" I responded with their customary greetings.

The girl had her arms filled with a tray of numerous small cups and saucers filled with homemade chai.

"Mista, chai?" she said.

From the turret I gestured over the side of the Humvee my thankfulness by putting my right hand on my heart and nodding in approval.

Simultaneously, I kicked Taylor down below me and asked him to grab what she was offering.

Taylor exited the driver's seat and took two cups off the tray before returning back inside the Humvee. I crouched down to take hold of the cup and saucer. Before I stood back up again, the little girl was gone. She had already moved on to one of the other Humvees to pass on her good gesture.

I can specifically remember each and every cup of chai I ever drank and how sweet it tasted. That night was no exception. Taylor and I both enjoyed our cups in reflective silence. It was a nice cool night; the moon illuminated my tilted machine gun muzzle, and I stood tall and leaned my back against the open hatch of my turret and enjoyed a cup of the sweetest, warmest chai. It wasn't long before Taylor popped me out of my relaxation bubble and ruined the moment.

"You know what I was thinking?" he stated rhetorically. "What if they poisoned this chai? They could wipe out a whole platoon right now."

"They're not that smart," I said back with a laugh. "Besides, it tastes so good that even if it was poisoned, I'd have to ask for seconds."

PARTY POOPER

"You all right, man?"

When we were off from a patrol, my close circle of buddies would usually congregate in Avery and Taylor's CHU and watch haji copies of American television shows. We would also steal someone's handheld radio and listen to what our leaders in our platoon said so we could monitor for any upcoming details. When we heard of a detail needing to be formed to do some undesirable chore, we would immediately lock the door, then turn out the lights and wait it out. If someone could not be found when a detail was being made, the sergeant in charge would just go find someone else. It was another tactic we devised that got us out of doing stupid crap.

With the little downtime we got, I started to set aside some of it to respond more to the letters I received in the mail, which stacked up from a lack of response on my behalf. People would always inquire as to what I needed and if they could send me anything. I always felt guilty when I asked for things, so I usually just told them letters were sufficient. If I really needed something, my parents would always send it.

One thing I never asked for, mostly because I was fearful of the sender getting caught, was alcohol. Some people in my platoon were getting frequent shipments of alcohol in their care packages from friends back home. They would be creative about it and get it shipped in salad dressing containers, Pringles cans, or best of all, brown Listerine bottles. Once in a blue moon did any of them ever share, but about three times during our deployment, and we made certain that we were not on QRF duty, we got a little buzzed.

With my luck, I knew it would backfire somehow. One night in March, we had just come off a mission. We were not on QRF duty so we retreated to our CHUs for the night. I went over to Avery's room, where he and Taylor hooked me up with a few drinks. We took some shots, played music, and talked about how bad we wanted to be out of Iraq.

I was getting a good buzz going and soon started to get a little drunk. We all did. Then a knock came on the CHU. We immediately stashed the drinks like underage kids in a college dorm and flung open the door. It was Hilmo.

"Hey, guys, get your stuff out to the truck immediately, except for Avery, you're off for the night." Hilmo spoke reluctantly, with his normal disgruntled face.

"You're kidding, right?" Taylor asked, straight-faced.

"I wish I was. We are supposed to be going out on some time-sensitive target with Third Platoon," Hilmo said.

"What the fuck? We're not even on QRF!" I yelled. My buzz was quickly sobering up.

"You know the LT. He can't say no to a mission," Hilmo jokingly said. "But hurry up 'cause we could be leaving shortly. Taylor, you're gunning. Conklin, you're driving. Avery, you're off for this mission," Hilmo finished and then took off.

Avery, Taylor, and I just stared blank-faced at each other. Avery broke the silence by laughing hysterically into his pillow. Taylor and I looked at each other.

"Dude, I'm fucking drunk," he said to me as he broke into laughter.

"*Hello!* I'm shit-faced, and I'm driving!" I yelled back. The three of us then broke out into unison laughter. Taylor immediately started throwing his gear on and I stumbled out of Avery's CHU. I could hear Avery's laughter continue as I stumbled back to my own CHU.

I threw open the door and tripped over the door frame, which sent me onto the floor. I looked to my left and could see Rod lying on his bed.

"You all right, man?" he asked casually and smiled.

"Yeah, I'm great. Just admiring the floor," I jokingly replied.

"Do you have to go out on that mission?" Rod asked.

"Yeah, and I'm drunk. This is not gonna be good," I said as I pulled myself up and gathered my equipment. I hastily grabbed as much of my gear as I could and ran out to my Humvee, which was parked near the CP. I dumped everything in the driver's seat and drove it over to our CHUs. I kept slapping myself and squinting, attempting anything to sober up. Once I'd parked the vehicle, I ran through the motions of checking the fluid levels and washing the windows.

"Ain't this some shit now, huh?" Reese said to me as he hopped in and started testing the radios.

"You're not gonna believe this. Well, you know me, so you probably will, but I'm drunk and I need a miracle that this mission gets cancelled," I pleaded with him.

"Yeah, I can smell you," Reese replied.

"Shit! Do you have gum? I'm gonna slam a Gatorade. Oh shit," I said, all paranoid. At this time, Taylor stumbled over and poured his gear on the roof of the Humvee. We both looked at each other and again broke into laughter.

"Oh man, you too, Taylor?" Reese asked.

"Yup," Taylor said.

"I love you guys," he said as we all broke into laughter.

Soon after the truck was all loaded up and ready to go, a call came over the radio which notified us to be on standby. Something had happened outside my control, and now our spontaneous mission was on standby. I immediately jumped for joy. A guard roster was initiated, and we all retreated back to our CHUs and played the waiting game.

Luckily for me and the rest of the platoon, the mission was scrubbed. Whatever Third Platoon might have needed us for was nixed. Taylor and I could not have been happier. We slept so well that night.

Drinking in Iraq was something that existed, but it never was a problem. It was rare when it happened, but I knew tons of people who did it. You could even look at the top of the sand-filled Hesco barriers and find beer bottles from even before we moved there. I'm even pretty sure some guys in Third Platoon brewed their own beer in one of the CHUs. No one really got busted for booze in our platoon, except for our scapegoat, Ly, who was caught drunk in his CHU by a squad leader who wasn't even his. Ly kind of brought it on himself by just barely hiding his Jack Daniel's bottle behind a Hulk Hogan plush doll. It prompted a thorough inspection from the platoon sergeant, of each and every person's CHU. Those smart about it never got caught, but they still did it rarely. Most of the time I did not even know when those closest to me had a stash.

MY TWENTY-FIRST BIRTHDAY

"This was my treasure chest."

With the end of March approaching, I wanted more and more to be home. Not only did I generally want to be home, but I had an important time in my life approaching. I was twenty years old, and on April Fools' Day, I would turn twenty-one—finally legal to drink in a bar. Unfortunately, I was two-and-a-half years into serving my country and was living in a combat zone, and I found it odd that until then I was still not allowed to drink alcohol in the States. A law that I hope will be changed in my lifetime.

As the day grew closer and the patrols got dumber, I was really getting depressed about spending my twenty-first birthday away from home. I had always heard stories from my buddies about how awesome and exciting their turning of legal age was. I always pictured myself drunk in a bar, halfway propped on a stool, preparing to hug a toilet. Thanks to Uncle Sam, I was now going to see that milestone come and go as just another day of patrolling in Iraq. So goes the story of my life.

On March 28 during one of our nightly meetings, an order came down to us to prepare for another air assault mission in the desert far out to our west. Everything began to transpire just as it had for Swarmer a few weeks prior. We did not know how long we were going to be out, but one day was long enough for me. Sadly, Fooks and Vinny were in the U.S. on their R&R vacations and Poston was back in charge. This made Avery and Taylor Gun 1, and left Chief and me on Gun 2. Being the more experienced one on the team, I was going to be the gunner this time and lug around the M240B instead of excessive amounts of ammunition and the AG bag like I was used to.

We were told very little leading up to the mission, and we had it scheduled for the next day. We cancelled our mission on the 29th in Tikrit to focus on preparation for the upcoming air assault. Chief and I ran through crew drills to demonstrate to Poston that we could execute together as an efficient gun team.

The day before our launch date gave us time to check and double-check that we all had our proper equipment and supplies. The line squads were going through multiple practice raids while our two gun teams kept rehearsing crew drills for putting the machine gun in operation. Poston had us running up and down the desert sands of FOB Remagen, and our only relief came from the light drizzle, the first appearance of rain since the season ended earlier that month.

As the new raid was scheduled for March 30, it was set in stone that I would be celebrating my twenty-first birthday out in the desert, sweating my ass off during the day and sleeping in a freezing hole at night. The story of my life continued.

The night before we left we decided to call in our Iraqi Army contingent from the Birthday Palace and have them drive into FOB Remagen. Trust was still an issue between our two forces, so they had no idea what they were about to do. We kept them on our FOB for the night and housed them all in our QRF tent. We had men throughout our company keep an eye on them and make sure all of them kept corralled. That night, they were informed that they would be joining our company in another air assault raid the following day.

I was pretty sure that this "big" mission, as it was hyped up to be, was a stab from 3/320th at a large-scale mission. Most of them had been left out of Swarmer because Colonel Steele stuck with the infantry grunts to handle the business while 3/320th Field Artillery stayed behind to watch Tikrit for us. Now they had formulated a mission to include their battalion with us as support. I saw it as a "whose nuts are bigger" quarrel. Either way, we knew who was better and we didn't need them to try to show us up. This was some sort of continuation mission to Operation Red Light that we had done a few weeks before Swarmer. Operation Red Light II was now about to kick off.

As the sun rose like a red fireball on the morning of the 30th, so too did our entire FOB come alive. Soldiers poured out of their CHUs with equipment stacked like hitchhikers', ready for another air assault raid. I traded my M4 for a 9mm and strapped it on my right leg. I didn't need my M4 since I was hauling the big gun. I grabbed my assault pack and threw my M240B gun over my back in order to spread the weight across my shoulders, and I held it steady with both hands. My platoon walked over to the airfield just like we had for Swarmer a couple weeks ago, but this time I was carrying less weight.

While we waited for the helicopters to come, we were accompanied by the presence of our Iraqi Army contingent. Poorly clad in their Desert Storm–era uniforms, AK47s, helmets, and blankets, they were already complaining of carrying too much equipment. They had to have had a hundred pounds less weight than the lightest American soldier, yet they declined to help us out, refusing to carry even something as light as a shovel. After a few arguments and close calls with beat-downs, we had to give in and carry the extra equipment while the Iraqi soldiers only carried their blankets. That set the tone right there for their approval rating.

As the wave of choppers arrived, which was not as massive as the Swarmer entourage, we prepared to load up. My chalk was to be QRF for First Platoon, who were flying out minutes prior to my helicopter. The eight of us were the equivalent of a small version of the BARF, which had left earlier in the morning while we prepared to drive around the sky and drop when requested.

The initial assault element loaded up in their wave of helicopters. This included my company, along with the entire two companies of 3/320th Field Artillery. All of the birds were going to different sites to surprise the homes and search them. Angel Company and the troop units of the Field Artillery also had selected sites of interest to arrest certain people for past crimes.

As the rest of the soldiers climbed into their respective Black Hawks and Chinook helicopters, my chalk did the same. We all lifted up at the same time, but instead of the massive attack formation we had with Swarmer, we all went our separate directions out into the western desert between FOB Remagen and FOB Speicher.

My helicopter had only men from First Platoon, about twelve in strength, with only my gun team as the heavy weapons team. Poston was with us to keep an eye on us, though Chief and I knew just what we were doing. We flew around solo for a while and monitored the progress of all units scattered about the desert at separate farm areas.

We heard news that First Platoon had hit their target, a known terrorist hideout, at full surprise. They immediately arrested all the males of the house and received no contact, so we kept on flying around the skies. The pilots would have kept flying all day, but those of us who were passengers on the bird were growing bored with the endless flight. We wanted to do something, so our platoon sergeant called up to the pilots and told them to land at the nearest farm.

The pilots lowered to the ground and we poured out of the Black Hawk in a nicely trained fashion. As everyone tactically and efficiently moved up to the house to search it, I scouted out the area with the highest peak, which mostly was a pile of dirt. The desert was so flat that when the assaulting element was inside searching the house behind me, Chief and I were in the prone position and could move our heads around and watch 360 degrees.

Nothing was found at the first home and no one called for QRF assistance, so we called the Black Hawk back and loaded back up for some more flying time. We flew for a few minutes before we all got antsy again and called up to be dropped off. I started to have flashbacks of the daily "drop and go's" we did during Swarmer, but none of us really wanted to be flying in a Black Hawk all day. We needed to stretch our legs.

We did not have anything better to do so we kept dropping and searching random farmhouses out of boredom. Each time, Chief and I would land and look for a good spot, then plop down and wait for the others to get done searching. Each time we lay down together, we would just spark into random conversations, mostly about music, movies, or anything but what we were doing.

After a few drop and go's, we all decided to just leave our assault packs on the helicopter. This helped out greatly because all of us could move more efficiently and quicker. One time we got off the bird and I looked back and saw that the last man out had forgotten to shut the door. The helicopter lifted off and I said a small prayer in my head that the bags remained in their place until it returned to pick us up. Thankfully, they did.

Sometimes during our spontaneous raids we switched it up and landed our helicopter right in front of driving cars out in the middle of nowhere and did flash searches. Each time we turned up nothing, but it was worth a try. Even if it was a terrorist and he was clean on that day, he would probably think twice the next time he loaded his car up with munitions, knowing that U.S. soldiers land helicopters in front of moving cars.

We continued our searches until we grew tired of coming up dry, finding nothing but good honest farmers out in the boonies doing no harm to anyone. We just told the pilots to fly around. We ended up flying a total of almost three hours in that Black Hawk. I kept dozing off in my seat until I looked around and saw that the entire squad was asleep, including Poston and Crisostomo. So I gave in to the sleep monster and slept too.

Around 11:00 A.M., we were woken up by the pilots and notified that they were going to drop us off for good with the rest of our platoon. We landed fifty yards from the target building of First Platoon. As I walked off the bird, Poston told Chief and me to grab some shade and take a break. The rest of the platoon was scattered around the compound pulling security, including Avery and Taylor's gun on the roof of the house.

Chief and I walked over under a tree with an adequate amount of shade. I grabbed an MRE out of my assault pack and watched a scene transpire that I doubt I'll ever forget. It was a scene I had seen before in war movies and never felt bad for, but this one was different. It was real.

As my buddies were handcuffing the main suspect we'd come for, they displayed in front of him multiple insurgent propaganda papers and DVDs that they had found inside the house. The DVDs were compilations of IED attacks and sniper shots on American soldiers. These recordings were outlawed and possession of them was punishable by arrest. The suspect also had a few too many AKs than one household could own.

But what got my attention more was that this man had a family outside with him. His wife wept uncontrollably, and we later made her go inside with her two small kids. The oldest of the man's children, a boy about ten, came back out and wept for his father. I could see the heartache in the man's eyes. It was the first time in my deployment that I didn't know who to sympathize with. I knew this man had done wrong and we were going to execute our order. I also knew that this man needed to provide for his family with an income, and since the fall of their government, most Iraqis could not find work, and insurgent activity brought a quick and easy lump sum of money that was awfully enticing.

As the kid kept crying and calling out for his father, while we took pictures of everything, one of the Iraqi Army soldiers stepped up in a big way. He took the boy aside and talked to him. He helped the boy get control of his emotions and stop crying. The soldier took the boy inside and stayed with him. It was the first time I saw real compassion displayed from an Iraqi to a fellow countryman, a stranger in a time of need.

I pondered to myself and openly talked with Chief about what was happening while we sat and ate our deliciously disgusting MREs. After having our turn in the shade, we relieved other guys in our platoon who were baking out in the sun. We drew them back, and Chief and I went to the rear of the house and propped ourselves against the wall to stare off into the desolate desert.

Now there were other men in the house who also were arrested. Luckily for us, we had linked them to other terrorists we had been looking for during Swarmer's raids. These men's cell phones showed frequent contact that linked them to many different terrorist cells in the area of Tikrit and Samarra. During this roundup, one of the detainees decided to pass out. Whether he was faking it or not, Doc immediately administered an IV of fluid into his system and he awoke to realize he was still flex-cuffed.

We waited for First Platoon to finish their investigation and for the cue to move on to the next target. We were again graced by the presence of the "sham-tastic" Headquarters Platoon and their Humvees. We let them pull outer cordon security while our platoon moved inside the house compound walls to relax. Now, when we were given the cue to relax, the Iraqi Army First Sergeant Kobe took it to the limit.

Instead of waiting around for our leadership to get their paperwork straight, he stripped down to his underwear and frolicked in the farm owners' well. There was built-up water in their stream, and the well was pumping more water out. Soon, other Iraqi Army soldiers followed their commander in shredding their uniforms and enjoying an afternoon bath.

We all got a good laugh out of it. Deep down, we all were thinking the same thing: We too wanted to strip down and jump in the water. The heat was at its slaughtering level, which it usually was at high noon, and all anyone wanted to do was jump in that water to cool off.

As bad as we wanted to, though, we refrained and kept our uniforms on. Helmets, gloves, vest, the whole shebang. After the Iraqi soldiers were satisfied, they hopped out and let the sun dry them off. Unlike in America, they were bone dry in less than three minutes. They put their uniforms back on and returned to duty. This meant that they all plopped down in a group circle and yelled at each other.

Once Captain Lesperance and Lieutenant Scher were satisfied with the capture, they loaded the men in Headquarters Platoon's Humvee and left the scene. We returned to the bare essentials of First Platoon with Iraqi Army attachments. The order was given to pack up and go, so we all prepared to move on for a good old-fashioned platoon foot patrol through the open desert.

Preparation for a foot patrol meant I went through my second-nature motions of getting ready to walk. I strapped my 9mm to my thigh, tightened my vest, canted my helmet, blew the sand off of my sunglasses, pushed my knee pads down to my ankles, threw on my assault pack, tightened my gloves, draped my M240B on my shoulders, and the last step was to let out a sympathetic sigh of depression.

We moved out in a textbook wedge formation, with First Squad first and Gun 1, then Second Squad, followed by Third Squad and finally my gun team. We walked straight from the initial target house to the next house on the horizon. We marched through thick clumps of freshly churned farm dust, what locals surprisingly called soil. Beads of sweat poured down my face like rain as we moved forward. With the occasional pause, we all took a knee and faced out.

When we finally reached the closest building, we went through the same steps we routinely did. Within fifty feet, First Squad rushed ahead and broke formation to enter the main house. Second Squad followed close behind with Gun 1 and headed for high ground on one end of the house. As Gun 2, Chief and I went opposite their lead.

Once the house was under control, Poston pulled both gun teams to post on the roof. This was the last place I wanted to be in that heat, but we met Avery and Taylor inside, and both their gun team and mine tried to maneuver in the thin and poorly constructed stairway that had to have been built by a small child. Despite the craftsmanship, we all made it to the roof, where we could feel the temperature rise.

It was a small roof, but both gun teams were on there. I did not mind because it meant I was close enough to hold "bitching sessions" with Taylor and Avery, the support I needed when things got tough. I knew things were sucking just as bad for them as me. Like always, misery loved company.

We stood on that roof looking out at nothing but smooth barren desert for over an hour. Every ten minutes we let the man who was not shouldering the gun squat down and take a break. Every minute it seemed that one of us would remind the others to not lock out their knees, to prevent passing out.

"But why not? It'll get me out of here if I pass out," Taylor said.

"No. Doc would just stick an IV up your ass, and we'd still keep you here." Avery always was the first to bring us back to the harsh reality.

Once the all clear was given, we were more than happy to break down and head downstairs. When I got outside, I saw the entire line squads of my platoon sprawled out in the shade and eating home-grown cucumbers from the house. The kicker was that they bitched about sitting around with nothing to do. I reminded them that they had that luxury courtesy of Weapons Squad, who'd pulled security for them. I still didn't get a cucumber to eat either. Bastards.

We formed up for another patrol and headed back where we had just come from. We walked back half a mile to the initial house and picked up where we'd left off. As the sergeants and Lieutenant Scher debated our route of travel, Chief and I found our old spot on the backside of the initial target building and sat back down.

Loose sheep kept walking around the house, and some were so curious that they would come within a couple feet of us. There were others that did not look that healthy and also looked mentally retarded. I don't know about you, but to me a cross-eyed sheep is pretty funny. Horrible as it may sound, you have to remember that, based on the lack of humorous events within a year in Iraq, the littlest things became comical.

I found alternative ways of entertaining myself by throwing rocks at Iraqi Army soldiers who incessantly kept falling asleep. If we were ever caught sleeping during patrols, the punishment would be strenuous "smoking" sessions where we would have to exercise until we practically collapsed. The IA on the other hand were pretty much left to do as they pleased. Through their eyes, we ran the show. They were just along for the ride. I took care of that by making it my job to throw rocks at any IA soldier I caught sleeping. I perfected my art while we waited at this house. From twenty feet away, I noticed one IA soldier spread-eagled in the shade, sleeping away. I got Chief's attention as I grabbed a rock and launched it in the narcoleptic Iraqi's direction. The rock drilled this guy in the neck. To my surprise, he didn't even move. I was now really pissed that he could be so relaxed and deep in sleep that a rock in the neck did not disturb him. As I reached for a heavier rock, one of the guys in my squad signaled for me to stop because I was being looked at by some sergeants in my platoon. Like a kid whose parents are giving him a displeased look, I dropped the rock and shifted my attention to gazing out into the nothing land known as the desert.

Before the sun set in the west, Poston decided to put Gun 1 up on the roof. He initiated a guard plan that rotated every thirty minutes with a pair of soldiers manning the gun, which was equipped with thermal devices. That became our only security element for the night. The best thing whenever Weapons Squad started a roster was that it usually meant the rotation would not regenerate and stick us with another shift somewhere in the early morning.

The order was given that we would stay put at this farmhouse for the night and resume foot patrolling of the desert in the morning. Chief and I got a guard shift in just as the sun was fading off in the west, which created yet another stunning orange sky that bounced off the desert sand. Postcard-worthy every night.

No one had the energy that night to dig holes to sleep in. The wind was nothing compared to the likes of Swarmer. I brushed around dirt and kicked rocks away to find a suitable place to call my bed, and finally nestled down for the night on the ground about thirty feet from my Humvee. Behind me, I could hear the Iraqi Army soldiers chowing down on some home-cooked whatever-they-eat, prepared by the wife of the man we took into custody earlier in the day. They put a lot of trust in that woman, but all was fine. They just squatted around a giant platter of pita bread and green, yellow, and red stuff and went at it. I turned over and for a while by myself looked up at the sky littered with stars. You'll never see a night sky in America like the ones over the open desert of Iraq. Shooting stars sprinkled through the sky like spilled glitter. After admiring the sky for a while, I pulled my black wool hat over my eyes and threw my poncho liner over my head and tried to sleep.

I did not have a sound night of sleep as the cold factor still chilled my bones through the desert at night. I woke up at 6 A.M., just as the sun was waking up with me. As I looked at my watch, the cold, hard reality of the day hit me. Simultaneously, Sergeant Pitchford, the closest guy near my location, walked up to me.

"Happy birthday, Conklin." Pitchford spoke in a smart-ass tone while he brushed his teeth.

It hit me like a ton of bricks that it was my birthday. I was now twenty-one, finally legal to drink in America, and here I was waking up covered in dust and dirt from sleeping on the desert ground and eating an MRE in a foreign country I hated. Oh, how I loathed deployment. The news of my twenty-first birthday spread like the topic of the day in my platoon. Every time someone wished me a happy birthday, I gave them a sarcastic but stern "fuck you" in return.

After the platoon tucked away their woobies and buried their MRE trash, we grudgingly donned our equipment and gathered in the courtyard of the house. Lieutenant Scher gave a rundown of the direction of travel and stated that we did not have any more actual targets. We planned on marching to a farmhouse, searching it, and then looking for another house close by, and so on until 3/320th's commander was sufficiently satisfied with his troop's progress to call the mission off and return to FOB Remagen.

News came to us that no one in the broader operation had found a thing yet. No caches were found by any unit at any location. This just made the task of searching more daunting and boring.

We formed up in the same platoon wedge formation we always did and proceeded to walk in the opposite direction to where we'd gone the day prior. The closest home was about a thousand meters away or, in military terms, a click away. It was a picturesque patrol, as we all looked like we were in a scene from a war movie. As we got closer to the farmhouse, we had to trek through a large pasture of deep green onions. The aroma of fresh onions permeated the air around me as if I were cutting open a sack full of them. The change of scenery was much different than the desert we were so used to patrolling. It reminded me of Vietnam patrols through rice paddies that I had seen in movies and photos.

Once we were in the depths of the pasture, we closed up our intervals some so we would not be so spread out in something so thick. Out of the blue, an Apache helicopter with two cocky pilots soared above us and stuck with us during our trek. They were always the best boost of confidence and we always felt almost impregnable when they were around.

Instead of draping the sling of the heavy gun which rubbed down my shoulders, I again threw my 240 up over my shoulders and continued pushing forward with our patrol. I could now see the guys at the end of the pasture coming to a halt and the farmhouse on that same horizon. First Squad was closest, with Gun 1, and they proceeded to break off and form a stack as they prepared to enter. We all picked up the pace as the line squads broke off and formed into stacks and the two gun teams went off on our own.

There was no way anyone could miss the giant natural dirt pile that loomed next to the house which we had used as a landmark as we drew closer. I decided that that would be the location of my gun, and I informed Chief of my plans, about which he was just not thrilled. Nothing really ever thrilled him. Some of us had nicknamed him "The Moper" since he always looked like he was about two seconds away from suicide.

We trudged up that hill, which proved to be a lot tougher than I'd anticipated. After we fought to climb up that hill, sometimes on hands and knees, with the enormous M240B slung across my back, we eventually made it to the top. We had stadium seating on that tall, pyramidlike dirt pile. We could watch what seemed like an eternity of desert. Down below, we watched our platoon as they wandered around doing their searches.

Though the weight was always an issue in Weapons Squad during patrols, I would not have wanted to be in any other squad during these types of raids. Once the interior of the house was searched, they all grabbed shovels and metal detectors and meticulously scoured the surroundings for anything that beeped on the detector. They did this at every house we came by. Chief and I really got a kick out of it as we tried to pick out the most sad and depressing expressions on the line squads' faces. Monitoring Sergeant Adams, I was convinced that he never really looked for anything. I'm pretty sure he was looking for a gym or at the very least some dumbbells.

After being on that dirt mound for over an hour, I noticed everyone seemed to be packing it up from this location. Chief and I moseyed on down the pile and reunited with the platoon. We formed up to go to the next home spotted, which was less than six hundred meters away.

As we got closer to that house, the same procedures took effect. The terrain was flat as compared to the last house, but as with most farmhouses, there were multiple dirt berms littering the property. We found a bump in the ground and lay there while the platoon searched the area.

Every now and then I would turn around to see the progress of the searching. This farmhouse we had come to happened to be abandoned. After about forty-five minutes, I noticed Avery walking my way.

"Avery, what are you doing? Where's your gun?" I asked him.

"I left it up there. I think we're going to be here awhile," he informed me.

"Why's that?" Chief asked him.

"Some of the guys found a grenade and some AK rounds in this abandoned house," Avery told us. He went on to describe the details.

After one of the squads had done an interior check of the empty home, someone had found a lone grenade. This set off a frenzy and reenergized the searching.

It was a one-room square house, so it didn't take long to look through all the garbage. Soon, one of the guys pulled an anti-tank mine out from a bag. They immediately called people inside as they carefully sifted through more garbage. After thirty or so of these mines were pulled out and neatly stacked outside, they notified Headquarters, and they promptly arrived in multiple vehicles.

With the influx of 3/320th Humvees in the area, we broke down our security and I became a curious onlooker. Then, like a rapid news feed, Sergeant Walters came over the radio and demanded people come to his location. He was with other Third Squad members in a large dirt mound about a hundred yards from the house. He had been using his metal detector when multiple beeps sounded. A sound no one had ever heard while using the detector.

Within seconds, Third Squad and others pulled out their entrenching tools and hastily began to dig. The sight of plastic garbage bags soon began to surface. I noticed an Iraqi soldier standing idle with a shovel and I immediately put my gear down and took his shovel from him and joined in on the dig. The bags we pulled were filled with wires and blasting caps. We knew we were on to something.

We kept digging all around the area and soon found what we had always been dreaming of finding. We pulled artillery shell after artillery shell from the ground. A treasure trove of rockets, grenades, land mines, RPG rounds, mortars, IED building materials, and cases of AK47 rounds were being pulled out by my platoon by the bucket load.

Joyous shouts of celebration and elation ran through the ranks of First Platoon. Everyone soon put down his rifle, took his helmet, vest, and shirt off, and began joining in the festivities. The Iraqi Army soldiers got in a group circle and began to sing and dance around the arsenal we were pulling from the dirt. Everyone again said, "happy birthday" to me, and this time it was returned with a genuine "thank you."

Thousands of feet of detonation cord, over forty anti-tank mines, and countless rockets were pulled by me and my platoon from the earth. It was amazing. I hardly noticed how badly I was sweating because I was working so hard that my adrenaline rush hindered me from noticing or caring.

We didn't stop here either. As soon as we figured out this much carnage could be hidden in this dirt berm, we decided to check all of the dirt berms around the area. Soon, news came from a neighboring dirt mound, from guys in First Squad who had found another sizable cache there. As soon as the first cache site had been sifted through and approved, we sprinted over to the next one.

All along the side of this hill were artillery shells buried lightly in the walls of this hill in rapid succession —155mm, 130mm, and 105mm shells were now being lined up in row after row. After one hundred of these, we stopped counting. Every time I pulled a shell out of the ground I would think to myself, *This is one less IED that could kill someone.* That's how we all felt about this. Finally, we were thwarting the terrorists' potential. Finally, we felt like we were doing something good in Iraq.

It seemed the day could not get any better, but then news came in from the opposite side of the farm that from the freshly tilled farmland, men from my platoon had pulled several hefty South African 155mm shells. News spread quickly, and soon Headquarters Platoon drove to our site and began with the multiple excavation sites. The field artillery command staff showed up and were elated. It dawned on me that their attempt at this mission had been intended to give their field artillerists the main effort, but they'd all come up dry. The only positive achievement was accomplished by my platoon, the infantry attachments.

While everyone was scattered across the farmlands and occupied pulling caches out of multiple sites, a couple of us headed back to the initial house where this all started. Sergeant Walters, Avery, Chief, and I were to meet EOD there and load up the mines that were located in the house. While we waited around, we were told that EOD would be coming just to blow the house itself up. So instead of walking back to this house in vain, we decided to celebrate and blow off a little steam by testing the craftsmanship of whoever had built this house and the walls that outlined the property.

The four of us lined up like an offensive line in football. On the count of three, we all charged the wall that surrounded the house. It did not take much effort before that wall bowed forward and crashed on the ground. We loved it. We loved it so much we did it for the three remaining walls that surrounded the house. The longer ones we had to split in half as we pushed them over, but in the end they all fell. It was great taking a little aggression out and being destructive. It really brought out the little kid inside of us. The house was then rigged to be blown up with all of the mines still inside.

We all headed back to the farm field that was the site of one of the large caches. There were so many people pulling things out that there was hardly any room to squeeze in and help. For once, there was a waiting line to use the metal detectors. Everyone wanted to be "that guy" who found the next large dump site, and there were many "that guys," so many that everyone was finding things buried all across the yard by himself.

We dug all afternoon and pulled hundreds of munitions out of the ground. If I'd made the decisions, I would have stayed there forever because I didn't want that feeling to disappear. It was just so great to see our hard work finally become rewarding.

In life, everyone has said he would love to find buried treasure. This was my treasure chest, and I had no problem digging on my hands and knees to pull this treasure out. I do remember getting ahead of myself once as I was digging in the field. I came to a plastic bag filled with something. As I yanked it out of the ground, the bag ripped and out fell numerous land mines. I froze in my tracks and stared at what had just happened. I then slowly lowered the bag and stood up. I still had a deer-in-the-headlights look on my face as I gingerly backed up. I decided I was going to let someone who had more knowledge than I did and was not so reckless handle these mines.

The cocky Apache helicopter from earlier in the day returned and gave numerous flyovers of our caches. Each time he would swoop in and shake his bird to signify a job well done. We always would return the gesture by screaming and waving back up at him.

As it got near evening time, the threat of darkness loomed. The initial fervor began to slow down, and it seemed that we had almost pulled all that could have been found in the area. EOD was already stacking the multiple caches into two separate dumps and slapping C4 on them to prepare them for demolition.

I cannot give a total amount as to what we found that day. After one hundred artillery shells, countless coils of detonation cord, and seventy South African 155mm rounds, everyone lost track. It was just too much. We called it quits when we started to feel satisfied we'd found what had loomed beneath the earth's surface.

EOD had everything rigged for the first cache and we all retreated a bit from the site. As they pulled out their detonator, which looked similar to a child's controller for a remote-control car, everyone kept a keen eye out.

"Hey, it's Conklin's twenty-first birthday," someone in my platoon shouted. Soon, everyone echoed the same thing and then broke out into the traditional "Happy Birthday" song. I got pretty embarrassed but found it amusing. The EOD guy came over to me with the controller and asked if I would like to do the honors. This floored me and I instantly turned into a child on Christmas.

Everyone broke into a round of applause as the EOD technician ran me through the steps of setting it off. My platoon gathered around me as I prepared to blow up the cache. A number of guys pulled out cameras and found a good viewing spot, and then it all came down to me.

"Five, four, three, fuck, you," I counted down and pressed the trigger. The EOD technician had not informed me that there would be a delay, and I instantly thought I had done something wrong.

"Aw, Conklin, you broke it," said Sunny to break the silence.

BOOOOOM! came the sound and sight of the now enormous mushroom cloud explosion as it rocked over the earth. It was the largest explosion I had ever seen or heard. Cheers and celebration again erupted through the ranks. Handshakes and high fives were being exchanged by everyone. Birthday greetings were again said to me. Everyone was in such a good mood. I even wrestled Lieutenant Scher out of playful fun. It seemed that on this day, there was no animosity between anyone. I even gave high fives to Poston, Ram, and Adams. For that moment in time it was like we were not even at war. Our gear was off, helmets and weapons were set on the ground. It felt like we were all back at Fort Campbell finishing up a field training exercise. For that small sliver in time, we were all back home. It was a great feeling.

As EOD rigged the next cache up, we were told that a Chinook was on its way to pick up the first half of our platoon. The other half would stay and blow up the next cache and then drive back in the Headquarters Platoon vehicles. I was informed that I would be on the Chinook, which made me even happier.

As the Chinook was spotted in the distant horizon, my platoon sergeant tossed me a smoke grenade and told me to throw it to make it easier for the pilots to navigate where to land. I gladly took the grenade, put my gear on the ground, pulled the pin, and launched the grenade out a bit from our location.

Smoke billowed out of the little canister as the chopper grew close and landed nearby us in the open desert. We all grabbed our gear and walked into the back of the Chinook. It was the first time I'd ever walked to a helicopter, because we had always been trained to sprint in and out. But for today, we were badasses. At least we felt like it. We were going to take our time getting into the Chinook.

I was one of the last ones in, so I sat in the back and had a good visual over the farmlands we had scoured through all day. It was a beautiful sight as we flew over and away. On the short trip back to FOB Remagen I kept replaying the series of events that had transpired over the course of the day. What had seemed destined to be an uneventful way to celebrate my twenty-first birthday had proved to be far better than anything I could have ever imagined. I never would have to worry about hearing other people's twenty-first birthday stories and feeling left out. I now had a story of my own.

No twenty-first birthday would be complete without drinking alcohol. When I'd gotten off the Chinook and walked back to my CHU, I got out of my uniform and into a pair of shorts. I prepared to head to the Internet room, where I was more than elated to send an e-mail to my parents to inform them about my wonderful birthday.

Before I left, Chief came into my CHU to give me one last present.

"A twenty-first birthday isn't complete without a shot of whiskey," he said as he handed me a Gatorade bottle with something other than Gatorade in it. I drank the beverage and thanked him immensely. Everything was now complete. My twenty-first birthday became historic. I will never forget that day.

TINY CHANGES

"It just began to piss us off because all we ever wanted was results."

When promotions came around, they always seemed to shift how we operated as a platoon. A handful of specialists in First Platoon were promoted to sergeant. We now had an influx of sergeants, which meant fewer specialists and privates. More importantly, it meant specialists would be treated more like privates when it came to stupid details and duties. My squad leader tried to convince Avery, Taylor, and me that we were next at becoming sergeants. We reacted the same way as if they told us Elvis was still alive. All three of us shot that idea down quickly. First off, none of us wanted it, and second, we were all supposed to transfer out of the Army as soon as we got back to America.

My team leader, Sergeant Fooks, had had a change in attitude when he was promoted back in February. He went from the sour "I hate the Army" mentality to the "do what I say, yes sir, yes ma'am" squared-away sergeant. He was a good sergeant though. Staff Sergeant Poston and Sergeant First Class Crisostomo decided to give him a line team in First Squad and swapped him out with Kemple's old amigo, Sergeant Woods.

Woods became my new team leader and he was tolerable. He was a recent transfer from Third Platoon, and I always got along with him.

Woods was built like a bodybuilder but was a very quiet, reserved, and respectful man. He may have not been the most motivating person in the platoon, but I personally thought he was amazing. He had quirks and they didn't slip past me. He always made weird noises with his mouth when he walked and hardly ever took his sunglasses off, even at night. Everyone had peculiarities, and when you live so close to so many people during a deployment, nothing goes unseen.

But overall, Woods was a great team leader. He always left Chief and me alone, and that was what we preferred. He was as consistent in the gym as Adams, but unlike Fooks, Woods did not demand I go with him every day. He knew my performance level. He knew I never quit when things got tough. He also knew my outlook in the Army. He even knew I was counting down the days to my final day. It was only months away.

The "April Fool's Cache" must have created a pause for the local terrorist cell, because we were not affected by any IEDs in April. We also tried out a new tactic—employing sniper teams to over-watch IED-prone Business 1 along Kadasiyah, Tikrit's northern edge. To pull off a standard mission like this, we would stage around 0300 hours on any given day. Our sniper team consisted of three well-shooting marksmen in desert camo uniforms and either Hilmo or Reese as the RTO. We would drive into Tikrit really late at night and drive out on Z Road. We would drive "blackout" to the open desert near the highway and drop off our sniper element. We would then either sit at the Birthday Palace and wait for word if they needed us, or we would drive around nearby Kadasiyah until called upon. Either way, the first few times we did this and nothing transpired, it just began to piss us off because all we ever wanted was results.

HAMMER TIME

"Hit him, Ram!"

Patrols in the LT's truck remained more enjoyable than the ones in Poston's truck ever were. Taylor and I would scrutinize and patronize Lieutenant Scher daily as our main form of entertainment. He took it all well and we were thankful for that. We would just bust him down on anything that got us going. His gung-ho attitude sparked so much fuel for our fire. Scher knew our jokes were our form of venting stress.

Each of our patrols was typically based on the funny things we could get away with. This started from the first day of patrols, and continued to the very last. Patrols were scheduled for a minimum of six hours, but more times than not they turned into seven or more.

During a routine patrol through a neighborhood, I was in the turret and we were driving through some narrow alleyways. My height elevation in the turret let me see over some of the walls around the homes. One house had several girls on the other side of the wall looking up at me. Some were attractive, while others were not. One girl, who had to be around twelve, looked at me, blew me a kiss, and pulled her cell phone out and motioned for me to call her. I just laughed so hard, almost uncontrollably.

During another afternoon patrol, we dumped off the dismounted element in the city before the mounted element drove to the other side of Tikrit to drive around and have our presence seen. We found an opening and parked our Humvees there while we took a piss break. While we walked around our vehicles and chitchatted with the others in the mounted element, we heard some shouting coming from a nearby house. Nothing alarmed us, as we knew that that was how most Iraqi people communicated—at the top of their lungs. We looked in the direction of the yelling and noticed a little girl walking our way and fully engulfed in tears.

She had to be about seven years old. She was soon followed by a young Iraqi man about twenty years old with a hammer in his hand. Almost in slow motion, we watched this man as he grabbed that girl and yanked her by the hair. Immediately, all of the drivers jumped out of our vehicles and began to yell at the man, who was oblivious to us.

In a sick form of punishment, this man then swatted at the girl's head with the hammer. Not like someone hammering a nail, but he used the side. It was enough obviously to inflict pain on the girl, and none of us wanted to watch. Instinctively, we all snapped and began to walk fast over to the man, who still paid no attention to us as he grabbed the girl and dragged her into his house. Ram watched from the turret in his Humvee but quickly jumped out. He himself had a young girl the same age back in the States and he snapped a little more than any of us did.

Ram lived up to his nickname and charged the man like a horned sheep, without any weapons in his hands except for clenched fists. As soon as Ram got within feet of the Iraqi, the man turned around and put the girl down. She immediately ran inside.

"What the fuck are you doing, motherfucker?" Ram screamed, inches away from this now scared and helpless man. "You don't hit kids in the head with hammers, motherfucker!" Ram continued to bark at him. I could tell immediately that the man didn't understand English, but Ram's universal body language was enough to tell this stranger that we were not happy.

"Hit him, Ram!" "Fuck that bitch up!" men yelled from our Humvees. Ram impulsively threw one blow to this man's head and sent him falling on his ass. The Iraqi immediately stopped talking and sat almost frozen with fear while holding his chin and looking up at Ram.

"That's how we do it in California, bitch!" Ram yelled one more time to him as he paced backward. His previous gang-environment life back home started to seep through.

"That's enough, Ram," Staff Sergeant Gibson yelled. "Come on back," he yelled in a thick Southern drawl.

The Iraqi man picked himself up and walked quietly inside his house. We hopped back in our Humvees and drove to another area to drive around. Though Ram and I weren't the closest of friends in our platoon, I was never more proud of his actions than at that moment.

MIDNIGHT CEMENT

"Grunts did whatever we were told."

Like I mentioned earlier, the "April Fool's Cache" put a regress in the number of IEDs in our area of operation, but it did not eradicate them. Just by chance, an element from Bandit Company of the 3/320th happened to drive through our area of Tikrit at a time that we were not driving through ourselves. It was even after a route clearance from one of our platoons, but still an IED found its way to exploding on a Humvee from Bandit.

None of the men were killed in that Humvee, but it was a powerful device and injured everyone with broken bones or minor shrapnel wounds. As everyone climbed out, the Humvee soon became fully engulfed in flames. It was a telltale reminder that things were never safe in Tikrit. That could have been any Humvee from my company since it was our area that Bandit just happened to drive through. IEDs do not show preferences, so one never knew when or if one would explode.

Also in April, another convoy of soldiers drove through our section of Tikrit when they had no right to be in it. This was a military police convoy that drove from Samarra to FOB Speicher. They detoured off of

MSR Tampa and drove through downtown Tikrit, my company's area, on their way to FOB Speicher.

While they drove through the choked, crowded, and bustling streets, someone threw a grenade at one of their Humvees. The gunner wasn't paying attention, but luckily the grenade didn't come inside the Humvee. Instead, it bounced down and blew out all four tires. The MPs reported the attack but kept on driving through on flats.

The news came to us that the vehicle was currently on fire. We were on QRF duty that day, so we reacted quickly. Frequent shotgun blasts from our gunners on the drive constantly cleared the streets, but we never found that patrol. Upon arrival at the suspected attack, we found nothing but the same mysterious and cluttered streets. We later found out that the patrol had made it to FOB Speicher, but boy was our command staff angry at that unit, whoever they were.

The recent attacks were enough for command to decide to do their homework on IED attacks in our area. Most of the attacks kept happening in the same areas. The concrete decorative stars on Business 1 were concealing IEDs, and bombed-out holes on MSR Tampa kept being reused. We ignored the stars for the time being and decided that it was time that we filled in the holes from previous attacks. This was a subject and solution that was brought up dozens of times to the lieutenant inside our truck during one of our several "bitch sessions."

Before this task finally became a job for the engineers like it always should have, the task came down to, you guessed it, us. Grunts did whatever we were told and it will always be that way.

During night patrols, there were a few instances where we filled in some holes on MSR Tampa that we had been attacked from. We added the supplies of concrete mix, water, and shovels into the trunks of our Humvees before we headed out. During the dead of night, about 3 A.M., we'd set up a roadblock on MSR Tampa and become construction workers.

Light beacons, chem lights, IR strobes, and flashlights were all safety precautions to make sure we were visible to other coalition troops that passed through. We utilized all hands to patch up the holes with concrete and even needed the drivers to get out and help. This left the gunners by themselves in the trucks, a tactic frowned upon, but at 3 A.M. and with the civilian curfew in effect, there was no traffic unless it was from other military convoys.

When other U.S. patrols came through while we were concreting, we waved them down, they halted, and then they followed the designated route on the opposite side of the road. This system worked and made it safe for us to continue our concrete pouring. It worked until a group of idiots came by, that is.

We were all scattered about the road, inside the safety net of our vehicles, busy filling in holes. I then heard the faint sound of military vehicles coming down the road, but I could see no headlights. As the sound got closer, I expected it was a unit driving blackout, but with my NODs, I could not see anything coming down yet.

We continued our work until someone from the rear began shouting.

"They're not stopping!" one of our gunners yelled while frantically flashing his flashlight.

"Who's not stopping?" I said as I dropped my shovel and walked closer to my Humvee. All of a sudden the sound of a convoy was right on top of us. It was a unit driving blackout and they had not seen us yet, even though we had numerous lights displayed.

"Hey, stop! U.S. soldiers, stop!" everyone began to scream in the road while simultaneously flickering any light source we had. The sound of screeching brakes soon resonated through the black night. The lead truck in the blackout convoy swerved at the last minute and barely missed one of our idle and helpless Humvees. A chain reaction almost ensued as the other trucks slammed on their brakes and slid off to opposite sides of the now halted first blackout truck.

"What the FUCK do you think you are doing?" Lieutenant Scher shouted while running over to the unidentified convoy.

"Who the fuck are you?" yelled back one of the unidentified men. Through bits and pieces of confusing rage-filled words between the two, I was able to put together the story. The blackout convoy was a group of Army Rangers who were apparently unaware of our activity despite our multiple lights. We were even displayed on the Blue Force Tracker computer, so their excuses were bullshit.

These Rangers were arrogant and refused to admit any fault, even though they'd been inches from slamming into one of our Humvees. They'd been seconds away from a total disaster, and yet they continued to bicker with Lieutenant Scher and three of our squad leaders. I was pretty proud seeing Scher so fired up. I also had a newfound disappointment in these arrogant Rangers.

Nothing was resolved from the shouting match, because the Rangers soon left our area, still ranting and raving. We finished up our concrete work and spray-painted our regimental symbol on it so we knew we were the ones who'd placed that concrete patchwork.

IN THE MERRY, MERRY MONTH OF MAY

"I could go for a good IED right now."

I looked forward to the month of May for a long time. The only thing on my mind every day about May was that it was the month I was to go on my R&R. I was supposed to leave at the beginning of May, but I switched with Sergeant Pitchford because he wanted to make it home for his sister's graduation. I was now scheduled to leave at the end of May. At first, I hated the idea of switching, because I was just so sick of waiting, but it worked out in the end for both of us. At the end of May, more of my friends would be home from college anyway, so the extra wait would be worth it.

On the last night of April, we had scheduled a night patrol through Kadasiyah. I hated night patrols because they required constant wearing of NODs, which strained the neck. I was scheduled to be a driver and I hated driving at night.

There was no one on the streets at night because of the curfew, so we had no one to come across to pass the time. That was where Lieutenant Scher came in handy. He was the closest person and easiest target in the vehicle. The jokes lasted from the beginning of the patrol to the end.

Avery was in the States by then, so Taylor and I were paired up more, which I loved. There was never a day he didn't crack me up.

"Sir, if you could have your choice of having a nice pen or having sex with Carmen Electra, which would you choose?" Taylor asked the hypothetical question.

"Honestly, I thrive and live for a good decent pen. Sometimes I . . ." Lieutenant Scher spoke before being cut off by everyone in the truck, who laughed and made fun of him. Scher just smiled while he continued to validate his statement.

"You know why I think you're gay, sir? Because of that statement right there," I said with a laugh.

"You're either a virgin or a homosexual," Taylor screamed.

Scher tried to justify himself. "I just like a good pen and I have never met Carmen Electra before. She's not my type, freak-heads."

"Holy shit, sir! It was a hypothetical question!" I yelled back while I tried not to laugh.

The patrol went on, as boring as the rest of them. Before the sunrise, everyone struggled to stay awake. It was impossible, especially as a driver, because I never got out of the vehicle. Sitting for hours on end in a hot environment, mixed with boring and tedious work, will knock out the most wide-awake person.

The sun began to rise as we continued to drive up and down every empty street in Kadasiyah. The ghost town slowly began to show life as people awoke and drove to whatever destination they were headed to.

"Wheeeeeeeeen's chow?" Taylor said in the most annoying and whiny way possible. It was an inside joke we always would bug the lieutenant with.

"Sir, we should head back early," I said to Scher.

"Why?" he replied.

"Because I'm sick of driving, sick of patrols, and sick of the Army," I jokingly stated back to the lieutenant.

"What? The Army is great. It gives you everything you need," Lieutenant Scher said with a smile. He hardly ever made eye contact from his seat as he kept staring out his dashboard window.

"Oh, God, shut the fuck up, sir!" Taylor yelled down from the turret.

"You know what, sir, you just changed my life. Wow. I love the Army. I have an idea, let's drive around all night and do nothing, and then drive around all morning and do nothing," Taylor said with a smirk. "And don't forget to attempt to win the hearts and minds."

This particular patrol seemed endless. We drove through the night, watched the sun come up, and the mind-numbing patrol still continued. It continued until Lieutenant Scher made the call to head back to the Birthday Palace to drop off our Iraqi Army contingent and then head home.

As we pulled out of Kadasiyah and onto IED Alley, the thought of IEDs came into my head.

"Sir, when was the last time our platoon got hit with an IED?" I said as I continued driving down the most feared strip in Tikrit.

"February 18, I believe. The one where the blasting cap went off on your truck." Lieutenant Scher spat out his hard facts like a contestant on a game show.

"February 18 to May 1? Damn. That's a long time," I thought out loud. I took a breath and then said something I shouldn't have said. "I could go for a good IED right now."

Before I could even get a reaction from anyone in my truck, a gigantic explosion occurred right in front of me. Within a split second, Second Squad's Humvee, which I was following, disappeared in a smoke cloud.

It was almost as if I'd triggered the IED with the period of my sentence. In that pivotal second, all that was normal changed to total fear and questions, and everyone was instantly shocked. Everyone in my Humvee uttered the same instinctive phrase of "oh shit," and then we popped back into reality. That always happened within the first two seconds of any IED attack.

I slammed on the brakes immediately before I drove through the billowing smoke screen. While Lieutenant Scher and Sergeant Hilmo networked their communications through the radios, my eyes were glued to the scene in front of me.

Like a viewer in a movie theater, my attention was locked to my front. I had the best vantage point for watching everything unfurl. I kept replaying in my head the images of the seconds leading up to the explosion.

The last thing I saw before the IED exploded was the back of Specialist Ly's head peering out of the turret. Staff Sergeant Hubert didn't like his gunners squatting down like the rest of our platoon. Moments before I spoke my lethal sentence, I was staring at the back of his helmet hoping he would at least get down through IED Alley. Now I wondered if he still had his head.

While the giant smoke cloud still shielded Second Squad's truck from visibility, I heard Sergeant Caruso's voice come over the radio. Here it was, the sentence everyone was waiting for.

"One-six, one-six, this is one-two-Bravo." Caruso's voice boomed over the speaker of the radio.

"Go ahead one-two-Bravo," the lieutenant retorted.

"No injuries, we're all fine. Truck is still running. Just a couple of cracks in the window, over."

A sigh of relief was expressed by everyone. Apparently, the IED's pressure blew most of the shrapnel over their truck, and just barely over the head of Ly. I was immediately rushed with the sense of calm upon hearing that longed-for phrase over the radio. The smoke cleared and Second Squad's truck became visible again. I could faintly see Ly's head back out of the turret and scanning around with his 50-caliber machine gun.

"One-six, this is one-three, my gunner spots a car with a large antenna on it driving like a bat out of Hell. We're gonna go stop them, over," Staff Sergeant Justin Jirkovsky's voice said over the radio.

"What's the description? Where are you looking at?" Hilmo questioned back.

After the explosion and the initial shock passed and we collected ourselves, chaos was the next phase. There was also instant chaos in the civilian traffic that surrounded us. They all wanted to be far away from us when an IED went off. There was confusion in the orchestration of what to do next. It was equally confusing when a million things were going on and they all transpired over the radio at the same time.

Within moments, our platoon unintentionally split in two. The rear Humvees chased after a certain car that the gunner for Third Squad, Sergeant Walters, identified as a possible triggerman, and Second Squad and I drove forward a little, all the while listening to Jirkovsky's radio messages.

Jirkovsky yelled for us to stop a certain car fleeing from them that was driving out with the detoured traffic and into the desert to our right.

"What car?"

"The black one."

"Which black one?"

"With the antenna."

"They all have antennas."

Confusion now swept through our platoon as we tried to work together.

"That car right there!" Lieutenant Scher yelled at me as he pointed out his side window. "Go after him."

I put my Humvee in gear and slammed my gas pedal to the floor. The truck went off the roadway and onto the sidewalk.

"*STOP!!!*" Taylor yelled down, panicky, from the turret. I slammed on the brakes instantaneously. Within seconds I could see why Taylor had screamed. On the other side of the sidewalk, the ground gave way and there was about a fifteen-foot drop-off, a ledge that led into the desert. I was about one second away from flipping my Humvee.

"Shit, I can't go, sir!" I yelled back at the lieutenant.

"SHIT!" Lieutenant Scher yelled back.

"Taylor, stop him," I yelled up to Taylor. He immediately shouldered his machine gun and took it off safety. Simultaneously I threw open my door, grabbed my M4, and stepped out. I pulled back my bolt to chamber a round and took aim at the fleeing car.

Chum, chum, chum, chum came the sound of Taylor's machine gun. I started firing away also. The sounds of the firing of the bullets and the empty shells hitting the hood and roof of the Humvee rang in my ears.

As I fired, Taylor's voice interrupted my concentration.

"What the hell am I shooting at?" Taylor yelled down.

"Stop that black car out there." I yelled up at him as I kept my eyes glued on the herd of cars moving sporadically out in the desert.

"Shoot the car or what?" he screamed back.

"Do whatever to stop him," I yelled while turning toward Taylor.

As I turned around and drew aim back on the speeding car, I could see to my left that Sergeant Caruso was out of his truck and taking aim at the same vehicle. Taylor and I reopened fire on the car, which was about five hundred yards away. Small pockets of smoke shot up around it and displayed where our bullets were landing. The car was moving so fast, but our bullets still hit it. The car eventually slammed on its brakes.

"Cease fire!" I yelled back at Taylor while motioning the signal with my hand. I turned my attention back to the halted car and saw a man jump out. Jirkovsky and the other Humvee were not far behind the car, ready to detain the man.

Before I saw the outcome transpire, Lieutenant Scher yelled for me to get in the truck.

"What the fuck is going on here?" I confusedly questioned the lieutenant.

"Get in, get in, let's go. IA is shooting at a dump truck down the road. I don't know, get in, let's go!" he yelled at me. Scher was as confused about the situation as I was.

I immediately hopped in and reversed my Humvee. Down the road in the opposite direction I could see an orange dump truck speeding away, closely followed by an Iraqi Army pickup truck with soldiers opening fire with AKs from the back of it.

"What the fuck are they doing?" I yelled to myself.

"What the hell is going on, sir?" Taylor shouted.

"Catch up to them!" Lieutenant Scher shouted.

Everything happened so fast. So much had transpired in the last four minutes that I started to become overloaded with confusion. Everyone did. I flicked on my siren and slammed my foot on the gas pedal.

Zigzagging through the narrow streets of Kadasiyah at lightning speed was enough to let me feel my heart pumping through my vest. I felt like I was in a movie or a police video of a high-speed chase.

As I blazed left turn after right turn, around tight street corners, each turn I had a fear of running over children. The sound of AK47 bullets ricocheted through the area. All the while I was wondering what the Iraqi Army was shooting at. Each turn I made, I saw the scene of panicked civilians running around with their hands in the air. Mothers were scooping their children up. On a few occasions, I came within inches of running people over.

After the long chase through the streets, I came to an opening. I could see to my front the IA truck and the orange dump truck both still driving at intense speeds. The dump truck came to a lonesome house on the edge of the river. The IA stopped right behind the truck and I pulled up within seconds. The driver darted out of the dump truck and entered the nearby house.

As soon as I parked, I jumped out with Lieutenant Scher and we both ran up with our rifles at the high ready. I was still confused as to what the hell was happening. I turned around and noticed that Caruso's truck hadn't followed us. It was just my Humvee alone. Hilmo stayed inside the Humvee with Taylor and relayed our progress over the radio.

As Lieutenant Scher and I approached the house, the IA began to come out of the house with the driver in their possession. They were punching and kicking the helpless man until I intervened.

"Hey, hey, hey!" I yelled at the IA. "Back the fuck up."

I took control of the driver. He was obviously frightened out of his mind. He was about twenty-five years of age and was terrified, practically frozen in fear. I grabbed him and walked him over to my Humvee. I searched him and found nothing on him. I ran his hands through one of our bomb tests kits. I was never actually properly trained on how to do the swab test, so I just "faked the funk" and quickly discarded the final test.

The family who owned the house came out frightened at the sight of the commotion. Lieutenant Scher went to speak with them and calm them down. I found myself practically running the show outside. It was just me, the man I was flex-cuffing, and a handful of Iraqi Army soldiers who kept looking at me for guidance. The emergence of an Apache helicopter soaring over the skies filled me with the best feeling of security. I had nothing for the IA soldiers to do. They were more in the way than anything, so I gathered them up and began to learn what the reason was for their chasing of this man.

They told me an elaborate story in a hard-to-understand broken English. They said the driver opened fire with an AK and drove off. During the chase, they said, he threw the weapon out the window. I attempted to explain that they needed to walk back and find that rifle they were talking about and bring it back to me. It was hard to instruct someone based on hand gestures, but I did my best and they all walked away, back toward Kadasiyah.

After a few confusing minutes, Lieutenant Scher came back and told me the family had no idea who this man was. I informed him that I had not found anything suspicious on him, so I turned him over to the Iraqi Army soldiers. They never did find that AK they were referring to.

The other half of my platoon was still near the site of the IED, and they were also wrapping things up. They successfully arrested the guy who they initially suspected was the triggerman. Sergeant Walters's split-second decision in identifying that man proved to be the best pick he could have made. The man actually confessed to what he had done. Third Squad arrested him and placed him in their Humvee for transport back to FOB Remagen.

I drove my lone Humvee back through Kadasiyah and linked up with the other Humvees in my platoon. As I drove by the car that Taylor, Caruso, and I had shot at earlier, I could see about five bullet holes scattered across the exterior. Two bullet holes were literally an inch above the driver's head. If he had been an inch taller, his brains would have been smeared on the opposite window. Turned out later I found out this man was a cousin of Saddam Hussein.

Back together as a platoon, we were more than ready to call it a day. During our drive back to FOB Remagen, I kept replaying the events that had occurred earlier. It never ceased to surprise me that everything could go from normal to hell in literally a split second.

MESS WITH US, LOSE YOUR HOME

"Typical Rakkasan 'zero tolerance' for bullshit"

A couple days later, our platoon received a different style of mission. We were to roll out of FOB Remagen with some extra assets. We brought some engineers with us to a site that we rarely ever patrolled. This mission came about after a bust was made somewhere in Iraq where a man was connected with firing rockets at FOB Speicher but was nowhere to be found. With typical Rakkasan "zero tolerance" for bullshit, we found out where he lived and set out to demolish it. During the mission brief prior to leaving, the news put a smile on everyone's face, and I'm sure gave an erection to some guys.

The rotation in our truck put me as the gunner. We were scheduled to drive through Tikrit and then take a right turn over Route Clemson and toward Ad Dwar. Driving Route Clemson was always a fear of mine, and Avery was always quick to remind me of his IED experience on Clemson.

We pulled out of the front gate with sirens blaring and lights flashing, which made traffic control so much easier. Only when we got into the heart of Tikrit did I have to pop off a few shotgun blasts at cars. Shooting shotguns at cars never got old. It was fun every time and thoughts of actually killing someone with those shots surprisingly never surfaced. We mostly fired bird shot, so all it did was crack windshields. There were times though that some buckshot made it into my barrel, and I didn't know it until I saw the holes in some cars. Gunners always responded with the standard "warning shot, no damage." The car was halted and that's all we really cared about.

As we crossed onto Route Clemson, we stopped on the bridge that went over the Tigris River. Staff Sergeant Poston called an immediate halt to our patrol since he was in the lead vehicle. He saw a large clump of grass on the median just at the opposite end of the bridge, about four hundred yards to his front. This was obviously a good call to halt because we had all heard of large out-of-place clumps of grass used to conceal IEDs. The median was nothing but a concrete slab running parallel to the road, so there was no reason for grass to grow there.

As soon as we stopped, we did our systematic and routine placement of cones to avert traffic around us. Since gunners had the elevated position in the turrets, we all grabbed our binoculars and peered out into the distance to survey the situation. I could clearly see this small pile of grass and knew it had to be something. I yelled down the turret hole to Lieutenant Scher and narrated all that I could see.

Since we viewed this as a potential IED, we decided we were going to try to cordon off the area and shut down the route. As I slumped down in my swing, I peered through the little crack between my turret and the hood, out into the distance. As soon as we began to reshuffle our vehicles in an eastern direction to lock the road down, we saw an oncoming patrol in the distance headed west, toward the potential IED.

Lieutenant Scher quickly began trying to find the oncoming patrol on his Blue Force Tracker, but no one was showing up. I stood up and waved a fluorescent flag to get their attention, but it was too late. As soon as their first vehicle drove past the grass clump, a gigantic cloud of black and gray smoke in a V form shot out of the clump in silence. Two seconds later, the sound of the incredible explosion rocked through the air and thumped in my chest.

"Holy shit!" I yelled, freely standing in my turret. The convoy didn't miss a beat and kept driving through the smoke. One by one, other vehicles popped through the giant smoke cloud. Sergeant Hilmo called the report into the company to inform them of the situation.

We all thought the patrol would at least halt next to us and tell us their condition, but they didn't even give a thumbs-up. They drove right next to us, as we were still parked on the other side of the road. I inspected their first vehicle as they passed us and noticed only a few slight cracks and dings on it. I figured that if anyone was injured, they would have stopped. They just kept on hauling over the bridge like nothing had happened. So went another close call in my life. Glad Poston had noticed it and didn't let us venture into the impending doom. It could have been a different story.

After the anonymous patrol passed through us, we headed farther down Route Clemson going east. We drove untested along the highway until we came upon a farm on a hill. We did a little off-road driving until we reached the home of the guilty man.

Upon arrival, we found it to be an empty and desolate farm. Three buildings in total, all vacated. The man's family had to have known we were coming. A recent radio address from Colonel Steele on all Iraqi radios had stated that we were going to demolish the homes of any guilty terrorists. We were no longer going to let homes harbor terrorists.

First Platoon, along with a few Humvees from Headquarters Platoon, parked all around the farm and let the engineers do their job. I spent all morning watching their large construction bulldozer demolish home after home within our cordon. What were once cheaply created dwellings were now piles of brick, stone, and mortar, piled up in crushed lumps on the hilltop. Families all across the plain had a clear visual of us on top of the hill wrecking these homes. I hoped it sent the right message to people. As soon as nothing was left on that hilltop but rubble, we packed things up and drove back to FOB Remagen, wiping our hands clean of another successful day in Iraq.

SATURDAY BLOODY SATURDAY

"The look of terror was still visible on his face."

The next day, May 6, we all woke up and hoped for a calmer day than the last. This usually meant we would not get one. Little did I know that this day would become a scar in my memory. I saw firsthand a different type of killing tactic. A desperate ploy used by extremists I prayed I would never bear witness to caught up to me. May 6 turned into a day that I would never forget.

We got up early that morning to try another one of our sneaky sniper over-watches. Very early in the morning we loaded up our Humvees to the maximum capacity, with the exception of leaving two or three men from the platoon back at the CHUs. Before daylight set in, we drove to a factory building across the street from the Birthday Palace.

As we drove toward the tall building we had chosen, we tried to be quiet. We drove with all of our lights off, and when we got to the factory, the main gate at the entrance was locked and we didn't want to bust it down. The noise we generated in attempting to override the locking system forced the owner of the gate to come down and open it. We then conjured up a story and informed the man that we were going to conduct a routine search of the premises. The man had nothing to hide, so he let us into his property.

Anyone who was not a driver or gunner got out of the Humvees and headed inside the factory to make it look like a full-blown search. It was a prime place to put a sniper team, as it was the tallest building in Tikrit and was adjacent to Saddam Boulevard, the Birthday Palace, and the stretch of Business 1 that included IED Alley.

Once all twelve dismounts were inside the building, they hung out for a few minutes before exiting with nine soldiers. The three that remained on the roof of the factory were there in order to watch over Business 1's IED Alley section. It was a great tactic and I was glad we were doing it.

Once we loaded back into the Humvees with everyone except our detachment, we crossed the street and zigzagged through Saddam Boulevard and into the Birthday Palace. We decided not to drive around Kadasiyah, so it would make the area look less patrolled and hopefully entice someone to emplace an IED.

I did not mind sitting at the Birthday Palace all morning. In fact, I would have rather done that every patrol. We were in a secured compound, but I use that word loosely because it was controlled by the Iraqi Army. We still felt somewhat separated from the terrors of the outside enemy though. An occasional accidental discharge from an Iraqi soldier and his AK was common, but we still did not wear any of our body armor when we were in the Birthday Palace compound.

All morning, our platoon sat in our trucks and devised ways to pass the time. My truck did so by doing the same thing we always did. Taylor and I would razz Lieutenant Scher. Hilmo and the interpreter slept in their seats, and the other three squads in their trucks did the same thing. Some slept in their Humvees, while others slept on the roofs of their Humvees.

Those who didn't sleep mostly listened to their iPods or watched portable DVD players. I had my iPod on that morning hooked to our portable speakers and pumped tasty jams for our whole truck to listen to. Lieutenant Scher never liked my music, since he only enjoyed West Point Academy speeches and Army marches. All he did was criticize every song that ever came on, and we, in turn, criticized him. He never let a song play through its entirety, so I revoked his privilege of touching my iPod.

Once Taylor and I were content with our joshing of the lieutenant, we averted our attention to the Iraqi soldiers who walked aimlessly around the small base. Taylor sat in the swing of the turret and I in the driver's seat, and we made fun of how stupid the Iraqi Army soldiers looked and acted that morning.

One Iraqi soldier stuck out from the crowd. He was wearing a BDU camouflage uniform. All Iraqi soldiers wore the desert camouflage uniform that U.S. soldiers wore during the Gulf War, but this soldier, an officer, was the first soldier I'd ever seen who wore green woodland camouflage BDUs. To say the least, he stuck out from the crowd, and we picked up on it.

Taylor and I were so bored that we kept on making fun of that soldier from the vantage point of our seats. Now, we weren't deliberately saying anything to his face; we were inside our Humvee and just passed words between the two of us, essentially talking behind his back. We were so bored that we were coming up with the story of his life based on the way he was walking. You would be surprised what extremely bored and bitter soldiers talk about when they are stuck in another world.

As the morning got older, the sun got hotter. We all threw open our doors and peeled open our vests. I put my iPod back on, and Taylor and I continued to talk about anything and everything. Then, like a lightning strike of reality, my surroundings changed faster than I could blink.

KAPLOOOMPH! came the loudest and closest explosion I had yet witnessed. About seventy feet from my vehicle's left was the origin. It was so close, I could feel my hair move on my head and my chest thump from the concussion.

"Holy shit!" I screamed as I instinctively tucked my leg in the truck and slammed the door. The sound of everyone slamming his door happened simultaneously. Everyone's eyes bulged out while we all scrambled with our gear and tried to figure out what had happened.

"I think that was a mortar," Lieutenant Scher said as he fumbled awake and reached for his radio.

Then the sound of bits and pieces of something began to splat all over and around the vehicle. I looked out the window and saw pieces of human flesh falling from the skies and hitting the pavement like wet clothes hitting a floor.

"Suicide bomber," I said faintly. I was so scared I could barely talk.

"What'd you say? How do you know?" Lieutenant Scher asked me while we all haphazardly tried to put our vests and helmets on.

"Because I'm looking . . . at . . . what's left . . . of . . . them," I said while I started to process what I was seeing. From the vantage point of where I was parked, I could not see the whole scene. I could see blood splattered with black powder next to the Iraqi Army crest at the entrance to the main building. Bits and pieces of human meat spotted the grounds in every direction. Some small pieces still trickled down from the skies.

Sergeant First Class Crisostomo appeared next to Lieutenant Scher's door and opened it. The look on his face was unforgettable. The sheer carnage of death was on his face, and I'm sure it was on all of ours. His struck me because this man was obviously shaken by what he'd just seen transpire, and it immediately spooked me. I kept thinking he was about to tell us bad news.

"Is everyone OK in here?" Crisostomo asked with an undeniable tremble in his voice.

"I'm good," I said, then everyone else went in turn. Jerry the interpreter, Taylor, Hilmo—we all gave the thumbs-up to the platoon sergeant.

"All right, sir, I checked on all the trucks. Everyone's present, every-one's fine," he said quickly.

"Send that up to company, Hilmo," Lieutenant Scher ordered as he hopped out of the vehicle. Jerry hopped out, too. Hilmo, Taylor, and I stayed put and kept our doors shut while we were glued to our windows.

"Holy shit" was the only phrase that kept being passed around in our truck. I looked at my watch to see what time it was, and that was when I realized my hand was trembling, but I'd been unaware. I cracked my knuckles, punched my steering wheel, and it stopped.

None of us moved out of our Humvee for a while. We all had a fear that there could be a secondary device somewhere. Lieutenant Scher, Ser-geant First Class Crisostomo, and Sergeant Pitchford were seen running all over the place. I could not take my curiosity much longer because I wanted to inquire as to what had just transpired. I needed to take a look for myself.

Stepping out of my Humvee, I immediately stepped into Hell. The closer I got to the bloodstained wall, the bigger the chunks of human flesh got. I tried gingerly to avoid stepping on large chunks. As I surveyed the ground, an occasional finger, a knee joint, teeth, gray brain matter, and hundreds of unidentifiable slabs of body parts surrounded me. I noticed one Iraqi soldier on his knees who wept uncontrollably while being comforted by a fellow soldier.

Next to the crest, on the ground were spread the remnants of four bodies in mangled pieces. One body looked more like a twist of mixed meats with unscathed legs, still with jeans and shoes on. A pair of legs with red meat pouring out of the pelvis area, oozing like a busted piñata.

A few feet away, another mangled body lay motionless. The evidence of a shredded military uniform gave away the identity of an Iraqi Army officer. His face was wiped clean away as if he'd been scalped. I located it several feet away and it was perfectly intact from ear to ear and looked like a discarded rubber mask. The main chest area was riddled with punched holes. One leg was separated from the body and spread about ten feet away from the rest. You could trace the body as the owner of the severed leg from the blood-smeared skid mark on the pavement connecting the two.

A third body was scarcely identifiable. Mostly pieces scattered in a pile. A hand, a leg, part of a skull, pounds of shredded-up red meat, and bits of fabric from an Iraqi Army uniform. Toes, teeth, an eyeball, a lung—parts were everywhere around me. This was the most ground-up human body I saw there, and I immediately knew this had to be the suicide bomber.

A few yards from the piles of what used to be living souls minutes ago was the last body visible. The situation hit me like a ton of bricks when I realized why this body was so significant. The body was poked through multiple times like Swiss cheese and the face was squashed like a flattened globe. The look of terror was still visible on his face. What astonished me from this body was that it was the Iraqi officer in green fatigues who Taylor and I had just been exchanging jokes about in our Humvee. Two minutes ago, this officer was walking with such youthfulness and life, and now he was sprawled out lifeless on the blood-soaked pavement before me.

As I stood in place and turned around, I paused and took in the whole situation. There were seconds where I had to look away to halt any nauseous feelings I had. I tried to look somewhere else, but there was meat everywhere. There was no escaping it. Everywhere I gingerly stepped I would see body parts and blood. A foot, bloodied uniform bits, or a severed finger curled up next to my boot with the tendon pulled out like string cheese. I was careful how I stepped, and tried to avoid stepping on any of it. I avoided the large chunks at least. I was surrounded by death.

Other Iraqi soldiers were coming out of their building with garbage bags and stretchers and beginning to pick up the large pieces. As they haphazardly moved the bodies from the ground to their truck, one of the soldiers accidentally dropped a stretcher with the remains of one of the shredded-up bodies and sent it slapping onto the pavement. The situation was too much for that soldier and he turned away and threw up. After this, I realized I had seen enough and tiptoed my way back to the Humvee.

"What piece do you think this is?" Specialist Sanchez yelled from his turret as he held up his vest. The vest had been draped outside his turret and was exposed to the rain of flesh. A chunk of meat clung to his canteen. The whiskers on the flesh gave notion that it was a cheek from one of the slaughtered men.

I couldn't sit idle very long amid the commotion, so I decided to walk to each Humvee and personally check up on my buddies. I knew everyone was uninjured, but I wanted to individually confirm for myself that everyone was really all right. I felt terrified myself after witnessing the carnage, but freely talking about it among my closest friends who were going through the same ordeal seemed like the best counseling available. In situations this traumatic, you could always guarantee that us infantrymen could spark laughter out of it somehow. Laughter was the essential key of turning yourself on and off to this lifestyle.

After I was satisfied in knowing that everyone was fine and dandy, I got back inside my Humvee and talked with Taylor. Soon, Lieutenant Scher and Jerry the interpreter returned to our Humvee as well. It was the first time we all sat in there and had a serious conversation. There were no jokes, no put-downs or snide remarks. We comforted each other without really knowing it.

The conversation eventually turned to religion. We all talked about our own spirituality, and I had never felt closer to any of those guys before. With terror and fear still fresh in our minds, I toned everything down as I reached for my iPod. While we were still on the conversation of religion, I remembered I had an album of songs written and performed by my parents' Christian band. I asked permission if I could play the music for everyone else to hear. No one objected.

I found so much comfort hearing my parents' voices as I sat in the Humvee still stricken with such trepidation. The others intently listened and hopefully found some sort of comfort as well. We all sat quiet and heard my parents sing about a brighter tomorrow and other songs of faith. It was such a moving moment in my life, I had to fight back tears. As body parts surrounded me outside my door and I focused on the songs of my folks. Never had I wanted more to be home safely than at that moment.

As the album neared an end, Sergeant Hilmo received a call from CP that informed us we could head back to FOB Remagen early. We spread the word out to the platoon and left the Birthday Palace. When we arrived back at the factory across the street, the sniper detail could not believe the scene we were painting for them. In fact, no one can ever get a good visual based on only words. Not even pictures will accurately portray the full extent of the carnage. I tried my best to describe it in words, but I'll never be able to describe the smell. It will never escape me though. It was indescribable.

As soon as we got back, I immediately headed into my CHU to play my stress-relieving guitar. I played straight up to lunch, when Taylor, Hilmo, and Reese came into my CHU to scoop me up for the meal. We walked across FOB Remagen to the chow hall, and I could not order the chicken wings that afternoon because all I could keep replaying in my head was the chunks of meat that had surrounded me that morning. I settled for a salad.

With First Platoon's usual luck of being busy while on QRF duty, we did not get far into our lunch before we were called up on our radios to gear up and head back out. We were not informed of what we were about to get into, which was standard. In the middle of the chow hall it was no contest getting every pogue to lock eyes with us as our entire table of thirty men stood up at once, grabbed our half-eaten trays, and stormed out. Time was of the essence, and those pogues must have been mesmerized to see soldiers in a hurry. I didn't worry about those assholes. I just worried about saving the ice cream cone from my tray as I threw the rest of my food away.

As we all ran to our vehicles, we threw on our damp-from-sweat gear, and we staged our vehicles near the gate. We were given the news on what we were to do and ventured out of the gate. The same job roles were still in effect from the morning, so I found myself driving again, with Taylor on the gun and Hilmo in the back on the radio, plus Lieutenant Scher as TC (truck commander) and Jerry, our interpreter.

As our convoy headed north on the bypass, Lieutenant Scher updated the platoon on the situation we were about to encounter. Iraqi Police had notified our headquarters of an IED emplacement gone wrong. They said they had a vehicle in flames on the bridge on MSR Tampa after two men tried to emplace an IED and it prematurely exploded.

I have to say, as I heard the news from Lieutenant Scher, I was overly excited. This was good news to me because I knew I was not about to get hit with an IED, and on top of that, two terrorists who planted IEDs were now dead. This could not have been better news.

As I neared the bridge, I could see a small smoke plume billow out from the crest. One Iraqi Police truck was parked before the burning car and traffic had already been diverted to the desert as a detour. With no immediate threat in the area and our four Humvees on the highway, I parked my Humvee next to the Iraqi policeman's truck north on the southbound lane. The first Humvee parked parallel to us on the northbound lane, and the third and fourth trucks went down the northbound lane to secure both lanes on the other side of the bridge.

We didn't have a lot of dismounted elements, so I told Hilmo to climb into the driver's seat in my Humvee as I got out with Lieutenant Scher and Jerry to converse with the policeman. Through Jerry, the policeman told us the story on what had happened. A white four-door car had parked briefly on the bridge with two men in it. The passenger got out with an IED and attempted to emplace it along the guardrail while the driver remained behind the wheel. Somehow it prematurely detonated, which sent the man nearest it into hundreds of pieces around the road. The car was unwrapped like an orange peel and the driver was instantly killed, but his body remained mostly intact, although the car continued to burn in flames, the driver included.

By the time I arrived, the flames still sizzled like a campfire. Jerry, Scher, Crisostomo, Pitchford, and I walked over and surveyed the car up close. It barely resembled the shape of a car. It was mostly a mangled twist of metal with patches of white that showed its original color. Everything was black and either burned or still burning. Lying in the center of the twist of metal were the remnants of the driver. The wheel of the car still remained in front of him. The man was barely identifiable as such. His carcass was still smoking by the time I came up to him. His arms were raised while he was on his back like an upside-down turtle. He was so charred that he looked like he was covered in tar. He was black from head to leg, his feet having been blown away. Parts of his skin glistened from the sun like flakes of glitter. The smell was uncanny and unforgettable. It was a mixture of burned hair and meat and was putrid to the nose. The smell alone was almost unbearable. I had to swallow hard to prevent losing what little lunch I'd managed to eat. The burning man was obviously dead. He lay stiff as if he had been dead for days. He was naked by all accounts and his skin was charred black as coal. Cracks in his skin peeked out slivers of khaki, which made it look hard. His knuckles were curled, both feet were blown off, and his face was black with a blank look. His mouth was curled like an O, as if his last words were "Oh shit!" but he didn't quite have enough time to say "shit."

While I walked around the burned vehicle, I saw that the road surrounding it was strewn with pieces of metal, shrapnel, and scattered body parts from the other man. Feet, fingers, a liver, intestines, and other body parts coated the bridge in all directions. I found the heart of one of the men about sixty feet from the vehicle. I traced it from the line of blood that it created when it skipped down the road.

Pitchford yelled for me at the crest of the bridge. We peered over the edge and looked down at the ground underneath and found the torso of the man who had emplaced the bomb. There was no head, arms, or legs, just the main chest cavity. It was motionless, with the stomach on the ground, and a blood trail had poured out from it after it briefly went airborne after the explosion, flew about fifty feet from the car, and slammed into the ground below the bridge. It was a disgusting sight. The blood trail was like a massive paintbrush stroke of red and black.

I continued to peruse the area and attempted to identify parts of the car, pieces of the IED, and more scattered body parts of the men. I tried my best not to step on any body parts, but since they were so prevalent all over the bridge it was impossible to walk so gingerly that one did not step on a finger, a kidney, or some brains. When I did, I tried my best to stomp my foot and get rid of whatever body part clung in the traction of my boots.

After EOD was notified and I was sick of being surrounded by burned human flesh, I walked back with Lieutenant Scher to our Humvee. I got back in my seat and tried to explain the scene to Hilmo and Taylor.

While we waited for EOD to arrive and collect whatever data they were looking for, air support in the shape of an Apache helicopter hovered over our cordoned area. Being the Humvee with the most radio monitoring, we frequently sent transmissions back to the pilots and explained the situation.

These Apache pilots were quite comical and obviously quite daredevilish in their flying antics. It passed the time admiring them. Taylor's father was about to be deployed to Iraq in the next few months, and he was an Apache pilot. Taylor couldn't stop talking about how he wanted to go to flight school and become one after his time as a grunt was over.

"Those guys have it made," Taylor said, as he stared out his hatch at the helicopter.

"They don't ever have to worry about IEDs," Hilmo said.

"I really want to go to flight school. LT, would you think I'm a lifer if I became a pilot?" Taylor asked Lieutenant Scher.

"You do whatever you want," Lieutenant Scher said, not really interested in the conversation. He was busy playing around with his Blue Force Tracker.

"Dude, it's still the Army. You still got a uniform on." I tried to put some sense into Taylor.

"Hey 'Mo, give me the hand mic," Taylor said as he grabbed the mic from Hilmo.

"Widow-maker three, this is Angel one-six Romeo, over," Taylor said into the hand mic that was connected to the Apache pilots.

"What the fuck are you doing?" Scher shifted his attention to Taylor.

"This is Widow-maker, go ahead with your message, over." The pilot's voice sounded on our speaker as the helicopter continued to do acrobatic flight patterns above our vehicle.

In the annoying little child's voice that Taylor always joked with, he started to converse on the radio. His cartoonish voice made me crack up. "I just want to say, you guys are freakin' awesome, over."

We all laughed in the Humvee, including Lieutenant Scher. That voice Taylor made always got me laughing, but having him do it on the radio was just too funny.

"Ha-ha. Roger that, over," came the pilot's voice.

"Roger, you're just amazing, and I love you, out," Taylor finished as I was plainly heard in the background laughing.

Joking around on the radio was already starting to get a little out of control this far into the deployment, but not in the way to impede legitimate conversations. In the past couple months, we'd been serious when we needed to be, but when times were boring or bleak, a small joke or sound effect over the airwaves was enough to cheer anyone up.

EOD did eventually come and collect whatever shrapnel they needed. Iraqi firefighters also came out, to hose down the bridge and clean off whatever body parts and blood were left scattered on the bridge. We sat in our truck for about two hours without air-conditioning because our truck never could get it fixed. Taylor and I continued to speak about how much we hated our jobs and being deployed in Iraq, and we also made fun of the lieutenant until it was time to head back to FOB Remagen.

We didn't go out that night. We were still on QRF duty, but we weren't called back up again that day. Saturdays tended to be busy because that was the Iraqi equivalent of our Sunday. Most things were closed and they had more time on their hands. We lounged in the dreaded QRF tent that night and swapped stories with some of the others in the platoon who hadn't been on patrol that day. It sounded glorious retelling the day's events, but I couldn't get over the fact of how lucky we all were. So many things could have shifted differently and the outcome could have been altered. I wondered if others ever felt that way. It was part of that luck in life that you have to keep your chin up and pray to whomever one prays to and wish for continual safety. My R&R time was just around the corner, and I feared I wouldn't make it even two more weeks. That was the life of an infantryman: uncertain about tomorrow. It was the life I'd chosen, so I kept positive and pulled out a book and read that night in my cot until I fell asleep.

OPERATION IRON TRIANGLE

"Operation That Which We Do Not Speak Of"

Being so close to my vacation back in the States, I didn't want to do anything until I went home. I didn't want to eat another MRE. I didn't want to do any patrols. I didn't want to guard stupid crap that didn't need guarding. I didn't want to be bothered with maintenance on Humvees; I just wanted time to fly by. The last thing I wanted was another mission on the scale of Operation Swarmer. I should have seen this next one coming.

At first I thought I would bypass it and that it would get postponed until after I left for my R&R, but the order came down fast to prepare for a May 9 launch date. Colonel Steele himself came to brief Captain Lesperance on what was to be called Operation Iron Triangle. This was going to be another air assault mission with our company alongside Charlie Company and Headquarters Company, all from my battalion. Of course there were to be some nameless pogue attachments in the area as well.

When the news finally filtered down to me, we planned for another Swarmer deal. This was going to be the first time I would operate as an AG for my new gunner, Sergeant Woods. I knew by now what to pack and to prepare for. Everyone in Weapons Squad knew what to expect, and we kept the complaining to a minimum.

The day before we left our FOB, Colonel Steele took the time to give us yet another classic pep talk to prepare us for the mission. I cannot remember what all was said, except the dialogue he spoke really struck us. He repeatedly assured us that we were going to land at a hostile area, that Army intelligence showed that the island (our objective) held dozens of Al Qaeda fighters.

"Guys, you are going to get shot at coming off the helicopter," Colonel Steele said with a powerful voice while he stared deep into the eyes of each of us. "If you don't get shot at, you ought to be surprised."

The words were hard to swallow, but we were all busy soaking up all that he had to say. We had each individually prepared ourselves to come face-to-face with this type of situation for months. It was easy to accept the rationale of facing imminent danger after a Colonel Steele speech. He was such a charismatic man, you wanted to kill anyone who was not a Rakkasan after any one of his speeches. He stated that the area we were to land at was going to be so dangerous that a fierce firefight would be expected. His speeches were always filled with this kind of bravado. Landing at a suspected Al Qaeda compound, he suggested that we should approach with the fiercest aggression toward all males of military age who didn't surrender. "Kill the sonsabitches before they kill you." He was convinced we were about to be thrown to the lions, and of course, we were prepared to fight tooth and nail.

After the uplifting morale-boosting pep talk from our "General Patton," the harsh reality of preparing for such a feat was at hand. The only thing that I was excited about was that Charlie Company would be on this mission with us. "Chopping" Charlie Company was Derek Borden's company. I had not seen him since Kuwait, so I really anticipated seeing how he was faring with the deployment thus far. Charlie Company came to FOB Remagen from their base in Samarra the day before we were to kick off Iron Triangle.

I looked for Borden all day, but I could only find people who knew him, but not his whereabouts. It wasn't until I went to the chow hall that I ran into him.

I was with some guys in my platoon, carrying my tray, when I noticed Borden sitting by himself in the chow hall.

"Derek!" I yelled as I veered away from my buddies to sit with him.

"What's up, buddy? How you been?" Borden said as he extended his hand. I placed my tray in front of him and sat down.

"You like my tooth? More like the lack thereof?" I asked him as I smiled and exposed my half-missing tooth.

"What the hell happened?" Borden said, choking back laughter.

"Shotgun didn't like my smile. Long story short, I'll get it fixed when I go home in two weeks."

"You lucky bastard. I went in December, way too early. You'll miss some of this heat," he said, obviously jealous.

"So you hear anything on Iron Triangle?" I asked him.

"Yeah, oh my, some people are going to die tomorrow." Borden began to talk with a smile. My attention was now fully his. "We were briefed today to expect heavy contact when we land. We're landing early morning, and it's an Al Qaeda training camp. It should be pretty interesting."

"Yeah, we weren't told much. I think we're landing at some old factory building doing the same thing on the other side of the hill that you're landing in. We'll see how fucked up this mission can get. It is the Rakkasans," I stated.

Borden and I continued to talk like schoolgirls and caught up on the latest gossip. We swapped stories about IED experiences and other close calls we'd shared. We didn't stop talking until they began to shut down the chow hall. I had some time on my hands, so we continued to talk for a while outside. I had to ditch him in the evening when my squad prepared to run through some last-minute rehearsals before the day of attack.

The information we were given the night before was not very detailed. We knew my platoon was to land at some compound and search it and expect enemy contact. A nearby compound about a click or two away was to be simultaneously secured by Charlie Company. Enemy contact was constantly reiterated. We were to leave FOB Remagen about two hours before daybreak and fly down south toward Samarra and our objective, near Lake Thar Thar.

We did not get much sleep that night because we had a 2 A.M. wake-up and we had to be staged by 3:30 A.M. In a sleepy haze and lit by the moonlight, I staggered out of my CHU and waited for Sergeant Woods outside of his. Together, we both dragged our zombie-like bodies to the staging area on the tarmac like we had done quite a few times before.

The birds were already parked and lined up there as we ran through roll calls, sensitive item checks, and last-minute changes to anything. They kept reiterating the fact that landing on a hot LZ was highly probable. These were not the words I wanted to hear, since I was scheduled to go home in less than fifteen days. Nevertheless, there was no backing out now. I climbed into my dark Black Hawk and settled in my seat. I hooked my NODs up on my helmet, buckled myself in, and leaned back to shut my eyes.

The flight was going to be longer than the one we had taken back during Swarmer. We were headed down to our objective, which was an area of rural desert near Samarra. With everything quite dark in the helicopter and the sun hours from rising, when we got adjusted to the sounds of the Black Hawk, it was easy to fall asleep. There was nothing better than a power nap before a raid. It also helped in calming whatever nerves we had worked up.

There was always tension when we flew, but flying on our way to a raid where we did not know what we were about to run into always invited butterflies in our stomachs. One thing I did to reduce my own jitters was to stare at other guys and see if they displayed any signs of anxiety. It sounds stupid, but it helped me. Specialist Ly would constantly swing his head as if to crack his neck without hands. Sergeant McCaskill, who sat in front of me, would stare out the window even though it was pitch-black out. I subconsciously would tap both my feet.

We had a bit of a scare halfway through the flight. One of the gunners in my helicopter opened fire with his machine gun. I immediately opened my eyes, just in time to see McCaskill across from me bolt in his seat. I'm convinced if he had not been secured down by his seat belt he would have literally cracked his helmet in half on the metal ceiling. I still don't know why the gunner opened fire during the flight. It was only for three seconds, but it was enough to get my nerves going in high gear. It was black as the ocean floor outside our windows, so I can't imagine what the gunner must have seen to spark him to open fire. The longer the ride got, the more nervous I got. I just wanted to land and get this over with.

"Five minutes!" yelled one of the pilots. Everyone else echoed the command. I reached into my ammo pouch and pulled out an ammunition magazine. I blew into the top of the magazine to get rid of sand that accumulated hourly. I clipped it into my M4 and began quickly to replay in my head the steps of what we were about to do. "Two minutes!" everybody yelled. I pulled back on the charging handle on my M4 and chambered a round, ready to fire. I glanced over at Sergeant Woods, who was busy readjusting his pack and shifting around his machine gun to prepare for a speedy exit. I could also see his lips moving, reciting a prayer. "One minute!" everybody yelled. I closed my eyes and muttered under my breath, "Here we go." Oh, how I wanted to be at home. I couldn't help but see visions in my head of my friends all drinking at their colleges again, and then here I was. "Thirty seconds!" was yelled and re-yelled by everyone. I pulled down my NODs and turned them on. I looked out the window and could see black silhouettes of a silo backdropped by a neon green sky.

As soon as our helicopter touched ground, the door gunner threw open the door and away we went like marathon runners, only we were hunkered down by a few hundred pounds. Within seconds, everyone was out and the Black Hawks were up and away. Silence now surrounded us. Looking through my NODs, I tried to gather in my surroundings. I scanned left and then right, and soon I found myself walking in a line, almost shoulder to shoulder with the rest of my platoon. Everyone was slowly creeping forward with his weapon at the high ready, expecting the bullets to hit us at any second. Each second that passed without gunfire, the higher pitched the thoughts of an inevitable ambush. This shoulder to shoulder–type Napoleonic tactic of approaching the compound was not what we had planned. Nothing ever seemed to happen the way we wanted it to.

As we quietly crept closer and closer to the nearest building, I was just waiting for someone to open fire from one of the windows. I could not believe how quiet everything was. It was definitely one of those times when you say to yourself, *It's almost too quiet*. I looked left again and found Sergeant Woods's silhouette. I ducked out of the assaulting line I was in to link up with him.

Woods and I took a knee in place and removed ourselves from the line. As we tried to get orientated to the surroundings, I saw Second Squad break off and fly into the first building. I held my breath as I anxiously awaited the sound of gunfire. Silence was all I heard. I told Woods to watch the area to our rear, and I turned around to monitor my platoon's advance on the buildings. I feverishly refocused my optic lens to see Third Squad assault and enter another adjacent building. Other than the occasional shouts of demands from my buddies inside the buildings, all seemed to be running smoothly.

Staff Sergeant Poston's voice stuck out over the frequent radio transmissions. I waited to hear my team's next block of instructions. He soon ordered both gun teams to the building in the middle of the compound. It apparently was the tallest building with a roof and accessible by stairs. It offered prime visibility of the surrounding area. Other than the silo next to our building, it did offer the most commanding view of our objective from which to watch my platoon at work.

I met up with Gun 1 at the base of the stairs. The Edwards, consisting of Taylor Edwards and Vinny Edwards (no relation) comprised Gun 1, since Avery was still home on leave. Poston was with Gun 1 and directed them as to which side of the roof to occupy. He then did the same for my team, and Sergeant Woods and I trudged up the stairs and took the opposite end of the roof. We were atop some type of water purifier building judging by the way it looked. The area smelled like the water one would encounter at a pool. It certainly made me think of better times, lounging at the side of a pool.

As I approached our corner of the roof, I saw a large blanket near where I was headed. It was plump, as if a body was underneath. I shifted the selector switch on my M4 from safe to semi as I neared the corner. Expecting a possible booby trap, I didn't want to touch the blanket. Instead, I stomped my feet on the ground next to it and hoped it was someone I'd caught sleeping. Roof sleepers were common to come across in Iraq, since it was a simple way of staying cool during the hot season. In this case, I'd chosen right. Seconds later, the blanket started shifting and a head appeared. A young man about my age pulled the blanket off his face and adjusted his squinty eyes. Within a split second he realized that the muzzle of my weapon was pointed at his face, with me behind it, smiling.

"Good morning, sleepyhead," I said in a sarcastic nurturing tone. "Time to get up for school," I continued as he immediately threw off the blanket and stood up, frightened out of his mind. I searched him quickly, and called to Poston that I was bringing down one male subject. With his hands on his head, I escorted him back down the stairs and turned him over to Third Squad.

I went back to the roof and sat down next to Sergeant Woods, while the rest of the platoon searched the surrounding buildings. We were only a few stories up, so I stayed awake by shouting phrases at the rest of the guys such as "Hurry up, you're slacking" or "Why are you so tired?" They were all things that made them snicker, but that was our style of camaraderie. They got justice whenever they saw me carrying my heavy load.

As the sun began to rise, activity in our compound began to settle. The tall silo to our front was scaled by Ly and his M249 SAW after he'd been ordered to climb it and over-watch the area. He dangerously climbed up this tall silo with all his gear and miraculously made it to the top. He spread his body out and didn't move for hours. I was afraid he would fall asleep and slide off the top.

Another thing I started to make out as the sun rose was the activity of Charlie Company. About two thousand yards away on the opposite hill was the objective of Charlie Company. I could not see the compound they were in because the hill next to it was too large, but I could make out soldiers milling around on the horizon of the hill. An Apache helicopter circled their compound much more than it circled around ours. I wasn't near the RTO to find out what they had encountered, but I hoped for the best.

While time passed and I fought to stay awake, I noticed that Sergeant Woods had lost that struggle. He was slumped over the gun, sleeping like a bear. I didn't wake him because there was no sense. Both gun teams weren't needed. I wasn't part of the few in my platoon who were busting their asses metal detecting the sand. I had my share of that crap, so I was relishing my vacation. We did serve some kind of purpose, since we were the highest point; whenever a car ventured toward our objective, we would call it up on the handheld radio and Third Squad would be in position to stop and search it. I always wondered what would go through an Iraqi man's mind during a routine drive when he'd suddenly see us. That facial expression was something I looked for in my binoculars that made me chuckle and pass the time.

The sound of sporadic gunfire faintly resonated across the valley, off in the distance. It originated from Charlie Company's position. It really aroused the suspicion of most of us, but nothing further was said. I really hoped the best for Borden and all of Charlie Company.

It was almost 9 A.M. before Poston decided to send one gun team down. Woods and Vinny stayed up on the roof as one team while Taylor and I walked down. On the ground, I could see that my platoon was just about done. All males had been handcuffed and separated as usual. Captain Lesperance and Lieutenant Scher discussed with each other their next steps. Overall, operations were pretty much at a close.

One of the men captured was able to pass valuable information on to the captain and the lieutenant, who, with the help of the interpreter, hastily interrogated each handcuffed man. This one coughed up some names of men on some kind of "wanted list" the higher chain of command had. The named men were living in the area, closer to where Headquarters Platoon was conducting searches.

Elements from the Iraqi Army quickly came to our objective and collected the captured Iraqi who was freely giving information. They took him to the home he was confessing about and met up with Headquarters Platoon there. The platoon set up a cordon around the home and let the Iraqi Army take over the raid, followed closely behind by some Angels.

Over the radio transmissions, we soon found out that they'd procured the man in question, who was indeed on the high-value target list. His neighbor, who was also his brother, was home, so they raided that house too. A more in-depth search turned up three extra AK47s and magazines wrapped up in a blanket. Two Angels from Headquarters Platoon found the weapons in a well on the property. The platoon ended up arresting six men, five of whom were on the high-value target list. Our company had come through on the positive spectrum within the first few hours of Operation Iron Triangle, and no casualties.

While that scene was sorted out, I was busy wandering around at my objective. I ventured into the main building, which I found to be abandoned much like all the poor homes I had been in lately. I found a door that was padlocked and a couple of us took turns at trying to break the lock. We ended up just breaking the door off, and found an empty room.

When I came out, I saw that most of my platoon were eating their MREs. Those who weren't were sent sifting through the sand with the metal detectors. I knew I had to either find a spot to eat an MRE or get caught up in the useless search.

"Conklin." I heard my name shouted by Sergeant Caruso. I knew what was coming next. "Go with Sanchez, grab a shovel, and dig anything that registers on his metal detector."

Almost immediately, I reached into my pocket of lies and pulled one out. "I can't, sarnt. Sarnt Poston wants me to relieve Sarnt Woods on the gun on the roof."

"All right. . . . Heiple, go with Sanchez," Caruso finished. Just like that, my lie worked, and it suckered someone else into doing the drudging work. I went back up the stairs to the roof and relieved Woods. Taylor and I ate our MREs up there and talked all morning while the platoon continued to pass the time searching in vain. They were to continue searching until we were given the OK to leave.

As much as I did not want to waste time looking for the nonexistent "weapons of mass destruction," I couldn't take the pounding heat from the tin roof much longer. I yelled down for Woods to come and relieve me, which he did, and I walked down and helped kick sand with the line squads. The only thing I found was garbage, dead sheep, and tin cans.

Soon enough, two LMTVs with pogue drivers came to pick us up, which put an end to our fruitless "dirt kicking." An LMTV (Light Medium Tactical Vehicle) was nothing more than a military truck with a canopied cover over a flatbed end that we would pile our platoon into. We loaded up and sat on MREs and assault packs in the center so we could all face out as we went. We had no room whatsoever for the Iraqi soldiers, so someone stole (commandeered) a blue KIA Bongo truck from the objective, got everyone piled in, and drove that between our two LMTVs. None of our trucks offered any protection, but the threat of IEDs was unheard of in that area of open desert, just like in Operation Swarmer.

One of the benefits of being on a gun team was that we were guaranteed a spot with some room on the truck. Gun 1 decided to be on the lead truck, so they would face their gun forward by placing it on the roof. We took the second truck, so Sergeant Woods and I were guaranteed the rear spot of our LMTV. Everyone had to squish in tighter to make room for our gun, which we just stuck with the barrel hanging off the end and held on to tight while we faced the rear and bounced along.

The first priority we had after we left our objective was to get to the makeshift regimental headquarters operation base, roughly in the middle of our thirty-six-square-kilometer area of operation. On our drive, we all talked about what we grunts would usually talk about: sex, beer, and things we would rather be doing at home. The guys in my platoon who were on their second tour in Iraq kept explaining how much this drive reminded them of how they operated missions during the initial invasion. That opened the discussion on how much the theater of combat had changed since 2003 and speculation about what the future might bring. It was a long but enjoyable ride, except for the numerous bumps in the trek that made the task of not breaking our tailbones troublesome when the truck hit a good one.

On our drive, we could start to see the chemical factories that we had been briefed about prior to the mission. We were now in the center of an old chemical factory from back in Iraq's heyday, known as the Muthana Chemical Complex. We were told all the buildings were sealed off, but who could we really trust? The battalion headquarters contingent was grouped in a large circle in several different vehicles. Around them we saw nothing out in the desert but random piles of extremely flat rubble. These piles were evidence of a once suitable and sturdy building, but now nothing more than the foundation was left visible. They dotted the desert all around. The closer we drove in, the more prevalent the rubble got. Remains of old chain fences still stood in place in some areas, where the fences no longer served any purpose. Soon, giant mounds of dirt that could not be missed were visible across the land. They were about three stories high, with concrete driveways that led into one side of the mound where the remains of the bunker was still intact. In addition to joking that we were all going to die down the road from breathing in the silent death that no one could detect, we joked that we were going to be the platoon that found the imaginary "weapons of mass destruction" our president kept talking about.

As we pulled into the makeshift headquarters, the first thing we saw, other than the grouping of several different military vehicles, was the "POW Corral." It was a roped-off circle with captured Iraqi civilians in it. They sat, squatted, or paced around. Armed Americans were posted like sentries around the ropes to make sure order was present. I wasn't sure what these captives were doing here, how long they'd been here, or what information they had. For the most part, I didn't know who they were, nor did I care.

It was good that we pulled into the battalion headquarters at the time we did, because our LMTV immediately broke down as we entered. At first, we saw this as impending doom, but then reality hit us and we all realized that we would not have to do anything until this problem was fixed. My platoon dismounted both trucks and tried to round up some mechanics. Nobody was in any immediate hurry, but eventually a mechanic was found and he went to work to repair what was busted.

At the battalion headquarters, they naturally were never without goodies, which we quickly partook in. We raided their spread on the table and collected what was a constant staple in Army chow halls in Iraq: muffins and twenty-ounce Gatorades. We all filled our assault packs and left the table practically empty for the pogues.

After I devoured a couple blueberry muffins, I found my platoon next to our disabled truck. They were already engaged in doing what they did best when passing time: sleeping. Everyone was propped on his assault pack in an odd line stemming away from the truck. I followed the dirt bump their bags rested against, dropped my gear at the end of the line, and joined my platoon in getting some shut-eye. It was no easy task for the weak to sleep in the afternoon Iraqi heat. It ranged from an average of 105 to 115 degrees during the daytime. We were all now accustomed to it, but it still hurt every time. The heat sapped whatever energy the weight we were carrying had not drained already. It made plopping down at any moment an easy task.

Before anyone wanted it to happen, our truck was ready, which meant we were too. My platoon loaded back up on the LMTV the same way we had earlier, but instead of taking two LMTVs, we took one and added two platoon Humvees. Gun 1 split up and helped operate the Humvees' turrets, while Sergeant Woods and I stayed together on the LMTV.

Third Platoon was already off in their own designated area doing whatever they were supposed to do. Headquarters Platoon was also off on their own, and my platoon had our own agenda ahead too. Second Platoon was still detached from the company in order to run the prison back on FOB Remagen.

As reluctant and unmotivated as we all were, we headed out into the great wide open with gusto. I think we had an agenda like a certain area to check, but I certainly didn't know, much less care. That was for Lieutenant Scher to worry about and us to shut up about and execute. Wherever we drove and needed to search, that's what we would do.

We drove a few miles out into the empty and unthreatening land-scape, until we came across our first objective. It was what looked to be an old gas station, with nothing else nearby for miles. It had obviously been abandoned for several years. Everyone in my platoon acted like it was Operation Swarmer all over again, only in slow motion. Nobody jumped off the truck to go kick in a door. Instead, soldiers climbed down the sides of the trucks and began to look around the buildings as if we had all day. There was no threat. Sergeant Woods and I gingerly hopped off the back end of the LMTV and lounged with our gun, next to a con-crete island where gas pumps used to be installed.

It was a miserable and boring task. As a perk of the gun team, I just spread out and got comfortable in one spot and never moved. Woods, who had to be narcoleptic, fell asleep in place while still propping his head up. I had to hand it to him; I was jealous of how easily he could escape the uncomfortable feeling of sweat-soaked clothes in the heat and still fall asleep. With no immediate threat and nothing to be alarmed at, I let him keep sleeping. I remained on my side of the gun and watched everyone meander around the empty shacks.

It was no surprise that nothing was found and there was nothing to report. The squads spray-painted their symbols signifying the search complete for the surrounding area, and we loaded back up on the LMTV. Woods and I were once again the last two on and aimed our gun out.

We drove out to another location, and it quickly dawned on me: This was definitely Operation Swarmer all over again, only no Black Hawk helicopters. The looks on the faces of my platoon as they fruitlessly searched house to house were comparable to soldiers' on the Bataan Death March.

Seeing that Woods and I disembarked from the truck with the gun at every stop, I devised a plan that would benefit both the platoon and my gun team.

"Sarnt Poston, I have a theory," I said to him before I began to get off the LMTV at another objective.

"What's that, Gaylord?" Poston amused himself by thinking up a forgotten nickname The Hodge had once called me in 2004.

"Ah funny, but seriously, wouldn't it make sense to leave my gun team on the LMTV each time we drive up to a new objective? Because in essence, we can be a mobile gun truck, and if shit hits the fan, the driver will drive us where needed. That way we could be anywhere quick, like a Humvee, dismount, and not keep lugging around ammo and mounting and dismounting each time we park." I pleaded my case as hard as I could to him.

"You just want to sit on the truck under the shade of the canopy, dontcha?" Poston said with a smirk.

"That's always a benefit," I said quickly back at him.

"All right. Besides, there ain't shit that's gonna happen anyways," Poston finished.

I had pleaded a successful case and enjoyed the spoils of my victory. Sergeant Woods and I quickly built a bench out of MRE boxes and remained facing out the back end of the LMTV. We were now living "shamtastic," chilling on the truck while the squads searched for imaginary weapons.

I got quite a lot of resentment from everyone, but once I asked them if they would like to join Weapons Squad, I would get the same negative response. I kept harassing younger soldiers in my platoon, saying that they were someday going to replace me in Weapons Squad. It always scared them. I especially loved catching Sergeant Fooks gazing at my machine gun from time to time.

"You miss her, don't you?" I said with a grin.

"Fuck no. I did my time," he said as he snapped out of his stare.

"You're welcome back to the 'dark side' anytime you want," I said from my shaded bench, while looking down at him.

"Hey, Dexter!" Vinny yelled from across the ways to Fooks. Dexter was a nickname he always called Fooks. The origin of Dexter came from how much Fooks looked like the popular cartoon character from *Dexter's Laboratory*. To me, Fooks looked like a young Michael Caine.

"Dexter, you want to carry my gun for a while?" Vinny continued to yell at Fooks until he got the answer he was looking for.

"Fuck you, dude," Fooks replied.

"Weapons is definitely shamtastic, living it up here on this truck while we search for things that don't exist," Staff Sergeant Jirkovsky would always say to me.

"Hey, don't hate the player, hate the game," I said in reply, with a witty smirk on my face.

So the day continued much like they all had during Operation Swarmer. This time it was from the comfort of MRE boxes on the LMTV, as I watched the rest of the platoon kick dust around numerous abandoned buildings. I did from time to time step off the truck to stretch my legs a little and help search, but I loved being in Weapons Squad for once.

During a search of one of the countless farmhouses we came to, Staff Sergeant Hubert and Sergeant McCaskill uncovered a small cache. They found two improvised hand grenades in a small hole that had been dug into the side of a berm. With our recent success of the April Fool's Cache, a close inspection of the sides of berms was our specialty. Along with the grenades, they also found two bags of propellant and about twenty blasting caps.

This immediately changed the pace at which we searched because now everyone searched more in depth. Lieutenant Scher did his usual interrogation with the landowner, who happened to be a woman. Her husband was suddenly absent. It seemed that every household we came to, all the men were "gone" and the women left to run the farm. Makes you wonder if a little bird tipped people off.

Nothing more was found at that farmhouse. We called EOD to come collect what we'd found and we were off to the next farmhouse to continue our search. First Platoon continued all day, until the sun began to recede and brought a close to the day's searching.

Other than the joint task in the morning of rounding up five highly valued targets and Second Squad's small cache, it had been a boring day. After the final house for the night, we piled into our LMTV and had a relaxing and joyous ride back to the makeshift battalion headquarters. There were old jokes and inside jokes passed between us, such as old Hodge tales, anecdotes about our former platoon sergeant Quinn, and the quoting of dozens of comedy films. Overall, it was a happy time in the back of the LMTV. It reminded me a lot of returning from the field after a training exercise at Fort Campbell, Kentucky.

When we got back to the battalion headquarters, we all immediately opened up some MREs. With some pogues watching the perimeter, we for once were not required to run guard, which was fully embraced by all. First Platoon just spent a couple hours walking around our vehicles, chomping down on some MREs and enjoying some good old conversation.

At one point we did hear some words through the grapevine about Charlie Company getting into a firefight and killing a few people. Things were still being hashed out, and Charlie Company was not present at the battalion headquarters that night, so we couldn't hear it from the horse's mouth. I just kept hoping Borden was all right.

The night was enjoyable, much like a mass slumber party. Since our company did not have to pull guard, we all pulled out blankets and slept in close proximity to each other under the stars. Going to sleep under the Iraqi night sky was always breathtaking because the sky was just lit up like a Christmas tree every night. I had a good night's sleep, except for being woken up by the sound of Sergeant Woods sleep-talking. It was startling at first, because he seemed to be weeping and shaking, and reciting some prayer out loud. I stared at him in the dark to make sure he was OK.

"Sarnt Woods," I said to him as I shook him awake.

"Wha-what's up, man?" Woods said to me with his eyes still closed.

"I'm just making sure everything is all right. You OK?" I asked.

"Yup, just fine," he said as he rolled back over. The next morning I asked him about his dream, and he said that he had no recollection of sleep-talking or of me waking him up.

The next day started off like any normal day at the office. We were awakened by each other and prepared to pack up our ponchos. Some men dry-shaved with razors, while many just "roughed it" and kept their stubble.

As we were all preparing for another day of searching random farmhouses, a rumor arose that we were to be sent back to FOB Remagen. This came as great news to all except Lieutenant Scher, who loved his job too much. The main suspicion as to why we were being scrubbed so soon was that the rumor we'd heard about Charlie Company on their objective was much more complex than we had thought.

We heard rumors such as that they had killed a couple of people on their objective, they had killed an old innocent man, or they had killed prisoners as they attempted to run away. We even heard that some members of Charlie Company had been wounded. You name it, we probably heard it. Whatever had actually happened, one thing was certain: we were being sent back earlier than planned. Oh, how we rejoiced, shook hands, and high-fived each other in celebration, as if the war itself had ended.

As my luck would have it, however, Lieutenant Scher was quick to ruin this good thing for me and those I shared his truck with. Instead of waiting for the helicopters to transport my company back to FOB Remagen, he elected our Humvee to stay behind with another company Humvee for a detail.

Oh, how Taylor, Hilmo, Reese, and I fumed over this selection. Lieutenant Scher, if he could have had his way, would have lived outside the wire, to be available to do any mission that came his way. This was the only drawback to being in his Humvee, as none of the rest of us wanted to be outside the wire. Taylor and I really abused our relationship with Scher and made fun of him, but we all laughed about it at the same time too, so the tension didn't really exist, but this time I was pissed. This meant that instead of a safe flight back to FOB Remagen, we would then have to drive back on the highway, over an hour on the road. I hated IEDs and this drive back was not something I looked forward to.

The detail we were held back for was to "clean up" after the previous day's searches. Things we had marked, such as empty shacks and homes, were to be demolished. If nothing else, it sounded like an opportunity to properly extinguish pent-up anger by destroying things.

Naturally, however, the things marked along our premeditated route of carnage were not what any of us expected. As we drove to the first grid coordinate, we found a tiny brick wall about two feet long and two feet high, out in the middle of nowhere. How this could ever be a threat to anyone puzzled us. Nevertheless, Taylor and I kicked it down with zest.

We thought that tiny bump to push over would be the smallest of our destruction, but boy were we wrong. Every time we arrived at a place we were plotted to visit, we came upon one of these little dinky piles of rocks out in the middle of nowhere that all we could do with was push them over. It was fruitless and redundant. The "Bitch Wagon" was not a quiet Humvee. Taylor and I really poured it into Lieutenant Scher, and begged him to tell us what idiot had devised such a stupid task. We were wasting time out in the middle of the desert to push over abandoned mud walls. My deployment once again earned another notch demonstrating how poorly our superior infantry soldiers were being utilized in Iraq.

After a dozen pointless stops, we finally broke Lieutenant Scher. I knew he did not want to call headquarters and bitch, so he just said on the radio that we were asking for an end of mission. The bitching immediately ceased. It was almost dead silent while Taylor and I secretly basked in our victory. We had finally broken Scher, but there wasn't a real victory. I could tell he was quite perturbed himself with the task. I quietly whispered, "I love you, sir," and peeked with my peripherals to see him produce a miniature smile.

We drove across the desert on our way back to the battalion headquarters, which was by now breaking camp. It remained a quiet ride. We did stop at one last location to search through old rubble, walking on what looked like a former small shopping mall, now two inches in height. Just a massive stretched pile of rubble in the middle of the desert. I played around the area while kicking the rubble to do a look-over for any loose arsenal.

I got an eerie feeling as I walked there. Knowing that this was a military compound at the start of the war stood as proof as to how accurate and destructive our bombing campaign had been. It was now three years after the "shock and awe" bombs had leveled Iraq's military might. I never saw any human bones or body parts among the rubble, but I did not rule out the chances of them being lower than surface level or of wild dogs having taken off with any exposed meat left. There were plenty of ripped uniforms and empty sandals scattered about, and an occasional gas mask, helmet, or piece of an AK47 was also sometimes spotted.

We finished up with this final place to check. Lieutenant Scher decided not to head back to the battalion headquarters, where they were still breaking down their camp. He knew that we would be tasked out as soon as we arrived. Scher was finally thinking like us instead of like "Captain America." He decided to leave our Humvees parked where they were and have lunch while we waited. Finally, some enjoyment was achieved. Despite the blistering heat and no wind, everything was peaceful. We all broke out some MREs, took our helmets off, and yapped our mouths off in conversations that now escape me.

As we waited for headquarters to pack up, I decided to relieve myself now that I had time before the long journey home. I grabbed a shovel, took some toilet paper we kept in the truck, and walked up on one of the sand bunkers that still existed, looking similar to a small pyramid. I found a nice spot high up, dug a hole, and the rest is history. Afterward, I got back in my truck just in time to hear that the battalion was staging for a convoy back to their respective FOBs. Some units were going to their FOB in Samarra; we were the only contingent going to FOB Remagen, and the rest of the elements were continuing north to FOB Speicher. We all formed one mass convoy and drove north.

We had many miles to travel until we reached more familiar territory near Tikrit. I was apprehensive at first with traveling on roads I had never been on before, which meant I didn't know what to expect. I had a useless position in the Humvee, as I was seated behind the driver. Within the first few minutes on the sad excuse for a road, I knew that I was in a dangerous place. I think people were calling this Fallujah Road, but I could not be positive. I didn't even know where Fallujah was and I didn't want to know. The sizes of the craters on the edges of the road, the apparent scars from IEDs, were so large I could have used one as a foxhole. It was no surprise that within moments of getting our convoy under way, we came to a halt.

Someone at the head of the column had called over the radio that they had spotted what they believed to be an IED. My Humvee was near the end, but I did not mind this stop. I knew that we were near the end of a convoy of over twenty vehicles, so the likelihood of an IED bypassing all who were before my truck was very small.

It was going to be a long journey back in our sauna of a Humvee. Our air-conditioning still never worked, and all the fan did was blow hotter air around. As we waited inside our truck while some EOD contingent removed whatever device had been spotted up ahead, I just tried to survive our oven-on-wheels that was set to bake. The excessive heat made it impossible to find any comfort. It would get so hot at times in that Humvee that I would get sick of wiping the rivers of sweat off my face. It occurred every three seconds, so I just let the sweat collect and fall and soak my vest and thighs. It was something we all had to adapt to, but it was never easy.

Soon enough, the all clear was given over the radio and our Humvee continued to trek along with the convoy. With the heat so high and the slight vibration felt when my back was against the seat while we were in motion, it was almost impossible not to fall asleep. We had a long ride back, so I knew it was going to be a tough battle for all. Instead of fighting it, I just shut my eyes, and that's all it took. I was out like a newborn baby.

I was surprised to find that nobody woke me up. It was not until we were at our weapon-clearing barrels inside the compound of FOB Remagen that I finally woke up.

"That was an enjoyable mission," I said with a yawn and plenty of sarcasm. Nobody cared that I was sleeping. Hilmo caught a couple minutes of shut-eye along the way and so did Lieutenant Scher. It was in that moment that I realized my Humvee crew was the best crew I could be stuck with. We were all complacent enough on missions when we should be, and I knew we could have our head in the game when shit went sour.

Operation Iron Triangle was now officially over for us. We got back to FOB Remagen in time to enjoy some cooked food in our chow hall. When I walked in, I was surprised to see men from Charlie Company and Scouts sitting down as well. I had forgotten that they were still on our base. I parted with my crew, filled up a plate, and searched for Borden. I soon found him sitting with another one of my close friends within the battalion, Specialist Jason "Stack" Stachowski from Scouts Platoon.

"What's up, ladies?" I said as I sat down next to Stack and across from Borden.

"Hey, man," said a somber Stack.

"What's up, buddy," mumbled Borden.

"I don't want to interrupt what you guys are talking about, but why is everyone so depressed? I know that mission was once again a giant goat fuck in the ass, but I didn't think it was that bad. Whatever happened with your company, Derek?"

"It's just that . . . ," he said to me.

"You didn't hear?" Stack said to me, and his tone broke any smile I had. In the gossip world, that one phrase he'd just stated grabbed my full attention.

"No! What happened?" I said, wide-eyed. I'm surprised I didn't choke on the piece of pineapple I was eating.

A cloud of dark suspicion hovered over Charlie Company. In time and through several firsthand accounts, the gloom of the incident at Charlie Company's objective came to light. Rumors and facts flew like an uncontrollable fire, and slowly I could put together piecemeal what had happened.

Simultaneous to my company's landing at our objective, Charlie had landed at theirs and come upon similar conditions. For reasons unknown to me, some of the soldiers fired upon a man in a house. Other Iraqi males within the vicinity were quickly rounded up and detained. All seemed close to protocol, but what happened next was the action everyone was talking about.

It had been only a day since the event took place, and already it had become hard for me to ascertain accurate facts. A statement was issued to all Rakkasans to enact their own version of remaining silent about the mission, but it is a hard task to seal the lips of soldiers. It would take me almost a year before I would hear any verifiable statements of what happened.

On Charlie's objective, some soldiers rounded up some "military-age men" and handcuffed them like protocol asked. Through some twisted changes of events, a couple soldiers decided to release the prisoners and stage an escape. In cold blood, the unarmed Iraqi men were shot down dead and a story was concocted to protect the soldiers.

As I sat in the chow hall, I took a couple seconds to let things wrap around my head. I scanned around and could tell everyone was talking about the same thing. Eyeballs and fingers kept being pointed in the direction of two soldiers: Specialist Hunsaker and Private First Class Clagett of Charlie Company. Hunsaker had a large scrape wound on the side of his face. Part of his story was that one of the prisoners supposedly grabbed his knife and slashed his face. It did not take a genius to tell that the scrape was across the whole side of his face, yet the chin strap on his helmet was intact. No one ever had his helmet off during a raid, so that just made Hunsaker's alibi all the more unbelievable. He slowly poked at his food next to Clagett, in silence, ostracized from everyone.

Contemplating this dark cloud of an evil deed that hung over Charlie Company and the entire Rakkasan regiment, I find solace in knowing that good eventually outweighed evil. Through months of interrogation, interviews, and sworn statements, three soldiers would eventually be convicted and sent to prison.

I could sense the tension in Borden and Stack's demeanor. They were both afraid as to what was going to happen to Charlie Company. With filling out so many statement forms, someone was going to get burned. A lot of people's careers were on the line over something that a few bad apples had done. In one mission, the future of Charlie Company had been put in turmoil. I hoped that Colonel Steele wouldn't be a target for this investigation, because that would put the future of the entire Rakkasan regiment in jeopardy. It took everything I had not to go punch Hunsaker right in the face in the chow hall.

We were not going on any missions on the day of our return, and our patrol area of Tikrit was still being temporarily patrolled by some field artillerists who'd taken over while we were out on Iron Triangle. Charlie Company was supposed to leave that afternoon, but instead their commanders were being debriefed and numerous people were still filling statements out. I parted with Borden and we wished each other the best of luck for the remainder of our deployment.

Our nightly squad meeting held in Staff Sergeant Poston's CHU gave us an extensive debriefing of Operation Iron Triangle. We were informed that some general would probably be on our FOB any day now and would randomly pick soldiers to ask what our escalation-of-force measures were. I never did see a general. One thing though was certain. We were told we were no longer allowed to talk about Operation Iron Triangle. It notoriously became known between us as "Operation That Which We Do Not Speak Of."

SNEAKING AROUND AT NIGHT

"Everything smelled like death, piss, and shit."

Our company got back into the groove that sucked. Daily patrols began the next day. A week of "partnership patrols" and then a week of QRF, rinse, and repeat. Things could not have been any more routine and monotonous.

On May 15, we tried another one of those sniper drop-off missions. This time around, I was on the team that would be cooped up in a house to watch IED Alley. Around midnight, our platoon staged and left FOB Remagen. We drove to Kadasiyah and were dropped off with everyone that was dismounting that early morning. After walking a few streets, the rest of the dismounted element got back into the Humvees while four others and I broke off and looked for a house to enter. I still carried the most gear out of them all, because I was carrying the tons of ammunition and equipment for the M240B for some unknown reason.

Our objective was to enter a house in the dead of night and remain on the roof to monitor any activity on IED Alley, without our presence being known. These missions had always sounded cool to me, but I'd always been in the mounted element. This was my first dismounted sniper drop mission, and I was happy with that decision.

It was a lonely feeling sneaking around homes in the dark of night with just four other soldiers and an interpreter. We knew the mounted element was not far off, but they still were not close enough for comfort. I never really liked using NODs at night, but they sometimes helped when the moon was the only light we had.

We walked by a few homes before Staff Sergeant Hubert found one that we would be entering. Naturally, he chose one that forced us to cross through some rubble between two houses first. It was a typical garbage pile and no one really knew what we were walking through. Everything smelled like death, piss, and shit, but that was Iraq in a nutshell and we were mostly accustomed to it.

I followed the man in front of me and tried to make sense of the uneven ground through my crappy night vision. A mixture of the shifty ground and my excessive weight sent me crashing into the garbage face-first and it made a lot of noise. We were trying to sneak around, and I felt like I'd just blown our cover. The curfew was in effect, so we knew there should not be anyone out this early in the morning, but we also did not want to wake anyone up. I slowly tried to pick myself up, and I could hear the others around me laughing quietly.

"Fuck you, bitches," I whispered loud enough for them all to hear me. My gloves and knees were soaked in something I did not want to know. As our small element neared a wire fence, Hubert began to cut it with his wire cutters. We made it through the nasty obstacle and came to the front of the house.

As with every Iraqi home, an eight-foot-tall concrete wall surrounded the house. We quietly checked the front gate to ensure that it was locked. Without making any chatter and knowing what needed to be done, I moved toward the wall and got down on all fours. Quickly, one of the guys stepped on my back vest plate and maneuvered over the wall. He unlatched the front gate and we all quietly entered the home.

It was always unnerving when we entered a house, especially knowing that we were seconds away from scaring the living hell out of whoever lived there. We quickly and quietly began to walk into black rooms with guns raised and flashlights shining. Two of the guys found a man and his wife sleeping in bed and woke them up. They were scared but completely cooperative.

Hubert corralled them in the center of the house and interrogated them. He asked them simple standard questions such as whether there were any additional people in the house and if there were any weapons. The man mentioned that he had a pistol in one of his rooms, and I went ahead and searched the room in question.

I performed a thorough inspection and found several Iraqi Army uniform bits from when Hussein ruled with an iron fist. I also came across a shiny silver pistol. It was probably some type of gift, and damn was it beautiful. Hubert, a gun enthusiast, just about shat himself when he saw it. Probably out of fear more than gratitude, the Iraqi man told us we could keep it, but sadly we knew we could not, but we kept it in our possession for safety while we remained in the house.

After the house was cleared, we set up an over-watch position on the roof. We set rotations to watch over IED Alley with our thermal device and to make sure no people were ever spotted on the road. It was a boring shift on the roof, but everyone was alert because we all wanted desperately to find someone emplacing an IED.

On my rotation away from the vigilant watch, I spent my time off downstairs keeping company with the nervous man and woman. I could tell they were scared beyond words. It was about three in the morning, and I knew they would rather be sleeping than being babysat by armed American kids in their own home. With the help of the interpreter, I tried to break the tension and talk with them. The man did not say much, but his wife was more open for conversation. Their tension and nervousness never did ease up though. I did not win any hearts and minds that morning.

After several hours of our rotating eyes on IED Alley, the sun was coming up and we were about to break down our observation post. But just as soon as we called our mounted element back from the Birthday Palace, an explosion shook through the air.

"What the fuck?" Hubert said as we made eye contact with each other while standing next to the husband and wife. Hubert ran upstairs to the roof to ascertain the situation. Apparently, although we had been watching a large portion of IED Alley, an IED had gone off on Third Platoon at the opposite end of the road, along the northern portion of Kadasiyah, a stretch of the road that we could not see from the house we were in. Third Platoon was conducting a route clearance for the standard QRF run in the morning, and luckily the IED did little damage, without any injuries.

We collected our gear and gathered back in the center of the house on the first floor. We spoke through the interpreter to apologize to the older couple for the panic we had put them through. We did our typical hand gestures over our hearts and proceeded out their front door and gate. The mounted element was outside waiting for our arrival.

"Way to go, fuckers. Were you sleeping?" Sergeant Fooks said from the turret, in his typical sarcastic way, as soon as they saw us.

"Dude, it was on the opposite end of what we were watching," I said in a serious tone.

"Chill, dude, I don't give a fuck," he responded with a chuckle. I smiled in return.

PASSING THE TIME

"Wow, sir, I admire your chivalry, but get the fuck outta here!"

The summer had definitely arrived in Iraq. Not only was it always hot, it was now deathly hot. There were some benefits to the excessive heat. We were no longer doing PT such as running around the FOB, since the word around was that there was no sense running and getting so dehydrated unless you were on patrol. The best thing about the heat was that when I needed to shower, I never needed a towel. I just put on a pair of PT shorts and sandals and walked to the shower trailer, which was located about two CHUs away from mine. I would shower, and when I was done, I just walked outside. About the time I was back in my CHU, I was practically dry.

I don't know if it was because I was heading home soon or what, but I started to get in a good mood. There also was a rumor floating around that FOB Remagen would be shutting down and we would have to move to FOB Speicher. That was a great rumor to us. The rumor started to gain credibility when I was told to pack my stuff up in my CHU in case everyone moved while I was on leave. Yeah, the heat was bad, the patrols were boring, and the air conditioner in our truck still didn't work, but nothing seemed to faze me. All I could think about was what I was going to do at home.

Days before my R&R departure, things became fun again. I was refusing to be left off the patrol roster, and instead I let other guys in my truck have the missions that I would have had off. I did this because I was leaving soon and the chance of them getting more time off would then be slimmer.

More than six months into constant daily patrols, it wasn't hard to tell who the certain people were who were burned out. I myself was way beyond burned out. Taylor too. One of the reasons we ridiculed and made fun of the lieutenant so much to his face was that he was the polar opposite of us. It seemed that he enjoyed the drudgery of patrols more and more each day. I guess the positive and negative equaled out, because Taylor and I had a lot of fun picking him apart. He let us. I knew it was Lieutenant Scher's way of keeping us from flipping out. That was how we vented and enjoyed things during patrols.

I realized how important it was to add humor to our daily lives because being deployed was a really, really, really lonely experience. I appointed myself the guy who never really cared much about anything but was always reliable. I tried to be the clown of the platoon to lighten things up. It could be anything, from as little as telling a joke to one buddy, to acting like a complete idiot in front of everyone just so they could crack jokes at me.

One gag I did days before I left for R&R came during our pre-patrol briefing. It was the same spiel every day. The words were ingrained in everyone's head because they'd been repeated so often. It always came to a time when the lieutenant or whoever was in charge of the mission would point to someone at random and that person would describe things verbatim, such as a quick first-aid lecture, and cover the levels of escalations such as the shout, show, shove, shoot method.

When my turn came, I took it upon myself to rat off the speech from memory but with a little spice. I reached into my pocket and pulled out two hard, white, square pieces of gum. I put one on my full front tooth and the other on my other front tooth that was still broken in half. I knew I looked like an idiot, but I didn't care. I kept my hand over my mouth until just the right time.

"Someone give me the escalation of forces," Lieutenant Scher said, opening the floor to the platoon.

"Shout, show, shove, shoot. You shout to signal. . . ." I kept right with the whole dialogue without hesitation while everyone laughed. I must have looked like the White Rabbit from *Alice in Wonderland.* Everyone had at least a smile on his face. I knew that as tedious and boring as our job was, the littlest thing could change someone's day. And this far into our deployment everyone's patience was thin.

During routine patrols, we would always stop for dead animals in the road. We had learned the hard way months prior when a dog packed with an IED exploded on my platoon. Whenever we came to a dead animal in or on the side of the road, we would immediately stop. Sometimes we would shoot a couple rounds through it, but most times we would call the nearest Iraqi Police and tell them to get out there and drag it off the road.

One patrol, we actually witnessed a civilian car hit a wild dog and just kept on driving. Instead of creating a headache for a future patrol, we decided to get it off the roadway. We locked down the road and stopped the traffic. I knew we had a shovel in the trunk so I headed back to the trunk to retrieve it. By the time I'd grabbed the shovel and proceeded to the dead carcass, I saw that Ram had literally picked up the dead dog by the bloody tail and was dangling it in the air. He then satanically shook it in front of all the traffic that we had halted. He had his tongue out like some devil worshipper as he flung the dead dog meters away from the roadway. I just dropped my shovel and busted up laughing. So did everyone else. The best part was the look on the faces of the people in their cars. If they'd thought we were sick and twisted before, this proved it certain.

Things were definitely getting better near the end of May. To top it off, Avery had returned from his leave a couple days before I left.

"Avery!" I yelled when news of his return hit my ears. I ran into his CHU to find him lying on his bed. "Welcome back to Hell, mother-fucker!" I said to him as I jumped on him.

"Ouch! Get off! I fucked up my arm," Avery said with minor laughter.

"What the hell happened?" I asked him. I'd known him long enough to know when he wasn't joking. Apparently, his last night in America was the cause of his pain, but he only vaguely remembered it. He had been completely drunk, and deservedly so, and hurt himself. He believed the injury stemmed from jumping onto a picnic table and breaking the table in half, with his shoulder taking the full force.

I went out to clean my Humvee from the prior mission and Avery came with me. We talked about every little thing he'd done when he was home. I was so thrilled to have him back, plus it motivated me thinking on my travels back home due shortly. We talked nonstop, all the way through dinner and into the preparations for the evening route clearance of MSR Tampa. He helped me check all the oil levels and otherwise get ready for the mission. I was so glad to have Avery back. Things were now full circle.

Everyone who came back from leave always said how much he actually missed the platoon when he was gone. I would always say to those guys, "Not me! Screw you all. I'm going to have so much fun forgetting this place." It was all said with humor, as I was known for my sarcasm in my company. One thing Taylor and I were really pushing for was that Lieutenant Scher still did not have a date set for his R&R leave.

"Sir, when are you taking leave?" became the question of the year in our truck.

"Never," he would always say. "Why would I take leave? And miss this stuff? No way, man. I told the commander I'm not taking my leave," Lieutenant Scher said.

"Wow, sir, I admire your chivalry, but get the fuck outta here!" I would plead with him while I laughed.

Taylor would always conjure up some witty and comical story. "Why don't you want to go home, sir? You can do whatever you want. We'll even let you take some MREs home with you, and you can drink minimal amounts of water, and you can suck in the U.S."

We were both begging for a break from Scher. He was a great guy and truly loved what he was doing, but his love for something we despised so much boiled our blood.

"Sir, whatever you do, please don't take leave while I'm gone, because when I return, it'll be like you never left. You should plan it that you leave when I return, so we won't see each other for, like, two months. Doesn't that sound awesome?" I jokingly asked him.

"Fuck that," he said in return. Internally, I was happy he was swearing, which was a complete 180-degree spin from the beginning of the deployment, when he never swore. "Freak-head" was his choice of swear word then. This late in the deployment, he used the big-boy words such as the F-word. Oh, how proud I was. I'm certain Taylor and I had corrupted him, from the shining example of a fresh soldier to a hardened, bitter veteran.

"These are sexy missions and one day you'll miss them," Scher said with a hint of sarcasm.

"Sir, this is definitely *not* sexy," I retorted with a deadpan expression.

One patrol worth remembering was during another day of gas station checks. In the middle of the afternoon, we arrived at one of the gas stations in the heart of Tikrit which was lined up with cars that stretched what seemed like all the way out of the city limits. It was our job to get inside the walled-up gas station and see how the police were controlling the pumps.

"Ha-ha-ha. Yeah right, sir. How the hell are we gonna get through this traffic jam?" Avery asked Lieutenant Scher once he saw the magnitude of the melee. Avery turned on the siren on our vehicle, but all that did was make any car on the road move off to the side, which actually created more chaos.

"Fire some warning shots and wave your arms and tell them to get the hell out of the way," Scher yelled up to me since I was in the gunner's turret. "Get out of the way!" he continued to yell from the door that he had now opened. Our windows could not roll down because of the extra body armor plates we put in there.

"I have a better idea," I said as I squatted down inside the vehicle. "Kill the siren, Avery, and give me the mic to the PA system."

Avery cut the wailing siren as I handed the mic to Jerry, our interpreter.

"Take this and tell them that if they don't move every car out of sight in the next thirty seconds, I'm gonna open fire." Jerry had begun to shout orders in Arabic over our loudspeaker, when I abruptly interrupted him. "And tell them I'm fucking crazy and trigger happy," I said as I stood up with my head outside the turret.

Within seconds, people came out of every nook and cranny, and vehicles disappeared like some crazy magic trick. It reminded me of a scene from a movie where a place is filled with illegal immigrants, and one man from the INS appears and people skedaddle. It was hilarious. I do not know for certain if our interpreter said everything I wanted him to say, but it worked. Avery was laughing uncontrollably.

"That's our new trick from now on," I shouted down the hole. The way I acted inside the Humvee and outside the turret was like a split personality. Inside the vehicle was where I laughed and smiled, but as soon as I stood up and was eye-to-eye with the people, I was deadpan and intimidating. I would frequently lock eyes with civilians who fumbled for their keys as they worked feverishly to open their cars. I would produce a sinister smile to expose my missing tooth. I looked like a crazy man.

Within my allotted deadline, the cars were gone and we locked down the road. The dismounted elements entered the compound and inspected how the gas station was run.

A PIT STOP HOME

"Hey there, high speed."

When the word came to leave, I was more than ready to go. On the morning of May 23, I was scheduled to leave FOB Remagen by a Black Hawk ride around ten in the morning. I was more excited at the fact that I could sit and eat breakfast in the chow hall and know I would not be called away for a QRF mission or something else stupid.

I went into the chow hall and saw most of my platoon sitting down for breakfast. First Platoon was still on QRF duty that week, so I joked with them all by saying that I hoped something happened so they would have to throw their meal away and drive off base. It happened so often that it was not an outlandish statement.

As I sat with Avery and Lieutenant Scher, I could not help but rub in the fact that I was going home while the others "enjoyed" the heat. Then Scher asked me something that I'd never expected.

"Do you know a Robert Seidel?" Scher asked me.

"Huh? Seidel?" I questioned back.

"Do you know any Seidels from Gettysburg?" he clarified.

"Um . . . It sounds familiar, but off the top of my head, I can't think of one. Why?"

"A Robert Seidel was killed in Iraq a few days ago. He's from Gettysburg," he said while he poked at his omelet.

"Seidel? From Gettysburg? You sure he was from Gettysburg? Where did you hear this?" I broke out several questions too fast.

"Yeah, he's listed as being from Gettysburg. We were both at West Point at the same time." Scher spoke in a dismal tone.

"What happened?" I asked.

"He is a lieutenant with Tenth Mountain. Killed by an IED in Baghdad," Lieutenant Scher continued.

"Holy shit. From Gettysburg? Damn, I'm sure it's front-page news in my town. Wow. That sucks," I said in a soft voice. "I'll call home and find out more while I'm at Speicher." Not a word was spoken until I was done with my meal and I bid everyone a farewell as I took my tray away from the table to leave.

I walked back to my CHU to pick up my assault pack, weapon, and a duffel bag. I stopped at the company arms room and dropped off my sensitive items. As soon as I'd turned them in, it was like I entered a new world of freedom. It was like the difference between night and day when I no longer had a rifle in Iraq. With just my bags and helmet, I walked with a kick in my step to some pogue office to sign my name out of some roster before I could await the Black Hawk bound to pick me up. I signed a few papers, not knowing really what they all were, but I didn't care.

"All right. You're good to go," said one of the female pogues. "Would you like someone to drive you down to the airfield on a golf cart?"

"No, no. That's all right. It's not that far. I'm used to walking," I said humbly back. It really wasn't far at all. The airstrip was a little more than a football field away. Being the grunt that I was, I never really took many favors from pogues.

"You sure?" she asked again.

I quickly realized, *Hell, I'm on vacation. The good times start now.*

"Sure. I guess. If it's not a problem," I said back. So I walked outside the finance office trailer and found a golf cart which I threw my duffel bag and assault pack on. Out came a stereotypical pogue, extra large in size, with a helmet that was two sizes too small.

"Headed home?" he asked me while he slowly walked to the golf cart.

"No. I want to take this golf cart out on a patrol with me," I replied sarcastically.

"You don't want to do that. It won't offer much protection from roadside bombs," he said back with a laugh.

I smiled to show him I thought that statement was humorous. Simultaneously in my head I thought of saying, *What do you know about IEDs you fat-fuck!* Good thing I had a strong inner monologue. My short drive was over before another word was said. I sat there on the edge of the airstrip with my duffel bag and waited for an inbound Black Hawk.

I did not have to wait long until I could hear the familiar sound of the blades of a Black Hawk slapping in the air at a distance and gradually growing louder. Soon, the beautiful aircraft came floating in, glistening from the bright afternoon sun. As soon as it touched ground, I had my bags in hand, helmet on, and I dashed the thirty yards to the bird. I guess it was force of habit to do that, because there was no rush on this ride. Someone was slowly getting off while I stood like an overeager soldier until there was room to get inside.

After I quickly buckled into my seat harness, we were up in the air and making a straight shot to FOB Speicher. I couldn't get over the fact that there was so much open space in the Black Hawk, with only three people. I had grown accustomed to being packed in like sardines, with enough gear to sink a ship. With two others inside and hardly any baggage, it was a comfy ride. We even rode with the doors wide open. I had a great view of the desert, sarcastically speaking. It was actually very bland, the usual—nothing but sand with the occasional house dotting the ground. If you looked for five seconds, you knew the scenery would never change, so I got comfortable in my seat and shut my eyes.

The two men also seated in the Black Hawk with me were obviously fobbits. You could always tell a fobbit by how he acted, talked, and dressed. These guys were no different, with their happy faces, wide-eyed look at the interior of a Black Hawk, and especially how unused their boots and uniforms looked. It was as if they were brand-new. They were snapping pictures of each other looking tough, as if they were on some kind of combat raid. Me on the other hand, wore worn-out boots with scuffs, rips, and sweat stains throughout. My uniform was sun-bleached and caked with layers of salt stains.

After about a five-minute flight, we landed and I found my way to a temporary tent with plenty of room. It was to be my home until my flight to Kuwait, whenever that was. The tent was air-conditioned, so I grabbed a cot and lived a life that I saw as luxurious.

I knew I had some time on my hands, so I called home and prepared my family for my arrival. I checked with my father about this Seidel name from Gettysburg that my lieutenant had spoken of earlier that morning. The story turned out to be accurate. First Lieutenant Robert A. Seidel III, age 23, was killed in Baghdad on May 18, by an IED that killed three other soldiers from the 10th Mountain Division. Seidel was an Emmitsburg, Maryland, resident, but he was listed as being from Gettysburg because his parents lived there. Just to show how small Gettysburg really is, it turned out they lived on the same street as my parents. That really made for an eerie feeling, undoubtedly more for my parents. Here came two Gettysburg soldiers coming home from Iraq at the same time, just that one of them wasn't coming home the way anyone would have wanted.

Throughout the second day and the start of the third day, more and more people trickled into the tent and it soon got full. I really hoped I would run into someone I recognized from the Rakk. There were a couple guys from 1st Battalion that I didn't know, but I could tell they were Rakkasans without seeing the torii patch on their helmets. Their demeanor, their attitude, and especially their uniforms—I could tell they were grunts. The feeling was mutual when they walked by me and said "Rakkasan" and I said it back. They didn't say it to anyone else. I guess it was a sixth sense we all shared. Misery loves company, right?

During one of the briefings in the afternoon of the third day, I finally ran into someone I recognized. Specialist Johnson was about to embark on leave the same as I was. He was in 3rd Battalion of my regiment, but in Bravo Company. Johnson was in the same platoon as my buddy Scud, who was still healing at the Walter Reed Medical Center in Washington, D.C. Johnson had also been close friends with Corporal Nyle Yates, who was killed back in March. I had known Johnson for quite some time, basically because we were together from the start. He was in the same basic training company as Borden and I back at Fort Benning, when we were all brand-new to the Army.

I was glad to see a familiar face. With Johnson, there was a staff sergeant and two other specialists I didn't know personally, all from Charlie Company the same company as Borden. I recognized their faces, but without their names being Velcroed onto their uniforms I would have never known who they were. The five of us from 3rd Batt soon became inseparable. Rakkasans always stuck together. Time passed by quicker with those guys around. There were plenty of stories we swapped. Bravo and Charlie Companies seemed to be having some pretty intense times in Samarra, which made for some intriguing tales.

There were about a hundred soldiers from across northern Iraq who were preparing to leave together on the next flight out of the country. Out of the hundred or so, I only gave the time of day to four, and I've already named them. All the other pogues were busy trying to be the one to take charge of everything. They always had time to spot-check other people to make sure they were wearing their hats right and other uniform gigs. No one ever said anything to us ragamuffin grunts. We distanced ourselves on purpose, but our uniform wear and tear kept people away anyway, reminding them that not everyone was in the same mind-set that they were. Life was not as cushy for us as it was for them. I was wearing a uniform that I had been wearing for sixteen days straight, and I had not showered for about eight days. I just did not have much time to do anything else but sleep, patrol, and work on our Humvees, which seemed to break down daily.

We crammed into a shuttle that brought us out to the center of the large-scale tarmac. We exited and filed through a series of Jersey walls, then formed a long single-file line. I remember standing there in line watching as the C-130 came lowering from the sky. Once again it was another beautiful sunset, making the sky bright orange and the air a cooler warm than the intolerable afternoon heat. It reminded me of warm summer evenings at the beach.

Once the C-130 landed, it lowered its rear hatch and dozens of soldiers came pouring out. They were walking toward us to get on the shuttle we had just exited. It was apparent these soldiers were just returning from leave.

"Look at their sad faces," I chuckled to Johnson.

"'Cause they're returning to this shit-hole. I'd have the same expression on my face, if not a gun in my mouth!" Johnson laughed back.

We filed into the hull of the plane and took seats. I never was one to stay awake during a flight on a C-130, so I immediately got as comfortable as I could and shut my eyes.

Hours passed and I woke up intermittently. The few buttons that were illuminated in the hull gave use as a minimally effective night-light that spread enough light over everyone to show the rest were all as sleepy as I was. I was not going to fight to stay awake, so I shut my eyes some more. After the incessant ear-popping, I knew we were lowering elevation and preparing to land. Pilots of C-130s always seemed to slam the wheels hard into the ground when landing. I like to think it was because they too were sleeping during the flight and they were just awakening like everyone else. Either way, I'd made it to my next rendezvous and I didn't care how I got there.

Once landed in Kuwait, we downloaded from the plane and quickly transferred onto an awaiting bus. I was a little apprehensive to see an Arab driver. I remembered the last time I trusted a Kuwaiti behind the wheel, at the beginning of the deployment. and how he almost flipped the bus on several occasions.

The bus came to a halt outside a large tan warehouse where we were to start and finish whatever paperwork was required to leave the country. When one of the National Guard soldiers who was stationed at this post passed out papers to a lecture that someone else was giving, his look when he saw our appearance made a lasting impact. It hadn't really hit me how truly out of the ordinary we were until I saw this guy with his recently shaved military haircut, pressed and starched desert camouflage uniform, and newly issued boots. We must have given a rugged impression, since all our uniforms were sun-bleached and stained, and all of us had stubble and dirt on our faces.

We filled out some paperwork to get our R&R certified. I realized one of my papers was missing my company commander's signature, so I quickly signed an unreadable chicken-scratch doodle for a signature, which slipped by them with no problem. We were given a couple of short briefs, most of the time during which I zoned out. They kept reiterating to take it slow while at home. "Don't cram everything in at once," and then I tuned the rest out. No one was going to tell me how to enjoy the time off that I'd earned.

After the final brief was over, everyone who was going home walked over to another warehouse to store our helmets and body armor. I waited my turn alphabetically, turned in my helmet and vest, and exhaled another sigh of relief. I stuck around outside the warehouse and waited for Johnson to finish up. Soon enough, he came out with the same happy face I was still sporting.

"Hey there, high speed, take your hands out of your pockets!" came a booming voice directed at us from behind. Some pogue sergeant was going on a power trip and I was his target. "You can fix your headgear as well." The sergeant shifted his attention to Johnson, who had his hat cocked back like a ball cap. "What, do you think you guys are back on the street already?" This sergeant continued his quest for inner satisfaction. We on the other hand attempted everything we could to not punch this guy in the face.

"If I wasn't stop-lossed, I would be," Johnson wittily retorted.

"Would be, what? How about addressing me as sergeant?" the pogue said.

Just before Johnson and I could not hold back anymore, our fellow Rakkasan staff sergeant came out of nowhere.

"Hey, big sarge, take it easy," he said to the unknown and disgruntled sergeant.

"You guys Rakkasans? Think you can do whatever the hell you want?"

"Hooah!" Johnson said in return while I refrained from laughing. The sergeant, knowing he'd lost his battle, walked away.

"Rakkasan!" I sounded off.

This sadly happened often. In my line of work, my main job was to stay alive. This was where my hatred came from for pogues who made it their job to correct a uniform flaw, or to tell me to straighten my hat, or blouse my boots. This was the fine line between grunts and pogues that will always exist. People in the Army who went on ego trips in combat zones were what backboned my hatred for the Army and what drove me away from it; they were one of the main reasons to not reenlist.

When we were released, it was near two in the morning. For some reason I could not sleep. I remained wide-eyed all night. I had not really received a good night's sleep since my first night at FOB Speicher. I was tired but couldn't sleep. It was too hot and it was in the dead of night. Overall, I didn't care. I would be home soon and that was where I would catch up on sleep.

The ever-increasing heat prevented a lot of people from sleeping. Being awake all night in our small tent, I noticed a lot of tossing and turning and numerous "fuck, it's hot" statements throughout the night from various people. It wasn't long before I gave in to fighting the heat. It was hot. These tents were not air-conditioned. Stepping outside to find a close latrine was a dreadful task, especially now that the sun was coming up. Kuwait was much hotter than Iraq, a feat I thought was impossible except for in Hades.

My buddies and I decided to skip the morning brief. It was pointless. We did hear, however, through those who went that we were to be leaving the camp around 11 A.M. This was good news, as I was bored out of my mind with finding ways to avoid the heat. When the time did come, I was ready to go.

With bags in hand, we all gathered down near the warehouse, where our names were read off a roster and we walked a pathway to awaiting buses. The ride was a quiet one. I was separated from my posse and the curtains were drawn, so passing time was another job for my iPod.

Once we got to where we were going, I was able to look out of the front window of the bus at a real airport. It was a welcoming sight, since it was so different from an airfield on any given FOB. The Kuwaiti heat was still ever present, but the thought that this all would soon be over made it bearable. I believe we might have been in Kuwait City again.

"I need some volunteers for baggage detail!" came a booming voice on the bus. I quickly was the only one who raised my hand on a full bus. What everyone didn't know was what I'd learned from other guys who went on leave before me. If you volunteer for baggage detail, you sit in first class. I was selected and got off the bus before everyone else. I wasn't surprised when I was reunited with all of my fellow Rakkasans, who apparently had good informants as well.

With the use of a conveyor belt, a total of twenty or so lower enlisted soldiers packed the plane up with everyone's baggage. An easy job for an easy victory. Once we were done, we walked up the flight of stairs and got comfortable in our seats. There really was no first class section on this jumbo plane, but at least we had first dibs on where we sat. We naturally all sat together in the back.

Once everyone else loaded into the plane and got in their seats, we were soon off the ground, bound for Germany. It was getting near night-time, and most people were thinking about getting sleep, but not my circle of friends. With Johnson as the ringleader, we broke into a few songs we sang out loud. We were noisy and obnoxious and no one else seemed to be taking part in our joyous activity, but we couldn't have cared less. From popular songs, to Christmas carols, to Army songs, there were no limits. We kept this up for about fifteen minutes before we decided to scream the Screaming Eagles song. We knew by now that our mission was complete. Everyone on the plane hated us, and that was exactly where we wanted to be.

It was nighttime in Germany when we arrived, but I had no clue what time it was. With just my hat as my baggage now, I joined the herd of people slowly filing out the only hatch we had open. As soon as I got out in the air, my body almost went into shock. I was so used to the incredible heat of Iraq and Kuwait that when I stepped out on the stairs I shrunk into a walking fetal position. Everyone was going through the same shock upon exposure.

It was cold, so people started hurrying down the stairs to the awaiting shuttle. To me it felt like winter with summer clothes on. As bad as all this was, one thing was noticeable. The air was breathable. I don't know if it was the sudden cold-weather shock or the clean air that made my lungs feel heavy, but it was just great to be out of the Middle East.

We were corralled into a small secluded section in the basement of the airport just long enough for the smokers to have one cigarette. I didn't want to wait any longer. Next stop, America!

My whole fight against trying to stay awake was finally about to pay off. With my bloodshot eyes, I finally decided to shut them and sleep on the flight home. And sleep I did. I don't remember much other than that the occasional flight attendant would wake me and give me food and drinks, which I gladly thanked each of them for.

Over the PA system, the pilot's voice resounded in a good phrase.

"We are now flying over American soil," he said, and away went the cheers. The excitement level was ever increasing, and the lackluster expressions on faces were soon replaced with smiles of happiness.

It wasn't long after that I could hear the landing gears kick in underneath and my heart started to pick up. As soon as our plane landed, we all cheered and clapped and shook hands with everyone around us. Me and my group were no different.

I was in America.

REST & RELAXATION

"I'm a flight risk?"

We landed in Atlanta, Georgia, around 9 A.M. on a Sunday. I did not know how much time had passed since I left my platoon, but I didn't care. We slowly proceeded off the plane, and I foolishly thought I would have to help unload it. I forgot that there were professionals that took care of that. I needed to get in the mind-set that I was on vacation, starting now.

Our large group was ushered into the airport, where we followed each other, ducks-in-a-row, to wherever we were headed next. It was amazing just to see fellow Americans. Everywhere I looked, people stared and smiled and shook our hands as we proceeded to walk through the terminal.

"Isn't this great?" Johnson shook my shoulders as we kept walking.

"Dude, we're home. We're home!" I just kept saying to him with a huge broken-tooth smile.

Our group was headed to an area designated for soldiers returning for leave. We were headed there supposedly to get our duffel bags in an orderly fashion. Before we got to our section of the airport, we had to pass through this large corridor that was the main section of the airport, where all the food vendors were located. While we proceeded to walk together, a voice came over the loudspeaker.

"Ladies and gentlemen, please join me in welcoming back our fighting men and women in the Armed Forces who just returned from Iraq and Afghanistan." Before the man on the PA system finished his sentence, every single person dropped what he or she was doing and turned and cheered as if it were a sports game. I was speechless. It was a moment ingrained in my memory that I hope I never forget. It was a euphoric feeling and quickly erased all the negatives that being deployed in Iraq brought with it. Men, women, and children stopped eating their food, turned away from their phones, and put their papers down to join in the cheering. Simultaneously, instead of us being bombarded by people shaking hands, the crowded halls parted like Moses himself had separated everyone just to let us go unmolested. Everyone continued to cheer. Each "thank you" and "welcome home" I heard through the cavalcade of civilians crippled me for being able to express anything in return other than a big smile while fighting back tears.

We finally got to the area in the airport specifically designated for returning soldiers on leave. They read us a few rules for what to expect upon getting our gear and making connection flights home. Our names were read off another roster while we walked to a secluded baggage claim area to be reunited with our duffel bags. Once I got my bag, I went to get my final signature on my official leave paperwork and I was free.

"Wait up for me, Conklin." Johnson spoke to me while I finished up.

"Hurry up, I want to get a drink," I eagerly said. I'd turned twenty-one in Iraq, so I'd still never officially and, more important, legally, bought a drink for myself.

Johnson did not take long as he quickly got his bag, and we were free to go.

"Wanna get something to eat first?" I asked him.

"I want a fuckin' drink, dude," he said to me.

We then had a conversation while walking, but both of us never looked at each other. We were like children at Disney World trying to take everything in and see as much as possible.

Johnson and I both had about three hours to kill before our flights departed. He was headed to Tennessee, and I was headed to the Baltimore airport, to my awaiting parents.

"Let me call my parents real quick," I said to Johnson when I passed a row of pay phones. I reached into my pocket and pulled out a bunch of cardboard "AAFES coins," the only non-dollar currency accepted in combat zones.

"Damn AAFES!" I yelled as I threw my useless currency back in my pocket. I went to a nearby vendor to break a dollar to call home.

"Mom, I'm back in America" were the first words I spoke to my mom on the phone. We talked briefly about scheduling to time it right for her and my dad to pick me up in Baltimore. I didn't talk long, as Johnson got antsy. "Mom, I gotta go. I gotta get a drink," I said, and before I knew it, it was all easy going from there.

We sat down in a nearby restaurant and immediately asked to order drinks, but we were turned down because of some rule that prevented them from serving at a certain time on a Sunday. They weren't going to start serving until after my flight departed, so I decided to change my flight immediately.

After my lunch, I changed my flight and called home to update my parents. I'd always told my buddies in my platoon that the first thing I was going to do in America was to get a drink, and I wasn't going to retract what I was determined to do.

Johnson missed his first flight like I did so we could both find a bar. We knew where one would be close to his departure gate, so we proceeded through the security checkpoint to find it. I found it ironic that the security staff still checked us as thoroughly as everyone else. I found it funny because it had been announced that we had just returned from fighting the very terrorists that they were trying to prevent from getting on planes. I guess it was protocol, and I was just happy that security was so tight that they didn't show favoritism to anyone.

Once past security, we didn't have to look far before we found a bar tucked away in a small kiosk area. We walked in, set our bags down, and leaned against the bar.

"I'm sorry, sweethearts, I can't serve to men while they're in uniform," the sad-faced older woman behind the bar said to us.

"Are you serious?" Johnson said in quick reply.

"I'm afraid so," she reluctantly said as she transitioned to pour a drink for another patron.

Then it was as if Johnson and I had rehearsed it. We looked at each other, stood up, turned around, and took off our uniform tops so we were both in our khaki T-shirts. Just to make sure our experiment worked, I reached into my bag for a civilian polo shirt that I had tucked away in my assault pack for just this occasion. I put it on and we both turned around and sat down.

"What would you like, sweethearts?" the same bartender said with a clever smile.

"Two Jack and Cokes, please," Johnson said back with the same happy smirk.

And so it was, we were doing exactly what we wanted to do. We were drinking at a bar in America when only a few days prior we were running combat patrols through the streets of Iraq. It was a good feeling.

A man at the bar bought us our next round, and before I knew it, I was catching a long-sought-after buzz. Some Nascar race was beginning on television and we started watching it. They opened up with the traditional national anthem and it never sounded more beautiful. There were soldiers on television and the broadcaster kept thanking the soldiers fighting overseas. It was perfect timing, and seeing that stuff on television had never meant anything until that very moment. I looked through the corner of my eye to see tears fill up Johnson's eyes as he was staring at the KIA bracelet on his wrist, which bore the name of Nyle Yates. I looked down on my own KIA bracelet and was reminded of Andrew Kemple.

"To Yates," I said to Johnson as I raised my glass.

"To Kemple," he said back at me.

"And to every other motherfucker who doesn't make it out of that shit-hole," I finished as we downed another gulp.

It didn't take long before I was legally drunk. We were both cutting it close to our departure times too. Before I knew it, we were ordering another round. I knew this one would set me over the tolerable limit, but I didn't care. We polished it off in no time and put our money down.

Johnson and I sloppily shook hands and wished each other the best of luck and to enjoy the time given. He darted off while screaming, "I'll see you in a few days, motherfucker!" which he continued to scream half-way down the hall, amid a crowd of people, while haphazardly dressing himself back into uniform.

I stood there outside the bar almost frozen in time, mainly because I was drunk and didn't know I was standing so idly.

"What time is your flight, sweetheart?" came the familiar voice of the gentle bartender inside.

"I don't know!" I screamed while I dug into my pocket to seize my ticket. I gave her the stub and let her look at it.

"You need to go to Concourse B, honey," she cautiously said.

"Is that far?" I drunkenly asked.

"It's a bit of a ways from here. You'll need to hurry," she said.

"Just poin . . . ma . . . in the right diregjon," I said while I attempted to sober up. Before I knew it, I was dressing back into my uniform and looking as goofy as Johnson had just looked.

I eventually made it to my departure gate and realized there was no one there. Everyone had already been seated on the flight. I panicked and darted forward anyways.

"Are you Specialist Conklin?" asked the lady at the door.

"Yeah?" I said embarrassingly back at her. I was still missing my tooth, and I could really feel it when everyone I talked to kept staring at it like it was some kind of tractor beam. Now I know what women with big boobs feel like.

"Good. You made it. We were waiting for you," she finished as she tore my stub. I felt so embarrassed. I kept apologizing, not realizing how many times I must have said it. The stench of Jack Daniel's mixed with the smell of my dirty uniform and the fact that I had not showered in a few days were all permeating the atmosphere around me in one horrid cloud.

As soon as I entered the plane, all eyes were on my drunken and sad face.

"Sorry, everyone. I apologize for being late, but I sincerely apologize for the way I smell," I yelled as I walked through the main aisle to find my seat. As soon as I got comfortable, the flight attendant came over to me.

"Sir, we have a seat in first class that a gentleman is holding open for you," she informed me.

"Are you serious? Hell yeah. Pardon my language, and sorry if I smell, everyone!" I yelled again as I walked down the aisle, drunkenly bouncing off of the arms of aisle seats.

I sat down in a first class seat and quickly reiterated my drunken spiel as to apologizing for my stench. I repeatedly thanked the man who gave me the open seat next to him. I don't remember much of the flight, not because I slept through it, but because I was wasted. I didn't sleep at all. In fact, I had another Jack and Coke on the plane, as if I needed it. I talked that man's ear off and remember him telling me on several occasions to "keep my voice level down" and "try not to swear so much."

The stranger talked about being a chef in Baltimore and I vaguely remember him telling me recipes to food I don't recall. I was wasted. He asked a question about my KIA bracelet with Kemple's name on it. For some reason, in my drunken stupor I remembered a conversation I'd had with Kemple in Baghdad and how he talked about taking leave in May, around Memorial Day. I realized that I was fulfilling that exact request he'd had and wondered who would have gotten this slot from my company had he not been killed. This set me in a depressing spiral, which turned me into the stereotype of why people should not drink, because of its depressant capabilities.

Drunk out of my mind, I began crying. We changed the subject several times, but I found myself crying over everything. The rest was a blur from there on. I don't remember landing. I don't remember getting off the plane. I do remember the chef physically helping me off, and taking me for a quick stop in the bathroom before I was reunited with my parents. That didn't help much, as I was already in such a drunken state, I was hysterical.

I composed myself as best I could with the aid of the chef. Before we came out of the bathroom, he shocked me.

"Now, Ryan, I want to tell you something before you are reunited with your parents," he said to me as I tried my hardest to compose myself and tune in with what he was saying. "I'm not a chef. I love Italian food, but I'm not a chef," he went on to explain.

"Huh?" I said, now completely confused.

"I'm a U.S. marshal. It's my job to prevent flight risks while in flight," he continued.

"Wait, wait, wait. I'm a flight risk?" I asked back while poking a smile behind my tears.

"No. I could smell you a mile away with that booze and I didn't want you to do anything foolish, so I took you under my wing. Now, how about we go meet your parents? I'm sure they're anxious to see you," he said while handing me paper towels to wipe away the tears.

"All right. My parents are gonna be so proud that I'm wasted," I reluctantly said. With my arm over his, together we walked out of the bathroom. I soon saw the familiar faces of my father, mother, and sister down the hall. I immediately broke back into tears. I hugged my parents and kept apologizing for my current state. It was undoubtedly the most embarrassing moment in my adult life. To top it off, on the drive home we had to occasionally stop so I could puke. I have the most patient family in the world. I love them. The ride from the airport was the first of many uncomfortable instances. Being on the highway and driving next to guardrails and medians, and having cars pass us, was downright horrifying. I shut my eyes during the ride home and tried to ignore it all.

The first full day at home was Memorial Day. I went to the parade in Gettysburg and tried to lay low with my family. Word got out that I was home, and several people stopped by the street corner where we stood for the parade, to say hello. I did not want to see too many people too soon because my tooth was still broken in half and I looked like a redneck goofball.

I remember going to the cemetery for the Memorial Day speeches, and it was all going fine until they played Taps. I could not hear it because I chose not to. Unlike before, I could now vividly see the faces of those that I'd served with who'd been killed, and I knew this call would forever have a different sound for me. I chose not to hear it and walked away while I plugged my ears.

The next morning I had a scheduled appointment with a local dentist to get a new bond for my tooth. The dentist fixed me up real good, and it was done free of charge out of the kindness of the dentist's heart. Now I was officially back to being me.

Driving a car by myself was an experience of its own. I had to obey street signs, watch out for other cars, and especially abide by speed limits. I felt very restricted and unsafe when I drove. The simple things such as having the windows down, wearing nothing but shorts and a T-shirt, or sitting in a comfortable seat all felt foreign to me. My bare feet on the shower floor felt exhilarating, since I was so accustomed to wearing sandals whenever I bathed. The smallest things I never imagined became odd yet refreshing.

Driving around town opened the floodgates to many fears that I'd never expected to have. Subconsciously, my heart would pick up its pace when cars got near me. Garbage on the sides of the road and especially guardrails filled me with anxiety when I passed them, sometimes swerving unknowingly to avoid them and causing a scene on the road. I realized that my mind had been in such a high-stress environment in Iraq that it was hard to switch off in America. I tried not to drive much during my stay.

Most of my nights were spent drinking at bars, having so much fun, if not too much fun, catching up with friends. Crowded rooms somehow made me feel nervous, and I always felt like I was on the alert, planning escape routes and scenarios for a possible suicide bomber attack. One of the nights out, I looked up at the television and there was a breaking news story out of Iraq. My attention was now glued on the screen. My friends followed my interest. The story of terrorist ringleader Al-Zarqawi's death flashed across the screen and I was elated. I was never so happy over the death of someone before. I had spent countless missions giving all that I had to round up people connected with him, and now the head boss was dead. I figured my buddies must have been celebrating over that news, and it dawned on me how much I missed them all of a sudden. As euphoric as I was to be drinking in a bar in America, I just wanted to be back with my brothers in my platoon.

One night of drunken stupor worth telling about was a night spent at a friend's house in town. Unbeknownst to me at the time, there were scheduled fireworks at the nearby college. So here I was again, drunk beyond reason, and all of a sudden the night sky flickered with lights and the sound of explosions ripped through the air.

In an instant I was back in Iraq; I was never fully capable of blocking it out. I dove to the ground and attempted to scratch my hands at the "soil," as if to begin digging a hasty fighting position. The explosions kept getting louder and louder and my screams went with them. My mind was both in a war zone and drunk. A dangerous combination. The tears I shed were like a faucet left running. One of my friends picked me up and ushered me into his car, bound for home. The sound of the explosions increased while we drove and I kept thinking we were getting attacked by roadside bombs.

"Avery! Where's Avery?" I kept yelling in the car while I hunkered down and cried. It was like I was in the middle of everything Iraq could offer all at once and I felt defenseless, unarmored, and vulnerable. The next thing I remember was waking up the next day in my bed and being too embarrassed to see anyone.

I decided to stay away from alcohol for the remainder of my stay. That didn't last long because I soon spent a couple days in Ocean City, Maryland, with my best friend, and later returned to Gettysburg to pick up where I'd left off. I also gave a short impromptu speech in my church during which I displayed numerous photos and talked about what I was doing for those many curious members who had been praying so much for me.

Overall, it was a nice enjoyable stay in my hometown. The fifteen days I had went by quick. It was so good to relax and spend time with my family until it was time to return to work.

BACK TO IRAQ

**"I began to get a little nervous and came to the
conclusion that I was doomed."**

As bad as it felt saying good-bye to my family again in the Baltimore airport, I didn't feel as bad as I thought I should have felt. I truly didn't want
to go back to Iraq, but something within me really missed it. I knew what
the longing was and it was that I simply missed my buddies. I'd had no
word from them through e-mails or calls. Nothing. That was exactly how
I'd wanted my trip home to be. But now that I was preparing to go back, I
began hoping and praying that nothing catastrophic had happened while
I was gone.

   As I went through the airport security and eventually to my plane, I
realized people treated me different because I was wearing my uniform.
They were more polite to me than they would be if I was in civilian
clothes. Strangers would smile more when they passed by. People would
move aside out of my way when I walked past, even if I wasn't close to
them. I'm sure they'd acted like this the first time I came through the airport two weeks prior, but I'd been in no state to recollect.

   When I made it to Atlanta, I was eager to see those fellow Rakkasans
I'd clung to on the start of my R&R. I immediately received stunned
reactions from them the minute they saw me. I had the appearance of

having been through a total transformation. Here I was wearing a clean ACU uniform, with a fresh haircut, clean shaven, and most of all I had my tooth back. I was looking like a squared away soldier once again. I even smelled clean. I was so unused to the smell of laundry detergent. I didn't want it to ever go away.

It was good to see the few Rakkasans there were and swap stories about what each of us had done on our leave. I never found a single Rakkasan who didn't drink heavily while at home. After we'd swapped a few stories, it became apparent that we just weren't as cheerful as we'd been when we were headed home for the start of our leave. This was understandable.

The plane rides to Atlanta, then Germany, and lastly Kuwait didn't seem important enough to remember. The most memorable moment was the initial landing back in Kuwait. The heat struck me like standing too close to an open fire. My first breath felt like breathing in steam. I could feel the climate change in the core of my body. As soon as my first foot hit the sand back in Kuwait, I was already pouring sweat. I pondered that it would be hilarious to be a flight attendant on that flight, just for the sheer fact of viewing the expressions on our faces when we first touched ground in Kuwait. As everyone stepped out of the plane, almost every soldier's first word was an expletive.

So I was back in the same camp in Kuwait where I was before. As much as I didn't want to be there, I didn't mind staying longer than scheduled. Johnson was right with me in hoping for some divine intervention to get us bumped off a flight or for someone to lose our paperwork and keep us in Kuwait indefinitely. We did run into three infantrymen from another brigade of our division whose flight had been postponed on several occasions, and they had been in Kuwait for four days. How jealous we were. Johnson and I wanted to be those guys, but with my luck it never happened.

We were not in Kuwait more than twelve hours before we were bound for a flight back to FOB Speicher. As bad as it sounded, I wasn't that down in the dumps. I really missed my buddies and I still couldn't confirm if something had happened while I was gone. I was just hoping for the best. I was also wishing that the heat would somehow be less than that of Kuwait. Now that the month of June was under way, summer was in full swing and Hell hath no fury.

I was stoked to find that Iraq was a little cooler than Kuwait. Instead of the outside temperature being 125 degrees, it was 123 degrees. Oh, joy for small miracles. When I eventually landed back at FOB Speicher, I was now part of that sad-looking crowd that exited the plane and saw the small crowd of soldiers entering the plane about to go home for their R&R. Everyone had his time and my time was done, so I continued in the long line of pitiful sad puppies all the way to the tents.

The next day we woke up at the crack of noon and took a shuttle into the PX area. We had to be the only ones left from our R&R group. That night, I decided to be more proactive in arranging a flight back to my platoon. I told Johnson that I would attempt to see if prior arrangements were set for me to be picked up, or set some up if there weren't. We shook hands and I bid him adieu.

That evening, I got the answers I was looking for from the R&R headquarters about getting a ride back to FOB Remagen. It wasn't long before I learned that a Chinook helicopter would land soon to pick up some people and supplies and would be visiting most of the FOBs within the area. I decided to hop on that flight.

I took a seat with some other soldiers in the cargo hold and expected it to be a short ride, since FOB Remagen was the next closest FOB, about a five-minute flight. After forty minutes up in the air, I began to get a little nervous and came to the conclusion that I was doomed. I was convinced that someone had mistakenly put me on the wrong flight and I was flying to Whoknowswhere, Iraq. It was about midnight and I had no clue where I was, who was with me, where I was headed. And I had no plan. Oh, and needless to say, I was still unarmed.

I could feel the shift of the flight preparing for landing and I was anxious to find out where I was. Being as proud as I was, I did not want to freak out and ask questions of the people around me, so I just kept quiet and waited for someone to say, "This is FOB Remagen," but they didn't.

Instead, the Chinook gunner yelled as we landed, "This is Balad!" Some soldiers picked their gear up and headed out while others transitioned inside. I was still confused as ever. Balad was way off course from FOB Remagen. I knew I had to start thinking, for I knew I was in for an ass-chewing when and if I ever got back to my FOB.

We lifted off shortly and ascended back into the black sky. After the thirty-minute flight away from Balad, we landed yet again at a place un-known to me. We were at yet another FOB that was not mine. I was now really pissed. I could have walked to FOB Remagen from FOB Speicher if I'd known this was going to happen. I did not know if I was getting closer to Remagen or farther.

We soon transitioned more cargo, and up and away we went to yet another FOB I had never heard of. This cycle would happen yet again before I heard the greatest news I ever eavesdropped on: "Next stop is Remagen." I was elated, but I kept my composure and put on the front that I'd never been worried from the start.

Finally, around 3 A.M., the Chinook landed on familiar ground on FOB Remagen. I was the only one who stepped off that bird. As I walked away from the helicopter with bags in hand, I watched it lift back into the night sky with the small red and green lights blinking as it disappeared. I then realized that the pilots must have been running some kind of sched-uled shuttle service from FOB to FOB, and the story of my life, I was just unlucky enough to have the shortest distance to go from FOB Speicher, but yet get the longest trip and the last stop.

It was a weird feeling being back at FOB Remagen. My eyesight tran-sitioned to the pitch-black base as the cement walls and sand barricades that surrounded the area came into view. The sensation of walking into my platoon's CHU area was one I would never forget. It felt good to be back home, as weird as that sounds. Not a soul in my company was out walking around at this time. They were probably preparing for an early mission in the morning.

I unlocked the door to my CHU and entered. I immediately heard the snoring from Rod and I flicked the light on to see him sleeping. I threw my bags down on the ground to make as much noise as I could. The snor-ing ceased.

"Welcome back," I heard from Rod, still half-asleep and facing the wall.

"Oh, did I wake you? Sorry. I'll only be a second," I said to him. I doubt he heard me because he was back snoring before I finished taking my boots off. I crawled into my familiar bed and went to sleep.

The next morning, I slept in for quite a long time, until Rod came back from an afternoon patrol and reversed the role and woke me up. I decided to put some PT shorts and sandals on and walk around the CHU area and see everyone.

It was just great to see everyone again. Of course they were all inquisitive about my adventures at home. I told them as much as I could remember and they all got a kick out of my stories. They were all stunned at the return of my normal smile and I received a rain of compliments. I must have looked so incredibly different since everyone had grown accustomed to my broken tooth. When I asked them what the platoon had experienced while I was out, I always got the same reaction. The person I would ask would pause, stare off in the distance, and always reply with the same response: "Nothing. Same old shit."

RALPHIE WON'T GO HOME

"I'm being forced to take a vacation."

Indeed, nothing had changed. I was out running patrols the next day like usual. I was disappointed to find that Lieutenant Scher still had no plans to take his leave. After almost a month of not seeing him every aching moment, I thought I would miss him a little, but he annoyed me from the moment I saw him again. He quickly grew even more irritating to Taylor's and my nerves. I was not surprised to notice that Scher's highly educated responses and elementary comebacks and mannerisms had taken a toll on the others in my Humvee while I was gone.

Lieutenant Scher refused to go on R&R because he still did not want to miss a second of constant patrols. I give him credit looking back on it now. He never missed a single patrol. No other platoon in Angel Company could say that about their PL. Being stuck with him was not as unbearable as I may be portraying it. He was fun to be around, mainly because of fun that was at his expense. Lower enlisted should never treat an officer the way we did, but he was around the same age as the rest of us in our truck and he was really cool with the good-spirited camaraderie.

Captain Lesperance soon noticed the tiring effort put forth by Lieutenant Scher. Whether it was a measure of good faith, or Scher was on

Lesperance's last nerve as well, he made it mandatory for him to spend a week in Qatar. Anyone else would have flipped crazy at the chance, but not Scher. He tried to fight it, but lost.

"Ralphie, what's the matter?" I jokingly asked Lieutenant Scher while driving during one of our millions of patrols.

"I'm being forced to take a vacation," Scher replied, with a hint of sarcasm. I knew the vacation was much deserved, yet he fought it at first until he finally succumbed to his commander's decision.

"What? God bless Les," I shouted with a laugh.

"Yeah, whatever. I'll be drinking nice cold beer while you're going to be running these sexy patrols." Scher's sentences were a definite sarcastic poke at himself.

"Sir, you think that fazes me? I just got back from all of that. The only thing that's gonna be missed on your excursion is you missing sweaty-ass patrols," I said back to him. "Oh, and do you even drink beer?"

"Sir, you're the type of person that will be in Qatar and realize it doesn't suck so bad, so you'll like . . . dehydrate yourself, and only eat MREs in the prone position in some foxhole that you make." Taylor spoke down from the gunner's turret.

Everyone in the truck erupted in laughter except Lieutenant Scher. He just did what he always did and smiled, but Taylor wasn't done.

"And I bet you won't get laid, sir!" Taylor finished off amid my laughter.

"Put your fucking gloves on!" Scher yelled over to me.

"Don't turn this on me! He said it." I pointed to Taylor, who was still laughing. "Besides, we go over this every day. Our air conditioner doesn't work, it's hotter than a brothel in Zimbabwe in this motherfucker, so why do I have to push my core temperature up by wearing gloves in this vehicle?" I always tried to fight that issue, every day, yet I never won. Everyone had to wear gloves at all times.

"Because I said so," Scher finished.

"Roger, sir."

GAS, GAS, GAS

**"We would always 'pucker up' when we drove down
Business 1 through IED Alley."**

My vacation at home did not resolve the tension or hatred I had about running patrols. We still kept our routine of driving around, anticipating something to blow up, and then being able to do nothing about it. We would still bounce between QRF patrols and daily "presence" patrols in Tikrit and the surrounding areas. It was easy to lose track of what day it was and almost impossible to remember every patrol. Only the ones with significant differences were memorable.

One of the kinds of patrols that we seemed to repeat frequently was to monitor the gas stations. Our presence was important to ensure the people got equal access to reasonably priced gas and that it wasn't hoarded by anyone. Those missions proved to be hectic. Gas stations were run by the IP and only open at certain times, so every car in Tikrit seemed to flock to the different gas stations all at once. It would only be comparable in America if for one day every gas station in town was selling gas for 10¢ a gallon.

If we weren't on QRF duty that week, we were monitoring gas stations. All we would do was drive out to a gas station, park, and the dismounted elements would converse with whoever was in charge at that station. There was one gas station in Kadasiyah, and we would always "pucker up" when we drove down Business 1 through IED Alley.

One day at the Kadasiyah gas station, I was in the turret gunning for my vehicle. Everything was so routine by now. We parked, looked around a bit, and then deemed it safe to dismount. All the vehicles dropped their dismounted elements and the drivers got out to set out orange cones to make it obvious to the locals not to drive through our cordon and get too close to our vehicles. When the dismounted element walked away, it was left to the gunner and driver to hang out until everyone was done.

Back to this day in question, there were the usual cars lined up and down the road in front of us. In line, I saw this one beat-up car coming at a slow crawl in the direction of my vehicle. It was a ways off, so I didn't really think anything of it. It did keep creeping and inching forward, so I let my driver know, just in case it picked up speed. Still it didn't change course, though it looked like it was attempting to join the line of parked cars. What made it a little out of the ordinary was that I could not see a driver. There was no one in the car. I was afraid it was a possible VBIED, pushed in the right direction with the requisite prayers said.

While I kept my eye on the driverless drifting car, I ran my hands over my weapon, making sure it was cocked and on safe. I blew the dust off the top rounds seeded in my machine gun and wheeled my turret in the car's direction. Still the vehicle kept rolling, as if the emergency brake had died. This far into the deployment, I was not risking anything. I was willing to do whatever it took to get me home alive, and so I was prepared to open fire with a warning shot in the hood. Something inside me told me not to, so I reached for a rock that I would routinely stock in the turret for wild dogs.

I lobbed the rock far away in the direction of the car and saw it land on the hood. At first, I was impressed with the throw, but then also with the fact that the car stopped. I raised my rifle, took my selector switch from safe to fire, and aimed on the space where a driver would be. Slowly, the driver's door opened and then shut. Out stepped what looked like a six-year-old boy. He walked away from the car and joined a group of men who stood in line with their cars.

"Holy shit! Did you see that kid?" I yelled down inside the truck.

"Oh my God! That kid has to be five or six years old," Reese yelled back up. Hilmo just laughed from the RTO seat below me. We all busted up in unison laughter. The sight of such a young boy behind a wheel was mind-blowing, but then I realized there must not be an age limit to drive in Iraq. It turned out this little boy had been sitting on blankets and still barely saw over the wheel. Like all piece-of-shit cars the Iraqis drove, this one was indeed stalled. The boy, who was filling up the gas tank for his absent father, received help from other men in line and pushed the car to the back. Oh my, just when I thought I had seen it all.

A SPECIAL RAID

**"Avery fired his shotgun so much that it felt like
I was in an old Western film."**

At the end of June, we conducted another patrol that would stand out from the routine ones we did every day and night. We had always known about the American Special Forces group stationed in the heart of Tikrit. We used to drive by their tiny base, surrounded by numerous walls and towers. On one night, they specifically requested our platoon to go with them as added support on a raid. This was the moment we'd all talked about and that got everyone fired up.

The mission brief in the evening was the same as usual. Staff Sergeant Gibson may have been the most excited. He stepped away from the huddled platoon during the brief and puked a large-sized funnel of brown out of his mouth. It was horrific, but everyone broke the discipline of listening to the brief to gawk at Gibson. It turned out he had swallowed his chewing tobacco and it had lodged in his throat. It was a sight almost as gruesome as the dead bodies I had seen in Iraq. Almost.

It was my rotation to be the driver in my truck for this mission. I didn't mind it. Avery was for the first time "excited" to be a gunner in our truck. He was always the most hesitant to be in the turret, but who wasn't?

We drove into Tikrit as usual and drove untested into the SF compound. It was a totally opposite environment to our own from the moment we drove in. The men walked around in tennis shoes, T-shirts, and ball caps, with guns strapped to every part of their bodies it seemed. Beards were also not uncommon. Jealousy in us began immediately. All of us were quite giddy to be working with SF anyway, but we all played it off as just another patrol.

We received a quick brief from the SF group and pieced together what we were to do and where we were headed. My vehicle was designated the number one truck in the whole convoy, since it had one of the best working Blue Force Trackers. Lieutenant Scher plugged the grid coordinates into the screen and we waited for the thumbs-up from the SF leader. All our vehicles K-turned around inside this small compound to turn out and head to our objective.

It was now about 11 p.m. and completely dark out. We had to cross the bridge into Route Clemson, which I was a little hesitant about. The SF guys gave me the only block of instruction that they felt I needed: They requested that as the lead vehicle, they wanted my foot on the floor at all times. In other words, time was of the essence, and they wanted to hit this objective as fast as possible. Also, to make it tougher for both sides, we were to go under blackout. I had to drive with my NODs on. I hated doing this. I still had not ever received training with driving under NODs. I could only rely on the other times I had done it on patrols in Iraq. It was a talent that was considered suitable for "on-the-job-training."

I drove like a bat out of Hell through town, over the bridge, and along the country road east of Tikrit. I loved it, but my heart had to have been pumping faster than the pistons in the engine of my Humvee. Avery, with floodlight in hand, constantly shined at oncoming traffic and shot his shotgun to force cars off the road. Avery fired his shotgun so much that it felt like I was in an old Western film and the stagecoach was being ambushed. He was soon asking for more shells. The sound from the engine working so hard slightly muffled Avery's shooting, but all the elements of a high adrenaline rush were present.

Lieutenant Scher frequently called out the mileage closer to the target. Avery kept shining his bright light and firing his shotgun. Reese kept vigilant with the hand mics. The interpreter behind me must have been sleeping, as erratic driving never seemed to faze Iraqis. I seemed to be getting accustomed to driving heavily armored wheels of destruction to the breaking point.

The convoy made it through Route Clemson without any difficulty. I kept my foot on the floor as I sped through the less populated area without street lamps to guide my travel. It was like driving in a dark cave. Still, I kept my foot on the floor.

All of a sudden, a large Hesco barrier appeared in front of me, larger than a Humvee in size and filled to the brim with sand. Hesco barriers were used all around our FOB and also utilized at IP checkpoints. I knew it wasn't going to go anywhere if I hit it. Especially head-on, which was where I was headed.

As soon as the Hesco came into view, Avery simultaneously screamed, "*HESCO!*" and I screamed, "*SHIT!*" and slammed on the brakes. No one ever wore a seat belt in any truck, so if the interpreter had been sleeping, he just had a rude awakening by face-planting into the back of my seat.

The brakes squealed an unhealthy screech as I jerked the wheel to the right to avoid the Hesco.

"Alert the rest on the radio!" Lieutenant Scher screamed back to Reese, the RTO.

After a few seconds, with the situation under control, I put my foot back on the gas and sprinted to regain my lost momentum.

"You can slow down a bit, we're losing the rest," Avery chimed back down, "and thanks for making me get the Heimlich maneuver from my stomach slamming into the turret," he finished.

"It was a test, dod-damn it. You passed," I said in the old familiar voice making fun of our old platoon sergeant Quinn. Though he was long separated from our company, making fun of him never ceased.

After a few moments, the rest of the convoy maneuvered around the Hesco obstacle and we regained our attack speed. It wasn't much farther when we arrived on scene. As we drove through some country field, we came to a tiny village with only a few houses in it.

"This is it," I heard Reese confirm from the radio transmissions. I parked and turned my vehicle in a way to seal off a road with Avery's gun. I also had a good vantage point of the Special Forces group doing what they did best.

There was no better training than seeing SF go to work. One team ran up and attacked one building by emplacing some charge on the door, which blew the door down to gain entry. The other group hit the next house over and split the lock with their shotguns. Shouts and screams were heard inside, and they soon came out with nine Iraqi men handcuffed and escorted by SF soldiers to be placed into a Bongo truck. The soldiers were fast and intimidating. I will never be able to grasp how scary it must have been to be on the other end of one of their raiding parties.

When the SF group was done with their main target, they began to enter nearby homes with what looked like a lack of caution. They were split up and at times had soldiers running around solo. Good thing our job was outer security, because we just watched them run their show. It was far different from our strategy and rhythm for raids, but then again, that's why they were called "special."

After about fifteen minutes of them doing their job mixed with a little driving around the area to help shine our headlights on dark streets, SF called it a mission complete. We moved back out to our respective compounds at a much slower speed than the initial raid. The next day, news filtered to us in our evening brief that the arrests made by SF with us were an entire IED cell. That made me feel better, but not safe. Capturing a cell of insurgents was like killing a bee. It may feel good and proactive in the moment, but we knew there was a hive somewhere else with more angry and volatile bees.

GUARD, PATROLS, AND BOREDOM

"Chief, I think I broke it."

Around the beginning of July, our method of QRF duty changed dramatically and not in a positive way. QRF duty sucked as it was, because we had to spend our nights quartered in a big empty tent with the entire platoon always at the ready. The QRF's normal method consisted of returning to our CHUs after the morning route clearance and doing nothing unless called upon. Now, after the morning route clearances, we were to be housed in one building together, with gear on and ready to go. Oh, and did I mention that that building was located in the heart of Tikrit now? It was located in the Iraqi Army's Birthday Palace compound.

This was a horrible location in which to spend our days. The building had shoddy air-conditioning and we were given a small room to house our entire platoon. Some slept, read, or watched a movie on the one television in the room. Of course, those low on the totem pole of rank had rotating guard outside, two in the parked Humvees and one outside the building. Though our building was inside the Iraqi Army compound, feeling safe never existed. As much as I hated standing in that parked Humvee baking in the sun, and the feeling of redundancy ever present, I had to remind myself that I was parked about thirty meters away from the suicide bomber who'd exploded a few months prior on us inside the compound. In the compound there were always Iraqis in all types of military and civilian garments. They got close enough for me to yell at them whenever they got closer to my vehicle. I trusted no one.

It wasn't surprising to have the electricity shut off periodically throughout the day. What was worse was when the air-conditioning lost power, which happened about every three hours. There was no escaping the relentless heat. I can't write enough about how hot it was. Only those who were there, who wore the layers of uniforms and body armor, will ever truly understand. I can't think of an analogy that civilians can ever relate to.

If spending our days on QRF duty was not enough to test the ability of a man not to break, situations kept getting from bad to worse for Angel Company. One of the batteries from 3/320th FA was tasked out in another section of Ad Dwar, which left their Owja section south of Tikrit abandoned. Like the bitches we were treated like by the 3/320th, the task fell to us to embrace their section, making our area of operations much larger.

The mixture of all these new additions took a toll on our nonexistent motivation. The only thing I had left was to count down the days closer to getting back in the States, and getting out of the Army. If I hadn't been deployed, I would have been beginning the initial paperwork to out-process that same month. Scores of soldiers in my company were far more beyond their original contractual date of discharge than I was, so I never complained about it in front of those individuals.

With the impending closure of FOB Remagen inching nearer, many things were beginning to change. The MWR was one of the first things to pack up and move off our FOB. A lot of pogues around the FOB began to disappear as well. This meant that some of the inept people placed on the guard towers around our FOB needed to have their towers further manned. With two field artillery units on base who had plenty of manpower to supply the help, still our company once again had the task dumped on our priority list.

Tower 16 was directly parallel to our settlement of CHUs and faced out into the western desert. That was the tower that my platoon operated. Occasionally, I had to take my turn in the guard tower.

Guard duty was always the most boring duty a soldier was asked to do. Luckily I was with Chief. Sometimes I worked shifts with other squads, but Chief was my favorite. He was known as the "Guard King." He saw more guard towers than I saw turrets. He knew all the shortcuts for passing an easy eight-hour shift in Tower 16, doing radio checks and sneaking in short naps.

After one of our guard shifts, we got into our Humvee, which our relief had arrived in. First Platoon was off on a patrol in Tikrit and we were feeling pretty gutsy. Instead of driving straight back to our CHUs, which would have been a straight shot in less than a minute, I decided to take the Humvee for a spin in the open terrain on the FOB.

Chief was coaching me on how to fishtail the vehicle and do donuts. It was pretty fun. It was 6 A.M., so most of the fobbits were still asleep, I had nothing to worry about. Not until I saw a ditch in the sand and decided to floor it and ride the ramp. I slammed my foot to the floor and hit the ditch square on. Up went the front end and blue sky was in clear view. Down came the violent slam back into the earth, with the sound of thousands of metal parts banging together. Though my foot was still on the gas, the Humvee slowed to a dead halt.

"Holy shit! That was awesome, dude!" Chief screamed while laughing uncontrollably.

"Chief, I think I broke it," I said in a serious manner. Chief just retaliated with a louder uncontrollable laugh.

My mind immediately went into survival mode. I tried to think of ways to fix this without anyone of serious rank finding out. Chief just kept laughing. He made it easier for me to calm down as I could not stop smiling myself.

So between our CHUs and Tower 16 stood my Humvee stuck in the open. I had to get this fixed as soon as possible. Humvees broke down every day, so Chief and I concocted a story that that was exactly what had happened. I ran back to the CHUs and grabbed another Humvee of ours not currently out on patrol. I drove it back to our busted Humvee and linked them with a strap. Together, we drove the Humvees back to the mechanics bay on the other end of the FOB. We dropped the first one off and found the nearest mechanic we saw.

The mechanics were the only cool pogues on the base. They never asked questions when we delivered a dead truck. I told them that it just wouldn't start. They looked under the engine and determined that the Humvee had a broken half shaft. No questions were asked as to how this happened. A good amount of damage had been done by my joyriding, but it was now their job to get it back in working order as soon as possible.

While the platoon was still out on patrol around noon, I decided to check the status of the vehicle at the mechanics hangar. I found it completely repaired and able to be driven. I thanked them for their work and drove it over to our CHUs and right into one of the designated parking spots for our Humvees. No one ever did find out, that is unless they are reading this. Boys and their toys.

July was a month with a lot of changes. New approaches to the QRF, more land to patrol, guard towers, FOB Remagen was disappearing, and the heat kept getting worse. One perk about FOB Remagen's transition was our reacquiring of Second Platoon, who were finally off guard duty after several months in the Remagen jail, which had since been relocated. Second Platoon was immediately forced back out on patrol. They received many sneers and comments from First and Third Platoons, who frequently joked with them that they might have forgotten how to run patrols. It wasn't long before Second Platoon was out running missions and seeing a bit of the gruesome brutality that Tikrit had to offer. One day they had to clean up the scene after an SUV carrying foreign allied troops overturned and decapitated the gunner. Second Platoon got hit by an IED or two as well, which brought them up to speed.

Tikrit remained its same hellish world. News filtered to us of happenings in the city that we never reacted to, which was just bizarre. The first was another common retaliation attack in Iraq. On July 12, there was a huge Shiite retaliation on the Sunnis after a massive car bomb in Baghdad. Apparently, the governor of Tikrit's wife was the retaliation target and she was assassinated along with eight others. Oh, how the war in Iraq was a civil fight, and here was the proof that these people would continue attacks back-to-back in a who-can-top-this string of murders.

Another unfathomable murder occurred on the 14th of July. A girl was kidnapped somewhere in Tikrit. She was later found on Fortieth Street. Most of her that is. Her decapitated head was on a stick with a sign that read, "Only make round bread, and don't sell pickles." The news came to us during our evening brief and was confusing to digest. The murder was both puzzling and disturbing. They have been doing this for centuries, I guess. As for making only round bread, Jerry, our interpreter, stated that it was a religious thing. As for selling pickles as some crime, I never heard of the reasoning behind that. The girl who was murdered was a known prostitute in Tikrit, according to reports I heard. "Wait, they have prostitutes in Iraq?" That's how I ended the brief that night in Poston's CHU.

Even our favorite Iraqi Army soldier, First Sergeant Kobe, was a victim of violence. Apparently, someone attempted an assassination on his life and shot him in the face. Luckily, the bullet did more damage to his lower jaw than cause anything more severe, such as death. However, his time as a soldier was done, which came as a blow to us because he really was the workhorse behind the Tikrit soldiers.

News of the chow hall's inevitable move was nearing closer. Everyone began to stock up more, with their pockets full of bottles of Gatorade. Our platoon was planning on having a platoon grill day soon, so I figured it would be funny to grab a bunch of the non-alcoholic beer still in stock at the chow hall.

By mid-to-late July, FOB Remagen was becoming more desolate. First MWR packed up; second to leave was the laundry, followed soon after by the inept haji barber who also sold bootleg DVDs. The chow hall eventually moved and we were left with dreaded MREs to live off of. When I had the opportunity to clean my uniforms, I did so by stealing a bucket from a nearby building and filling it up with water and laundry detergent. I then hand washed all my clothes in that bucket. I would twist, scratch, and rinse out the layers of salt and sweat stains. The advantage of this hand-washing process in Iraq was the drying phase. I would just secure the clothes to my 550 Cord clothesline I had tied between my CHU and my neighbors'. They would dry within minutes. Pretty soon, everyone was hand washing their uniforms and using this same process.

THE DEATH OF JOHNNY 5

"You killed Johnny 5! You bastards!"

As much as we all could begin to see the light at the end of the tunnel, nothing made our constant patrols more enjoyable. I tried to find the littlest things that were funny that I could take away with me. Indeed, those rare but funny moments are still lodged in my memory.

During a route clearance trip, we were passing under an overpass at the south end of Tikrit where an Iraqi Police unit had already surrounded a small car accident. As we drove by, we looked over and saw the everyday clunker Iraqi car, but this time, and I don't know how it happened, the car was resting in the middle of the road and the engine was perfectly separated fifty feet in front of the car. How could that happen? Avery exclaimed, "Now I have seen it all. YES!" Avery, being the grease monkey he was, assured me that this was rare, and it was hilarious to witness.

Another patrol worthy of mentioning was Doc Gallegos's shining moment. One day on QRF duty, while we were housed in the much hated Birthday Palace, a call came over the radio to react to an IED attack. The message was passed and, as in an alerted fire department, everyone filtered out of our room with equipment on and ready. Our platoon darted out of the Birthday Palace with sirens blaring.

We drove out to the infamous Route Clemson to find, on the other end of the bridge over the Tigris, a small faction of Iraqi Police signaling for us as if we didn't know something had happened to them. As soon as we arrived, we could see the obvious damage. One of their SUVs was severely blown out from a roadside bomb. I drove by the scene and knew there could not have been any survivors in that car.

Doc however got out and reviewed the carnage up close. He found that one of the men who'd been presumed dead by the Iraqis was still alive, but barely. A nine-line medevac was ordered over the radio, and soon a Black Hawk landed and loaded up the man who was still alive thanks to Doc's constant effort. The wounded Iraqi was flown to FOB Speicher, but we never learned of that man's fate.

One good victory story that I can take away from the experience was a day we actually found an IED before it went off. On July 25, we were driving through the Stink Wadi area, the smelly and almost abandoned poor section of Tikrit. Amid garbage a small white bag was spotted that just did not look right. This far into the game of IED hunting, we trusted everyone's intuition.

I was the RTO that day, so I promptly requested EOD meet us at our location for further investigation. We hardly ever requested EOD unless we were almost certain of a potential device. They knew that too, so they reacted quickly whenever we did call.

They showed up and immediately unloaded their Johnny 5 robot. Most of us gathered outside the vehicle, about seventy-five yards away, and watched them do their magic. Down the center of the road came Johnny 5, rolling fearlessly to do a face-to-face inspection of the bag. Once he was up close, EOD controlled the robot's camera to angle in on the bag. Our curiosity was satisfied when it was confirmed that the bag was an IED. Holy shit! We'd found one by sheer vigilance!

While we all watched patiently as Johnny 5 deactivated the IED, we never expected what came next.

W-A-A-G-O-O-O-S-H! The bomb detonated for some reason right on Johnny 5's mechanical arm. Everyone who watched jumped and ducked instinctively at the same time. Very quickly, we all regained our composure and focused on the smoking black pile to see what was left of Johnny 5. The only thing left was what was falling from the air.

"You killed Johnny 5! You bastards!" shouted someone nearby. It was a scene much altered from what it would have been if Johnny had been an American soldier.

"Johnny 5 took one for the team," I stated. Everyone was laughing and replaying everything that had just transpired as if we had just witnessed a car accident. EOD quickly unpacked another Johnny 5 unit and had it inspect what was left of the debris, which wasn't much.

We were fortunate that day not only in finding an IED before it found us, but because when it exploded, many of us onlookers with cameras in hand were susceptible to the cross fire of flying debris, and miraculously, no one was injured. I do remember a couple small chunks lodged into the armor on some of our Humvees that we rode in. First Platoon had pressed the luck button again. It was a testament that our attitude had greatly changed since our first start at patrols. We were getting complacent and had a sense of not caring anymore. It was time for us to go home.

AN OVEN WITH FOUR WHEELS

**"The only thing I could hear was the sound
of my ear filling up with sweat."**

My platoon was on QRF duty when on August 3 our Company CP received a tip from a farmer. This farmer claimed that he'd seen people hiding bombs in the weeds on his farm in Owja. We all kicked into overdrive and piled into our Humvees in no time. It was quite possibly one of the hottest days I could recall, kind of like Hell in the summer. Whatever that feels like. I was so glad to be driving, but then again, without air-conditioning in our truck, driving slowly, I turned out to be in the worst position. Not only had the air-conditioning died months ago, the fans we had decided to die as well. My luck was at an all-time high. I wanted to slam my forehead into the steering wheel until I passed out, but I figured that would hurt, so I didn't.

We staged near the clearing barrels next to the gate of FOB Remagen and paused to get our mission brief from Lieutenant Scher. We all started talking among ourselves and seriously felt that this sounded too much like a baited ambush. The signs were too perfect. Some unknown Iraqi calling us to a specific location, at a specific time, out in the country. I did not like the sound of it. None of us did. In fact, we decided to take the farmer with us so he could show us firsthand. The Iraqi farmer rode in the first Humvee as we drove out of the gate.

We drove through the little village of Owja, right across the street from the entrance of FOB Remagen. We drove on some desolate road and stayed on it for quite a while. The farther and farther we got from our base, the more the landscape changed as if a genie were granting a wish. It was like we were in an oasis. The dry, light dirt disappeared and we were surrounded by green foliage. Brown was the color of the road and that was it for that color. Palm trees lined the roads; palmettos were prevalent all throughout. I seriously felt like I was in Florida. It was like a jungle. If only the heat cooperated, I would go back and build a Disney World.

As I admired the strange beauty, I retained in the back of my mind the knowledge that our patrol might be about to get ambushed. The tall trees, plants, weeds—all of it seemed the perfect place from which to ambush a patrol. To top it off, we were having bad reception with company headquarters and we could not talk to them. It was not a good feeling. We were out in the middle of nowhere, and the road we were on was barely wide enough for our Humvees. When the first Humvee in our patrol rolled to a stop, I knew we were there.

"Here it comes!" I said with a laugh to the rest of the truck, but no attack ever came. Thankfully. Dismounted elements stepped out and followed the farmer to where he was going to point out the area. After a few moments of everyone in the truck trying to fix the communication issue with the CP, we heard over the platoon radio that the dismounted guys had found some artillery shells exactly where the man had said they were. Two 155mm rounds and fifteen 57mm rounds sat in a pile among the weeds on his farm.

From the bake oven I was stuck in, my Humvee, I still hoped that nothing was booby-trapped. If it was and if it exploded, it was so hot that I wished the explosion would at least offer a cool breeze. We gave up trying to contact the CP, even though we were not far from the FOB. The truck was worse than a sauna. As we waited for the dismounted elements to pack up the found artillery shells, the rest of us in our hateful Humvee were placed in our own personal torment.

No one was talking. It was dead silent. The only thing I could hear was the sound of my ear filling up with sweat. Sometimes I would hear sweat from the gunner bead off and slap the metal floor. Some people's boots sweated so badly that it looked like they'd crossed a stream. On this mission, I was the driver, so I had never even stepped a foot outside, but my boots were a very dark brown from sweat. I was so soaked that I felt like I had showered with my entire uniform on. When I breathed, it was like breathing in air that was on fire, that burned my entire throat.

The silence continued as everyone dreamed of a million places we all would rather be. I scanned around over my right shoulder and could see that everyone had a "thousand mile stare." Zombies. Drenched zombies. I needed to break the suicidal look everyone had. I reached into the gap between the radio and the radio mount, where we kept our speakers and my iPod. I connected the cords, undetected by all in my Humvee, then scanned through my device in search of the perfect song. Once I found it, I turned the speakers on.

"It's Beginning to Look a Lot Like Christmas" by Bing Crosby filled the interior of our sweatshop on wheels, and everyone snapped out of the daze he was in and started laughing. I played a few more poignant songs, until after nearly an hour of constant sweat, we drove back to the FOB for a mission complete.

DEATH AT A FUNERAL

"For a split second, the entire landscape was lit up like daylight."

August 6 was our last night on QRF, and tower guard around the empty FOB started early the next morning. We all hoped that divine providence would step in and we would not be called up during our last night. We completed our routine route clearance around dusk and prayed that nothing would stir in Tikrit.

Around 8 P.M. on the 6th, we received a tip that there was a possible suicide bomber and/or suicide car driving around the Tikrit/Kadasiyah area and we needed to find it. "You have got to be fucking kidding me!" I screamed as everyone busted out of his CHU and donned his gear while on the run. As everyone was getting organized in the Humvees, I ran and hopped in the driver's seat of my own. Once I had ensured that the Humvee was ready, I progressed to my next step: complaining. Thank God Taylor was gunning, for he helped me rip into Lieutenant Scher.

"Here we go again, sir. Aren't you excited?" Taylor sarcastically chimed to Lieutenant Scher.

"Let's do this," he said in a manner similiar to a little boy's at Christmas.

"Sir, put your erection away. You know this is going to be chalked up as yet another stupid-ass mission where somebody cried wolf," I said in return. We all agreed that these types of missions were dumb. Chasing a potential suicide bomber and/or car? It sounded ludicrous, and we were rarely given anything substantial to go on. If we didn't get blown up, then we would think that there never was a VBIED. If we did get blown up, then we knew that there *was* one.

Just as our platoon exited out the gate, there was an explosion faintly heard in the air. Quickly, the radio opened with someone from the CP that the RTO was in quick conversation with. CP informed us that a suicide bomber had just blown himself up somewhere in the city. "Awesome!" I said as our convoy picked up the pace through the street lamp–lit road into Tikrit.

We drove down IED Alley to reach Kadasiyah and found in the clearing between residences a cordoned-off area that was blocked by Iraqi Police. Lieutenant Scher left the Humvee and joined the dismounted element to ascertain the situation. Judging from the scene around me—the flashing lights, several policemen—I knew something big had happened and I knew just where. Along a row of businesses, one of which had lights on, there were several people out and about looking curiously at one building. From behind the steering wheel in my Humvee, Taylor and I sank into our usual bitch session and tried to predict what had happened.

After a few moments passed, Lieutenant Scher came back to our Humvee and grabbed the hand mic. As he was relaying information back to the company, Taylor and I learned what situation we were dealing with. A man had walked into a funeral home during a funeral and blown himself up. He killed thirteen innocent men and women and wounded another twelve. No one had yet entered the small funeral home, because there was a car that was a suspected VBIED parked right in front of the building. I was several hundred yards away, and I could see there was indeed a maroon car parked in front of the small funeral home. Its back end sank lower to the ground than usual. I could tell that something heavy was in the trunk.

EOD was immediately dispatched from FOB Speicher and reached our location in about twenty minutes. The EOD team was the same cocky team that saw their Johnny 5 explode in front of us. These guys were gung-ho as usual and quickly launched another robot out to the car. The platoon and the EOD team were a couple hundred yards away. Some of us were outside of our vehicles to anxiously watch everything go down, but some remained inside the safety of their trucks. For me, it was a warm night, and I needed to stretch my legs. I got out and hung with others in my platoon along with EOD as they put their robot into action.

Slowly, it moved toward the trunk of the car and attempted to open it. For some odd reason, Johnny 5 could not open it up. They placed a small charge on it, but it did nothing. This enacted Plan B, which did not mean anything bad for me, but made me thankful for the job I'd chosen in the Army. As the robot rode back to the EOD team, one of their guys dressed himself from head-to-toe in some bulky protective outfit that looked like a primitive diving suit or a crude astronaut's space suit. The bomb suit he wore was something I knew nothing about. I didn't know what it could or could not withstand, but I would never have done what he was doing. Just another day at work for him, so I wanted to get a good seat, but I climbed back inside my Humvee in case things went flying.

The man shuffled his bulky self slowly to the car as if he walked on the moon. Everyone who watched held his breath. Not a single person in our platoon ever said he had the desire to do what this guy was doing. When the EOD "astronaut" reached the trunk, he placed his own charge around it and finished quickly. He returned as fast as he could move in that suit, which was like a sprinter in slow motion.

"Fire in the hole!" screamed the tech person who operated the trigger mechanism. *B-a-a-o-o-m!* The charge successfully flew open the trunk like nobody's business. They again sent Johnny 5 out there to inspect the contents with its camera. Lo and behold, two 130mm artillery rounds, a propane tank, thousands of ball bearings, and a Sanyo phone base station sat in the trunk. The entire device was remote controlled. Not knowing if some terrorist were still keeping eyes on his product or not, I decided to stay within the safe confines behind the wheel of my Humvee until that car was disposed of.

Several hours passed until EOD was finally ready to detonate the VBIED. It was then nearing 3 A.M, and we had been on scene for over seven hours. The order was given for everyone to get in the Humvees as EOD again shouted, "Fire in the hole!" All the gunners were told to sit down in their Humvees instead of exposing themselves, even though everyone's vehicle was at least over one hundred yards away.

I stared over the steering wheel and attempted to get the best view of the maroon car, lit by one street lamp and seconds away from becoming pieces of scrap metal. *W-A-A-C-L-A-M!* bellowed a gigantic fireball. For a split second, the entire landscape was lit up like daylight. The fireball was enormous and shot up high into the sky. I'd seen cars blow up in Iraq before, but this one was as if a supermarket exploded. Instantaneously, the sounds of hundreds of those ball bearings started to strike in and around our vehicle.

"*SHIT!*" everyone screamed. "Taylor, get down!" I yelled while simultaneously grabbing his leg. He was white as a ghost when he slammed to the floor.

"Fuck, dude!" he screamed. *Ping, flang, ding,* went the sounds of metal that slammed into our truck, even before the giant fireball disappeared. Right before my eyes I saw a huge chunk land on the hood directly in front of me about a foot away. The piece of shrapnel connected to my hood like a magnet on a refrigerator.

"Is everyone all right?" Lieutenant Scher asked everyone nearby, simultaneously holding the hand mic down so he could relay the same question to the rest of the platoon. Yeah, everyone was all right. Just got a rude awakening. My heart raced just as fast as at some of the other IEDs I had experienced.

Everyone was entirely lucky not to have been accidently decapitated or filled with shrapnel. I think the EOD team did not dig the impressive charge deep enough, because that explosion had not come off as planned. But everyone was all right, and that's all that mattered. The threat was gone, and the dismounted elements finally proceeded into the funeral house of death.

As they left to go investigate the funeral home, I hopped out and inspected my Humvee for damage. We knew we were lucky once again, but it was definitely hair-raising. Around the truck were several chips, dings, and even holes in the body of the armored Humvee. I grabbed the chunk of metal that was right in front of my windshield. It was the size of a computer mouse and was still hot when I grabbed it. I conversed with other drivers who all had similar cracks and dings in their trucks. We all swapped stories of our perspective on the "nuclear bomb" explosion.

It wasn't long before the dismounted elements lumbered back to our trucks. "What was it like? What happened?" I asked some of them as they came back.

Specialist Ly just looked at me and said, "Hell. A shitty, bloody mess. You don't want to see it."

Jerry, our interpreter, was always in a jovial mood during patrols. He walked back from the funeral home visibly shaken and disturbed.

"Jerry, are you OK?" I asked him. He looked like he had seen a ghost.

"Fug diz shit, Coglin," he said, and began to tear up. I knew it was bad. I did not need to see it. I had to remain with Taylor anyway, so I couldn't go. I felt bad for some of the guys in the platoon who had to see it. Lieutenant Scher said it was "Hell on earth." Hollywood apparently would not be able to paint a more gruesome scene than the likes of that small funeral parlor that had become a whirlwind of death. Scattered body parts of men and women were plastered all over the walls and ceiling, and a river of blood coated the floor like a carpet. It was like an explosion in a microwave.

Jerry was still able to help in the investigation and stated that the suicide bomber was Jordanian or from some African country. When I asked him how he knew that, he said that only his head survived, and he could tell the difference between an Iraqi and a Jordanian head.

Leaving the mess up to the police to clean up, we all finally prepared to head back to the FOB around 4 A.M. As I started up my Humvee and prepared for the order that everyone was ready to go, a power line directly in front of my truck surged and sent blue sparks flying everywhere. It was like a firework exploded only a few feet away from my face. It startled us all, but Taylor acted like he had been shocked with electricity himself. He wiggled, freaked, and screamed. He was all right, just completely taken off guard and I could not stop laughing. Everyone kept laughing, and it helped change the depression of a miserable mission.

During the entire ride back to the FOB, I could not stop laughing at Taylor's "girlish" reaction to the power line spark. He laughed too, but I was near tears. He was the gunner, so his feet were only inches away from me and he frequently kicked me while I drove. As horrible as that mission went, it ended on a high note.

LEAVING FOB REMAGEN

"It was a mundane task."

On August 11, First Platoon took over the towers at FOB Remagen. Second Platoon continued running presence patrols, and Third Platoon finally took over QRF. Over the next several days, no one from my platoon left the wire and it felt glorious. Having the guarantee that nothing bad would happen to us made us all sleep better. There were several towers around FOB Remagen, but only really about four or five were actually manned. My squad maintained the tower in the southwest corner of the FOB, which faced toward one small mosque out in the distance.

Our rotations were much easier than they had been during our stay in Baghdad. We operated in pairs as usual and did four hours in a tower with eight hours off before the next rotation. Four hours with the same person was much easier than eight hours. I was with Sergeant Fooks a few times, but I was mainly cooped up with Sergeant Vinny Edwards. He was much more fun and relaxed. Same tower rules applied, which meant anything and everything about our personal lives was open to be discussed. The location of the tower was perfect because the fence in front of it was close enough that no sergeant of the guard could step in front to see us up in the tower. Plus, we were the farthest tower from the inhabited section of the FOB, which made it fruitless for anyone to ever attempt the two-mile walk to our tower to surprise us. We would hear a Humvee from a mile away. To our front, there was nothing but open desert, with the exception of that lone small mosque way off in the distance. It gave us an opportunity to chill out on the stools we were given and take off our helmets. We kept our vests on, but unsecured the Velcro part so our chests could breathe.

The best rotation to have guard was during the night. The temperature was far cooler than during the daytime. As soon as the sun came up, the heat came with it. I always wished it would rain, but it never did. We had not seen rain since the short rainy season several months before. I guess that's why it's a desert. The other remaining shifts were always uneventful, but with good goofing off the time passed smoothly. Activities we did were basic guard etiquette. Random conversations filled our void of music, except we usually all slipped our own iPods to guard and listened to music as well. Reading the ignorant, comical, and mostly always sexual graffiti written within the walls of the cement tower always amused me. I especially loved the giant chipped hole in the back of our tower above which someone had written "POGUE GLORY HOLE." There was also a plethora of penises, vaginas, naked women, and the Rakkasan symbol of a torii blasted all around the cement tower in black marker.

One other activity that occupied our precious time off was so incredibly redundant, but typical of the Army. Since we were turning over our FOB to the Iraqis and my company was the only one left on it, we were left to "police call"[18] the FOB. Yes, we had to clean up loose trash that spotted the landscape inside our fenced-in FOB. This was the climax of stupidity at its finest. All day, soldiers from my company spent their eight hours off from the towers walking and driving around and picking up trash all around FOB Remagen. Iraq was the dirtiest country I had ever seen, and garbage blew like tumbleweed. As soon as one area was cleaned it seemed that some lonely bag of potato chips would come blowing in the wind and settle right where we had just cleaned. It was a mundane task. It sucked. We knew the place would be trashed again within a week

---

[18] *Police call* was the term for meticulously combing the grounds to collect and properly dispose of trash.

under Iraqi control. We gathered several bags of garbage and steel scraps, which we unloaded at the burning pit on the FOB. We made several trips during the day.

My circle of friends would still utilize Avery and Taylor's CHU as the focal point of congregation for those in the platoon who could all tolerate getting together. No matter how well we got along with everyone, everyone had his own days when he was on edge. I was notorious for pushing the limits of those days.

I can't remember how I pushed Sunny over the edge one night, but it happened. We were soon in violent death grips with each other on the wooden deck Avery had built outside his CHU. A few punches were thrown by both of us. It wasn't until the tussle prompted a slight chip in my newly fixed tooth that I immediately ended the fight and let the victory go to Sunny. I didn't want to lose my tooth again. The chip I did get was unnoticeable, but I didn't want to take my chances.

By August 15, everyone was since packed and living out of the top portion of his duffel bag. There were no more TVs to watch movies on or video games to be played. Every night, the guys in my platoon built a roaring fire in one of the steel barrel drums outside of Avery's room. We usually burned all our addresses from our mail in there to prevent them from falling into someone else's hands.

The fires that we burned every night consisted of anything and everything we could get our hands on. One night I passed the steel drum right when an explosion ripped out of it, sending sparks high into the air. The fire was so fierce and quick that I checked that I still had eyebrows. Apparently someone had thrown away something that contained a bullet or two.

Another activity that some of the guys in my platoon picked up on at night was Glow Ball. We had a football that we taped several fluorescent glowing chem lights to with duct tape. We split up on two sides in the gaps between several CHUs. We would then throw the ball back and forth and watch it glow in the air while we fought to catch it. It was a fun game, and we played for almost an hour while others burned things. The game quickly ended when the ball was eventually thrown into one of the burning barrels.

At 8 A.M. on August 16, Vinny and I scaled down the metal ladder inside our guard tower and were relieved by two others from our platoon for the last time. That day was the official turnover day from us to the Iraqis. That would be the last time I ever saw a morning dawn in Iraq from the comfort of a concrete tower. I was glad to be done, but I knew I was in for a fast-paced and busy day.

Our CHU area was more alive than it had been the past week or so. Several Iraqi soldiers wandered around our CHUs and inspected what would soon be theirs. There also was some sort of change of command ceremony that involved the passing of flags between the two armies. Several soldiers and representatives from 3/320th came to the FOB to perform this dog-and-pony show. They took all the credit too. Nothing was ever mentioned about our company, even though we were the only people still living on the deserted FOB. Ceremonies like that were always bullshit to me anyway. I was glad we were not forced to attend. I chilled with others in our CHUs and blasted the air conditioners one last time. Avery and I also walked through other empty CHUs in search of anything of value left in refrigerators. We found several Gatorades and sodas. We even found a lot of frozen meat in some freezers, which I gathered in my arms and brought to my refrigerator.

We all loaded our Humvees with our own belongings. I packed my bags with everyone else's in my patrol truck just the same. It was tight, but we managed to make it all fit. It would only be a short trip up MSR Tampa to FOB Speicher.

By mid-afternoon, we'd gotten the go-ahead to proceed as a platoon out of the gates of FOB Remagen one last time. We gathered all our men and now knew the FOB was under the control of the Iraqis. None of us wanted to stay long. I felt sad leaving my CHU. It had become my home, my oasis, my haven from all that pissed me off during our endless patrols. It was my sanctuary. I felt anger for some reason seeing the Iraqi soldiers walking around unappreciative of their new gifts. Everyone in my platoon felt similar feelings. It was like I was being evicted from my apartment and now I was seeing the Iraqis dancing all around what was just my CHU. While our Humvee was still running, I ran back into my old CHU after almost forgetting the meat that I had stashed in my refrigerator. As I walked in, there were two Iraqis standing inside. I completely ignored their presence and grabbed my meat. I figured they did not need it or deserve it. I carried the armful of frozen meat and put it in the cooler in the trunk of our Humvee.

During the hottest time of the day, we all bid adieu to FOB Remagen and left the gates for the last time. Some of the Humvees were so overloaded with gear that some men's bags were strapped all around the outside of the trucks. It looked like a patrol of hillbillies were moving to Beverly Hills. To us, FOB Speicher was our Beverly Hills. It was luxurious to us. It was gigantic and offered a plethora of food and activities. It was a move we were happy to make.

FOB SPEICHER

"Everyone was more focused on the wall of sand headed our way."

The drive to FOB Speicher was uninterrupted by "evildoers." As we rolled inside the gates of our new base, it felt good to be in a place with "luxury." We drove through the now recognizable base all the way to the far back northwest corner of living areas. We passed several trailers, large tents, and cement barriers until we pulled up to what was now our home. Large green Army tents. This was a change of pace, but as little time as we had left in country, we knew it would be temporary. The tents were accessible by two wooden doors on both ends and the floors inside consisted of plywood. Each tent could comfortably house two squads. Our company occupied several tents in close proximity. There were other units in the numerous tents in the row. With all of the tents precisely aligned, it earned the nickname of "Tent City."

Once we arrived at our designated tent, the task of unloading everything ensued, with the sounds of cots being erected, the shuffling of boots on the floor, the wooden door slamming shut, the dropping of heavy gear on the ground, and the ever-recurring grunting and snickering from everyone.

I quickly unloaded my gear and organized my cot space to my specifications. I set up my cot and made it as comfortable as I could by using an Iraqi blanket I had been sleeping on at Remagen that I collected from 3ID on Christmas. I almost didn't bring it, but Poston had found room in his Humvee for it. I slept in my Army-issue sleeping bag and my woobie, but I never felt the uncomfortable stiffness of an Army cot because of that wool blanket. I set up my *FHM* calendar next to the air conditioner, which was right next to my cot. That calendar gave me the most satisfaction every day when I woke up and put a large black "X" on the day that had passed. One day closer to home. Oh, and the photo of the near-naked model didn't hurt to see either.

The move in was quick and painless and surprisingly absent of the absurd needless stupidity that usually occurred from micromanagement. Everyone was busy making his cot space as comfortable as possible. 550 Cord was strung up all over the inside of the tent, making an instant clothesline to hang whatever we needed: towels, laundry bags, uniforms, knee pads, hygiene kits, etc. We did not even have to run a patrol that day, so everyone was happy. We all just wanted to go out and roam around the base and take advantage of all that was offered: fast food, Internet, phones, MWR, PX—you name it. We were no longer living at a desolate FOB.

An advantage to living in the same tent as the platoon sergeant and platoon leader was that we heard more information. Every night the platoon sergeant met with the squad leaders to disseminate information to them. In turn, the squad leaders relayed the information to their team leaders, and finally the team leaders reiterated the news to us lower enlisted in the squad. Sometimes Sergeant Vinny Edwards and Sergeant Woods, our two team leaders in the squad, misheard information or forgot to write things down to pass on to us. Now that we were in the same tent as the head honchos, we were able to wipe out the middlemen and hear straight from the horse's mouth. It was good to finally get accurate information every night for a change.

The day after we moved in, we were back out in the streets of Tikrit. As Hilmo and Avery were getting our Humvee ready for the mission, the unmistakable smell of rotting food overwhelmed the inside of our truck. In the trunk, the smell fumed out of the cooler that was in there. The meat that I'd taken out of my freezer before I left FOB Remagen had been sitting in that empty cooler for over a day of intolerable heat. To say the least, the meat was way past spoiled. The cooler was too for that matter. I spent that afternoon cleaning it out but could not cure it of its smell. The car fresheners we had in the Humvee were useless against the power of the stench.

We were stuck on the rotation of patrolling the gas stations again. It was an easy task but still outside the wire. It was also significantly shorter than normal patrols. We also had sham missions where we had to escort people who held meetings in Tikrit. Sometimes we would be out for only a couple hours. I believe everyone was just tired and ready to go home. We had days left before our replacing unit was to take over. We were told that the unit was already in Kuwait, so we knew for a fact that we would be going home. Everyone slacked off a lot more during patrols, but we still were cognizant of the dangers of certain areas, and gunners still kept their heads on a swivel. Luck seemed to be in the air, though, especially when on the 19th of August we were notified that the Iraqi Army stationed at FOB Remagen had been hit with a rocket. Glad we left.

FOB Speicher was amazing to us and we loathed the pogues who took it for granted. The MWR was nearby our tents and offered movies, comfy chairs, Internet, and phones. The return of having a place to drop off dirty clothes and get a one-day turnaround of clean, fresh-smelling, and folded uniforms was fantastic. There were also a few shops near the PX which were run by TCNs.[19]

The port-a-potties, also nicknamed the "jack shacks" for obvious reasons, were located to our rear behind an empty tent and on the other side of the dirt berm that surrounded our tents. The first few times walking to the jack shacks at night were treacherous, but then it became second nature. Several times I would trip late at night from the tent pegs that ran along the tents. Trudging over the large dirt berm formed of loose sand made it easy to lose my shower sandals at night, but luckily I had my head lamp with me. I later transitioned to unlaced boots in the middle of the night, but that did not stop my boots from filling with sand. Later, paths were created with stomped-down trails, making the route more passable.

---

[19] *TCN* stands for third country nationals. They were civilians contracted by the United States to work on a United States base and were neither American nor Iraqi.

The showers were also nearby and consisted of trailers like we had seen at FOB Remagen and Camp Buehring. There was usually also a line for them because other units used our showers.

FOB Speicher was also host to several sandstorms. I hardly ever recall any sandstorms at FOB Remagen, though we were only about fifteen or so miles away. At Speicher, we usually passed sandstorms in the comfort of our tents. We could see them coming when we were outside. We would all gather on the dirt berm outside our tents and watch the impending swirl of brown clouds like a curtain about to fall on our Tent City. We would then run inside and wait it out. Sandstorms occurred roughly every day during our time at FOB Speicher. It was always a little nerve-racking when they happened when we were inside the tents. The tent walls shook violently and we all expected someone's tent to fall. We got used to them and carried on our normal routine inside, but sometimes it got so bad that we would pause and stare at the tent ceiling with the "wait for it" look in our eyes. Luckily, no tents ever collapsed.

The largest sandstorm we ever experienced occurred at the most inopportune time. A few days into our temporary stay at Speicher and with a few more left to go, our company decided to have a layout of every item that belonged to the company that soldiers had signed for and hopefully still had. When it came to layout events, everyone had to keep a close eye on what he had signed for because sometimes things "magically" disappeared.

Each squad loaded up a Humvee with personnel and equipment and spent the afternoon outside a small building with everything spread out. It took hours. Weapons, NODs, bags, lasers, base plates, PAS-13s—you name it, we had it. Each platoon had its chance to have the XO walk through and have serial numbers read to him to verify each item's existence.

We spent several hours waiting around kicking sand out of boredom. The XO only used a few soldiers to read off the numbers, which led to the rest of us being insanely bored. What grabbed and held most of our attention was staring off into the desert and seeing the sky off in the distance completely brown. After several hours, the brown sky had gotten closer and bigger, and we knew that a gigantic sandstorm was on its way, but it was still too early to predict its path.

As we neared the end and last of the equipment serial numbers to be read, everyone was more focused on the wall of sand headed our way than if we had all that we had signed for. Luckily we did. As soon as the go-ahead was given, everyone scrambled to grab what he had signed for and stash it in the Humvees. By then, it was almost too late. The sky had turned a dark brown and the wind was picking up. Everyone was running around laughing like a child awaiting a downpour of rain. Sand was already kicking up all around us, but we had to take off our sunglasses because it had gotten too dark. It was around two in the afternoon, but it felt like dusk because the sun was choked out from the floating sand wall.

Just as soon as all of the equipment was packed or secured by someone, everyone was on his own. Several men sprinted into nearby vehicles and waited it out inside the Humvees. I ran with others toward the nearby building, but we didn't move as fast as we could. I felt blind. It was like opening your eyes underwater in a sea full of salt. Sand pelted my entire body as I stumbled like a man blindfolded. I could not see past five feet. I followed the laughter and shouts from others and found the door. I entered and found about six others from my platoon. Everyone was laughing hysterically.

After about ten minutes, we walked back outside to find everything much calmer. The eye of the storm was gone and had left everything in its path covered in sand. We all cleaned ourselves off as best we could and got in our vehicle. We'd left the hatch open, so sand was everywhere inside. That was the best sandstorm experience I ever had.

My old friend Borden from Charlie Company stopped by one day and looked for me, but I was out on patrol. I had not seen him since the debacle by his company during Operation Iron Triangle. He heard through the "Rak-vine" that my company had been transplanted to FOB Speicher. He was making a pit stop at Speicher to have work done on his vehicle, which he drove up from Samarra. He ran into Vinny and Avery and they told him to come back later in the day. Thank God they told him that, because he did return shortly after I got back from a patrol. It was great seeing Borden and hearing officially from someone in Charlie Company what was happening to them. Their company was still under an extensive investigation and their commander and first sergeant had been temporarily removed from their own company for an unspecified time. I saw them both at the chow hall at Speicher several times when I went there. Borden also mentioned that their company had been stuck on tower guard in their area ever since the investigation began. At least he was safe.

TO THE VERY LAST PATROL

"First day on patrol and they saw death and blood."

By August 27, two guys from each platoon in my company had already been sent home and arrived in the U.S. as part of our advance party. We knew we were soon to follow them. We were told that half of the remaining platoon would leave on the 1st of September. I was part of the second half, and we were scheduled to leave on the 5th or 6th. This information I did not wait to send home. Another good sign of our impending departure was the arrival of our replacement unit at FOB Speicher. The unit was the 1st Battalion of the 505th Infantry Regiment, from the 82nd Airborne Division. The 82nd and 101st had always been sort of rivals to each other, since World War II, but we were pretty happy to see the new guys and embraced them quite warmly. It was also funny that our area of operations in Tikrit, which had been patrolled by a company, would now be patrolled by a battalion. Proof of how much coverage we did. The soldiers from our replacement unit were housed in newly constructed CHUs built specifically for them not far from our Tent City. Their CHUs were much larger and newer than ours were at Remagen, but they fit more people into each one.

The replacing unit wasted no time in "ripping" with us out in sector.

By the end of August, we had started taking the platoon leader, platoon sergeant, and other squad leaders from our replacing unit out on patrol with us. This meant that we had to drop several people from each truck to fit them in our vehicles. After a day, we incorporated more of the new lower enlisted soldiers to sit in our Humvees during patrols, which let more guys from our platoon stay back.

For about three days we did a lot of "sightseeing" around Tikrit, showing the boys from the 82nd the "hot spots" for activity. We did not let them operate important jobs yet, such as driving or gunning. Each Humvee had three from our platoon and two from theirs. They mainly sat and listened while we drove around. When I was gunning, I made it a point to not be so complacent while out on patrol. I wanted those boys to see us "in the game" even after a year. I remember several months back when I was watching the unit we replaced and how they operated in theater. I remembered the first time I jumped when I saw one of the 3ID's gunners open fire with a shotgun. I continued that tradition of sorts when I fired a couple warning shots in busy intersections like we did every day. In my peripherals, I could see one of the soldiers from the 82nd flinch near my feet. *Get used to it,* I thought.

This was not the 82nd's first deployment. Whether they felt like they were ready or they just did not care for us to chaperone them on patrols, they decided to cut our time with them in half. By August 31, we were looking at only two more patrols outside the wire. I was ecstatic.

On that last day in August, it was my rotation out of my Humvee. I lounged around the tent, checked my e-mail, and picked up my laundry while my platoon was out on patrol. I kept running through scenarios on how elated I was about to feel over leaving Iraq for the last time in my life. Sadly, my excitement was shattered when the harsh reality of the war caught back up with me.

As I relaxed on my cot and read a book, I overheard my platoon sergeant talking to one of the squad leaders about some soldiers from the 3/320th being ambushed a few hours ago out on patrol. There were a couple casualties and one was fatal. With my ears perked like an alerted dog's and unable to focus on my reading, I sought out Sergeant Hilmo for more information.

As soon as I saw Hilmo's face, I knew that something bad had happened. The 3/320th was the unit we were attached to our whole time in Tikrit, and it was impossible not to intermingle with them at any given time. Most of us had grown friends within each other's ranks, and I hoped it was not anyone I knew that was killed.

While out on patrol in their sector in Ad Dwar, a convoy of Humvees from Bandit Company of the 3/320th were "sightseeing" areas in their sector with their replacement unit from the 82nd. They were on the other side of the Tigris River when a complex and groundbreaking ambush took place.

While driving through a street that was flanked on either side by tall buildings, the last Humvee in their patrol was singled out and attacked. Terrorists used an innovative tactic of throwing an anti-tank mine with a parachute to explode right above the hood of the Humvee. The explosion ripped through the hood, and the main blast was literally in the lap of twenty-eight-year-old Staff Sergeant Michael L. Deason of the 3/320th. He was killed immediately. Deason was commanding that vehicle in the front passenger seat, opposite the driver. The other four soldiers in the truck were wounded with shrapnel. The confusion and chaos that occurred created a break in contact with the other three vehicles in their convoy. The patrol kept on rolling through, unaware of the attack on their last vehicle. The wounded driver and his bloodied cargo turned around and sped all the way back on a twenty-minute drive to FOB Speicher, alone. I can only imagine the looks on the faces of the pogue guards at the gate when they saw this charred and bloodied Humvee fly in solo to the gate. The soldiers immediately drove to the ER and began their medical attention. Deason was a great NCO from what I'd heard, though I knew very little about him. But I knew exactly who he was when I first heard the name of who had died. He had talked to Staff Sergeant Poston a few times, and that was how I was introduced to him. Deason was a good soldier and an even better man. A Farmington, Missouri, native, he left a young wife and two young children both under the age of three. That was to have been Deason's last patrol. He was like all of us itching to come home. It truly became his "last patrol." Of the other four in the Humvee that received wounds, all recovered. Two were from the 3/320th on their last patrol. The other two were from the 82nd on their first patrol. What a hell of a way to start. First day on patrol and they saw death and blood. I felt bad that this had happened on their first outing outside the wire. They and the rest of their unit must have had horrific fears that this could be an everyday occurrence. Welcome to Iraq, fellas. Enjoy 364 more days.

When the rest of my platoon returned from their patrol, the information traveled faster than bullets. The mood and attitude in the air was almost like that among children stuck indoors during recess while it rains. The harsh reality that there was still combat stabbed us out of our complacency and boredom. Thoughts of Kemple's death came to light, and we knew firsthand what the artillerists were experiencing with the passing of one of their own.

Because of Deason's death and the wounding of the others, the Internet and phones were shut down on FOB Speicher. This was done every time a U.S. soldier was killed or wounded in our area. They were temporarily shut down only for about two days, to prevent the word from being spread back home before family members were contacted by the Army. The deadly attack also delayed the original departure date for the first wave of my platoon. It was pushed back a few days so everyone could collect himself and take part in a memorial service in Deason's honor.

On September 1, I woke up in my cot and prepared myself for my last time outside the wire. The day had finally come and I was, of course, scheduled as a gunner and I would not have had it any other way. As much as I was burned out from every position (gunner, driver, RTO, and dismount), I preferred to be the gunner on that day. It would be my last time seeing Iraq out in the open and from the best vantage point.

As our Humvees left the gate of FOB Speicher, everything felt final to me. I actually tried to enjoy it and take in everything as I left the gate. As much hatred as I had experienced in seeing the country while I was there, I knew I would miss it in a strange way. As soon as we left the front gate and traveled down the long, straight road that intersected with MSR Tampa, I waved at the kids who lined up along the road like they had done for every passing patrol every day. I waved with my open hand instead of the normal finger that the gunners usually responded with.

Driving down MSR Tampa, I felt completely carefree and stood up more than usual. I relished the feeling of the hot wind blowing on my face as I stood up in the moving Humvee. I smiled as I looked around and gazed at the scenery and tried to imbed the images in my brain. Seeing

Kadasiyah, Evil Mosque, Fortieth Street—it was all surreal seeing everything for the last time. It was a hell of a feeling.

Our patrol visited every place there was in and around Tikrit. It was a great mission to end with. It was also great for the men of the 82nd who were with us to see where everything was located. We even went back and entered the gates of FOB Remagen to show them what it looked like if they ever needed to go there. It was really weird to revisit it, seeing nothing but Iraqi Army soldiers walking around. Even though it had been only about two weeks since I was there last, I really missed it. Oh, and I noticed several pieces of trash blowing around the grounds of the FOB. So glad I spent an entire day cleaning it up for nothing.

Toward the end of the patrol, we entered the Birthday Palace in the heart of Tikrit for one last time. There, we introduced the men of the 82nd to the Iraqi Army, their new "allies" in the area. Some of the guys explained to our replacing unit the story of when the suicide bomber detonated himself next to the wall we were standing by. I was impressed by how well the stains of blood had been removed and how there was no trace of that bloody afternoon except for the chips and crevices in the marble facade. We also had one last Iraqi lunch with the soldiers on their base. The yellow rice and nasty chicken they served was something I would never sit through again. It was awful.

After lunch and our farewells with the Iraqi Army were completed, we drove back to FOB Speicher. The patrol had gone according to plan and was very enjoyable. As I neared the Twin Tits on the MSR Tampa for the last time, I lit a cigar that Avery had given me earlier that day. My "victory cigar." After we passed around the double arches, I was being a little uncouth by standing fully erect in the turret with my hands on the side, leaning back and puffing away on my cigar. The wind blew hard in my face but it felt wonderful. As we pulled into the gate and over the speed bumps, I turned and faced toward Tikrit and shouted at the top of my lungs, "Good-bye, Iraq! Never again will I walk your shitty-ass streets!" I felt so alive once inside the gate. Unloading my weapon systems of their ammo near the clearing barrels felt so awesome. Never again would I ever be locked and loaded. Everything felt so spine-tinglingly good.

As soon as we got back, the entire platoon came out of their tents in order to clean out the Humvees. We were all pounding fists and high-fiving each other. We knew we were done. Here we were cleaning out the Humvees of everything that would not be turned over to the 82nd guys. Within an hour, each Humvee was stripped of our personal belongings, like extra magazines, iPod speakers, lucky charms, and other equipment. One by one, each truck was turned over to soldiers in the 82nd and we watched them drive off. It felt like sending a child away to college. As much pain, as many maintenance problems, and as much sweat shed in those trucks, it was still sad to see them driven off by soldiers other than members of my platoon. *Treat her well,* I thought.

The Iraqi interpreters that we worked with throughout our time in Tikrit also showed up to bid fond farewell to us. It was a bit sad to see them go off with the 82nd guys, because we had grown close to the interpreters. We actually trusted them, and they were great assets, intriguing conversationalists, and proud citizens of a crumbled nation. I learned so much about their culture and especially pronunciation on several helpful Iraqi phrases, something the Army never taught me. Jerry presented me with a small silk Iraqi flag that he'd bought in his hometown of Mosul as a gift. I always would ask him during patrols where I could find one. He said he would get me one someday, but I never thought he would come through with it. I was moved but felt bad because I had nothing to give to him.

We were done. With no Humvees, our time outside the gate was over. Even the inside of our tents began to become very tidy on account of everyone's gear all packed tightly away in duffel bags and rucksacks. We all lived out of the top half of our duffel bags from then on.

Throughout the day, Angel Company began turning over everything that we had that needed to remain in country with our replacement unit. When I ran into some members of Second Platoon, I found out that they had been hit by an IED earlier that day but with little to no damage. We were all glad that that life was now over for us. "Enjoy Tikrit" was the unofficial catchphrase we passed to the men of the 82nd.

THE LAST RENDITION OF TAPS

"Never again do I ever want to see those makeshift memorials in the deserts of Iraq."

On the 2nd of September, the 3/320th Field Artillery held their makeshift memorial service for Staff Sergeant Deason. It was a hot afternoon when we gathered out in a flat open desert not far from our tents. Just like Kemple's ceremony but with the roles reversed, the 3/320th lined up in formation in the front and my company formed up behind them. I was impressed with the entire battalion of the replacement unit from the 82nd lining up in formation for the ceremony also. They never had the privilege of knowing the soldier being honored, but he was a soldier nonetheless. It was a gesture that was more powerful than words.

Sweat poured down my face and back as I stood in formation with the rest of my mixed company. Occasionally we saw pogues walking out of ranks in fear that they would pass out due to the heat. Others literally did just that and were carried away. It was quite comical to watch, and several soldiers around me snickered and chuckled.

A couple people from the 3/320th spoke at the podium, but the sound system was so muffled that nothing was audible. We were also so far in the back that we never heard a single word said. When the command to salute during the playing of Taps was over, followed by the guns fired by a squad, it brought back memories of Kemple and was depressing for everyone. At the completion of the ceremony, everyone broke ranks and joined a very long line to have the opportunity of saluting the memorial up front by himself. The wait in line was quiet and everyone had time for silent reflection. I saw several soldiers from the 3/320th Field Artillery cry as they stood before the overturned M4 between two combat boots. I knew just how bad it felt. We all did. When my turn came, I walked before the box by myself, saluted, and said a short prayer as I stared at the photo they had of Deason. I made a sharp left turn and shook hands with the commanders of the 3/320th, Colonel Steele, and Command Sergeant Major Camacho. Never again do I ever want to see those makeshift memorials in the deserts of Iraq.

Later that afternoon, Angel Company had a formation behind Headquarters Platoon's tent for an awards ceremony. Almost everyone in my company that had not yet been presented with the Combat Infantryman's Badge was formally given the badge on that afternoon. The badge was presented to infantry soldiers who survived any type of contact with the enemy. It was a great honor to have the most coveted and respected badge in the Army officially pinned onto my ACU top. The others in my platoon who had already received theirs from the invasion deployment were quick to pound it into our chests, letting the pins on the back of the badge break skin and draw blood. It was an old infantry tradition. It was a good lifter on a dismal morning. We always joked with Chief that he was the only one in our platoon not to receive his CIB since he was stationed on guard duty almost the entire year. I noticed that the certificate I got with the badge was signed and stated, "Presented at FOB Remagen, Tikrit, Iraq on this 2nd day of April 2006." I guess it had taken some time to catch up with us, it being September 2, 2006, and at FOB Speicher. April 2 was Kemple's birthday. Rest in peace.

GOOD-BYE, IRAQ

"My day had finally come."

With the waiting game of days to pass, time actually moved pretty fast. There were still plenty of boring and dull moments in the tents. Movies continued to run and everybody kept pondering what he would be doing in America in a couple of days. Boredom and tight living spaces still provided for very funny conversations. Conversations looking retrospectively back on the past year were almost always funny.

One of the funniest moments that occurred in our tent was a dare I would never do myself. Avery was known for having the worst smelling feet in the platoon. Several individuals dared Chief to suck one of Avery's toes for ten seconds for money. Amid everyone's dying laughter, both parties seemed all right with the dare and soon money was presented. Sixty dollars was rounded up and Avery ripped off his putrid moist sock. While wearing a white cowboy hat and surrounded by almost the entire platoon, Chief was ready and willing.

"Are we ready? Are we ready?" Chief yelled while others of us got our cameras ready.

"Get ready. Go!" MacMillan yelled from the back of the circle. Away Chief went and stuck Avery's nasty toe into his mouth. We all screamed in unison, stunned that Chief actually went through with the bet. A rowdy crowd, including Lieutenant Scher, joined in the unison laughing, clapping, and shouts of "suck it." That he did. For ten seconds he held that toe in his mouth. As soon as he let go, the look of utter disdain was on Chief's face. Everyone continued to laugh as Chief stuck the three twenty-dollar bills into his pocket.

"That is a stupid fucking human trick right there," Sergeant Vinny Edwards shouted in the background.

"That was fuckin' nasty," Avery said while laughing himself. The things infantrymen did when bored would shock the prim and proper civilians who have never experienced living life in a fraternity where shenanigans were multiplied by a thousand. I ended up drawing another doodle of an Indian Chief like I had on a sandbag in Baghdad, only this time I labeled it "Chief Suk-A-Toe" and left it on his cot. He got a good kick out of it.

The following day, the last day our company was all in Iraq at the same time, we were presented with a special memento by our esteemed colonel. We had rarely seen or heard of Colonel Steele since the Operation Iron Triangle mishap. He took the time that day to present each soldier with an American flag that held more symbolism that anything I've ever been given. Unbeknownst to us, Colonel Steele had set aside a special detail of men during the past year that operated the flagpole at the Brigade Headquarters at FOB Speicher. Every nine minutes and eleven seconds (in honor of 9/11) the flag that flew over the headquarters was changed out with full military honors. This ceremony was done roughly every ten minutes for the entire year. I thought that would have been horrible to be on that detail for the deployment, but I was greatly appreciative of the gesture. No other brigade commander would do something so special like Colonel Steele did. He gave a short speech to our company within the concrete walls that surrounded the brigade headquarters. It was a powerful and inspiring speech, as all of his were. He reiterated the importance of the flag and explained the process that each flag went through every nine minutes and eleven seconds. He then individually placed a triangle-tucked flag into the hands of each of us and thanked us personally by looking into our eyes and addressing us by our last names. It meant so much to all of us. He did this presentation to every soldier in the entire brigade, and that was what was most impressive. We loved Colonel

Steele. I would not have wanted anyone other than him commanding us. There were times that we had said negative things among ourselves back in the rear at Fort Campbell in regards to the constant strain, stress, and training he threw upon us, but his reasons and professionalism were understood and appreciated.

On September 4, the first half of my platoon left Speicher and proceeded to Kuwait. There was more room in both of our tents, but everyone was itching to join them and leave. With the first half finally out of Iraq, I decided to head to the nearby Internet shack and tell the good news to my family. On the return to my tent, I found there were now two big stories buzzing in everyone's conversation. As happy and giddy as everyone was to be leaving Iraq, the biggest story on everyone's mind was the death of the Crocodile Hunter. World-renowned animal lover Steve Irwin had been fatally wounded in an attack from a stingray. It took no time for the story to pass through the ranks of every soldier in Iraq. Pop culture and news were always things one strived to be "in the know" about so as not to feel so separated from society.

Two days later, my half of my platoon finally got the order to leave FOB Speicher in the afternoon. My day had finally come. It was a glorious feeling to walk on the sand of Iraq knowing that each step would be one of my final steps. The trip reminded me a lot of our mid-tour leave procedures. We processed through the same trailer and filled out similar paperwork. The whole day was a little fuzzy due to taking in so much and the level of excitement I was in.

When it came to lining up and walking in the back of the C-130, I focused my attention down to my boots as I walked. I knew that each step was a countdown to the last time the bottom of my boots would touch Iraqi soil, even though it was an American-made tarmac. When I'd walked right up to the ramp of the plane, I paused, took a deep breath, and then stepped inside and off of Iraqi soil. I smiled the biggest smile I could cook up. Everyone was cheering and hollering like we had just witnessed our favorite sports team win a championship. I took a seat and got myself comfortable. I put the earbuds of my iPod in while I looked around at everyone situating himself. I turned on the song "The War" by the band Mêlée, put it on repeat, and shut my eyes. The song's lyrics reverberated in my head, paralleling what I was doing, and the chorus almost moved me to tears.

ON OUR WAY HOME

**"There's plenty of beer waiting at the company
as soon as you guys get back."**

We touched down on a Kuwaiti tarmac on an American base on the evening of September 6. We landed at what was called Camp Virginia, and it was as dark as night but as hot as an afternoon. It was a lucky break that we landed while the moon was out. I knew that it was going to suck once the sun came back up. As we dismounted the plane, everyone followed the long procession of ducks-in-a-row soldiers to await our duffel bags to be unloaded from the C-130. Once everyone was reunited with his duffel bag, we were all ushered into an awaiting bus that took us to our tent for the duration of our stay.

We arrived at several large white tents in one of which we were placed. They were the same kind of tents that we had not seen since our first arrival in Kuwait one year prior. Our company only occupied about half of the tent, so there were plenty of cots to go around. I remained within that air-conditioned tent the rest of that night and most of the day. The only times I ventured outside the tent were for meals and port-a-potty breaks, because it was just so horribly hot. Luckily, the order was given that we could remain in our PT uniforms for the remainder of our stay. It was welcome news and actually got me out of the tent more than I usually would have been.

On the evening of the 7th, we had U.S. Customs agents come into our tent to inspect the packing of our duffel bags. This was a much more relaxed inspection than the one for mid-tour leave. Everyone dumped the contents of his duffel bag on his cot and agents freely walked around looking for anything we weren't allowed to have such as ammo, guns, absurd amounts of cash, and certain small souvenirs. I had the small silk Iraqi flag that Jerry had given me, but I did not think it would be a problem. The agents mentioned that the flag was on the list of things not to send home, but they were so passive that I just stuffed it in my bag anyway. Once our belongings were packed back in our duffel bags and secured with a padlock, the bags were placed on a wooden crate outside our tent and loaded on our plane. We were told that the Customs packing would be the hardest part about our stay in Kuwait.

A few hours later, we put on our ACUs and took our minimal belongings to the next base we were sent to. We arrived to Camp Ali Al Salem and began our paperwork process. The next day, we boarded several buses that took us to what I believe was Kuwait City. It was not the same airport we'd arrived in a year before, but it was an equally long bus journey to this airport. It was a hot evening to say the least. Around sunset, a baggage detail was needed to load equipment into the cargo basement in the belly of the plane. Just like on mid-tour leave, my hand was one of the first to be thrown in the air. Several other lower enlisted in my company did the same. The word must have been out by now.

We packed the plane in very little time. Working together in a chain made things move fast. Cohesive working habits were second nature. When the order to board the plane was given just as the sun was slipping down the horizon, one more sensitive items check was conducted. Yes, the last one in a foreign country, I thought to myself. As I boarded the plane, I held on to the sides of the ladder and took it all in. As I entered the plane and saw my first glimpse of female flight attendants, it was impossible to not be turned on. Everyone was and the blunt flirting must have been nauseating to the women, but they played it off very well. They must have done this a few times before, and they knew where we were coming from.

I walked up another small set of stairs that led to the first class section. Apparently there were two floors on this plane. It was the biggest plane I had ever been on. It was so good to be on baggage detail because I was looking at my seat and it looked like it was built for a king. I sat in the well-cushioned blue reclining chair and my body tingled. There was water, peanuts, and plenty of room to relax. A multi-swiveling television was inches from my right hand. I made myself as comfortable as I could, put my iPod on, and went to sleep.

Halfway through our flight to Germany, I noticed that some soldiers from first class were venturing into the cockpit. Post 9/11, that was unheard of. But the plane was full of armed soldiers who had just been fighting terrorists, so security was much different. I noticed that Lieutenant Scher was already in the cockpit, so I left my seat and joined him. We talked to the pilots and we were fascinated with the complexity of all the buttons laid out in front of them. We asked several questions about how the plane flew. There was not much to see out of the window because it was pitch-black. They did let me sit in the pilot's seat behind the wheel for a photo opportunity. I knew that never in my lifetime would I ever again get the opportunity to sit behind the wheel of a moving airplane. I needed proof.

We arrived in Germany at the same exact building our company had come through on our initial journey. The plane was refueling, which gave the smokers time to smoke, the chewers time to dip, and I had time to order a coffee. A lot of people took the time to wait in line to call home. Almost all the soldiers had some family or friends waiting for their initial steps off the plane. My family wanted to so badly, but I foolishly talked them out of it because I knew it would be tough for them to miss work and drive ten hours to see me for only a few minutes. We were not scheduled to be released as soon as we got back to the base anyway. The logic behind our immediate return to work was to begin our reverse deployment checklists. These would consist of a lot of paperwork and medical screenings. It was hard to tell my parents not to come, but I would have missed them more if I saw them for a brief second and then not again for a while. I would go home a few days after my arrival anyway, so I told them to wait. I was not the only soldier who took this route.

When we got back on the plane, I was anxiously awaiting and speculating about our return to American soil. I knew I did not have any family or friends awaiting my arrival, but I wondered how many people would actually be there on the tarmac to receive us. As soon as we got over American soil the pilot took over the loudspeaker to inform us, and the announcement was followed by hundreds of "hoo-ahs" from all parts of the plane. The excitement level was building. I was still a little subdued and tried to take it all in.

As we neared the end of our eighteen-hour flight, I began to gather my belongings and join in the joyous atmosphere. As soon as the wheels touched down on the American tarmac, everyone screamed and celebrated. I shook the hand of everyone around me and I had a smile almost sewn on my face. It was near four in the morning on September 9. Soldiers began to scramble around the seats and peek out of every window to see into the dark morning and look for a congregation.

The plane crept to a standstill and we were instructed to put what gear we had left on. I put my heavy sweat-stained vest back on and grabbed my assault pack. My helmet and weapon were the next to be donned. Slowly, each person took the slow shuffle toward the exit of the plane.

When I passed the flight attendants, they all responded with the desirable phrase of "welcome home." Yes, I was home. I followed the man in front of me until it was time for me to turn left and out of the plane. As I took my first steps onto the stairs out of the plane I looked toward the hangar nearby. The tarmac was covered with people behind a roped-off barrier. I mean, it was *covered* with people, despite what time it was. Thousands of people screamed at the top of their lungs, and I felt like the Beatles landing for their American invasion. Countless signs, balloons, whistles, screams—it was too much at once. My whole body tingled and I had goose bumps that I could feel through my ballistic plates.

At the bottom of the steps, I shook hands with some general and saluted him as I passed the colors of our nation and my division. I followed the long procession of soldiers as we neared the loud crowd. I felt like a celebrity, or a sports star walking into a stadium. My joy overwhelmed me and I began to dance with all my gear on. Flashes of camera bulbs began to flicker as people continued to cheer and laugh. The soldiers around me laughed as well.

We proceeded to an area where we were congregated and ordered to drop all of our gear, including our weapons. We were still separated from the families, but they were entering the hangar that stood to our right. The hangar was the standard large structure found on any military airport. It took a while before the last soldier came out of the plane, but each person was greeted by a loud and thunderous crowd. As we stood outside the closed hangar and anticipated the next step of our arrival, the happy crowd inside grew increasingly louder. Our excitement built to an all-time high. We just had to wait for the formal orders to march in.

"Mark time, march!" screamed an NCO from somewhere nearby. Soon, hundreds of combat boots smacked the pavement in sharp unison. Slowly, the gigantic hangar doors split open. The screams inside began to spill out and fill the early morning air. Once the doors were finally open, it was a magnificent scene to witness. The back of the hangar was covered with the largest American flag I had ever seen. A stage was erected before it and was balanced on each side with bleachers filled with screaming family members who were more audible than an IED.

"*Forward, MARCH!*" came the order, and we entered the building in unison step. We looked sharp, tough, and mean. We marched to the sound of the military music that was played by a band in the background but almost drowned out by the cheering crowd. We were commanded to halt, but many of us did not hear it because of the family members' screams.

"Welcome home" was the only thing the officer at the podium needed to say to increase the screaming. The whole experience was sensory overload and it was hard to register all that was happening. My adrenaline was pumped so high that I could have exploded. Our division song began to play, and every soldier shouted the verse and chorus as loud as I had ever heard it before.

I tried to refrain from looking around, because I was afraid that if I did I would burst into tears. Everyone I saw had glossy eyes as they tried to fight it themselves. Some had streaks of tears already falling. I smiled and took the whole celebration in, not caring that I had a single tear streak down my cheek. Once another "welcome home" was said, we were dismissed and released from our formation. Like stands full of crazed fans storming the field at a sporting event, family members overran our ranks. It was so amazing to see my fellow soldiers immersed in embraces with their parents, wives, girlfriends, and children. It hit me hard that I regretted telling my family not to come. Nearby I found Brice, who also did not have family attending. His wife never showed because during the deployment she had cheated on him and spent all his money. We hung together and enjoyed the atmosphere. We mingled a bit with some of the guys' families. I was surprised by being tapped on the shoulder by an older gentleman that I had never met before in my life.

"Would you like to call home to your family?" the man asked. He must have realized I had nobody clinging on to me.

"Sure, thank you," I said to him, not even asking him what his name was. I called home quickly on his cell phone and just said to my parents that I was home. I was off quicker than a minute because I did not want to hog this man's time or phone minutes. Brice and I walked outside of the hangar and collected our gear. Outside, I saw the familiar face of Sergeant Armstrong, who had been part of the early group from my platoon that arrived two days prior.

"There's plenty of beer waiting at the company as soon as you guys get back," Armstrong stated with a big smile on his face. Let the celebration begin, I thought. A group of us boarded a nearby shuttle that took us back to the area on Fort Campbell where our unit was located.

Fort Campbell and especially our barracks and brigade buildings was a welcome sight. Even before the sun came up, I could see how beautiful the brigade neighborhood looked. There were "Welcome Home" signs everywhere. Seeing the large red toriis standing tall over each battalion building was a magnificent sight as well.

Once we were dropped off in the back of our company area, everything felt both foreign and familiar. It was like an out-of-body experience. Everything looked just like we had left it one year before. It was so good to see the things that I'd never thought I would ever miss.

Walking into the always crowded company bay area, I saw that it was filled with soldiers I had just returned with. People were still whooping and hollering like undersexed fraternity boys. It was weird to see some of the guys from the company who'd left on the first wave dressed in civilian attire.

I hopped in line with the rest of my anxious company to drop off my sensitive items. Everyone was so eager to be released that I forgot what I was doing. I quickly became the front of the line and shouted out my four sets of serial numbers on my sensitive items. After the match was con-firmed, I turned them in. As I let go of my M4, I felt like I was breaking up with a girlfriend. My weapon, my confidant, my closest friend, was gone in an instant. No last "thank you" or "I love you" at all. Those few sad seconds were quickly replaced by two beers. A decent trade-off, I guess. Fuck it, I deserved this beer. Members of the company who'd arrived days before us started showing up with cases of cold beers and began passing them out like good behavior stickers in school.

I went upstairs to the company office area and signed for my barracks room key. It was not the same room I'd had before I left. It was actually Kemple's old room. I left in a hurry and ran across the street.

As soon as I entered the barracks, the party started. I was still in my uniform, bags in hand, and it was almost six in the morning. Every-one's body clock was set for mid-afternoon, and that was exactly how we treated it. Music pumped from those who were on the early flight and had had time to buy a stereo. Others had bought something I had never seen before: "Guitar Hero." Everyone in the company freely walked the halls and entered any open door. Each time someone did, they were given a shot of alcohol. It turned into a drunken mess, but damn did it feel good to be back home.

FROM SOLDIER TO CIVILIAN

"It was time for me to leave."

We were released for the rest of the day and that gave us a little time to catch up. None of us had any clothes other than Army uniforms. No vehicles, no televisions, nothing. Highly intoxicated, several of us got a taxi and headed to the nearest mall. After a year in which we all collected tax-free paychecks and spent nearly none of it, we were coming home to more money than any of us had ever seen in our bank accounts, and we were in desperate need of everything. The afternoon was spent buying the essentials: clothes, cell phones, beer, shoes, liquor, food, beer, hats, beer, televisions, cars, beer, stereos, liquor, guns, etc. Dinner at Hooter's was the first and best meal I had back in the U.S. We ordered more food than any of us could eat. We mainly just drank and flirted with the waitresses. For shits and giggles, I bought a suit and wore it to dinner, topped off with a fake mustache. I did not care about anything. I was on cloud nine being back in Clarksville, Tennessee.

The following day we showed up at the company area around eight in the morning, but that was still too early for everyone. Every morning we gathered for formation in uniform and then loaded up on a bus to be shuttled to whatever building we needed to be at that day for paperwork and medical screenings. Each morning, the bus smelled like a bar. Everyone was hungover from the previous night, and still stank of it. We were just making up for lost time and celebrating. We finished our required tasks near lunchtime, and the rest of the day was spent doing what infantrymen did best. We drank. I and several others from my platoon went out and rented a boat on King Lake in Kentucky, where we drank and fished. A long weekend in Nashville was also spent in a four-star hotel, and there was little I remembered from that trip.

The week at work that I remember was spent signing a lot of forms, most of which I had no clue what they were. Most everyone was half-drunk or still drunk. Typical infantrymen. The only thing I ever remember filling out regarding mental health was a paper questionnaire about whether I had ever seen anyone killed or wounded in theater. No shit! We were infantrymen in Iraq. It was the dumbest shit ever. Those of us who were getting out skipped most of the paper because we were afraid that we would be held in longer awaiting doctor appointments and that would hinder us from getting out of the Army sooner. I listened to everyone else around me and did the same, because I was already supposed to have been clearing from the military at that time. I did not want to prolong it any longer.

Once we finished all of our medical, financial, and paperwork-from-Hell week on September 16, we were released on leave for about a month. I only took about ten days so I could get out of the Army quicker. I went home and it was great. I wasted no time readjusting to society. I bought a car, hung out with friends and family, and got stuff situated for a job back home.

Upon returning to Fort Campbell, I spent a few weeks clearing post and being discharged. Getting out of the military was a process that took much longer than I expected. I had to gather a million signatures from several different installations on post. The hardest process of all of them was turning in my gear. They were like Nazis when it came to the inspection of the cleanliness of the gear.

After several boring mornings and drunken nights, it was time for me to leave on November 6. Others in the company had already left, and now it was my turn. The Angels from Hell was already not the same company it had been a month prior. A huge wave of stop-lossed soldiers disappeared as soon as we got back. Now it was my turn to cut the umbilical cord between me and the Rakkasans. It was bittersweet leaving the men I had gone through so much with. People were dipping out from the ranks daily. The company was shrinking, but I knew there were new "cherry" soldiers waiting to fill our vacant spots.

On November 5, 2006, I signed my last signature in front of Lieutenant Scher and Captain Lesperance. I know I joked a lot with Lieutenant Scher, but I took the opportunity to be sincere when I thanked him for his tireless effort with how he ran our platoon. He was a workhorse. We shook hands and pulled each other in for "the man hug." I turned my attention to Captain Lesperance and thanked him for what he had done, and before he said thank-you in return, I went into an appreciative spiel about how he'd handled the situation of Kemple's death and how he'd fought off the confusion of the field artillerists who wanted to clog the scene and complicate the situation. I'm not a big fan of awards, so I'm unsure what he deserves, but that man earned my undying respect. With the signature I signed in front of them completed, I was officially out of the Rakkasans, out of the 101st Airborne Division, and out of the Army. In my newly purchased civilian clothes I walked out of the company room for the last time and proceeded to my car. It was a whirlwind return back from Iraq and back to society.

It was hard to bid farewell to the men in Angel Company. They had become my family, and we had gone through so much bullshit not just within the past year but during all the training we had done also. There was a camaraderie that is hard to explain. With each person, I knew his strengths and weaknesses, and we all knew where we fit together to work as a cohesive team given any situation. It's rare to have and feel that with other random young adults. We bled, we sweated, and we cried at times, but we did it together. It was like an amazing band ending or the series finale of your favorite television show. My life with this family was at its end. Never would we all be in the same place at the same time again. Never would this band of brothers have the world on their shoulders and be asked to do the things we'd done.

The night before my long drive back home I spent with my buddies. We drank and talked about so many good times, bad times, and drunk times we had shared over the past few years. There were hugs, tears, and a pillow fight. The next morning I woke up with a severe headache in the apartment of one of my buddies and looked around the room. Almost all of the specialists and privates from my platoon were passed out in different arrangements on the floor and couches. Once again, I took it all in and said quietly without waking anyone, "Rakkasans." I had said my good-byes the night before, so I didn't want to wake them all and redo it. I tore off a little note and posted it on the refrigerator. On it I wrote, "Till we meet again . . ." and I signed my name and walked out of the door.

In the middle of my ten-hour ride back home, I received a text message from my brother that informed me that Saddam Hussein had just been convicted of his charges and was scheduled to be hanged. I turned up the music in my car, and with my windows down I screamed victoriously. Then all the thoughts quickly came to mind that I had been at that site. I lived outside the courthouse. Then the previous year flashed before my eyes and I couldn't help but say to myself, *Did I just do that?* I'd just spent a year in Iraq as an infantryman. Holy shit.

EPILOGUE

I never intended to write this book. When I returned to my home in Gettysburg, my parents gave me a stack of e-mails that I had sent over the course of my year in Iraq. When my mother turned them over to me, she said, "Now, you know what to do with these." Being a military enthusiast and avid collector of family records, I thought it would be a unique "down the road" project to do and have as a personal narrative of my time in Iraq.

Obviously, because I was twenty-one years old, the idea quickly vanished from my "things to do" list. I celebrated being back from Iraq and, especially, being a civilian again. I felt like I had to make up for lost time. I drank heavily, grew my hair out, and slept in every morning.

After a month, I felt completely out of my element. I was missing everything that had been my life for the last several years. I couldn't find the closeness and camaraderie with my friends that I had gained with my Army buddies. I even contemplated joining the National Guard to find that void I was missing. After my irrational thought processing passed, I decided to stay a civilian and in the Individual Ready Reserve (IRR) and take my chances of being called back, which were slim to none. I kept up the only pastime infantrymen had and that was to drink. I was used to drinking all the time with my buddies, but now I found myself doing it alone and yearning for the good times I used to have. I could never fill that void of missing happiness and security, and I found myself doing a lot of things by myself. As much as I had missed my friends and family, I returned a bit of a loner. There was no real explanation for it and I never knew why. I just felt shut off.

I'd left for the Army right after high school and I'd rarely ever returned home except for the occasional ten days of leave for Christmas and summer. It had now been more than three years, and a lot of my friends had changed since high school. I'd changed myself. The past year in Iraq I'd had little to no communication with my friends and family, and I'd missed a lot out of their lives and they'd missed a huge chunk of mine. I was a small-town kid who'd done big world things. I returned to a town full of small-towners who would never understand the things I spoke of. I rarely talked about my experiences because I couldn't figure out how to make them relatable, for people to understand. I had a scrapbook full of pictures, but no one ever wanted to see them as much as I was willing to share. I got annoyed that my friends and family weren't as inquisitive as I had hoped they would be. On the flip side, my blood would instantly boil whenever I was asked the question as to whether I had ever killed anybody, which seemed to be everyone's first question. I was missing my Army family bad and the conversations and bullshit pain we had all shared.

I became enraged when I saw or heard people complain about the pettiest things. Kids complaining that they had a scuff on their new shoes, people fuming at waiting in line at the grocery store, or how hot the temperature was. I bit my tongue from saying something like *You don't know how good you got it*, or *You have no idea*. The news seemed to focus more on what famous celebrity was adopting a new baby from a foreign country, instead of covering the progress in Iraq. I was living in an age where a soldier's death wasn't making the top headline. I took my anger out on my body at the gym.

Driving was never the same for me. Garbage on the side of the road, dirt piles, and dead animals still jump start my heart and make me think of IEDs. A year driving countless hours on the roads in Iraq and waiting for something to blow up on me is something that I find impossible to turn off. I know America is a safe place, but the trepidation is ingrained in my brain and it won't go away. Walking by a construction site and hearing an explosion or heavy equipment slam makes my heartbeat flutter fast. If I'm with company, I try to put on my best acting face and pretend like nothing happened. I don't like going places that are crowded with people. I like my space. Being crammed in with people makes me feel like I can't be on guard as much as I would like.

I grew up the kind of person who ignored his feelings and wouldn't let things bother him. When I got back from Iraq, I knew there were some internal, emotional issues that were out of place, but I wouldn't let them get the best of me. My alpha male instincts made me think I was stronger when it came to my feelings. I had too much pride to talk with anyone other than those who were there with me in war. Post-traumatic stress disorder was something I knew I didn't have. I didn't want to be labeled as living with a disorder. There are plenty of people who go to Iraq and see tons more carnage and combat than I saw, so I watered down my problems and ignored them. I figured it was a syndrome for people who went through endless days of running out of ammunition and slicing people's throats to survive. That wasn't me. So what was my problem?

I was living in small town Gettysburg and I seemed to be the only Iraq vet around. I needed an outlet, but I didn't know what to do. I joined the local VFW in hopes of finding people who had the understanding of each other without questioning each other. I was the youngest member by like forty years. After visiting once, I never returned. I spent most of my days in a gym and most of my nights in a bar.

I needed a new direction in life and desperately looked for things to focus my attention on. I started attending school at a local community college and I loved it. It kept me busy and kept my mind occupied. My brother hooked me up with a job working security for Gettysburg College. After six months in civilian life things were going well for me and I was becoming happy again.

Once I got settled in my new routine in life, the stack of my Iraq e-mails continued to sit idle on the dresser next to my bed, almost staring at me. Out of boredom one day I decided to flip through them. It was fun to reminisce about my time in Iraq, even though a year had not yet passed. I started toying around with expanding the e-mails from what I recollected, and writing in extreme detail about what had happened from the start of my deployment. Soon, I found it quite fun to write everything as I remembered it. I would do a little here and a little there. If there was something I felt was missing or that I couldn't remember, my buddies were a phone call away and it was a great excuse to hear their voices again.

With my writings saved onto a tiny hard drive, I began taking them with me wherever I went. I would sift through my e-mails and then set them aside while I wrote about what was covered in one specific e-mail. I found myself writing at work, at home, at friends' houses, and anywhere else I was with a computer. I would sometimes call my buddies and clarify certain details and then plug those in. At random times during any given day, a memory would come to mind and I would jot it on a piece of paper and plug that into the story as well. I still never thought about ever publishing my memoir; I just wanted to write down everything that was in my head as it had happened. It became therapeutic for me to write the story in my head that I wanted out and possibly viewed by others. Soon, I saw the big picture and realized I was doing the best thing for me to do. I was getting my thoughts, experiences, and adventures out of my mind and my heart and putting them on paper so they didn't dwell inside of me anymore. In turn, my memories were now on paper and able to be viewed by anyone who wanted to read them. This was the therapy that I happened to devise for me. It worked.

After eighteen months of school and writing my memoir, I finally felt normal. No longer did I carry a rucksack with MREs and ammunition, but a backpack filled with textbooks and pencils. I could always be found wearing a ball cap with long hair protruding out of it. The fresh-faced soldier was hidden under the Abe Lincoln–style beard I was attempting to grow. I blended in with the crowd and people would have no idea that the quiet hippy-looking punk in the back of the class had lived the life I had. I also cut my drinking down and went several weeks without ever even touching it. It didn't become a problem anymore. The Army was in my past and I had a lot of plans for my future. My ambitions kept me busy and focused.

In February of 2008, I literally stumbled across a casting call for a reality television show while I was spending a weekend in Pittsburgh. Soon,

I remembered the joke that I'd made with Fooks up in the guard tower in Baghdad, when I told him I would someday get on a reality show. While walking down the streets of downtown Pittsburgh, I saw hundreds of hopeful eighteen to twentysomethings waiting in line for their chance to show why they should be picked, and I figured I had nothing to lose if I joined the line. While awaiting my turn for my first interview, I remember calling Fooks, Hilmo, Avery, and Taylor on my cell phone and telling them what I was about to do.

After that first interview things kept spiraling in my favor. The casting directors kept calling me back for another interview and I laughed every time. *Why would they choose me?* I kept asking myself. They asked me to make a ten-minute video about myself, and filmmaking was what I was going to school for, so it was no problem. I sent it to Los Angeles, and soon I was sent to Cincinnati, and finally Los Angeles for the last interviews. After a few months of answering every question about my life except my blood type, I was chosen and in complete disbelief. It made the joke I'd made in Baghdad more humorous than ever intended.

Life was finally on a track that I loved. In the summer of 2008, I packed up some belongings and moved to Brooklyn, New York, to start filming the show. Opportunities were opening up for me in several avenues that I had always wanted but could not find in my small hometown. I loved what I was doing and I had little motivation to move back home.

Life in Angel Company moved on without me and they again came under deployment orders. They deployed to Baghdad, Iraq, in August of 2007 to begin a fourteen-month deployment. The company was a skeleton of the company I deployed with, but I knew about two-thirds of the men on the roster. The Angels from Hell returned from Iraq in early November of 2008 while I was finishing up filming in Brooklyn.

They returned unharmed with the exception of Third Platoon's Sergeant Ben Miller, who committed suicide. Suicide is a major problem in the military and at times outnumber the casualty rate for deaths in Iraq and Afghanistan combined on a monthly basis. I remember Ben from his first day in Angel Company up to my last day. If I was the comic relief for First Platoon, then Miller easily earned the same honor for Third Platoon. I'll never forget the way he tried to motivate us all before we loaded the helicopters to launch Operation Swarmer. His suicide was hard for the entire company, both those serving and those he'd served with. Miller was still in the Army at the time and was home on leave from Iraq when he committed suicide in his hometown in Minnesota. He is buried right behind Kemple at Fort Snelling National Cemetery in Minneapolis, Minnesota. I find great comfort in knowing that they are with each other, both in the ground and up above.

On November 11, 2008, Veterans Day, I marched through downtown New York City with Iraq and Afghanistan Veterans of America (IAVA) and relished the appreciation from the public for my past service in Iraq. I felt like I had come full circle to be marching on behalf of veterans in the city that fell victim to the 9/11 attacks, my overall reason for joining the service. I could finally put some closure on the Army chapter of my life. Little did I know that on that exact day a package from the Army arrived at my parents' house in Gettysburg. It was the letter I was dreading. The Army had just called me out of the IRR and back to active duty.

I was being sent back to Iraq for another year.

Fuck.

AUTHOR'S APPRECIATION

The making of this book has been a pleasurable and entertaining project. There are many people to thank that had a hand in the initiative, construction, and support that went into these pages. First and forever I would like to thank my parents for everything they have done for me. I could list the things I'm thankful for, but there is not enough paper in this world to write them on. There is only one word that sums it up perfectly and that is the word *everything*. Thank you for everything.

My story would not be the same if it wasn't for the men I served with. Fate brought us together, and we forged lasting friendships that made our time together what it was. We found joy and made memories in the worst of situations. Though our hair may fade, our bond never will. Ryan Avery, you will always be a man of great talent. You are my personal "Yoda" and I will continue to call and visit whenever I'm in need of wisdom in whatever random adventures I get into. Taylor Edwards, you're a man of your words and dreams. May the best experiences come your way as you fly through the sky in your Apache helicopter. Jimmy Poston, though we had a bumpy ride at first, we overcame and learned to respect each other. To my dying day I will always say I wouldn't want any other squad leader to go into combat with than you. Adam Scher, you are one hell of a guy. Thank you so much for being so understanding in dealing with my shenanigans. Most lieutenants would have punched me, but you held your ground and together we had a blast. You are one hardworking officer and there should be more leaders that follow in your footsteps. A special acknowledgment goes to Ryan Matson, our combat camera for the Army during Operation Swarmer, who took amazing snapshots. To Fooks, Vinny, Mo, Chief, Pitch, Scuba, Nick, Reese, Mac, Ly, Cho-Chay, Sunny, and all the others from First Platoon, I thank you for your friendship, strength, teamwork, and patriotism. To the greater band of Angel Company, I say thank you. Please continue to keep your heads on a swivel as you continue to answer the call in Iraq and Afghanistan. My thoughts and appreciation is extended to the Kemple family and the Miller family. Thank you for producing and sharing two of the finest examples of soldiers I ever had the pleasure to serve with.

A special and sincere appreciation goes out to Darren "Sub" Subarton who sadly passed away just months before this book was published. Not only did he always provide a smart-ass remark to everything I ever did or said, but he helped me immensely with unwavering support, tracking down buddies, donating countless photos, and giving the eulogy at Kemple's memorial. Sub was the first friend to read a rough copy of this book, and I find great comfort knowing that he read it before his unexpected passing.

To Kurt and Dana Kluck, who supported me when I was deployed and held out their arms when I returned, and kept the beer cold, I say thank you. To all my other friends who dealt with my excuse for "staying in for the night," so I could write this book, I am thankful for your patience; Megan Shaffer, Chad Heidel, Shaun Grenan, Becky Martin, Alex Bigler, JD Ordonez, Tara Reyka, Katelynn Cusanelli, Devyn Sims, Michelle Bert, Derek Borden, Chet Cannon, Baya Voce, Scott Herman, Sarah Rice, William Lafferty, Gary Boynton, Matthew Ruecker, my extended family, and so many others. To Eric Lowman, who shares the passion of military history, thank you for your support and for pushing me to write my story hours after I stepped off the plane. I told you I'd do it. To Frank and June Conklin, who smiled at all my adventures in life, thank you for your love and your gift at remaining so close to such a large family. A special smile goes to Charles "Ed" and Waunettia Allen. I wish we'd had more time and I know you'd be proud. A sincere thank-you goes to Dan Hans, Lou Nyiri, and my church, who supplied me with constant prayer and gave me strength when I thought I had none. Carrie and Greg Trax, thank you for all that you have done and continue to do. To my brother, Aaron, thank you for living an almost parallel life to mine. We've done a lot together and shared so much that some twins would be jealous. Good luck with the remainder of your deployment in Iraq. Make it home safe and I'll be there waiting for you when you return.

I would not be doing the things I'm doing now if it wasn't for Jon Murray and the rest of the hardworking and adventurous souls at Bunim-Murray Productions. May a million showers of thank-you fall upon Jon, Jim Johnston, and the casting department for allowing me the opportunity to open my life for the world to see. If "all the world's a stage," then thank you for giving me that platform.

To the founder of IAVA, Paul Rieckhoff, thank you for everything you have done and for continuing the better fight. You have an amazing gift to turn your voice into results. I am indebted to you for the directions you have pointed me in. You have a natural leadership both as an officer and advocate. E. J. McCarthy, you have proven to be an amazing agent and wonderful friend. My circumstances in life have been less than ordinary, but you have rolled with the punches right along with me. Without you, this book would be sitting on my hard drive collecting digital dust. Likewise, without Michelle Vega and Natalee Rosenstein at Berkley, this book would not be. Thank you for remaining excited and helpful for the entire process it takes to get published. It's been a very rewarding experience.

I would like to broaden my appreciation to all veterans of the Iraq War both before and after me. I know where you've been and I know where you can go. Dream it, then live it. Lastly, I'd like to thank you, the reader. I don't speak for every soldier, but every veteran has a story and this one is mine. Thank you for reading.